Reevaluating the Third Reich

Reevaluating the Third Reich

Edited by
Thomas Childers and Jane Caplan

FOREWORD BY CHARLES S. MAIER

EUROPE PAST AND PRESENT SERIES

HM

HOLMES & MEIER
New York / London

Published in the United States of America 1993 by
Holmes & Meier Publishers, Inc.
30 Irving Place
New York, NY 10003

Book design by Adrienne Weiss

This book has been printed on acid-free paper.

Library of Congress Cataloging-in-Publication Data

Reevaluating the Third Reich / edited by Thomas Childers and Jane
    Caplan ; foreword by Charles S. Maier.
        p.   cm. — (Europe past and present series)
    Based on presentations at a conference in Philadelphia in 1988.
    Includes bibliographical references and index.
    ISBN 0-8419-1178-9 (cloth: acid-free paper). — ISBN
0-8419-1228-9 (pbk. : acid-free paper)
    1. Germany—History—1933–1945—Congresses.   2. National
socialism—Congresses.   I. Childers, Thomas, 1946–   .   II. Caplan,
Jane.   III. Series.
DD256.5.R384   1988
943.086—dc20   91-37761
                                                                CIP

Manufactured in the United States of America

TIMOTHY MASON
1940–1990

DETLEV PEUKERT
1951–1990

By a tragic coincidence, the untimely deaths of Tim Mason and Detlev Peukert were announced when this book was in progress in the spring of 1990.

In mourning them as friends, we also grieve the loss of two brilliant and dedicated historians of National Socialism. Though different in nationality, temperament, and training, Tim and Detlev shared a common effort to understand this grim epoch of human history, and a common commitment to the democratization of history and to socialism as theory and practice. Precocious in their maturity, each had produced a string of dazzling publications whose impact on their colleagues and students will not soon disappear.

This book is dedicated to their memory.

Contents

Abbreviations

AHA	American Historical Association
ADW	Archiv des diakonischen Werkes, Berlin
AOG	Arbeitsordnungsgesetz
AWI	Arbeitswissenschaftliches Institut (of the DAF)
BAK	Bundesarchiv Koblenz
BoE	Bank of England
CDU	Christlich-Demokratische Union
DAF	Deutsche Arbeitsfront
DNVP	Deutschnationale Volkspartei
DZA	Deutsches Zentralarchiv, Potsdam
DVC-A	Deutscher Caritas-Verein-Archiv, Freiburg
EAF	Erzbischöfliches Archiv Freiburg
Gestapo	Geheime Staatspolizei
KPD	Kommunistische Partei Deutschlands
IfZ	Institut für Zeitgeschichte, Munich
IMT	*Trials of Major War Criminals before the International Military Tribunal*
Kripo	Kriminalpolizei
NCA	*Nazi Conspiracy and Aggression*
NSDAP	Nationalsozialistische Deutsche Arbeiterpartei
Orpo	Ordnungspolizei
PA	Politisches Archiv (of the German Foreign Office)
RDI	Reichsbund der deutschen Industriellen
REFA	Reichsausschuss für Arbeitsstudien
RGI	Reichsgruppe Industrie
RSHA	Reichssicherheitshauptamt
SA	Sturm-Abteilung
SD	Sicherheitsdienst

SPD	Sozialdemokratische Partei Deutschlands
SS	Schutzstaffel
Sipo	Sicherheitspolizei
StAM	Staatsarchiv München
StAW	Staatsarchiv Wiesbaden
VfZ	*Vierteljahreshefte für Zeitgeschichte*
YVA	Yad Vashem Archives

Foreword

CHARLES S. MAIER

The essays that comprise this collection emerged from a remarkable conference on Nazi Germany in the spring of 1988. Certainly there have been many academic discussions of Nazism. Nonetheless, this colloquium at the University of Pennsylvania generated some particularly memorable moments of intellectual confrontation. Most notably, the intense debate suggested that a major generational break in the understanding of Nazism was taking place.

The political and moral stakes of such a reinterpretation seem very high. Nazism, after all, provides one of the basic examples of political evil. How we define its ideology or analyze its system of governance, how we categorize its murderous violence, to whom we attribute its coming to power and support, testify to our underlying political values. The Philadelphia discussions revealed that these commitments were in possible conflict, and certainly open for re-definition.

The participants invited by the conference organizers, Jane Caplan and Thomas Childers, did not represent the entire spectrum of scholars engaged in research on Nazi Germany. Those whose work tended to focus on Hitler himself, his personality and his decision making, were not present. Instead, those taking part spoke for the more institutional or collective interpretations of Nazism, which have generated most scholarly interest and controversy over the past two decades. In the debate between those whom Tim Mason had aptly labeled "intentionalists"—those who focused on Hitler's will and ideology—and the "functionalists"—who ascribed policy to collective, bureaucratic outcomes—the conference participants tended either to be functionalists or to argue that neither term could encompass the way the regime worked.

It is not surprising that those of us at Philadelphia were not intentionalists. By virtue of temperament and prior work, this group included those who have followed collective structures of decision making within the Third Reich. Not that discussants denied the central role of Hitler. Rather they tried to contextualize it or at least to show, as did Christopher Browning, that while Hitler remained at the center there was no unchanging script. Hans Mommsen, the historian most prominently associated with a "functionalist" explanation both of the regime and of its policies of extermination, sought in fact to turn the intentionalist argument around. His paper in effect accepted its premises, only to argue that Göring more than Hitler should be regarded as the central decision maker of the regime.

The second major historical issue to be raised concerned Nazi political economy. Often applied with a Marxist bent, this approach asks how National Socialism interacted with the leadership that dominated the economy until 1930, and in some cases remained important even later. Historians engaged in this research have been preoccupied by the question of the degree to which the Nazi rulers modified or even overturned the "capitalist" organization of the German economy. It is a vexing issue first raised by the social democratic and Communist interpreters of Italian fascism in the 1920s, then applied to the Nazi regime in successive decades. Through the 1980s it has continued to orient some of the most revealing contributions to the history of how Nazism functioned, what transformative effects it exerted, or to what degree it can be envisaged as radical.

Perhaps the most poignant moment at Philadelphia came with Tim Mason's effort to meet the frequent critics of his earlier controversial thesis that Hitler had been constrained to go to war by the very economic tensions that his rapid rearmament drive had generated. Mason's concept of an inner crisis had been sharply attacked. So too had his argument that the working class had remained a source of opposition and resistance. Mason presented an important self-criticism (and self-defense). He acknowledged his critics' objections, but simultaneously sought to rescue the concept of an inner crisis of regime by focusing on a wider range of contradictions, and not just the demands of labor. It is a moving experience to witness someone who takes ideas seriously endeavor to rethink earlier assumptions and findings. In this case, the awareness of the depth of Tim's personal battle with depression made his effort at intellectual reconstruction all the more impressive.

It would be a mistake to understand Mason's paper simply as a strategic retreat from a position that had become untenable. On one level his presentation exemplified in microcosm the abandonment of some of the cherished starting points of Left historiography. But that historiography, from Franz Neumann on, had not simply been wrong. It had contributed to some of the most revealing insights about Nazism. It had emphasized the uneasy yoking together of classes under an imperialist program, its suspension of old elites alongside the new party elite, its ability to tap the deep populist resentments of German capitalism even while buttressing the organizational strengths of the economic sector. Although this writer often found Mason's theses of inner crisis problematic, they had always opened new perspectives. In what turned out to be Tim Mason's last public scholarly intervention on the Third Reich, he attempted a painstaking balance—an effort to redeem what seemed valuable about a half-century historical project, and to be faithful to evidence as well.

The third major controversy was raised by the contributions to what may be called National Socialist "civil society." Historians engaged in this research have tried to determine the degree of complicity, the sources of collective loyalty, and the impact of the regime on associational life. Such research can logically include the restructuring of economic hierarchies, but historians have tended to treat the economy as part of a different agenda, originally suggested by Marxian analysis. (Peter Hayes and Harold James address these issues from different, often revisionist stances.) Investigations of civil society under Nazism have tended to focus on the receptivity of noneconomic associations: Nazism's permeation of churches, schools, youth groups, and family—what Simmel called the web of group relationships. Understanding the penetration of Nazism was the objective of the major research project on Bavaria in the National Socialist era organized by the Institut für Zeitgeschichte and its director, the late Martin Broszat. Among conference participants, Ian Kershaw has made a major contribution to that research agenda. Outside the Bavaria project, Detlev Peukert's studies have comprised another innovative contribution to the "everyday history" of the Third Reich.

It was precisely the implications of this research program that provoked some of the most intense discussion and soul searching. In retrospect, I think that there were two reasons for debate and unease. The first is the now familiar criticism that studies of National Socialist civil society often seem to downplay the organized brutality of the regime. At the local level, much of life—so the critics tend to portray the thrust of "everyday history"—apparently went on as "normal," at least until late in the war; Nazism almost fades from the picture. Ian Kershaw's essay argues against this objection, which, in fact, is too encompassing. Kershaw himself, for example, has carefully argued that mass silence on anti-Jewish policies must be understood as a major constituent of the regime. Indeed, Robert Gellately's essay, which examines letters of denunciation to the Gestapo, suggests that "civil society" was a major resource for the enforcement of terror—and not just the locus of life as usual.

The second source of uneasiness about the "civil society" agenda was different. It emerged with the discussion of Detlev Peukert's paper and did not focus on any tendency to "normalize" local life. (In fact, none of Peukert's work argues for life as normal; it argues for a permeation of society by Nazi projects but

it conceives these projects differently than did an older generation of historians.)
What Peukert proposed was that the regime merely acted, albeit radically, on the
long-standing belief in German—and perhaps Western—society in the differential value of human life. German medicine and popular science had long agreed
in effect that some human life was more worthy than others. There had been an
argument for denying reproductive rights since the nineteenth century; the Nazis
added a broader eugenic repertoire that included euthanasia, de facto enslave-
ment, casually inflicted murder, and, ultimately, organized extermination. The
German "great chain of being" led downward to degradation and death.

Peukert's analysis provoked debate and controversy. Tim Mason tren-
chantly suggested that the conference was confirming a new paradigm: Nazism
as an expression of "biological politics." The concept of Nazism as a biological
project—crassly eugenic, categorizing humanity hierarchically along racial
lines—has become a major theme in the literature. The responses to Peukert
indicated that some conference participants found this view troubling on several
grounds. To be sure, it suggested that Neo-Marxian class interpretations were
irrelevant (although electoral analysis, such as that of Thomas Childers, had
already undermined this venerable approach). But Peukert's essay also was
received as a disquieting attack on the uniqueness of the Final Solution. Peukert
insisted on the barbarousness of Nazi genocide, but refused to accord primacy to
its most massive component, the plan to kill European Jews. He insisted on
viewing the Final Solution as one of the most extreme efforts in a broad denial of
human value to Gypsies, homosexuals, and all those deemed less worthy of life
than the *Volkskörper*. As Marian Kaplan argued, it was good to have German
historians fully acknowledging the Holocaust, but it threatened to become a
Holocaust without Jews.

In retrospect the confrontation seems especially poignant since Peukert
also died, sadly prematurely, in the period following the conference. Certainly
he has left some of the most original social history of the regime, with special
attention to the groups who remained at the margins of the Nazi project. He was
a major contributor to the difficult debate on the texture of *Resistenz*, that is,
selective, low-level dissent, or even partial disobedience. But Peukert's essay also
testifies to the continuing difficulty that the German Left has had in coming to
terms with the specifically anti-Jewish thrust of National Socialism. Despite his
full avowal that the Nazis envisaged the most monstrous projects, there is still
some desire to dissolve victimhood into broad abstract categories ("less-valued
life") and to diffuse agency among German or even Western scientistic tendencies. This is not to argue that Gypsies did not suffer equivalent ethnic slaughter,
nor that the regime was more tender toward Jehovah's Witnesses or homosexuals.
Nor is it to argue that genocide was foreordained; Browning's remains a plausible
narrative of escalation. But why the final reluctance to accept the unique and
central role of the anti-Jewish agenda? The Philadelphia debates suggested that if

an older generation of the Left has found it intellectually wrenching to renounce a residual class view of Nazism, so a newer Left finds it equally difficult to accept that ethnic hatreds might be atrociously motivating in their own right. Somehow they have found it easier to consider Nazism as a perversion of a universalistic scientific project, a view not without some kinship to Ernst Nolte's problematic conceptualization.

I linger over Peukert's and Mason's contributions because, first of all, both these historians were engaged in some of their last public debates. The loss of each diminishes the profession. At Philadelphia, furthermore, each spoke directly concerning the most problematic issues of today's historiography. If Nazism is construed as a monstrous German eugenic project and no longer bears any inherent relationship to capitalism, or to the hierarchical structures of political and economic power, then, as Tim Mason recognized in his last published essay (included as the appendix to this volume), the generic concept of fascism has little relevance. Comparison with the Italian and other authoritarian, paramilitary, anti-Marxist, often aggressively expansionist, interwar movements seems to retain little heuristic value. I agree with Tim Mason's fear that much will be lost if the fascist paradigm is abandoned.

Perhaps there is an irony that Mason did not have time fully to explore. If Nazism is generalized as a project of exterminating "life unworthy of life," if asymptotically it tends toward a murderous eugenicism that is shared at least in degree by other Western cultures, then it also loses its anti-Semitic particularity. So Peukert's intervention suggested. But in this case, National Socialism also sheds the very specificity, its murderous anti-Jewish phobia, that the centrist and conservative interpreters from the late 1960s through the mid-1980s insisted upon to establish its uniqueness. As the debates at the massive 1983 Reichstag congress indicated, Nazi anti-Semitism was cited precisely to undermine any generalized theory of fascism.[1] In a polarized academic culture, fascism had become a taboo concept by 1980, a code word associated with a crude Marxism that seemed to assail the universities and debase political discourse in general. But if a new "biological" paradigm emerges, one extrapolated less from German particularity than Western pseudoscientific hierarchies, does not the new historiography on the Left allow for the rehabilitation of a new generic fascism based on eugenic categories or even dehumanized technocratic longings? There were such traits in the Italian project, crude racialistic overtones among Magyar right-wingers, and obvious anti-Semitism at Vichy. It would be an intriguing irony if by downplaying the economic context of fascism, the new Left made the concept of fascism "safe" for non-Marxist social science and political language once again.

[1]Martin Broszat et al., eds., *Deutschlands Weg in die Diktatur. Internationale Konferenz zur nationalsozialistischen Machtübernahme im Reichstagsgebäude zu Berlin* (Berlin: Siedler Verlag, 1983).

The essays in this book exposed the contradictory implications and shifting paradigms of the newer historical literature. The Philadelphia conference from which they emerged was a moment of intense debate, when historians, often in profound disagreement, could still recognize the personal authenticity of opposed scholarly views. The Philadelphia conference required all participants to reflect on their moral as well as intellectual commitments. When such issues explicitly come to the forefront among historians who are seeking to master an important subject as a community of scholars, the experience is memorable.

Reevaluating the Third Reich

Introduction

THOMAS CHILDERS
JANE CAPLAN

Interest in the history of Nazism has endured unabated since the demise almost half a century ago of the "Third Reich"—a period that neither the passage of time nor the accumulation of research has yet robbed of its historical significance and moral urgency. Within the historiographical continuum, shifts in emphasis, theme, and method are readily discernible. From the first tentative studies of tyranny and resistance in the postwar decade, through the massively documented reconstructions of the Nazi Party's growth and the regime's policies that began to appear in the late 1950s, to the revival of interest in theories of fascism in the 1960s—and the subsequent development of a new concern with the social history of the Third Reich and with the relationship between political structure and ideology in Nazi decision making—historical research on both sides of the Atlantic has generated a succession of different themes and approaches that have vastly expanded our knowledge of this most challenging episode in modern European history.[1]

At the same time, works on National Socialism have always developed in the context of moral, political, and public claims that are surely more intense and intrusive than for research on any other period. Analysts of National Socialism and the Third Reich operate with an almost inescapable sense of engagement, usually self-imposed but sometimes also mandated by pressures from the wider political world. The frontiers between knowledge, morality, and politics; fact, interpretation, and fiction; scholarship, popular education, and commercialism, are nowhere more fragile than here; and policing them or redrawing them has been a difficult and sometimes painful process, as the recent *Historikerstreit* (historians' dispute) has demonstrated once again.

1

That debate was precipitated in the spring of 1986 when the Berlin historian Ernst Nolte argued that the Nazi regime and its crimes must be viewed in the brutal context of other twentieth-century atrocities, a context in which Nazi genocide emerges as simply one variant of a pattern of mass murder, from the Turks in Armenia to Stalin's crimes to Pol Pot's Khmer Rouge. If the National Socialist past was comparable to other national experiences, Germany might ultimately claim a national acceptance that few have denied to the perpetrators of other outrages. The nation might—as Michael Stürmer, the conservative Erlangen historian and advisor to the Kohl government, implied at the outset of the debate—be able at last to put its troubled Nazi past behind it and concentrate on the solid achievements of postwar democracy. When, in response, the Frankfurt philosopher Jürgen Habermas charged that Nolte, Stürmer, and other prominent West German historians were guilty of apologist reasoning and were seeking to "relativize" the Third Reich, the stage was set for another major debate on the nature of the Third Reich and its place in German history.[2]

Over the next three years the *Historikerstreit* became the subject of several conferences and symposia in both Europe and North America, and yielded a small mountain of articles in both scholarly journals and the popular press, as well as several book-length treatments. Yet, for all its sound and fury, the *Historikerstreit* has produced little new of substance about either National Socialism or the Third Reich. This should, perhaps, hardly be surprising, for ultimately the *Historikerstreit* is less concerned with an analysis of the Third Reich as such than with the proper role of the Nazi past in the political culture of contemporary Germany. The debate is, in essence, an important political struggle for a "usable past," as Stürmer would have it, or, alternatively, for the acceptance of "an unmasterable past," as Charles Maier has argued.[3] Yet, while the *Historikerstreit* has significant and revealing implications for contemporary German politics, its impact on historical scholarship has been disappointing. Unlike the Fischer controversy of the 1960s or the *Sonderweg* debate of the late 1970s and 1980s, both of which inspired new paradigms and spawned important research on a wide range of topics,[4] the *Historikerstreit* has, to date, broken no new ground in our understanding of the National Socialist movement or the regime it created.

Although overshadowed by this highly public and politicized conflict, other more significant shifts in the historical interpretation of National Socialism have been underway in recent years, shifts that promise to influence and, in some important regards, reshape our understanding of the Nazi phenomenon over the next decade. These shifts of focus, theme, and paradigm constitute a major force for the revision of current interpretations of National Socialism and are vividly reflected in the following essays, which have been substantially revised since they were originally presented as papers at a conference held at the University of Pennsylvania in April 1988.[5] The conference brought together a group of American and European specialists in the history of National Socialism in an effort to examine and reassess the most important recent scholarship on the Third Reich.

Although the authors hardly embrace a single interpretive view or adopt a uniform methodological approach, together they provide a challenging reassessment of existing analytic paradigms and the crystallization of a set of new ones. Some provide a reevaluation of older categories of interpretation—the intentionalist-functionalist debate, for example—or the reworking of others—best captured here in the essays on the Nazi economy—while others, particularly those dealing with Nazi racial policy, offer a significant, and controversial, new paradigm for understanding this most brutal and central feature of National Socialism. The essays collected here stand, therefore, at the crossroads between older and newer contexts of interpretation and offer, we believe, a powerful insight into the varied directions of current research.

Among the most significant changes in the recent scholarship on National Socialism, as Tim Mason points out in his short essay in the Appendix, is the virtual disappearance of the generic concept of fascism, which presided over much of the historical discussion of National Socialism in the 1960s and 1970s. Increasingly, scholars have concentrated on the more localized and, in Mason's view, less meaningful study of National Socialism alone. Closely linked to this eclipse of fascism by National Socialism is a second and highly revealing shift: the marginalization of class as an analytic and explanatory point of departure in the most recent literature. Class was, of course, the bedrock of the classic debates on fascism and also played a paradigmatic role in efforts to explain the sources of popular support for National Socialism before 1933. The sociological literature associated with the fascism debate was, in fact, a major stimulus of the recent close attention to the social history and everyday life *(Alltagsgeschichte)* of Nazi Germany.

Yet, paradoxically, both the new social history and the sociohistorical examination of political mobilization, although initially launched from a class perspective, have ultimately had the effect of weakening the purchase of Marxist class concepts. The class-based interpretation of the rise of National Socialism has been undergoing sharp revision for over a decade now, and the nuances of experience and behavior disclosed from the perspective of *Alltagsgeschichte* have proved to be not always compatible with older class paradigms.[6]

In addition, feminist scholarship of the past decade has also intervened to disturb some of the smoother assumptions of class theory and to force a reassessment of other well-established interpretive approaches to National Socialism. The feminist interest in reproductive politics, for example, has led to the emergence of a new eugenic paradigm for Nazi racism, reflected here in the essays of Detlev Peukert and Claudia Koonz.[7] In this new conceptualization of Nazi racism, the specificity of Nazi anti-Semitism is submerged in what is seen as a broader Nazi project of national eugenic or sociobiological renewal, in which not only Jews but also other so-called carriers of racial degeneration, whether defined by race or gender, were targets of the Nazis' murderous policies.

Certainly, among the most important substantive and methodological departures of the past decade in the research and writing on National Socialism has been a new interest in the social history of Germany between 1933 and 1945. Traditionally, the social history of the Third Reich had been assigned a secondary position, after analyses of political and economic developments. However, beginning in the 1970s, scholars have increasingly directed their attention toward the nature of German society, and especially to the fabric of quotidian social relations and of individual experience under the impact of National Socialist rule. The perspective in much of this work has been "from below" and has been increasingly influenced by new historical interests and methods such as *Alltagsgeschichte* and women's history. The task has been to examine patterns of everyday life and the subjective perceptions of "ordinary" Germans far removed from the Reich Chancellery or the other halls of power.[8]

In the process of examining the special characteristics of social relations in the Third Reich, this new research has at the same time drawn attention to continuities, revealing ways in which certain trends or patterns of social interaction preceded, continued under, and emerged from Nazi rule. Such findings suggested that, in certain basic areas of German life, neither 1933 nor 1945 should be viewed as the absolute watershed each is so often portrayed as being. As Ian Kershaw points out in the first essay of this collection, the *Alltag* approach suggests that

> below the barbarism and the horror of the regime were patterns of social "normality" that were, of course, affected by Nazism in various ways but that pre-dated and survived it. The role of Nazi ideology hence becomes "relativized" in the context of a "normality" of everyday life shaped for much of the time by non-ideological factors.

Thus, beneath the brutality of Nazi politics, "society in Nazi Germany can . . . be more easily related to other eras in German history, and more easily compared with other contemporary societies."

It was this conclusion, derived from the massive project entitled "Bavaria in the NS Period," a decade-long undertaking in which the *Alltag* approach was most extensively and systematically employed, that prompted its director Martin Broszat in 1985 to call for the "historicization" of the Third Reich. By this he meant a new, more nuanced, conceptualization of Nazi experience in German history that would take into account elements of both continuity and change, subjective perceptions as well as "objective" developments, and patterns of everyday experience as well as high politics.[9] The implications of Broszat's emphasis on everyday life, and on the contribution, however unintentional, of the National Socialist regime to long-term structural changes or the modernization of German society, are both profound and controversial.[10] As Kershaw points out, "this perspective challenges—and in some ways displaces—the traditional emphasis on the ideological, political, and criminal terroristic aspects of Nazism."

   Although the focus of *Alltagsgeschichte* has been largely directed toward social developments, it has also contributed significantly to discussions of political control, accommodation, dissent, and opposition. The work of Kershaw, Detlev Peukert, Robert Gellately—all contributors to this volume—as well as that of Reinhard Mann, Klaus Tenfelde, Jürgen Reulecke, and other participants in the Bavaria Project, has broadened our understanding of the possibilities of "opposition" or *Resistenz* in everyday life. They have also suggested a more textured and complex picture of the shades of accommodation or collaboration with the regime.[11] In his essay here, Robert Gellately uses the extensive collection of Gestapo case files in Würzburg to examine the implementation and enforcement of Nazi race policy. His analysis states that, in contrast to recent works that have tended to emphasize popular dissent or disaffection with various Nazi policies, "it is important to view opposition and dissent against the background of compliance, collaboration, and accommodation." He demonstrates persuasively that in their enforcement of racial policy, the Nazis were able to rely to a remarkable degree on informers who came forward to denounce fellow citizens. He goes on to conclude that

> given the vigilance of volunteer denouncers, official and semi-official snoopers, the extensive information gathering and police network, the many party operatives and so on, . . . the paucity of negative remarks aimed at the regime's anti-Semitism of one kind or another may be taken as an indication of the extent to which citizens accommodated themselves to the official line and, for all intents and purposes, did not stand in the way of the persecution of the Jews.

   In her essay, Claudia Koonz also uses the implementation of Nazi racial policy to examine Nazi efforts to generate "a new model of womanhood," to reshape "private life." Here, too, "compliance and accommodation, rather than a transfiguration of private life," were the effect of Nazi policy. The Nazis, Koonz argues, "recognized women's central importance in their racial schemes"; women were expected "to bear more children, select 'racially fit' mates, indoctrinate their children, and volunteer to help the 'racially worthy, deserving poor.'" They were also—and this is the subject of Koonz's analysis—expected "to target clients for forced abortion, sterilization, or euthanasia, to report 'suspicious' activities in the neighborhood, to boycott Jewish shops, and to refuse shelter to fugitives."

Koonz's essay traces the involvement of women in the implementation of Nazi eugenics policy, particularly the sterilization campaigns of 1933–36,[12] and she analyzes the correspondence written by women in the occupations most affected by the new laws—employees of hospitals, schools, welfare centers, and institutions for disabled people—to determine their reactions to Nazi racial policy. Their letters to church authorities in both Protestant and Catholic regions, Koonz suggests, "provide fresh insight into the success of the new eugenic rhetoric in transforming deeply felt moral values about life and death." They allow us to ascertain "how . . . women, as mothers, teachers, and health-care workers, react[ed] to the radical shift in gender prescription that replaced the traditional vision of woman as life-giving with a new image of woman as the heartless pruner of 'unwanted life.' " Using the techniques of *Alltagsgeschichte*, Koonz is not only able to examine women's attitudes on these matters but also to isolate differences between Protestant and Catholic reactions to National Socialist policy as well. The correspondence about eugenics, Koonz concludes,

> reveals a *Kirchenkampf* on gender lines within the Catholic and Protestant communities as well as the struggle between church and state. Because the issues had such a direct bearing on women's lives . . . , internal religious debates about race often pitted men against women, average people against their prelates.

While social history has perhaps come to the forefront of recent research, older political paradigms have also undergone major reevaluations. Among the numerous controversies that have emerged in the past twenty years concerning National Socialism, none is more central or more influential in the recent historiography of the Third Reich than the so-called "intentionalist-functionalist" debate. That debate centers on the question of whether the radicalization of the Nazi regime was the result of the implementation of its ideological program and its leaders' (especially Hitler's) intentions, or whether it must be understood as the less predictable consequence of the structure of the regime and its mode of operation. It raises fundamental questions about the role of Hitler, the nature of the Nazi state, and the place of ideological design in policy-making. These issues were prominent in the early political analyses of National Socialism—the works of Franz Neumann and Hannah Arendt come to mind—but they have been reformulated and systematically addressed for the first time in the scholarship of the 1970s and 1980s, especially in the work of Hans Mommsen and Martin Broszat.[13]

In his essay for this volume, Hans Mommsen presents his reflections on the state of that debate, using the relations between Hitler and Göring as his point of departure. In his view, the Hitler-centric interpretation of the Third Reich that is found in the works of Karl Dietrich Bracher, Eberhard Jäckel, and Klaus Hildebrand, an interpretation that clearly dominated the research of the

1960s, has been steadily undermined by numerous studies from the past decade that emphasize the "relative independence" of major figures within the regime such as Göring, von Ribbentrop, and von Neurath. These studies, and his own research, strongly suggest that "political responsibility and initiative lay to an important degree with the holders of high political and military office." These party, state, and military officials were "by no means committed to common goals," and it was only the interaction between them and the dictator, on whom they depended for "political and psychological integration," that "can adequately explain the political processes of the Third Reich." Rather than a Hitler-dominated monocratic state, Mommsen's interpretation of the Nazi regime thus emphasizes a decentralized "polycracy" that revolved around a "weak dictator." It focuses attention on the role of political and administrative structures and decision-making mechanisms in shaping the actual content of policy and argues that the former exerted a powerful, in some cases even decisive, influence on the latter. For over a decade this interpretation has had far-reaching implications for virtually every aspect of research on National Socialism, and its influence remains strong.[14]

Jane Caplan assesses the influence of this "functionalist" position, as well as other interpretations of the Nazi state, in her essay on state theory and National Socialism. She notes that interest in theories of the state tended to wane as research into the nature of the Nazi state became more empirically oriented. After assessing the course of theoretical writing on the Nazi state from Franz Neumann to Poulantzas, she shifts her attention to National Socialist political theory itself. Formulating a coherent theoretical position regarding the state proved difficult during the Third Reich, Caplan argues, in large part because "Nazi ideology was hostile to the concept of the state as well as to its practices." Among the greatest problems confronted by Nazi political theorists was conceptualizing, and then articulating, "the relationship between *Volk*, Führer, NSDAP, and state." The solution was "a series of largely formulaic representations, in which the concepts of the *Volk* and Führer took rhetorical and explanatory primacy." Since before the *Machtergreifung* (seizure of power) the Nazis had claimed to represent "the totality and universality of the (racial) nation," but once in power the party was faced with the challenge of "translating that proposition from the realm of ideology into that of politics." The idea that a "symbol of unity," in the person of Hitler, "could be made concrete pervaded the political and legal ideology of the Nazi regime," Caplan contends, and "helped to obstruct the development of any effective theory of state." It also meant unrelenting conflict among the party, the SS, and the bureaucratic proponents of administrative reform, who insisted on the achievement of real administrative unity, centralization. The result, Caplan concludes, was that the state in Nazi Germany "stood neither 'above' society, nor alongside it . . . ; rather, civil society experienced in violent form the consequences of an endemically fragmented political system."

Although the intentionalist-functionalist debate and *Alltagsgeschichte* have been major conceptual and methodological innovations of the 1970s and 1980s, more traditional empirical research has also yielded important advances in dealing with a number of long-standing issues in the history of the Third Reich. Nowhere is that more apparent than in the realm of economic history. The relationship between capitalism and National Socialism has, of course, been the subject of often bitter debate for decades. This complex issue has been broken down into a series of controversies, the most notable of which concern the role of big business in the rise of Hitler,[15] the ability of the regime to pull the nation out of the Great Depression,[16] the extent and effectiveness of Nazi economic preparations for war, the role that contradictions in German economic policy may have played in the timing of the outbreak of war,[17] and the extent to which one can speak of a distinctly Nazi or fascist economic order.[18] These issues have continued to attract considerable scholarly attention during the past decade, and Harold James, Tilla Siegel, Peter Hayes, and Tim Mason, all contributors to this volume, have been major participants in those debates.

In his essay, Harold James argues forcefully that 30 January 1933 "did not mark a major turning point in Germany's interwar economic history." In stark contrast to the conventional wisdom, James contends that Nazi economic policy was "anything but Keynesian," that its fiscal policy was "substantially orthodox." Rather than embarking on a new, distinctly fascist or ideologically determined economic policy, as the Nazis claimed, the economic actions of the regime, James argues, were "still dominated by the preconceptions and prejudices of the Depression Era." Until the introduction of the Four-Year Plan in 1936, which transformed Germany from "a controlled trade economy" into a "rearmament" or "state-planned" economy, the Nazis pursued "a rather unadventurous and conservative policy, following the lines laid down by previous governments' responses to the world depression." This policy "coincided with a staggering economic recovery," but the major structural shifts or breaks in Germany's capitalist economy, James contends, were not Nazi innovations but are to be found in the "bureaucratic/governmental response [to the Depression] by the Brüning government in the second half of 1931." The Nazis, of course, claimed credit for Germany's return to virtual full employment by 1935, but, James concludes, "the implication is that any government could have reaped the rewards that the Nazis harvested with such propagandistic insistence; or that— with regard to economic policy—'it did not have to be Hitler' to produce recovery."

Tilla Siegel, in her analysis of industrial relations under National Socialism, also stresses continuity, not only with the preceding Weimar period but also with the subsequent postwar period. Adopting a case-study approach, Siegel uses an analysis of labor relations in the shipbuilding industry to challenge a number of important theses concerning Nazi economic and labor policy. She notes that much labor history in the Third Reich has been focused on "the specific Nazi use of terror, ideology, and propaganda to integrate workers into the *Volksgemeinschaft*, and on how the regime was at times compelled to improve working conditions in order to prevent social unrest from threatening rearmament and war production." That research, she suggests, has tended to proceed from the assumption that "the irrationality of Nazi ideology and of the party often collided with the rationality of big business and the military." Her own analysis of labor relations in Germany's major shipyards indicates a strikingly different picture. She demonstrates that "on all fronts—government, Labor Front, and management—the politics of 'industrial peace' in Nazi Germany increasingly resorted to very 'rational' managerial concepts that had already been well developed in the 'rationalization movement' of the Weimar Republic, and that were well known in the United States." Moreover, this bundle of concepts, often incorporated in the term "Fordism," "were also later to become important features in industrial relations in the Federal Republic of Germany." The emphasis in Siegel's essay on both continuity over time and the comparative dimension in assessing Nazi economic policy reflects precisely the benefits to be derived from the "historicization" of the Third Reich that is suggested by Broszat.

The role of labor relations in the Nazi economy occupies a central role in Tim Mason's contribution to the volume as well. During the 1970s Mason developed the provocative thesis that "the accelerating dynamic of Nazi aggression in 1938 and 1939 was strongly conditioned by the *internal* problems of the regime." Mason contended that the dramatically accelerated drive to create an armaments economy to serve Hitler's plans for aggressive war created severe structural problems for the economy, problems that surfaced in the form of growing working-class unrest and dissatisfaction. In the original version of this view, Mason therefore concentrated on the problems of the labor market, which, he contended, had become acute by 1938. His contention—that growing concern about possible labor unrest pressed Hitler toward a *Flucht nach Vorn* (flight forward) in 1938–39—provoked considerable debate at the time, and recently a new round of that discussion has begun.[19]

In his essay here, Mason has developed a much broader definition of economic crisis. He argues that fiscal problems—the budget and the threat of inflation—had become "drastic at the end of 1938," and that foreign trade and agriculture had "also [come] under heavy pressure." These internal problems appeared as products of the forced rearmament after 1936 and constituted a major internal crisis of the regime. The regime's "needs to produce the biggest army in the world *and* to placate its working population with high real wages" had become incompatible by 1938–39," and thus, Mason argues, "Nazi Germany needed war and conquest in order to go on rearming at a high rate: the international arms race cannot be disassociated from the basic conditions of production inside Germany." Nazi determination to have both guns and butter, therefore, had produced by 1938 a "huge contradiction, which amounted to a fundamental crisis of policy choices, and thus to an (albeit hidden) crisis of the regime itself." This economic crisis, in turn, "brought in its tow political and then military problems of a basic kind that," Mason concludes, "could only be disguised, but could not begin to be resolved in peacetime."

Peter Hayes also takes up the question of Nazi economic performance, situating his essay within the context of the debate on polycracy or monocracy. He poses three basic questions. He notes that in dealing with the National Socialist economy both interpretations are in basic agreement that the proliferating organizations, overlapping jurisdictions, contradictory objectives, and un-coordinated administration characteristic of the Nazi regime resulted in an economic structure that was inefficient, one that ultimately undermined the Nazi war effort. In reevaluating Nazi economic performance, Hayes challenges this prevailing view from a number of perspectives.

He reminds us that "the Nazi state did carry out the most rapid recovery from the Depression among the major industrial nations," that full employment had been achieved by 1938, that "by 1939 Hitler had an operational air force, a massive army, an almost complete *Westwall* of fortifications . . . , and a domestic food supply that appeared (and proved) nearly immune to blockade." Key bottlenecks still existed in the economy, but, Hayes argues, "it is hard to ascribe the presence of these to administrative chaos." In contrast to Mason, Hayes denies the presence of an economic crisis in Germany in 1939, arguing that the key problem in that year and thereafter "was not between what Germany was doing and what [Hitler] wanted, but between what Germany *could* do and his growing requirements." Nazi failings, Hayes contends, "were ones of conception, not coordination. Germany simply could not marshal the wherewithal to 'arm in depth' and defeat a coalition of Britain, the United States, and the Soviet Union." The Third Reich was, in the end, "no more equal than the Second to the demands of fighting on multiple fronts and on the sea, not to mention in the air." Even a different organizational structure, Hayes concludes, "would not, in all probability, have overcome this fact."

Although the intentionalist-functionalist, or monocratic-polycratic, debate has exerted a powerful influence on research into virtually every area of the Third Reich, nowhere has it been more striking—and more hotly contested—than in the analysis of National Socialist racial policy.[20] Developed most forcefully by Lucy Dawidowicz and Gerald Fleming, the Hitler-centric intentionalist position essentially contends that Nazi racial policy was defined and driven by Hitler's own personal ideological obsession. From the outset of his career Hitler was determined to destroy the Jews, and Nazi racial policy, despite some tactical detours, proceeded more or less directly from the pages of *Mein Kampf* to the gas chambers of Auschwitz. While not all adherents of the intentionalist interpretation subscribe to the idea of a Nazi blueprint for action, they do agree that Nazi policy toward the Jews maintained an inner ideological logic, that it was linked to a basic set of other "final goals" in foreign policy, and that it proceeded by stages from the anti-Jewish boycott of 1933 to systematic physical extermination during the war.[21]

The functionalist interpretation, on the other hand, derives from an analysis of Nazi decision-making structures and their operational interactions. Its advocates maintain that rather than following an ideologically determined plan of action, Nazi racial policy evolved in an unsystematic, ad hoc, and improvisational manner. Competition between different party, state, and military organizations was inherent in the polycratic structure of the Third Reich, and the resulting conflict, the functionalist interpretation insists, is as critical to an explanation of ultimate policy outcomes as the content of the ideology itself. As rival state and party agencies competed to translate a loose, ill-defined set of ideological imperatives into reality or to deal with situations created by the actions of other agencies, a radicalizing dynamic was generated that pressed the regime to adopt increasingly extreme measures to resolve conflict. The "Final Solution" may have been a logical outcome of Nazi ideology, but it was hardly the product of a grand strategic design.[22]

While building on foundations laid by the existing intentionalist-functionalist debate, Christopher Browning and Detlev Peukert challenge, from very different directions, the adequacy of conceptualizing Nazi racial policy along these lines. Browning focuses on Nazi Jewish policy between 1939 and 1941, and contends that an examination of population resettlement and ghettoization, two major aspects of that policy, demonstrates the weakness of the traditional intentionalist *and* functionalist interpretations. He argues that contrary to the intentionalist position, the Nazis were quite "serious about expulsion as a solution to the Jewish question," and that it was the failure of these earlier expulsion plans, not "a long-term plan" for extermination, that "helped trigger the quantum leap to mass murder."

At the same time, Browning takes issue with Mommsen, Broszat, and the functionalists on a number of major points. He questions their emphasis on the role played by local Nazi authorities in radicalizing the regime's Jewish policy and thus disputes the efficacy of the related bureaucratic model, associated with Raul Hilberg and, more recently, with the work of Susanne Heim and Götz Aly.[23] Lower-echelon technocrats, social planners, and party authorities clearly "articulated the vision and presented the alternatives that shaped the decisions of those above them," but they did not make the crucial decisions themselves, Browning argues. It was Hitler, often acting indirectly, who played the crucial role in propelling Nazi racial policy, Browning contends. Indeed, "from September 1939 to October 1941," when the "Final Solution" had been decided on, "Hitler instigated and approved every major change in Nazi Jewish policy."

Finally, Browning argues that the mass extermination of the Jews cannot be explained as "a by-product of or companion piece to the anti-Bolshevik 'crusade,'" a position recently articulated by Arno J. Mayer,[24] or as a product of Nazi eugenics or "biopolitics." Both contributed in important ways to the "Final Solution," but, Browning insists, "the Nazi campaign to murder the European Jews had gained a great deal more 'autonomy' and 'priority' in its own right by late 1941 than these other models indicate." Browning concludes that while "anti-Bolshevism, eugenics, and bureaucratic momentum" all contributed to a growing consensus "that the 'Jewish question' was real, the war created "the fateful atmosphere" in which the Nazis were "increasingly able to impose their own image of the Jew as the enemy of the German people." Thus, in contrast to the eugenics, bureaucratic/structuralist, or anti-Bolshevik interpretations of recent years, Browning's analysis places the role of anti-Semitism at the center of the debate.

Detlev Peukert's examination of the genesis of the "Final Solution" disputes this emphasis. Peukert, whose argument is informed by the new literature on eugenics and Nazi social policy more broadly,[25] contends that all monocausal explanations of the origins of the "Final Solution" are inadequate. He suggests, however, that in the "tangle of causes" one central thread can be isolated, one that "might explain the origins of the decision, unparalleled in human history, to use high technology to annihilate certain abstractly defined categories of victims." That thread, he maintains,

> is not to be found in the traditional history of anti-Semitism and the persecution of the Jews. . . . Rather, what was new about the "Final Solution" . . . was the fact that it resulted from a fatal racist dynamism present within the human and social sciences. This dynamism operated within the paradigm of the qualitative distinction between "value" and "nonvalue." Its complement in practical terms was the treatment of the *Volkskörper*, or "body" of the nation, by means of "selection" and "eradication."

According to Peukert, the "Final Solution" was "a systematic, high-technology procedure for 'eradicating,' or 'culling,' those without 'value.'" It operated in terms of the dichotomies *healthy/unhealthy* with reference to the *Volkskörper*, *normal/deviant* with reference to the *Volksgemeinschaft*, and *Volk/Volksfremd* with reference to the nation and the race."

If the vision of a healthy, dynamic *Volkskörper* remained vague at best, "the catalogue of deviances . . . to be eradicated [became] ever more detailed and specific." It was "the negative radicalization of the racist utopia" that would, Peukert argues, "become the vital guiding thread in the evolution of Nazi policy." Before the war, eradicating these "deviant threats" to the *Volkskörper* ranged from segregation to sterilization. With the euthanasia program, initiated in 1939, calling for the systematic murder of those deemed "unworthy of life," the "crucial step [was] taken from the racist utopian dream to its realization in the 'Final Solution.'" Indeed, the process whereby the racist definition of the victims of the "Final Solution" was expanded, Peukert argues, makes plain that it was the eugenic, racial-hygiene variant of racism that provided the key component parts in the machinery of mass murder. "Anti-Semitism based on racial anthropology supplie[d] the graphic and traditionally legitimized scapegoat image that help[ed] serve as a basis for expansion of the category of victim. But," Peukert concludes, "the specifically modern character of the 'Final Solution' derives from the swing to racial hygiene in the human and social sciences."

The essays collected in this volume do not represent a unified school of thought or a distinct interpretation of National Socialism. Disagreements on emphasis and interpretation are readily apparent, and, of course, it has not been possible in the limited framework of a single volume to address all the issues or methodological departures of recent years. Yet, together, the essays assembled here are representative of some of the most important scholarship of the past decade on National Socialism, and they indicate a number of the most promising new directions for research. In the process they offer a valuable set of guideposts in a complex and demanding discussion that, we believe, must never be allowed to wane.

Philadelphia 1991

Notes

1. The best guide to the various debates concerning the Third Reich is Ian Kershaw's *The Nazi Dictatorship: Problems and Perspectives of Interpretation* (London, 1985, revised and expanded edition, 1989).

2. The major contributions to the debate have been collected in R. Piper, ed., *"Historikerstreit": Die Dokumentation der Kontroverse um die Einzigartigkeit der nationalsozialistischen Judenvernichtung* (Munich, 1987). For strongly conflicting views of the controversy, see Hans-Ulrich Wehler, *Entsorgung der deutschen Vergangenheit? Ein polemischer Essay zum "Historikerstreit"* (Munich, 1988), and Immanuel Geiss, *Die Habermas-Kontroverse: Ein deutscher Streit* (Berlin, 1988). See also Dan Diner, ed., *Ist der Nationalsozialismus Geschichte? Zur Historisierung und Historikerstreit* (Frankfurt, 1987); and Bernd Faulenbach and Rainer Bölling, *Geschichtsbewusstsein und historisch-politische Bildung in der Bundesrepublik Deutschland: Beiträge zum "Historikerstreit"* (Düsseldorf, 1988).

3. The best treatments of the debate available in English are: Charles S.

Maier, *The Unmasterable Past: History, Holocaust, and German National Identity* (Cambridge, Mass., 1988), which situates the controversy in the context of German historiography since the war; and Richard J. Evans, *In Hitler's Shadow: West German Historians and the Attempt to Escape from the Nazi Past* (New York, 1989), and Geoff Eley, "Nazism, Politics, and the Image of the Past: Thoughts on the West German *Historikerstreit*, 1986–1987," *Past and Present* 121 (1988): 171–208, both of which focus far more sharply on the political content and implications of the debate. The *New German Critique* has also devoted a special issue to the *Historikerstreit* (44 [Spring–Summer 1988]), with some translated pieces as well as original commentaries.

4. The most recent assessment of the Fischer controversy is found in the proceedings of the symposium, "The German Empire and the First World War: A Quarter Century After the Fischer Controversy," with contributions by Fischer, Samuel R. Williamson, and Konrad H. Jarausch, *Central European History* 21 (1988): 203–43. On its broader implications for German historiography, see Richard J. Evans, *Rethinking German History: Nineteenth Century Germany and the Origins of the Third Reich* (London, 1987); and Hans-Ulrich Wehler, "Historiography in Germany Today," in Jürgen Habermas, ed., *Observations on "The Spiritual Situation of the Age"* (Cambridge, Mass. 1984), pp. 221–59. The best guide to the *Sonderweg* controversy is Robert G. Moeller, "The Kaiserreich Recast? Continuity and Change in Modern German Historiography," *Journal of Social History* 17 (1984): 442–50.

5. We are deeply indebted to the Deutscher Akademischer Austauschdienst, the Council for European Studies, the Social Science Research Council, the Center for European Studies at the University of Pennsylvania, and Bryn Mawr College for their generous support of the conference that made this volume possible.

6. Despite sometimes acrimonious disagreements concerning methodology and interpretation, the sociographic literature of the past decade on the social bases of National Socialism is in fundamental agreement that the social foundations of National Socialism were far broader than the traditional lower middle-class interpretation suggested. For a cross-section of that literature, see Thomas Childers, ed., *The Formation of the Nazi Constituency, 1919–1933* (London, 1986). Few would suggest "a farewell to the class analysis" of National Socialism, but most agree that a far more differentiated approach to social identity and political mobilization is in order. For some attempts to break new ground in that, see Rudy Koshar, *Social Life, Local Politics, and Nazism: The Bürgertum of Marburg/Lahn* (Chapel Hill, N.C., 1986); Peter Fritzsche, *Burgher Dissidents: Populism and Political Mobilization in the Weimar Republic* (Oxford, 1990); and Thomas Childers, "The Social Language of Politics: The Sociology of Political Discourse in the Weimar Republic," *American Historical Review* 95 (1990): 331–58.

7. See especially Renate Bridenthal, Atina Grossmann, and Marion Kaplan, eds., *When Biology Became Destiny: Women in Weimar and Nazi Germany* (New York, 1984); Claudia Koonz, *Mothers in the Fatherland: Women, the Family, and Nazi Politics* (New York, 1987); Ute Frevert, *Women in German History: From Bourgeois Emancipation to Sexual Liberation* (Oxford, 1989); and Gisela Bock, *Zwangssterilisation: Studien zur Rassenpolitik und Frauenpolitik* (Opladen, 1986).

8. *Alltagsgeschichte der NS-Zeit: Neue Perspektive oder Trivialisierung? Kolloquien des Instituts für Zeitgeschichte* (Munich, 1984); Detlev Peukert and Jürgen Reulecke, eds., *Die Reihen fast geschlossen: Beiträge zur Geschichte des Alltags unterm Nationalsozialismus* (Wuppertal, 1981); Detlev Peukert, *Volksgenossen und Gemeinschaftsfremde: Anpassung, Ausmerze und Aufbegehren unter dem Nationalsozialismus* (Cologne, 1982), now translated as *Inside Nazi Germany: Conformity, Opposition and Racism in Everyday Life* (London, New Haven, 1987). See also the three-volume excursion into oral history edited by Lutz Niethammer, *"Die Jahre weiss man nicht, wo man die heute hinsetzen soll": Faschismus-Erfahrungen im Ruhrgebiet, 1930 bis 1960,* and *"Hinterher merkt man, dass es richtig war, dass es schiefgegangen ist": Nachkriegserfahrungen im Ruhrgebiet. Lebensgeschichte und Sozialstruktur im Ruhrgebiet, 1930–1960,* vols. 1–2 (Bonn, Berlin, 1983); and *"Wir kriegen jetzt andere Zeiten": Auf der Suche nach der Erfahrung des Volkes in nachfaschistischen Ländern,* vol. 3 (Bonn, Berlin, 1985).

9. Martin Broszat, "Plädoyer für eine Historisierung des Nationalsozialismus," *Merkur* 39 (1985): 373–85, reprinted in Broszat, *Nach Hitler: Der schwierige Umgang mit unserer Geschichte* (Munich, 1986), pp. 159–73.

10. This plea for a new contextualization of the Nazi years preceded the *Historikerstreit*, but it quickly emerged at the heart of that dispute. Nolte's call for a new comparative context in which to evaluate Nazi crimes, and Andreas Hillgruber's use of the tools of *Alltagsgeschichte* to defend German soldiers fighting tenaciously on the Eastern Front in the last months of the war, struck many as a fundamental misconstruction of Broszat's concept of "historicization" and as a misuse of *Alltagsgeschichte*'s emphasis on the importance of "subjective experience." Others, such as Saul Friedländer and Charles Maier, while careful to distinguish between Broszat and the conservative combatants in the *Historikerstreit*, nonetheless wondered if the very concept itself were not essentially flawed and prone to precisely such disastrous misuse. For Friedländer's response to Broszat's "plea," see Saul Friedländer, "Some Reflections on the Historicization of National Socialism," *German Politics and Society* 13 (February 1988): 9–21 (translated from his "Überlegungen zur Historisierung des Nationalsozialismus," in Dan Diner, ed., *Ist der Nationalsozialismus Geschichte?* pp. 34–50). Subsequently, Broszat and Friedländer agreed to publish an exchange of letters dealing with the problems and implications of "historicizing"

the Third Reich. As Andrei S. Markovits observes in his introduction to the English version of the exchange, their discussion raises issues that "may prove a good deal more lasting and significant for the larger debate and the future of German historiography than the well-known skirmishes of the *Historikerstreit* proper." The original exchange appeared in *VfZ* 36 (April 1988): 339–72; the English version, with Markovits's introductory comments, in *New German Critique* 44 (Spring–Summer 1988): 81–126.

11. Ian Kershaw, *Popular Opinion and Political Dissent in the Third Reich: Bavaria, 1933–1945* (Oxford, 1983); Robert Gellately, *The Gestapo and German Society: Enforcing Racial Policy, 1933–1945* (New York, 1990); Detlev Peukert, *Inside Nazi Germany* (New York, 1987); Klaus Tendfelde, "Proletarische Provinz: Radikalisierung und Widerstand in Penzberg/Oberbayern, 1900–1945," in Broszat et al., eds., *Bayern in der NS-Zeit: Herrschaft und Gesellschaft*, vol. 4, pp. 1–382; Reinhard Mann, *Protest und Kontrolle im Dritten Reich: Nationalsozialistische Herrschaft im Alltag einer rheinischen Grossstadt* (Frankfurt, 1987); Dieter Rebentisch, "Die 'politische Beurteilung' als Herrschaftsinstrument der NSDAP," in Peukert und Reulecke, *Die Reihen fast geschlossen*, pp. 107–25.

12. See also Gisela Bock, *Zwangssterilisation im Nationalsozialismus*; and Kurt Nowak, *Euthanasie und Sterilisierung im "Dritten Reich": Die Konfrontation der evangelischen und katholischen Kirche mit dem 'Gesetz zur Verhütung erbkranken Nachwuchses' und der "Euthanasie-Aktion"* (Göttingen, 1980).

13. The best introduction to the terms of the debate is found in Tim Mason, "Intention and Explanation: A Current Controversy about the Interpretation of National Socialism," in Hirschfeld and Kettenacker, *Der "Führerstaat": Mythos und Realität* (Stuttgart, 1981), pp. 23–41. The new wave of analysis that focused on structures and operations of the Nazi state broke on the historiography of the Third Reich in 1969 with the appearance of Martin Broszat's *Der Staat Hitlers* (Munich, 1969), translated as *The Hitler State* (New York, 1981); William N. Peterson's *The Limits of Hitler's Power* (Princeton, N.J., 1969); and Peter Hüttenberger, *Die Gauleiter: Studie zum Wandel des Machtgefüges in der NSDAP* (Stuttgart, 1969); R. Bollmus, *Das Amt Rosenberg und seine Gegner: Zum Machtkampf im nationalsozialistischen Herrschaftssystem* (Stuttgart, 1970); A. Kuhn, "Herrschaftsstruktur und Ideologie des Nationalsozialismus," *Neue Politische Literatur* (1971); M. Funke, "Führer-Prinzip und Kompetenz-Anarchie im nationalsozialistischen Herrschaftssystem," *Neue Politische Literatur* (1975).

14. The debate on the role of Hitler was precipitated largely by the work of Hans Mommsen, who has argued that Hitler was in many ways "a weak dictator." See Mommsen, "Nationalsozialismus," in *Sowjetsystem und demokratische Gesellschaft: Eine vergleichende Enzyklopädie*, vol. 4 (Freiburg, 1971);

"Nationalsozialimus oder Hitlerismus?" in Michael Bosch, ed., *Persönlichkeit und Struktur in der Geschichte* (Düsseldorf, 1977), pp. 66–70; "National Socialism: Continuity and Change," in Walter Laqueur, ed., *Fascism: A Reader's Guide* (New York, 1979), pp. 179–210; and "Hitlers Stellung im nationalsozialistischen Herrschaftssystem," in Hirschfeld and Kettenacker, *Der "Führerstaat,"* pp. 43–72. See also Peter Hüttenberg, "Nationalsozialistische Polykratie," *Geschichte und Gesellschaft* 2 (1976): 417–32. Mommsen's thesis has been attacked most consistently by Klaus Hildebrand and Karl Dietrich Bracher. See Hildebrand, "Monokratie oder Polykratie? Hitler's Herrschaft und das Dritte Reich," in Hirschfeld and Kettenacker, eds., *Der "Führerstaat";* and his "Nationalsonzialismus ohne Hitler?" *Geschichte in Wissenschaft und Unterricht* 31 (1980), pp. 73–97. See also Karl Dietrich Bracher, "The Role of Hitler: Perspectives of Interpretation," in Laqueur, *Fascism*, pp. 211–25.

15. For the most recent scholarship on this issue, see Henry Ashby Turner, Jr., *Big Business and the Rise of Hitler* (New York, 1984); David Abraham, *The Collapse of the Weimar Republic: Political Economy and Crisis*, 2d ed. (New York, 1986); Reinhard Neebe, *Grossindustrie, Staat und NSDAP, 1930–1933* (Göttingen, 1981); and Thomas Trumpp, "Zur Finanzierung der NSDAP durch die deutsche Grossindustrie: Versuch einer Bilanz," in Karl Dietrich Bracher, Manfred Funke, and Hans-Adolf Jacobsen, eds., *Nationalsozialistische Diktatur, 1933–1945: Eine Bilanz,* (Düsseldorf, 1983).

16. Harold James, *The German Slump: Politics and Economics, 1924–1936* (Oxford, 1986); Richard J. Overy, *The Nazi Economic Recovery* (London, 1982); "Unemployment in the Third Reich," in *Business History* 29 (1987): 253–81; Dan P. Silverman, "National Socialist Economics: The Wirtschaftswunder Reconsidered," in B. Eichengreen and T. Hatton, eds., *Interwar Unemployment in Historical Perspective* (The Hague, 1988); and J. J. Lee, "Policy and Performance in the German Economy, 1925–1935: A Comment on the Borchart Thesis," in M. Laffan, ed., *The Burden of German History, 1919–1945* (London, 1988).

17. See Tim Mason, "Innere Krise und Angriffskrieg, 1938/1939," in Friedrich Forstmeier and Hans-Erich Volkmann, eds., *Wirtschaft und Rüstung am Vorabend des Zweiten Weltkrieges* (Düsseldorf, 1975); Mason, *Sozialpolitik im Dritten Reich*, chap., 6; Alan S. Milward, *War, Economy and Society, 1939–1945* (London, 1977); Ludolf Herbst, "Die Krise des nationalsozialistischen Regimes am Vorabend des Zweiten Weltkrieges und die forcierte Ausrüstung," *VfZ*, no. 3 (1978); Richard J. Overy, "Hitler's War and the German Economy: A Reinterpretation," *Economic History Review* 35 (1982); David E. Kaiser, *Economic Diplomacy and the Origins of the Second World War* (Princeton, N.J., 1980); Hans-Erich Volkmann, "Zum Verhältnis von Grosswirtschaft und NS-Regime im Zweiten Weltkrieg," in Bracher et al., eds., *Nationalsozialistische Diktatur, 1933–1945: Eine Bilanz*, pp. 480–508; Volkmann, "Politik,

Wirtschaft und Aufrüstung," in Manfred Funke, ed., *Hitler, Deutschland und die Mächte* (Düsseldorf, 1978); William Carr, *Arms, Autarky, and Aggression,* 2d ed. (London, 1979).

18. Tim Mason, "The Primacy of Politics—Politics and Economics in National Socialist Germany," in Henry A. Turner, Jr., ed., *Nazism and the Third Reich* (New York, 1972), pp. 175–200; Charles S. Maier, "The Economics of Fascism and Nazism ," in idem, ed., *In Search of Political Stability: Explorations on Historical Political Economy* (Cambridge, 1987); Peter Hayes, *Industry and Ideology: IG Farben in the Nazi Era* (Cambridge, 1987); John R. Gillingham, *Industry and Politics in the Third Reich* (London, 1985); A. Barkai, *Das Wirtschaftssystem des Nationalsozialismus: Der historische und ideologische Hintergrund, 1933–1936* (Cologne, 1977); See also Dietrich Eichholz, *Geschichte der deutschen Kriegswirtschaft, 1933–1945* (East Berlin, 1969).

19. For Mason's original exposition of the thesis, see the references in note 17, as well as his *Arbeiterklasse und Volksgemeinschaft: Dokumente und Materialien zur deutschen Arbeiterpolitik, 1936–1939* (Opladen, 1975), chaps. 8–11. Richard J. Overy's recent objections to Mason's interpretation have sparked a new round of the debate. See Overy, "Germany, 'Domestic Crisis' and War in 1939," *Past and Present*, no. 116 (August 1987): 138–68. The responses of Mason and David E. Kaiser, as well as Overy's rejoinder, are found in "Debate: Germany, Domestic Crisis and War in 1939," *Past and Present*, no. 122 (February 1939): 200–240.

20. See Ian Kershaw, *The Nazi Dictatorship,* pp. 82–105; also, Michael R. Marrus, *The Holocaust in History* (New York, 1987); Saul Friedländer, "From Anti-Semitism to Extermination: A Historiographical Study of Nazi Policies toward the Jews," *Yad Vashem Studies* 16 (1984): 1–50. Otto Duv Kulka, "Major Trends and Tendencies of German Historiography on National Socialism and the 'Jewish Question' (1924–1984)," *Yearbook of the Leo Baeck Institute* 30 (1985): 215–42; see also his "Singularity and Its Relativization: Changing Views in German Historiography on National Socialism and the 'Final Solution,'" *Yad Vashem Studies* 19 (1988); Richard Breitman, "Auschwitz and the Archives," *Central European History* 18, nos. 3–4 (1985): 365–83.

21. The most vigorous statement of the intentionalist position is found in Lucy Dawidowicz, *The War Against the Jews* (New York, 1975); and Gerald Fleming, *Hitler and the Final Solution* (Berkeley, Calif., 1984). See also Eberhard Jäckel, *Hitler's Weltanschauung: A Blueprint for Power* (Middletown, Conn., 1972); Andreas Hillgruber, "Die 'Endlösung' und das deutsche Os- timperium als Kernstuck des rassenideologischen Programms des Na- tionalsozialismus," in Funke, ed., *Hitler, Deutschland, und die Mächte,* pp. 94– 114; and "Die ideologisch-dogmatischen Grundlagen der nationalsozialistischen Politik der Ausrottung der Juden in den besetzten Gebieten der Sowjetunion und ihre Durchführung, 1941–1944," *German Studies Review* 2, no. 2 (1979): 263–

96; and Helmut Krausnick, "The Persecution of the Jews," in Hans Buchheim, Martin Broszat, Hans-Adolf Jacobsen, and Helmut Krausnick, *Anatomy of the SS State* (New York, 1968), pp. 1–124.

22. The functionalist interpretation is associated most prominently with the works of Hans Mommsen and Martin Broszat. See especially Mommsen, "Die Realisierung des Utopischen: Die 'Endlösung der Judenfrage im "Dritten" Reich,'" *Geschichte und Gesellschaft* 9 (1983): 381–420, now translated as "The Realization of the Unthinkable: The 'Final Solution of the Jewish Question' in the Third Reich," in Hirschfeld and Kettenacker, eds., *Der "Führerstaat,"* pp. 97–144; Martin Broszat, "Hitler und die Genesis der 'Endlösung': Aus Anlass der Thesen von David Irving," *VfZ* 25 (1977): 737–75, translated as "Hitler and the Genesis of the 'Final Solution,'" *Yad Vashem Studies* 13 (1979): 73–125; Mommsen and Broszat have constructed their interpretation on foundations laid in the following works: Uwe Dietrich Adam, *Judenpolitik im Dritten Reich* (Düsseldorf, 1972); and his "Persecution of the Jews: Bureaucracy and Authority in the Totalitarian State," *Leo Baeck Institute Year Book* 23 (1978): 139–48; Adam, "An Overall Plan for Anti-Jewish Legislation in the Third Reich," *Yad Vashem Studies* 11 (1976): 33–55; Karl Schleunes, *The Twisted Road to Auschwitz: Nazi Policies toward the Jews, 1933–1939* (Urbana, Ill., 1970; new edition, 1990).

23. Raul Hilberg, *The Destruction of the European Jews*, revised and expanded edition in three volumes (New York, 1985); Susanne Heim and Götz Aly, "Die Ökonomie der 'Endlösung': Menschenvernichtung und wirtschaftliche Neuordnung," *Beiträge zur nationalsozialistischen Gesundheits- und Sozialpolitik*. Vol. 5, *Sozialpolitik und Jüdenvernichtung: Gibt es eine Ökonomie der Endlösung?* (Berlin, 1985), pp. 11–90.

24. Arno Mayer, *Why Did the Heavens Not Darken? The "Final Solution" in History* (New York, 1988).

25. See Ernst Klee, *"Euthanasie" im NS-Staat: Die "Vernichtung lebensunwerten Lebens"* (Frankfurt, 1983); Hans-Walter Schmuhl, *Rassenhygiene, Nationalsozialismus, Euthanasie: Von der Verhütung zur Vernichtung "lebensunwerten Lebens," 1890–1945* (Göttingen, 1987); Robert N. Proctor, *Racial Hygiene: Medicine under the Nazis* (Cambridge, Mass., 1988); Heindrun Kaupen-Haas, ed., *Der Griff nach der Bevölkerung: Aktualität und Kontinuität nazistischer Bevölkerungspolitik* (Hamburg, 1986); Götz Aly, Angelika Ebbinghaus, Matthias Hamann, Friedemann Pfafflin, and Gerd Preissler, *Aussonderung und Tod: Die klinische Hinrichtung der Unbrauchbaren* (Berlin, 1985); Michael Kater, *Doctors under Hitler* (Chapel Hill, N.C., 1990); and his "Die 'Gesundheitsführung' des deutschen Volkes," *Medizinhistorisches Journal* 18 (1983): 349–75. Robert J. Lifton, *The Nazi Doctors* (New York, 1986).

1

"Normality" and Genocide: The Problem of "Historicization"

IAN KERSHAW

Since 1986, scholars working on German history and related fields have been preoccupied with (or have found it impossible to escape from) the *Historikerstreit*, "historians' dispute," a major controversy on how West German society should handle the Nazi past more than forty years after the death of Hitler. This paper is concerned with an issue that, while intrinsic to the *Historikerstreit* and forming one significant strand of it, is separable from it, in fact preceded it, and raises distinctive theoretical and methodological problems best dealt with in detachment from the polemics of the *Historikerstreit* itself. This is the problem of the so-called "historicization" *(Historisierung)* of National Socialism, a term that first entered serious discussion when advanced by Martin Broszat in an important and programmatic essay published in 1985,[1] over a year before the *Historikerstreit* broke out. It revolves around the question of whether, more than forty years after the collapse of the Third Reich, it is possible to treat the Nazi era in the ways that other eras of the past are treated—as "history"—and what new perspectives such a shift in conceptualization and method would demand. In intellectual terms, the controversy that Broszat's article provoked, although more narrowly confined in terms of the number of participants and receiving (until recently) far less public attention, is much more significant and

This essay, in slightly different form, was originally published as a chapter in Ian Kershaw, *The Nazi Dictatorship: Problems and Perspectives of Interpretation*, 2d ed. (London: Edward Arnold, 1989), copyright © 1989 Ian Kershaw.

rewarding than the *Historikerstreit* itself. Interestingly, too, this controversy crosses the hardened battle-lines that rapidly formed in the *Historikerstreit*. And it involves consideration of the contribution and potential of what has, in many respects, proved a most fruitful approach in research on the Third Reich in recent years, that of *Alltagsgeschichte*, "the history of everyday life."

During the past fifteen or so years, new and exciting avenues of research have been explored in a massive outpouring of studies ranging over most of the important aspects of the impact of Nazism on German society. Yet, just as the time seems ripe—almost a quarter of a century since the appearance of Schoenbaum's wide-ranging social history of the Third Reich, which saw it as "Hitler's social revolution," and Dahrendorf's equally influential interpretation of Nazism as "the German revolution"[2]—for a new full-scale study that would synthesize and incorporate much of this work and offer a revised interpretation of German society under Nazism, the "historicization" controversy casts doubt on even the theoretical possibility of constructing such a social history without losing sight of the central aspects of Nazism that provide it with its lasting world-historical significance and its moral legacy. The first part of this chapter offers an outline of this important controversy, while the second part seeks to evaluate its implications for a potential history of German society in the Third Reich.

The "Historicization" Approach

A major breakthrough in the deepening awareness of the complexity of German society in the Third Reich, it is universally recognized, was the research undertaken and published between the mid-1970s and early 1980s within the framework of the "Bavaria Project." This project, run by the Munich Institute of Contemporary History and carried out under the rubric of "Resistance and Persecution in Bavaria, 1933–1945," helped to offer an entirely new dimension to the understanding of relations between state and society in Nazi Germany. It deliberately turned away from narrow, often morally loaded definitions of "resistance" and used instead a novel concept of *Resistenz*[3]—a term difficult to convey in English, but taken from the language of medicine, not politics, and suggestive of morally neutral impenetrability or immunity rather than actively motivated opposition. This approach allowed the opening up of research into the gray, overlapping areas of collaboration and opposition, political conformity and nonconformity, consent and dissent apparent in the actual reality of having to adjust to and come to terms with Nazi rule. The "Bavaria Project" was a landmark because it examined, for the first time in any systematic fashion, popular opinion, mentalities, and behavior, and because it tried—again a breakthrough—to write the history of society in the Third Reich "from below."

The project, it seems clear, was an important impulse, among others, in the rapid development of the "everyday life" approach to the Third Reich. The very concept of *Alltagsgeschichte* and the methods deployed by its exponents have provoked much stringent criticism—some of it well justified—particularly from the leading protagonists of the "critical history" and "history as social science" *(historische Sozialwissenschaften)* approach.[4] Such criticism has not, however, been able to stem the continued spread of *Alltagsgeschichte,* and some, even of its sharpest critics, have accepted that, properly conceptualized, *Alltagsgeschichte* can have much to offer in deepening understanding.[5] The remarkable resonance of the "everyday life" approach, exploring subjective experiences and mentalities at the grass roots of society, presumably reflects in part, not least through the opening up of previously taboo areas of consideration, a need, particularly strong among young people, to come to grips with the Third Reich not just as a political phenomenon—as a horrific regime providing a source of political and moral lessons in a postfascist democracy—but also as a social experience, in order to understand better the behavior of ordinary people (like their own relatives) under Nazism. By making past behavior and mentalities more explicable, more understandable, more "normal"—even if to be condemned—*Alltagsgeschichte,* it can be argued, has contributed to a deepened awareness of the problems of historical identity in the Federal Republic, and of the relationship of the Third Reich not just to political continuities and discontinuities, but now also to social strands of continuity predating Nazism and extending well into the postwar era. This further prompts the need to locate the Third Reich as an integral component of German history, not one that can be bracketed out and detached as if it did not really belong to it. These are some of the considerations behind Martin Broszat's well-known "plea for the historicization of National Socialism," premised on the assertion that the history of the Nazi era, as opposed to that of the political system of the dictatorship, still remains to be written.[6]

Broszat's use of the term *Historisierung,* "historicization," relates to the problems of historians, and specifically West German historians, in dealing with the Nazi past. Even forty years and more after the end of the Third Reich, the distance that the historian puts between him- or herself and the subject matter of Nazism provides, in Broszat's view, a major obstacle to the possibility of approaching the scholarly study and analysis of Nazism in the same way that other periods of history are tackled—with the degree of intuitive insight that "normal" historical writing demands. Yet, without the proper integration of Nazism into "normal" historical writing, he sees the Third Reich remaining an "island" in modern German history,[7] a resort for lessons of political morality in which routine moral condemnation excludes historical understanding, reducing Nazism to an "abnormality" and serving as a compensatory alibi for a restored historicism *(Historismus)* with regard to the more "healthy" epochs before and after Hitler.[8] The position is summed up in the following way:

> A normalization of our historical consciousness and the com-
> munication of national identity through history cannot be
> achieved by avoiding the Nazi era through its exclusion. Yet it
> seems to me that the greater the historical distance becomes, the
> more urgent it is to realise that bracketing the Hitler era out of
> history and historical thinking also occurs in a way when it is only
> dealt with from a political-moral perspective and not with the
> same differentiated applied historical method as other historical
> epochs, when treated with less carefully considered judgment and
> in a cruder, more general language, or when, for well-intentioned
> didactic reasons, we grant it a sort of methodological special
> treatment.[9]

A "normalization" of methodological treatment would mean the application of the normal rigors of historical enquiry in a meticulous scholarship
deploying "midrange" concepts susceptible to empirical investigation in place of
bland moralization, whether from a liberal-conservative perspective or from
sterile economistic-determinant theories of a Marxist-Leninist or "new Left"
variety.[10] This in itself would refine moral sensitivity through the increased
understanding derivable from greater differentiation, as in the relativization of
"resistance" through its "de-heroization" and recognition of the checkered gray
nature of the boundaries of opposition and conformity between the "Other
Germany" and the Nazi regime.[11] It would allow, too, Nazism's function as the
exponent of modernizing change comparable with that in other contemporary
societies to be properly incorporated in an understanding of the era, and hence a
deeper awareness of the social forces and motivation that the Nazi movement
could mobilize and exploit.[12]

The relevance of the Bavaria Project and of the emphasis on *Alltagsgeschichte* to this line of thought is self-evident. The underlying notion
beneath the whole concept of historicization is that below the barbarism and the
horror of the regime were patterns of social "normality" that were, of course,
affected by Nazism in various ways but that predated and survived it. The role of
Nazi ideology hence becomes "relativized" in the context of a "normality" of
everyday life shaped much of the time by nonideological factors. Nazism can be
seen to accelerate some, and put the brake on other, trends of social change and
development that form a continuum from pre-Nazi times into the Federal
Republic.[13] Beneath the barbarity, society in Nazi Germany can thus be more
easily related to other eras in German history, and more easily compared with
other contemporary societies. The long-term structural change and modernization of German society become thereby more explicable, as does the role of
Nazism—deliberate or unwitting—in relationship to that change. This perspective challenges—and in some ways displaces—the traditional emphasis on the
ideological, political, and criminal terroristic aspects of Nazism. One of Broszat's

critics has, for example, suggested that the approach that he advocates looks to a comparison with the modernizing tendencies of other advanced Western societies at the expense of attention to the crucial differences in the essence of their development. From such a perspective, therefore, "the racialist aspect . . . and particularly the 'Final Solution of the Jewish Question' seem to be regarded as somehow irrelevant" since the "unique duality" of the German modernizing experience is ignored. [14]

The suggested historicization can, therefore, be summarized in the following claims: that Nazism should be subjected to the same methods of scholarly inquiry as any other era of history; that social continuities need to be much more fully incorporated in a far more complex picture of Nazism and the emphasis shifted away from heavy concentration on the political-ideological sphere as a resort for moral lessons (since moral sensitivity can only arise from a deeper understanding, which historicization offers, of the checkered complexities of the era); and that the Nazi era, at present almost a dislocated unit of German history,—no longer suppressed but reduced to no more than "required reading" (Pflichtlektion) [15]—needs to be placed in a broader historical context. [16]

Criticism of Historicization

The main critics of Broszat's historicization plea are the Israeli historians Otto Dov Kulka, Dan Diner, and, especially, Saul Friedländer. They recognize the problem of historicization as expounded by Broszat as an important methodological and theoretical issue, as representing in some respects a legitimate perspective, and as raising a problem that "belongs within the realm of a fundamental scholarly-scientific dialogue" between historians who "share some basic concerns as far as the attitudes towards Nazism and its crimes are concerned." As such, they are anxious to distinguish it from the apologetics advanced by Ernst Nolte in the Historikerstreit. [17] Even so, it is noted in passing that the exhortation, forty years later, to treat the Nazi era like any other period of history is also Nolte's starting point. [18] Leaving Nolte completely to one side, there are still the implications of Andreas Hillgruber's approach to the historical treatment of the German army on the Eastern Front for the concept of historicization, to which we will return. [19]

The most direct and structured critique of Broszat's historicization plea has been advanced by Saul Friedländer. [20] He sees three dilemmas in the notion of historicization and three additional problems raised by this approach.

The first dilemma he points to is that of periodization and the specificity of the dictatorship years themselves, the period 1933–45. [21] The historicization approach seeks to incorporate the Third Reich into a picture of long-term social change. Broszat himself uses the example of the wartime social planning of the German Labor Front both as an episode in the development of social-welfare schemes that predated Nazism and extended into the modern system of the Federal Republic, and as a parallel to that which was taking place under entirely different political systems, as in the British Beveridge Plan.[22] These various long-term processes of social change, in this instance in social policy, can be seen, therefore, as taking place in detachment from the specifics of Nazi ideology and the particular circumstances of the Third Reich. The emphasis shifts away from the singular characteristics of the Nazi period to a consideration of the relative and objective function of Nazism as an agent forcing (or retarding) modernization.

The question of the intended or unintended "modernization push" of Nazism has, of course, been an issue ever since Dahrendorf and Schoenbaum wrote. Friedländer accepts that recent studies have extended knowledge on numerous aspects of this "modernization." However, in his view, when taken as a whole such studies reveal a shift in interest from the specificity of Nazism to the general problems of modernization, within which Nazism plays a part. The issue is, therefore, one of "the relative relevance" of such developments in an overall history of the Nazi era.[23] And, in Friedländer's judgment, the danger—in fact, the almost inevitable result—is the relativization of the political-ideological-moral framework peculiar to 1933–45.[24]

The second dilemma arises from the recommended removal of the distance, founded on moral condemnation, which the historian of Nazism places between him- or herself and the object of research, and which prevents him or her from treating it as a "normal" period of history. This raises, says, Friedländer, inextricable problems in the construction of a global picture of the Nazi era, since if few spheres of life were themselves criminal, few were completely untouched by the regime's criminality. Separation of criminality from normalcy is, therefore, scarcely an easy task. No objective criteria can be established for distinguishing which areas might be susceptible to empathetic treatment and which still cannot be handled without the historian's distance from the subject of inquiry.[25]

The third dilemma arises from the vagueness and open-endedness of the concept of historicization, which implies a method and a philosophy but gives no clear notion of what the results might be. The implications of historicization are, however, by no means straightforward, but might be interpreted in radically different ways—as indeed Nolte and Hillgruber demonstrate in their controversial interpretations of the Nazi era that provoked the *Historikerstreit*.[26]

Friedländer is prepared to discount Nolte's writings in this context. But he uses the illustration of Hillgruber's essay on the Eastern Front to demonstrate the potential dangers of historicization, and links this squarely with the problems of the "everyday history" approach itself, and with the open-ended nature of the *Resistenz* concept used in the Bavaria Project.[27]

Not only the relativization of distance from the Nazi era, he argues, but also the emphasis within *Alltagsgeschichte* on the ordinariness of many aspects of the Third Reich, on the nonideological and noncriminal spheres of activity, and on ever more nuanced attitudes and behavioral patterns, creates significant problems. Friedländer accepts that criminality is not necessarily excluded, and that a continuum can be constructed involving criminality in everyday life and normality in the regime's criminal system. However, he suggests that in an overall perspective of the Third Reich premised on the relativization and normalization of the Nazi era advocated in the historicization approach, the tendency to place too much weight on the "normality" end of the continuum can scarcely be avoided. Despite Broszat's disclaimers, fears Friedländer, the passage from historicization to historicism (*Historisierung* to *Historismus*) in regard to the Third Reich is a real danger.[28] Hillgruber defended his controversial empathizing and identification with the German troops in the east by comparing his approach with that of "everyday history," as applied to other areas of research.[29] Accepting that there is some force in this defence, Friedländer suggests that one might justifiably apply the concept of *Resistenz* to the behavior of the German soldiers defending the Eastern Front in the final phase of the war. Hence, many units were relatively immune to Nazi ideology and were only doing their job like soldiers in any army. On the other hand, of course, the *Wehrmacht* more than any other institution sustained the Nazi system as such. This reveals to Friedländer not only the fact that *Resistenz* is "much too amorphous a concept to be of any great use,"[30] but also the vacuous nature of historicization, which "implies many different things" so that "within the present context it may encourage some interpretations rather than others."[31]

From these dilemmas arise, in Friedländer's view, three general problems. The first is that the Nazi past is still too overwhelmingly present to be dealt with in the "normal" way with which one might, for example, tackle the history of sixteenth-century France. The self-reflection of the historian necessary to any good historical writing is decisive in approaching the Nazi era. The Third Reich simply cannot be regarded in the same way or approached with the same methods as "normal" history.[32]

The second general problem is what Friedländer calls "differential relevance."[33] The history of Nazism, he says, belongs to everyone. The study of everyday life in the Third Reich may indeed be relevant to Germans in terms of self-perception and national identity, and thereby be a perspective that commends itself to German historians. But for historians outside Germany, this perspective might be less relevant in comparison with the political and ideological aspects of the Third Reich, in particular, with the relationship of ideology to politics.

The same point is made in a slightly different fashion by other critics of historicization. Otto Dov Kulka sees the emphasis on the "normal" aspects of the Third Reich as a reflection of the present-day situation and self-image of the

Federal Republic as an affluent, modern society—an image into which Nazi ideology and the criminality of the regime can scarcely be accommodated. From this present-day West German perspective, he accepts the examination of, for example, long-term trends in the development of social policy as both justified and important. But the world-historical uniqueness of Nazism, he emphasises, resides specifically in the duality of a society where "normal" trends of modernization were accompanied by the slave labor and extermination "in industrially rational fashion" of those ideologically excluded from the "national community." And in the event of a victorious Third Reich, modern German society would have looked very different from the democratic welfare state of the Federal Republic and the socialist German Democratic Republic.[34]

The third—and most crucial—problem is, therefore, how to integrate Nazi crimes into the historicization of the Third Reich. In Friedländer's view—and he acknowledges that this is a value judgment—the specificity, or uniqueness, of Nazism resides in the fact that it "tried 'to determine who should and who should not inhabit the world.'"[35] The problem—and the limits—of historicization lie consequently in its inability to integrate into its picture of "normal" development "the specificity and the historical place of the annihilation policies of the Third Reich."[36]

Evaluation

The objections to the historicization of National Socialism that are raised by Friedländer, Kulka, and Diner cannot lightly be dismissed. They touch on important philosophical and methodological considerations that have direct bearing on any attempt at writing the history of German society under Nazism.

Friedländer's concern about the omission or downplaying of the political, ideological, and moral aspects of Nazism permeates his critique. But it could at the outset be queried whether the traditional concentration on the political-ideological-moral framework could lead to further major advances in the depth of that understanding that provides the basis of enhanced moral awareness. This "traditional" emphasis, epitomized perhaps most clearly in the work of Karl-Dietrich Bracher, produced many lasting gains.[37] A "historicized" treatment would not need to discard them. But to confine scholarship rigidly to the traditional framework would be sterile and perhaps ultimately even counterproductive, since it would put a block on precisely those approaches that have led in recent years to much of the most original—and most morally sensitive—research. Moreover, the implications of historicization might be less serious both in theory and in practice than Friedländer fears.

It seems questionable whether the first dilemma posed by Friedländer—the incompatibility between doing justice to the specific character of the Nazi era and concentrating on the unfolding of long-term social change—is a necessary one. It might, in fact, be countered that the specific features of the period 1933–45 can be highlighted only by a "longitudinal" analysis crossing those chronological barriers and placing the era in a developmental context of elements of social change that long preceded Nazism and continued after its demise. Friedländer's fear is that there would be an inevitable shift in focus to the problem of modernization, and that a "relativization" of the dictatorship era by its new location in a long-term context of "neutral" social change would be bound to lose sight of, or to reduce in emphasis, crucial events or policy decisions in the period of Nazi rule itself.

The fear does not appear to be borne out by recent works on social change, some of which have adopted a long-term perspective and have deliberately addressed the issue of modernization and the "social revolution" argument. Obviously, the "criminal" side of the Third Reich is not the dominant focus in such works. But in the stress on Nazi social policy, the significance of ideology is by no means underplayed, and the relationship of this ideology to the core racial-imperialist essence of Nazism is made abundantly plain. The wartime social program of Robert Ley—to take the example from Marie-Louise Recker's study of wartime social policy, which Broszat cites and Friedländer sees as an example of the dangers implicit in historicization—indeed reveals a number of superficial similarities to Beveridge's social insurance provisions in Britain. But what is most striking in Recker's analysis, although, admittedly, not in Broszat's reference to her findings, is the specific and unmistakable Nazi character of the program.[38] Not only is it legitimate (and necessary) to deploy a "longitudinal" and also a comparative perspective in analysis of Ley's program, but such a perspective contributes directly to a clearer definition of the peculiarly Nazi essence of social policy in 1933–45. The same can be said of Michael Prinz's recent admirable analysis of Nazi attempts to eradicate the status barrier between white- and blue-collar workers, in which the long-term perspective serves to depict in a particularly clear way both the specific features of Nazi social policy toward white-collar workers and the anchoring of this policy in Nazi ideological precepts.[39]

Applied to other subject areas, the "longitudinal" approach highlights precisely the political-ideological-moral framework that Friedländer suspects will be ignored or downplayed—if in ways different from, and often more challenging than, the traditional approach. An instance would be Ulrich Herbert's excellent analysis of the treatment of foreign labor in Germany since the nineteenth century, which allows not only the continuities that cross the Nazi era, but also the specific barbarities of that era itself, to come more clearly into view.[40] Herbert was, of course, a leading participant in the Ruhr oral history project that was so closely linked to perceived experiences of the "normality" of "everyday life." It is all the more significant, therefore, that he was the historian who contributed an outstanding monograph on foreign workers, one that offers the first major analysis of one of the most barbarous aspects of the Third Reich, and that he not only brings out fully the ideologically rooted nature of the regime's policy toward foreign workers, but also the extent to which "racism was not just a phenomenon to be found among the party leadership and the SS, . . . but a practical reality to be experienced as an everyday occurrence in Germany during the war."[41]

The moral dimension is also more than evident in recent research on professional and social groups—such as technicians, students, and the medical, legal, and teaching professions.[42] And such studies have found little difficulty in blending together long-term patterns of development and change (into which the Nazi era has to be fitted) and specific facets in such processes peculiar to Nazism. The same is abundantly true of research on the position of women. Continuities in antifeminism have not prevented an elaboration of the specific contours of the 1933–45 era, as in Gisela Bock's work, for example, in which a direct association is made between Nazi antifeminism and racial policy in the analysis of compulsory sterilization.[43] As in this instance, most other recent publications, many of them excellent in quality, on women in the Third Reich have placed particular emphasis on the central issue of race, precisely the issue that Friedländer fears will lose significance in a social, rather than political, history perspective.[44]

It is difficult to see how any scholarly attempt to construct an overall picture of society under Nazism could ignore the findings of such important research. We still face, however, Friedländer's second dilemma: the inability of the historian, having removed the previously automatic "distance" from Nazism, having taken the epoch out of its "quarantine," and having abolished the "syndrome of required-reading,"[45] to apply objective criteria in separating "criminality" from "normality" in the construction of a "global" picture of the Nazi era. Friedländer's worry is evidently that spheres of empathetic understanding might now be found in the "normality" of everyday life under Nazism. The previous general consensus resting on a total and complete rejection of this era would thereby be broken. But the historian, now faced with a choice other than rejection,[46] would have no objective criteria for drawing distinctions. In the context of the philosophy of "historicism" (Historismus), and in the realm of pure theory, the problem of "distance" or "empathy," which Friedländer poses, does indeed appear insoluble. But even at the theoretical level, the problem is hardly peculiar to the Third Reich, and poses itself implicitly in all historical writing. In many specific areas of contemporary history, one might think, the problem seems hardly less acute than in the case of Nazism. Whether the historian writing on Soviet society under Stalin, on the society of Fascist Italy or Franco's Spain, on the Vietnam War, on South Africa, or on British imperialism, faces a fundamentally different dilemma might be questioned. Objective criteria resting on the historian's "neutrality" arguably play no part in any historical writing. Selection on the basis of subjectively determined choices and emphases is inescapable. A rigorous critical method and full recognition of subjective factors shaping the approach deployed and evaluation of the findings provide the only means of control. In this respect, the historian of Nazism is in a position no different from that of any other historian.

Broszat's writings are in places certainly less clear and unambiguous than they might be on the difference between the method he advocates and the traditional or "restored" historicism that he contrasts to it.[47] He explicitly presents "distance" and intuitive insight or "empathy" *(Einfühlen)* as opposites, and speaks of the possibility of "a degree of sympathetic identification" *(ein Mass mitfühlender Identifikation)* both with victims and with "wrongly invested achievements and virtues" *(fehlinvestierte Leistungen und Tugenden)*. At the same time, however, he makes sufficiently plain that the counter to an un-critical, positive identification with the subject matter lies precisely in the critical historical method, applied to Nazism as to other periods of history, one that ultimately promotes enhanced moral sensibility precisely through a meticulous scholarship that includes empathy but does not uncritically embrace it.[48] The result is the methodological tightrope that all historians have to walk, in which the choice between empathy or moral distance is reshaped by the critical method into the position that characterizes a great deal of good historical writing—that of rejection through "understanding." This, the premise that "enlightenment" *(Aufklärung)* comes through "explanation" *(Erklärung)*,[49] seems the basis of Broszat's approach in his collected papers, and certainly in his own work on the Bavaria Project and elsewhere.

The best work arising from *Alltagsgeschichte*, in fact, clearly demon-strates that a concern with everyday behavior and mentalities by no means implies empathetic treatment. Detlev Peukert's work, in which "normality" is rooted in a theory of the "pathology of modernity," provides an outstanding example.[50] The dilemma posed by Friedländer is scarcely visible here. "Every-day normality" is presented not as a positive counterpoint to the "negative" aspects of Nazism, but as a framework within which "criminality," arising from a "pathological" side of "normality," becomes more readily explicable. Nor does Peukert uphold the concern that a continuum from "normality" to "criminality" inevitably means in practice that the dominant emphasis falls on the "nor-mality," and his work is all the more impressive in that so far he has offered practically the only wide-ranging attempt to synthesize research emanating from a wide variety of monographs in the genre of *Alltagsgeschichte*. And, although Peukert deliberately excluded it from consideration in his book, there is no reason why the "twisted road to Auschwitz" could not be fully incorporated into an analysis premised on such an approach to "normality." By expressly linking "daily life and barbarism," through association with the destructive potential built into modern society's emphasis on advances in production and efficiency, he has himself indicated how an "everyday history of racism," which is still in its beginnings, could contribute to a deeper understanding of the behavior and mentalities that made the Holocaust possible.[51] Here, too, the dilemma of empathy or distance would be premised on a false dichotomy and would not in practice present itself.

Friedländer's third dilemma arises from the vagueness and open-endedness of the term historicization, which is subject to different—some unattractive—interpretations. It can be readily conceded that historicization is indeed an imprecise and unclear concept.[52] In some respects it is ambiguous if not outrightly misleading. The proximity of the term to historicism, which is the opposite of what it denotes, does not help clarity. And it seems related to "normal" in at least three different ways: to the proposed "normalization" of "historical consciousness" (that is, the removal of the feeling that the Nazi era is to be bracketed out of "normal" German history and to be treated as the subject of moral lessons rather than of historical understanding); to the application of "normal" historical method in approaching the Third Reich; and to the "normality" of "everyday life." As an ordering or analytical concept, it has no obvious value, and is purely suggestive of a method of approach. The discarding of the term would arguably be no great loss. It confuses more than it clarifies. But the approach and method signified by historicization could not be dispensed with. Even so, it would be necessary to distinguish the three different uses of "normal." The application of "normal" historical method and the extension of the sphere of analysis of the "normality" of "everyday life" can be more easily defended than can the inclusion of the Nazi era in a supposed "normalization of historical consciousness." This last usage, as the *Historikerstreit* has demonstrated (and as Friedländer and others fear), indeed appears either to elide the Nazi era altogether or to erase or dilute the moral dimension by shifting the spotlight to similar (and allegedly "more original") barbarities of other "totalitarian" states, particularly those of Bolshevik Russia. It is in the context of such distortions that Friedländer poses his third dilemma, by pointing to the use, by Nolte and, implicitly, by Hillgruber, of the same term, "historicization," in the context of an intended "normalization" of historical consciousness in the face of a "past which will not pass away."[53]

The argument that the notion of "historicization" advanced by Broszat, with its connotations of heightened moral sensitivity toward the Nazi past, might be misused "in the present ideological context"[54] to result in the diametrically opposed "relativization" of the regime's criminality (as in Nolte's essays that prompted the *Historikerstreit*[55]) is certainly a serious criticism of the vagueness of the concept, but is not convincing in itself as a rejection of the approach—largely based on an "everyday history of the Nazi era"—that Broszat's concept is meant to denote.

If, however, as Friedländer himself suggests, Nolte's eccentric argumentation is left on one side, there still remains the question of Hillgruber's declared adaptation of the approach of *Alltagsgeschichte* to the problem of the troops on the Eastern Front, with the dubious conclusions he draws. [56] Friedländer astutely points out that the empathetic approach can produce startling results, and suggests that Hillgruber's essay demonstrates how Broszat's supposed historicization, aimed precisely at avoiding traditional historicism, can lead to a return of historicism, now dangerously applied to the Third Reich itself. [57] But the point about Hillgruber's essay is that it is squarely rooted in a crude form of the "historicist" tradition that presumes that "understanding" (Verstehen) can only come about through empathetic identification. It is precisely the claim that the historian's only valid position is one of identification with the German troops fighting on the Eastern Front that has invoked such widespread and vehement criticism of Hillgruber's essay. [58] The critical method—which in his other work (not excluding his essay "The Historical Place of the Extermination of the Jews" in the same volume as the controversial treatment of the Eastern Front) makes him a formidable historian whose strength lies in the careful and measured treatment of empirical data—has entirely deserted him here and is wholly lacking in this one-sided, uncritical empathizing with the German troops. Although Hillgruber claimed to be applying the technique of Alltagsgeschichte and the approach advocated by Broszat and others to experience events from the point of view of those at the base of society directly affected by them, it is precisely the absence of critical reflection that creates a gulf between his depiction and the work of Broszat, Peukert, and others, who indeed look to grass-roots experiences, but do not detach these from a critical and analytical framework of analysis.

The example of Hillgruber appears, therefore, to be misplaced. What, apart from the dubious value of the actual term "historicization," it illustrates is that, in his zeal to emphasize the need for greater empathetic understanding of "experience," Broszat appears to have posed a false dichotomy between that understanding and the "distance" that is an important control mechanism of the historian of any period, not just of the Nazi era. In reality, Broszat's own historical writing—even his latest short book in a series founded on the necessity to "historicize" German history—plainly does not abrogate "distance" in the interests of uncritical empathy. Neither here nor in Broszat's other recent writing could it be claimed that the narrative approach (Erzählen) that he misses in historical treatment of the Third Reich[59] has come to dominate or to replace critical, structured analysis and reflection. "Distance," as well as empathetic understanding, might be said to be vital to the historian of any period.

The preservation of a critical distance in the case of National Socialism is, in fact, far from being dispensable, a crucial component of the new social history of the Third Reich. But it is precisely the virtue of this new social history, located in description and structured analysis of "everyday" experience, that it breaks down the unreflected distance that has traditionally been provided by abstractions such as "totalitarian rule" and compels a deeper comprehension through greater awareness of the complexity of social reality.[60] If I understand it correctly, this is the essence of Broszat's plea for historicization, and for a structured *Alltagsgeschichte* as the most fruitful method of approach. And the findings of the Bavaria Project alone demonstrate how enriching such an approach can prove to be.

It seems plain that Friedländer is correct to stress that the Nazi era, from whichever perspective it is approached, cannot be regarded as a "normal" part of history in the way that even the most barbarous episodes of the more distant past can be viewed. The emotions that rightly still color attitudes to Nazism obviously rule out the detachment with which not only sixteenth-century France (Friedländer's example) but also many more recent events and periods in German history and in the history of other nations can be analyzed. In this sense, Wolfgang Benz is quite right when he claims: "Detached concern with Nazism as an era of German history among others and work on it devoted to purely scholarly interest seems then not so easily possible. The mere distance of forty or fifty years does not yet make the Nazi era historical."[61] But of course this does not rule out the application of "normal" historical method to the social, as well as to the political, history of Germany in the Nazi era. Even if a wide-ranging interpretative analysis of the Nazi era that is based on such methods will, as Benz adds, naturally be unable "to do justice to the longing of the citizens of the postwar society to be released from the shadow of the past,"[62] this does not mean that it cannot be written. And while the historian's relationship to the subject of study is different in the case of Nazism from, say, that of the French Revolution, it could be argued that, even accepting the uniqueness of the Holocaust, the problems posed by historicization in theory differ little from those facing the historian of, say, Soviet society under Stalin.

Like the French and Russian Revolutions, the Third Reich embraces events of world-historical importance. Its history can certainly be approached as part of the prehistory of the Federal Republic and the German Democratic Republic, but, as Friedländer rightly states, "the history of Nazism belongs to everybody."[63] Perspectives inevitably vary. The polarization of German and Jewish collective memory of the Nazi era—epitomized in the films *Heimat* and *Shoah*—is plausibly advanced by Friedländer as an important element in the current debates over approaches to the Third Reich.[64] The differences in emphasis are unavoidable, and each has its own legitimacy. It is difficult to see how they can satisfactorily be blended together in any history that, purely or largely based on the notion of "experience" and constructed on a narrative method *(Erzählen)*, attempts a "global" description of the Nazi era. Even if one suggests that in some ways the historian who shares neither collective memory possibly has an advantageous perspective, the attempt seems in any case bound to founder on the assumption that it is theoretically possible to write the "total" history of an entire "era" based on collective "experience."[65] Equally impossible is the construction of a history built solely around the actions or experiences of the historical actors themselves and detached from the often impersonally structured conditions that in good measure shape or predetermine those "experiences."[66] Only the application of constructs, concepts, and even theories that reside outside the sphere of historical experience can provide order and make sense of experience in a historical analysis that is bound to be less than "total" or "global."[67] If this appears to stand in contradiction to Broszat's historicization plea, it is scarcely out of synchronization with his practice in his own writing on the history of the Nazi era.

If we abandon the assumption that the history of the Nazi era (or any other "era")—in the sense of any "total" grasp of the complexity of all the contradictory and often unrelated experiences that occur in a given period of time—is theoretically and practically possible, then it becomes feasible to conceive of a history of German society under Nazism that could incorporate in a structured analysis the findings of recent social historical research, in particular that of *Alltagsgeschichte*, but that at the same time would embed this in the political-ideological-moral framework that Friedländer is anxious not to lose. Such an approach would have to jettison notions of the historicization of Nazism in terms of regarding it as any other period of history or "relativizing" its significance. But it would find indispensable the normal methodological rigor of historical inquiry, deployed as a matter of course in dealing with other eras (and already, one might add, deployed in countless scholarly works on Nazism). Applied to the social sphere of "daily life" as well as to the political-ideological domain, conventional critical historical method would be sufficient to eliminate the modern antiquarianism that has rightly been criticized as a feature of the poorer strains of *Alltagsgeschichte*. Finally, it would be not only legitimate, but essential, to proceed in such an approach by way of a critical exploration of the continuum that stretches from "normality" to barbarism and genocide, in order better to comprehend the social as well as the political context in which inhumane ideologies become implemented as practical policies of almost inconceivable inhumanity. Auschwitz would, therefore, inevitably form the point of departure from which the thin ice of modern civilization and its veneer of "normality" could be critically examined.[68]

The last, and ultimately fundamental, issue preoccupying Friedländer seems resolvable in such an approach. The integration of Nazi crimes against humanity into a "global" interpretation of society in the Third Reich ought to become, in fact, more rather than less possible in the light of the developments made in the empirical social history of Nazism in the past decade. Peukert's synthesis has, in many respects, pointed the way toward an integration of "normality" and "barbarism."[69] I have attempted in my own work explicitly to relate lack of humanitarian concern with regard to the "Jewish Question" to spheres of dissent and protest in "everyday" matters.[70] My working hypothesis in such research was the notion that, especially under "extreme" conditions, "normal" daily and private concerns consume such energy and attention that indifference to inhumanity, and thereby indirect support of an inhumane political system, is significantly furthered. Robert Gellately, building on the work of the late Reinhard Mann, has extended such suggestions to the areas of social consensus and active support for "policing" measures in racial issues.[71] To posit a clear divorce between the concerns of *Alltagsgeschichte* and the political-ideological-moral framework that focuses on the genocidal criminality of the Nazi regime is to adopt a misleading perspective. Out of recent work on the social history of the Third Reich, which Broszat has done more than most to promote, emerges the realization that there can be a social context in "civilized society" in which genocide becomes acceptable. Research on the grass-roots history of the Nazi era has significantly deepened our awareness of the troublesome reflection that "many features of contemporary 'civilized' society encouraged the easy resort to genocidal holocausts."[72]

Notes

1. Martin Broszat, "Plädoyer für eine Historisierung des Nationalsozialismus," *Merkur* 39 (1985): 373–85, reprinted in Martin Broszat, *Nach Hitler: Der schwierige Umgang mit unserer Geschichte* (Munich, 1986), pp. 159–73. All references that follow are to the latter version.

2. David Schoenbaum, *Hitler's Social Revolution* (New York, London, 1966); Ralf Dahrendorf, *Society and Democracy in Germany* (London, 1968), chap. 25.

3. Martin Broszat et al., eds., *Bayern in der NS-Zeit*, 6 vols. (Munich, 1977–83). For the concept of *Resistenz*, see Broszat's contribution on "Resistenz und Widerstand" vol. 4 (Munich, 1981), pp. 691–709, reprinted in idem, *Nach Hitler*, pp. 68–91.

4. See, e.g., Hans-Ulrich Wehler, "Königsweg zu neuen Ufern oder Irrgarten der Illusionen? Die westdeutsche Alltagsgeschichte: Geschichte 'von innen' und 'von unten,'" in F. J. Brüggemeier and J. Kocka, eds., *"Geschichte von unten—Geschichte von innen": Kontroversen um die Alltagsgeschichte* (Fernuniversität Hagen, 1985), pp. 17–47. And for a lively debate about the merits and disadvantages of *Alltagsgeschichte*, see *Alltagsgeschichte der NS-Zeit: Neue Perspektive oder Trivialisierung?* Kolloquien des Instituts für Zeitgeschichte (Munich, 1984).

5. See, e.g., the thoughtful assessment of the limitations but also the possibilities of *Alltagsgeschichte* by Jürgen Kocka in reviews in *Die Zeit*, no. 42, 14 October 1983 ("Drittes Reich: Die Reihen fast geschlossen"), and *Tageszeitung*, 26 January 1988 ("Geschichtswerkstätten und Historikerstreit").

6. Broszat, *Nach Hitler*, p. 167.

7. See ibid., pp. 114–20 ("Eine Insel in der Geschichte? Der Historiker in der Spannung zwischen Verstehen und Bewerten der Hitler-Zeit").

8. Ibid., p. 173. Historicism was the dominant historical philosophy in Germany from the time of Ranke until World War II. Its main thrust was "idealistic." That is, it regarded history as the unfolding of cultural progress and development formed by the "ideas," intentions, and motives of historical personages. The main task of historical writing was, therefore, to explain actions by the intuitive "understanding" *(Verstehen)* of the intentions behind them. This led to a heavy emphasis on the overwhelming importance of personal will in the historical process and, coupled with the Hegelian elevation of the role and nature of the state, to a positive evaluation of the unique features of German development and of the power politics of the Prusso-German nation-state.

9. Ibid., p. 153 (and back cover). For one who has written extensively and with great sensitivity about Nazi concentration camps, in which the term "special treatment" *(Sonderbehandlung)* was a euphemism for murder, Broszat's use of the same term in the present context seems a remarkable and unfortunate linguistic lapse.

10. Ibid., pp. 104 ff., and also pp. 36–41. In his exchange of letters with Saul Friedländer, Broszat speaks of a "plea for the normalization of method, not of evaluation"; "Dokumentation: Ein Briefwechsel zwischen Martin Broszat und Saul Friedländer um die Historisierung des Nationalsozialismus," *VfZ* 36 (1988): 339–72, here p. 365 (henceforth cited as "Briefwechsel"). I am extremely grateful to Prof. Friedländer for allowing me to see proofs of this exchange before its publication.

11. Broszat, *Nach Hitler*, pp. 110–12 and 169–71.

12. Ibid., pp. 171–72.

13. For an excellent collection of essays summarizing much recent research and locating Nazism within a context of long-term social change, see W. Conze and M. R. Lepsius, *Sozialgeschichte der Bundesrepublik Deutschland* (Stuttgart, 1983).

14. Otto Dov Kulka, "Singularity and its Relativization: Changing Views in German Historiography on National Socialism and the 'Final Solution,'" *Yad Vashem Studies* 19 (1988): 151–86. I am most grateful to Prof. Kulka for a preview of this article.

15. Broszat, *Nach Hitler*, p. 161.

16. See Saul Friedländer, "Some Reflections on the Historisation of National Socialism," *Tel Aviv Jahrbuch für deutsche Geschichte* 16 (1987): 310–24, here p. 313.

17. Friedländer, "Reflections," pp. 310–11 and 318; Kulka, "Singularity and its Relativization." The two contributions by Ernst Nolte, which were at the forefront of the *Historikerstreit*, are reproduced in *"Historikerstreit": Die Doku-*

mentation der Kontroverse um die Einzigartigkeit der nationalsozialistischen Judenvernichtung (Munich, 1987), pp. 13–35 and 39–47.

18. Friedländer, "Reflections," pp. 317–18; Kulka, "Singularity and its Relativization."

19. Friedländer, "Reflections," p. 320; Dan Diner, "Zwischen Aporie und Apologie," in Dan Diner, ed., Ist der Nationalsozialismus Geschichte? Zu Historisierung und Historikerstreit (Frankfurt a. M., 1987), pp. 62–73, here p. 66. The work referred to is the first essay ("Der Zusammenbruch im Osten 1944/45 als Problem der deutschen Nationalgeschichte und der europäischen Geschichte") in Andreas Hillgruber, Zweierlei Untergang: Die Zerschlagung des Deutschen Reiches und das Ende des europäischen Judentums (Berlin, 1986).

20. Friedländer, "Reflections."

21. Ibid., pp. 314–16.

22. Broszat, Nach Hitler, pp. 171–72.

23. Friedländer, "Reflections," p. 315.

24. Ibid., p. 314. Kulka's criticism in "Singularity and its Relativization" runs along similar lines. Diner ("Zwischen Aporie und Apologie," p. 67) also criticizes the inevitable loss of the specifics of the period 1933–45 when, as in the Alltagsgeschichte approach, the emphasis is placed on "normality." With reference to the oral history project directed by Lutz Niethammer on the experiences of Ruhr workers, he points out that "the good and bad times" in subjective memory by no means accord with the significant developments of 1933–45. A "considerable trivialisation of the Nazi era" is allegedly the consequence. The reference is to Ulrich Herbert, "Die guten und die schlechten Zeiten," in Lutz Niethammer, ed., "Die Jahre weiss man nicht, wo man die heute hinsetzen soll": Faschismuserfahrungen im Ruhrgebiet (Bonn, 1986), pp. 67–96.

25. Friedländer, "Reflections," pp. 316–17.

26. Ibid., p. 317.

27. Ibid., pp. 317–21.

28. Ibid., p. 318.

29. Ibid., pp. 319–21; and see Diner, "Zwischen Aporie und Apologie," pp. 66 and 69.

30. Friedländer, "Reflections," p. 319.

31. Ibid., p. 321.

32. Ibid., 321–22.

33. Ibid., p. 322.

34. Kulka, "Singularity and its Relativization," and, as cited by Herbert Freeden, "Um die Singularität von Auschwitz," Tribüne 26, Heft 102 (1987): 123–24.

35. Friedländer, "Reflections," p. 323. The phrase is taken from the closing lines of Hannah Arendt, Eichmann in Jerusalem (London, 1963), p. 256.

36. Friedländer, "Reflections," p. 323. Diner ("Zwischen Aporie und Apologie," pp. 67–68 and 71–73) is even more unyielding in his criticism, emphasizing the centrality of Auschwitz as a "universal point of departure from which to measure the world-historical significance of National Socialism," the impossibility of "historicizing" Auschwitz, the diametrically opposed experiences of "perpetrators" and "victims," and the theoretical impossibility of combining in one narrative history the "normality" experiences of the former and the experiences of the latter of an "absolutely exceptional situation." He adds (p. 68) that any notion of "daily routine" (Alltag) has of necessity to begin from its conceptual opposite, the "specifically exceptional." Accepting, it seems, if with grave reservations, that some synthesis might after all be possible (p. 71), he draws the conclusion that an "approximately comprehensible" history embracing both the "banality" of a merely apparent "normality" of "everyday life" and the horrors of "Auschwitz" (and all that the name stands for) is at best conceivable by starting from the uniqueness of the latter, and not from a misleading notion of "normality."

37. Most classically in Karl-Dietrich Bracher, The German Dictatorship (New York, 1970).

38. Marie-Louise Recker, Nationalsozialistische Sozialpolitik im Krieg (Munich 1985). See Broszat, Nach Hitler, p. 171.

39. Michael Prinz, Vom neuen Mittelstand zum Volksgenossen (Munich, 1986).

40. Ulrich Herbert, A History of Foreign Labor in Germany, 1880–1950 (Ann Arbor, Mich., 1990).

41. Ulrich Herbert, Fremdarbeiter: Politik und Praxis des "Ausländer-Einsatzes" in der Kriegswirtschaft des Dritten Reiches (Berlin, Bonn, 1985), back cover. See also Herbert's essay, "Arbeit und Vernichtung: Ökonomisches Interesse und Primat der 'Weltanschauung,'" in Diner, ed., Ist der Nationalsozialismus Geschichte? pp. 198–236.

42. Not surprisingly, moral issues are particularly close to the surface in research, which has made considerable strides forward in recent years, on the place of the Third Reich in the professionalization of medical practice. For surveys of the literature, see Michael E. Kater, "Medizin und Mediziner im Dritten Reich: Eine Bestandsaufnahme," Historische Zeitschrift 244 (1987): 299–352; and idem, "The Burden of the Past: Problems of a Modern Historiography of Physicians and Medicine in Nazi Germany," German Studies Review 10 (1987): 31–56.

43. Gisela Bock, Zwangssterilisation im Nationalsozialismus (Opladen, 1986).

44. See particularly Renate Bridenthal, Atina Grossmann, and Marion Kaplan, eds., When Biology Became Destiny: Women in Weimar and Nazi

Germany (New York, 1984); and Claudia Koonz, *Mothers in the Fatherland: Women, the Family, and Nazi Politics* (New York, 1986).

45. Friedländer, "Reflections," p. 316.

46. Some twenty years ago, Wolfgang Sauer pointed out that a characteristic feature of writing on Nazism was that the historian faced no other choice than rejection: "National Socialism: Totalitarianism or Fascism?" *American Historical Review* 73 (1967–68): 404–24.

47. See Broszat, *Nach Hitler*, pp. 120 and 161, for the phrases cited in the following sentence, and pp. 100–101 and 173 for comments on "historicism" *(Historismus)*.

48. See, in particular, the essay "Grenzen der Wertneutralität in der Zeitgeschichtsforschung: Der Historiker und der Nationalsozialismus," in Broszat, *Nach Hitler*, pp. 92–113.

49. Ibid., p. 100. See also "Briefwechsel," p. 340, where Broszat reemphasizes his dependence on a "principle of critical, enlightening [*aufklärerischen*] historical understanding which . . . is to be clearly distinguished from the concept of understanding [*Verstehens-Begriff*] of German historicism in the nineteenth century."

50. See Detlev Peukert, *Inside Nazi Germany: Conformity and Opposition in Everyday Life* (New Haven, Conn., 1987). Friedländer offers a qualified acceptance of the merits of *Alltagsgeschichte* in "Briefwechsel," pp. 354–55, although this is far from satisfying Broszat (see ibid., pp. 362–63).

51. Detlev Peukert, "Alltag und Barbarei: Zur Normalität des Dritten Reiches," in Diner, ed., *Ist der Nationalsozialismus Geschichte?* pp. 51–61, esp. 53, 56, and 59–61.

52. See the comments of Adelheid von Saldern, which offer some support to Friedländer's objections, in her critique, "Hillgrubers 'Zweierlei Untergang'—der Untergang historischer Erfahrungsanalyse," in Heide Gerstenberger und Dorothea Schmidt, eds., *Normalität oder Normalisierung? Geschichtswerkstätten und Faschismusanalyse* (Münster, 1987), esp. pp. 164 and 167–68. Meanwhile, Broszat himself acknowledges that the "historicization" concept is "ambiguous and misleading" ("Briefwechsel," pp. 340 and 361–62).

53. Friedländer, "Reflections," pp. 317–21. Nolte's article, "Vergangenheit, die nicht vergehen will," is in *"Historikerstreit,"* pp. 39–47. The Hillgruber work referred to is the first essay in *Zweierlei Untergang*.

54. Friedländer, "Reflections," p. 324.

55. See *"Historikerstreit,"* pp. 13–35 and 39–47. Klaus Hildebrand, for example, praised Nolte in a review for the way in which he undertook "to incorporate in historicizing fashion [*historisierend einzuordnen*] that central element for the history of National Socialism and of the Third Reich of the annihilatory capacity of the ideology and of the regime, and to comprehend this

totalitarian fact of the matter in the interrelated context of Russian and German history"; *Historische Zeitschrift* 242 (1986): 465.

56. See Hillgruber's remarks in *"Historikerstreit,"* pp. 234–35.

57. Friedländer, "Reflections," pp. 320–21. See the further debate between Broszat and Friedländer on this point in "Briefwechsel," pp. 36, 355–56, and 360–61.

58. See Diner, "Zwischen Aporie und Apologie," pp. 69–70; and von Saldern, "Hillgrubers 'Zweierlei Untergang,'" pp. 161–62 and 168 for comments on Hillgruber's argument in the context of the "historicization" problem. The most devastating critique of Hillgruber's position can be found in Hans-Ulrich Wehler, *Entsorgung der deutschen Geschichte?* (Munich, 1988), pp. 46ff. and 154ff. See also the excellent review article by Omer Bartov (whose own book, *The Eastern Front, 1941–45: German Troops and the Barbarisation of Warfare* [London, 1985], offers a necessary and important counterinterpretation to that of Hillgruber), "Historians on the Eastern Front: Andreas Hillgruber and Germany's Tragedy," *Tel Aviv Jahrbuch für deutsche Geschichte* 16 (1987): 325–45.

59. See Martin Broszat, *Hitler and the Collapse of Weimar Germany* (Leamington Spa, 1987). For Broszat's remarks on the concept behind the series *Deutsche Geschichte der neuesten Zeit,* see Broszat, *Nach Hitler,* p. 152; and for his advocacy of narrative *(Erzählen)* as historical method, see ibid., pp. 137 and 161.

60. See ibid, pp. 131–39, "Alltagsgeschichte der NS-Zeit."

61. Wolfgang Benz, "Die Abwehr der Vergangenheit: Ein Problem nur für Historiker und Moralisten?" in Diner, ed., *Ist der Nationalsozialismus Geschichte?* p. 33.

62. Ibid., p. 19. Norbert Frei's recent short book, *Der Führerstaat* (Munich, 1987), offers some pointers toward the potential of such an approach.

63. Friedländer, "Reflections," p. 322.

64. Saul Friedländer, "West Germany and the Burden of the Past: The Ongoing Debate," *Jerusalem Quarterly* 42 (1987): 16–17. See also "Briefwechsel," pp. 36–37, on the "dissonance between memories."

65. See here the pertinent remarks of Wehler, "Königsweg," p. 35. On the potential, but also the substantial problems, of "experience analysis" *(Erfahrungsanalyse)* with reference to the Third Reich, see von Saldern, "Hillgrubers 'Zweierlei Untergang.'" Friedländer emphasizes the limits of narrative as a method in "Briefwechsel," pp. 370–71, while Diner ("Zwischen Aporie und Apologie," p. 67) is adamant that "experienced everyday routine and existential exception can theoretically no longer be narrated as one history."

66. See Wehler, *Entsorgung,* p. 54, referring to the problems involved in Hillgruber's identification with the German troops on the Eastern Front.

67. See the comments by Klaus Tenfelde and Jürgen Kocka in *All-tagsgeschichte der NS-Zeit*, pp. 36, 50–54, and 63–64, and Kocka—on the need for theory in *Alltagsgeschichte*—in a recent review in *TAZ*, 26 January 1988.

68. See Peukert, "Alltag und Barbarei," p. 61, and Diner, "Zwischen Aporie und Apologie," pp. 71–72.

69. Peukert, *Inside Nazi Germany*; see also his "Alltag und Barbarei."

70. Ian Kershaw, *Popular Opinion and Political Dissent in the Third Reich* (Oxford, 1983).

71. Reinhard Mann, *Protest und Kontrolle im Dritten Reich* (Frankfurt a. M., New York, 1987); Robert Gellately, "The Gestapo and German Society: Political Denunciation in the Gestapo Case Files," *Journal of Modern History* 60 (December 1988): 654–94; and "Enforcing Racial Policy in Nazi Germany," in this volume, and idem, *The Gestapo and German Society* (Oxford, 1990).

72. Leo Kuper, *Genocide* (Harmondsworth, 1981), p. 137.

2

Enforcing Racial Policy in Nazi Germany

ROBERT GELLATELY

In his recent book, *The Highroad to the Stake: A Tale of Witchcraft*, Michael Kunze recounts Duke Maximilian's many difficulties in enforcing policies in Lower Bavaria at the beginning of the seventeenth century:

> In order to "eradicate vagrants the more quickly," the prefects received instructions from Munich "to conduct a general inspection and inquisition" in each judicial district in order to establish "which of our subjects is so bold as to harbor foreigners and persons unknown, without the permission of the authorities." Objection was raised to this order on the grounds that it was a pointless exercise, since "that manner of illegal lodging might not always and every day be inspected and raided by the authorities, the district courts being often far removed from such places." The Duke . . . announced even more emphatically that "the lodging of persons unknown in this our realm and not here resident is utterly and expressly forbidden to all, whoever they may be, whether dwelling in towns or markets, in villages or in wastelands." . . . The response was typical: here, as in similar cases where the Duke's resolve to impose law and order turned out to be impracticable on account of difficulties of communication and enforcement, the gracious monarch in Munich behaved like an obstinate child. In a sense he was saying in midsummer: It must snow. When they tried to explain to him that it was impossible, we can imagine him stamping his foot pettishly and saying: That's just why I want it to snow.[1]

In the three centuries between the rule of Duke Maximilian and the Nazi "seizure of power," many difficulties of enforcement were overcome. All parts of the realm became linked through such developments as industrialization, urbanization, increased literacy, and communications networks.[2] However, more than improved technology and communications is required by a regime intent on monitoring and controlling the thoughts and words, as well as the deeds, of the population. Hitler's dictatorship was dependent on information that was volunteered, solicited, or coerced. Information was required in such quantities that it could be produced only with the help of citizens; with it, the state found it possible to infiltrate all kinds of social spaces and, eventually, to override conventions to breach the most private spheres of personal and sexual life.[3]

The following remarks suggest that a key ingredient in the routine functioning of the terroristic regime created by the Nazis was the interaction between the police and the people. After a discussion of the Gestapo and its modus operandi in the context of German society, there will be an examination of how Gestapo cases were initiated. Then, after a brief discussion of official attitudes toward those who offered information through denunciations—inevitably a problem for a regime allegedly determined to institute the conflict-free "community of the people" *(Volksgemeinschaft)*—this essay looks briefly at the social origins and motives of the denouncers.[4] The concluding section draws on Würzburg Gestapo case files to illustrate the enforcement of and resistance to Nazi anti-Semitic policy. It will be argued that the regime's efforts to break all social bonds between Jews and non-Jews could be enforced, and were "successful," to the extent that it obtained cooperation or collaboration from the population at large.

The paper employs the notion of "policy"—instead of law—enforcement, primarily because institutions such as the Gestapo and even the NSDAP took it on themselves to enforce not merely laws (or decrees and ordinances) but to police the broad range of behavior that might be thought by them to fall outside the spirit of the "new order."[5] For example, the Gestapo sought to enforce the anti-Semitic laws and various regulations, but as well anathematized a whole range of behavior (such as "friendship to the Jews") made formally illegal only later.

The most important institution for the enforcement of policies of all kinds in Nazi Germany was the Gestapo, or *Geheime Staatspolizei*. It is true, of course, that all organizations of party and state were involved in the enforcing of policy, and the party in particular handled matters, often short of specific reference to the police and justice system.[6] As is well known, even Julius Streicher's anti-Semitic newspaper *Der Stürmer* played an enforcer's role by publicizing the names of those who kept up business contacts with Jews, when such behavior was still not technically illegal. Streicher and his paper did so because they could justify their acts as within the spirit of official Jewish policies *(Judenpolitik)*.[7] However, the Gestapo as the chief arm of the political police must be singled out for special attention, not least because it was charged with enforcing many of the most ambitious and sinister public policies of the Nazi state. Thanks to the systematic card files the secret police established on all those who became entangled in the enforcement process, it is possible to reconstruct its routine methods of operation.

Studies of the Gestapo have usually adopted the methods and perspectives of legal and administrative history, and a number of indispensable monographs have resulted.[8] Useful work has been done on the institutional history of the Gestapo as part of the SS empire, and there exist a number of biographies of key Berlin officials, such as Himmler, Heydrich, Kaltenbrunner, and Göring.[9] However, most of the scholarship to date has dealt with the national arena, and only rarely has there been more than cursory examination of the local context, in which the enforcement of policy invariably takes place.[10]

Social historians of Nazi Germany have been surprisingly reluctant to study institutions like the secret police, which played a prominent role in Hitler's "new order." For example, David Schoenbaum's innovative social history provides a detailed and lengthy treatment of the state and touches on nearly every branch of the civil service, yet the Gestapo is not mentioned at all.[11] Surely, any account of "Hitler's social revolution" ought to deal with the changing interrelationship between the police and the people. Even in recent *Alltagsgeschichte* (history of everyday life) relatively little is said about the enforcement process, although part of the reason can be traced to the destruction, nearly everywhere, of many essential sources.[12] Oral history projects might have been expected to explore this theme more extensively, because how the regime was able to enforce policies of various kinds should have marked memories indelibly.[13]

The Gestapo and the Nazi Party (in its policing function) turn up occasionally in some recent social historical literature. However, the terror system embodied especially by the Gestapo tends to be regarded as imposed "from above" or the outside, and there have been few attempts to integrate the local "inputs" of various forms of social collaboration into the examination of the routine workings of the police.[14] Further research in this direction should shed light on why many citizens of Nazi Germany believed that the Gestapo—which was numerically small—was omnipresent and omniscient. As is clear from autobiographical accounts and other testimony, many felt constantly under surveillance at work, in their leisure activities, and even in the intimate spheres of personal and sexual life.

Effective enforcement was not dependent on the existence of a numerically large police force, which in turn relied on the collaboration of an army of paid agents and spies.[15] A detailed study of the local Gestapo in Würzburg (as elsewhere in Germany, for that matter) shows, in fact, that the number of those involved was very small, and also that most were local career policemen before 1933 and not members of the NSDAP or the SS.[16] It is fair to say that given the increasing reach of the regime into social life, there certainly were far too few Gestapo members to have accomplished their tasks even with the collaboration of other elements in the police network. Exaggerated estimates of those involved in policing seems to have been a widespread contemporary misperception, in society at large and especially on the Left. One man otherwise knowledgeable of the situation in the mines around Bochum wrote in 1936, for example, that there was "one works spy" *(Betriebsspitzel)* "for every twelve to fifteen workers."[17] Such a report is clearly unreliable. How would the regime possibly go about finding so many spies willing to go down into the mine? In all likelihood, such "spies" were not the police plants often supposed, but insiders, at the very least, members of long standing in the same social milieu who came forward, more or less voluntarily, for all kinds of reasons, not necessarily or even primarily because of attachment to Nazism.[18]

A number of writers have offered suggestions as to how the Gestapo, in spite of its small numbers, attained its reputation. Franz Neumann rightly noted that the police represented "the most important instrument of the Nazi system," but said little about how it operated on a routine basis.[19] E. K. Bramstedt, who touched on several important aspects of the problem, was suggestive in pointing to the notion of "control by fear," but did not address the problem in its specificity.[20] Martin Broszat's renowned account of the Nazi state never mentions the question of enforcement as such.[21] The well-known *Anatomy of the SS State* delineates the institutional evolution of the political police, but, because it adopts primarily an institutional approach, it treats the enforcement process indirectly or by implication.[22] In this regard, Hannah Arendt offers some ideas that are worth recalling.

While Arendt probaby exaggerates the role of agents in the operation of the political police, she is closer to the mark in highlighting the significance of the "mutual suspicion" that came to permeate "all social relationships;" and that in turn created "an all-pervasive atmosphere even outside the special purview of the secret police."[23] This feeling of being subjected to "constant surveillance" could not have resulted merely from the existence of a large number of officials formally charged with enforcement tasks. "Collaboration of the population in denouncing political opponents and volunteer service as stool pigeons," while not without precedents, were in Hitler's Germany "so well organized that the work of specialists" was "almost superfluous."[24] If by specialists, Arendt here meant to suggest the full-time members of bodies such as the Gestapo, she was certainly correct. "In a system of ubiquitous spying, where everybody may be a police agent," but almost certainly is not, it becomes possible for the regime to enforce policy effectively.[25]

After 1933 the Gestapo operated as a kind of executive steering group that managed the information-gathering and enforcement effort; within a relatively short time, the powers of this well-organized and newly nationalized political police went virtually unchecked. It functioned as a kind of ultimate "thought police" about which Duke Maximilian could only have fantasized.[26] While there remained enormous obstacles—Hitler and his cohorts could not make it snow in summer any more than could Maximilian—the most striking feature that separated them from their predecessors in the seventeenth century was the increased ability to force, with pathological consequences, their visions and dreams on a historical reality. It is becoming ever clearer that these efforts required popular participation.

It is possible to gather a sense of how the Gestapo operated in general by looking at how it initiated cases. Werner Best, a leading Gestapo official and in a good position to understand the enforcement process (even if he was a somewhat dubious defense witness at Nuremberg), asserted that the cases that the Gestapo took up were "almost without exception on the basis of reports which were sent in from private persons or other agencies outside the Police."[27] He was not the only policeman from the Nazi era to suggest that, at least when it came to initiating cases, the Gestapo was primarily a passive organization.[28]

Reinhard Mann's recent quantitative analysis of a random sample drawn from 70,000 surviving Gestapo cases from Düsseldorf corroborates Best's assertions. From the sample of 825 cases, only 127 (or 15 percent) could be attributed to "the observations of the Gestapo and/or its spy network," and another 57 cases (or 7 percent of them all) began on the basis of information obtained from interrogations. However, the largest single source that led to the initiation of a case was constituted by "reports from the population"; some 213 cases commenced this way, (or 26 percent of the total), although Mann insisted that this figure was certainly conservative. An additional 24 cases (or 3 percent) were opened when businesses of one kind or another reported the matter, so that these cases should be added to those "from the population." Surprisingly, only 17 pecent (or 139 cases) began on the basis of information received from other Nazi control organizations (such as the Kripo, Orpo, SD, and SS). In addition, some information came via communal or state authorities (7 percent of all cases, or 57 out of the random sample of 825).[29]

Nazi organizations (such as the NSDAP and affiliates) put the Gestapo on the trail of 52 cases (or 6 percent of the total). On the basis of recent research in local Nazi Party materials, it seems likely, however, that the party was much more active in the policing process than this figure would indicate.[30] Its local officials exercised considerable discretionary powers and handled or cleared up many matters of potential interest to the Gestapo. It would seem that citizens offered more information on neighbors to the local party than the latter passed on to the Gestapo, so that there was a far greater frequency of denunciations over the entire course of the regime's existence than might be deduced simply from a study of Gestapo files. As revealing as these latter sources are, therefore, much remains hidden in them.[31] That point is made all the more obvious by Mann, who noted that 103 cases (13 percent of the total) contained no information as to the cause of initiating the proceedings.[32]

The enforcement process that can be reconstructed on the basis of Mann's analysis makes several conclusions inescapable. His work indicates that the regime's main enforcer was highly dependent on information outside the Gestapo, and that its chief supply came from denunciations offered by "ordinary" citizens. The Gestapo would have been seriously hampered without it. While Mann interpreted this striking propensity to cooperate as evidence of the way society was won over to Nazism, this conclusion does not necessarily follow for, as his figures show, when it comes to the question of motives, much circumspection is called for. He believed that only 50 (or 24 percent) of the 213 denunciations seemed based on "system-loyal engagement" (that is, affective motives), while 80 (or 37 percent of them all) were intended to "resolve private conflicts" (instrumental motives); 39 percent (or 83) of the files contained no hint on the motive of the informer.[33] In point of fact, virtually all and any denunciation functioned in support of the system and played a productive role (regardless of the intention of the informer) in the enforcing of policy.[34]

Reinhard Mann's figures pertain to the Gestapo in all of its many "political" spheres of activity—its enforcement practice, underground work, and general modus operandi. As the analysis below suggests, a different degree of cooperation from the population was required in order to enforce different policies. It seems clear as well that when it came to infiltrating the Communist and Socialist underground movements, the Gestapo may have had to rely more heavily on planted moles than on volunteered information; certainly, that was the opinion of the émigrés and at least some of their comrades still inside Germany.[35] Coercion may have been necessary to elicit this information, but it is an exaggeration to suggest, as one recent study would have it, that "circumstantial coercion" was invariably what caused informers to assist the police.[36]

Like any political police, the Gestapo was able to carry out its surveillance and enforcement tasks to the extent that it attained denunciations from the public. Political denunciations are understood as taking place when citizens inform the police or other authorities about instances of disapproved behavior that come to their attention. However, despite the significance of denunciations in making the "police state" come alive, the part played by citizens who provided them has been neglected by historians.[37] One of the reasons why this is the case, especially in the many works on "resistance and persecution," but also in the recent wave of books on *Alltagsgeschichte*, stems from the concern to deal with the victims rather than the victimizers, to give voice to the forgotten and silent. But whatever the explanation, there is certainly no doubt that in accounts of "resistance and persecution" very little has been said about denunciation, even though a study of it would contribute a great deal to understanding the context. "Persecution" and the many varieties and shades of behavior that were its essential prerequisites—such as compliance, conformity, adjustment, accommodation, cooperation, and collaboration—if not entirely lost sight of, have not received sufficient attention. As Detlev Peukert, himself a practitioner of the "everyday" genre, points out, it is necessary to recall that the "fondly drawn pictures of everyday nonacceptance" that began streaming from the presses in the Federal Republic with the approach of the fiftieth anniversary of the "seizure of power" took place "against the background of the majority's passivity, conformity, or even enthusiastic support."[38] His recent book reinforces this point[39] as do, for example, two recent movies, *Die weisse Rose* (which deals with student resistance in Munich) and *Eine Liebe in Deutschland* (which takes up the story of how far enforcing racial policy on the Polish foreign workers was carried), both of which prominently feature the role of denunciation.[40]

There is no doubt, however, that policy enforcement was dependent on the information provided by citizens about suspected "criminality." This was a point made by a number of Hitler's henchmen, at home and abroad.[41] The crucial question, however, is not what motivated the denouncer, but whether or not the information helped root out a specific "crime," or, if it did not do so in a given instance, whether it contributed to an atmosphere in which, indirectly, it worked as a deterrent to disobedience. The regime had to be hospitable and receptive to the tips, and made it clear that it would follow up the information, no matter how dubious its source or trivial the allegation. Only in rare, specific instances was there a need to make informing the police a legal duty, because a sufficient number of people came forward without having to be prodded officially.

Various ministries and institutions found it difficult to decide what to do in the case of careless or patently false denunciations. On the one hand, there would simply be no hope of enforcing racial policy (for example) when it came to policing social and sexual relations between Jews and non-Jews (as prohibited, for example, by the Nuremberg laws for such relations outside marriage) unless civilians could be encouraged to report misbehavior. On the other hand, as Minister of the Interior Frick pointed out in a memorandum to local officials at the beginning of 1939, it was wasteful to see Germans denounced "because they once bought something in a Jewish store, lived in the same house as Jews, or otherwise had business relations with the Jews."[42] In September 1939 the Gestapo and Justice Ministry, on the one hand, and the Propaganda Ministry, on the other, adopted conflicting positions. The secret police wanted greater severity applied to the knowingly false or careless denouncers—a massive problem for the enforcement people in the country—while Goebbels's very unpopular decree that sought to ban listening to foreign radio broadcasts simply invited a flood of frivolous tip-offs based on flimsy suspicions.[43]

A succinct statement of the ambiguous attitude of the regime came from the minister of justice in a letter of 1 August 1943 in which he offered his opinion of recent cases to judges as "guidance" in their future decisions. The minister observed that "the denouncer is—according to an old saying—the biggest scoundrel in the whole country." That was especially so of anyone who knowingly and maliciously denounced others for crimes they had not committed. When it came to the careless denouncer, of course, the judges were advised to be more cautious. While "we do not want to turn the people into denouncers and snoopers," he added, so that everyone spies on everyone else, the regime could hardly afford to do without informers. In sentencing even the thoughtless and careless ones, the minister believed that too strict a penalty ought not to be imposed because that might result in the drying up of "useful sources in the discovery of criminal activities."[44] Like other modern dictatorships, in the last analysis the Nazi regime preferred too much information rather than too little, and quantity over quality, to the point where the flood of information threatened to incapacitate the system.[45]

The social origins of the denouncers and their motives deserve more attention than can be given here. A number of accounts that deal with Nazi Germany, but also others that look at different societies in upheaval, maintain that there is a greater tendency for informers to come from marginalized groups, from those prone to spite and resentment, who use the political police to strike at their social superiors.[46] However, evidence can be found, especially in the eyewitness accounts, that indicates that no social class, vocational group, political camp, or religious denomination (including the Jews) was entirely free of informers. One suspects that denunciations lodged by and aimed at the socially disadvantaged and/or marginalized groups were handled by the police and/or the party with greater alacrity than those pertaining to privileged sectors such as the landed aristocracy, the officer corps, or the medical profession.

It is always problematic to attribute motives to people who offered information to the Gestapo, not least because, normally speaking, they sought to adjust the description of their motives to suit the occasion. As mentioned above, Reinhard Mann believed that only 24 percent of all the denouncers were probably motivated by "system-loyal" considerations.[47] The motives of those in the Würzburg Gestapo files that deal with those accused of deviation from the norms of the regime in the broad area of race relations seem to fit Mann's interpretation. Although the declared enemies of the regime, especially those in the Socialist underground at home and in exile, might have considered the informers as traitors to the cause who were on the police payroll, this certainly was not generally the case. While concerns about motivation continue to plague our moral sensibilities, only under exceptional circumstances did the Gestapo, other control organizations, or the political leaders in Berlin give the matter much more than a second thought. As indicated above, at the highest levels, in the RSHA and the Interior, Justice, and Propaganda Ministries, concerns about how to deal with denunciations persisted for the duration of the regime. When it came right down to it, the Gestapo and other official or semiofficial bodies checked out the information first and worried about motives later.

At the street level, effective enforcement required a minimal degree of popular cooperation; that is, enough citizens had to provide information about "criminal" political behavior. It was quite beside the point whether the denouncers agreed with the decisions taken at the highest level (part of the time, or at all), never mind whether they shared their leaders' political or ideological views. Thus, it is important for historians to distinguish the regime's popularity from the question of the degree to which it was actively or passively supported. Even after the opening of hostilities against the Soviet Union, when many citizens, especially in the working class and/or Catholic-peasant milieus, would have been happy to see Hitler ousted, the regime's efforts to enforce its racial polices of separating Jews from non-Jews, to keep to this example, were never jeopardized.

Any social historical study of Nazi Germany, as Ian Kershaw makes clear in two related monographs, must henceforth take into account what he terms "popular opinion."[48] He demonstrates on the basis of thorough and thoughtful local research that the regime worried a great deal about how it was doing with the public, and attained degrees of acceptance that varied from place to place, over time, and according to the issue. Far from speaking with monolithic unanimity, the German people counted in its ranks numerous grumblers, malcontents, dissenters, and opponents. Displeasure with how things were going, of one sort or another, could be witnessed on occasion in virtually all groups in society. Kershaw is quick to point out, of course, that particularly on the "Jewish question" by 1939 (if not earlier) there was a consensus "based on the passivity and apathy of the vast majority of the population," behavior that was nothing less than a "deliberate turning away from any personal responsibility." However, this moral abdication was reinforced by the more active participation of at least some people because "the conditions of Nazism encouraged the full flourishing of denunciation as an effective form of social control, in which neighbours and workmates collaborated with 'active' not 'passive complicity' in building the climate of repression and apathetic compliance."[49]

The existence and persistence of dissent that flared into opposition and even resistance on rare occasions does not seem to have seriously affected the ability of the regime to enforce its will, at least when it came to the broad and growing sphere of racial policy. An examination of the ways in which the regime went about the business of enforcement indicates that it could do quite well even in the face of some dissent. For example, a close look at the way it socially isolated the Jews reveals that, in spite of a few stumbling blocks and miscalculations that caused ripples of public consternation and some dissent, it was able to enforce policies with remarkable effectiveness. Kershaw has made a convincing argument as to the "indifference" and lack of concern most citizens entertained when it came to the fate of the Jews. (Others may prefer the notion of "passive complicity."[50]) For the enforcement of policy, of course, the indifference of the many was a stance not incompatible with the relatively smooth implementation of public policies aimed at gradually separating Jews and other citizens.

To the extent that political denunciations have been mentioned in the literature, their spread is most frequently attributed to the general atmosphere of terror and fear. According to this view, from the very first days of the "new order" brutality was applied on actual and potential enemies, not without considerable effect on people not personally at risk. As William Allen puts it, "in the atmosphere of terror, even people who were friends" concluded that they had to betray each other to survive.[51] He points out as well the "social reinforcement of the terror system," which is to say, how people such as a local school principal began to enforce rules he thought reflected the new state of affairs without ever having been ordered to do so.[52]

It is misleading to mention only the "negative" influence of terror and fear in the spread of denunciations, because more "positive" factors were also at work. The "legal" facade surrounding the "seizure of power" no doubt paid dividends in that many law-abiding citizens, out of respect for the legal norms, simply complied with the new regime. Because the takeover was not patently *illegal*, many could choose to ignore its revolutionary character, especially after the radicals were subdued after the purge in June 1934. The stoic acceptance, however, seems to have yielded to more positive attitudes.[53] Hans Bernd Gisevius, a member of the Gestapo in 1933, later recollected that many people fell in line of their own accord:

> There was, to be sure, a tremendous amount of bitterness and distrust, and frequently open revolt appeared. But there was at least an equal amount of enthusiasm and devotion, not to say fanaticism. Seldom had a nation so readily surrendered all its rights and liberties as did ours in those first hopeful, intoxicated months of the new millenium.[54]

What struck him most forcefully was what he called "individual *Gleichschaltung*," by which he meant a kind of willing self-integration into the new system: "Not one of these zealots would confess to another whether his principal motive was idealism or opportunism. But all of them understood that they could no longer hang back."[55] As Fritz Stern rightly points out, in a suggestively titled essay on "National Socialism as Temptation," it would also be a mistake to say the chief motive was opportunism (this he calls a "thoroughly uninteresting subject"), when the "voluntary, preemptive acceptance of the conformity ordered or expected by the regime" grew "out of a whole range of motives."[56]

In Hitler's Germany, a combination of these "positive" and "negative" factors contributed to a social situation well described by Foucault's notion of the "carceral society."[57] Not all members of a such a society will lend a hand by actually informing the authorities. By the looks of it, however, a sufficient number did so to make the enforcement of policy, not to say the elimination of political opposition, possible.

Two Gestapo case types drawn from the surviving Würzburg Gestapo materials can function as specific examples of the way in which the enforcement process operated. The first demonstrates the drive to separate Jews and non-Jews socially. The second shows how the regime was able to enforce strict guidelines on expressions that indicated nonacceptance with the letter or spirit of official anti-Semitism.

In her recent book, Sarah Gordon used two major file types from the Düsseldorf Gestapo—namely, those accused of being a "friend to the Jews" and those accused of "race defilement" *(Rassenschande)*—as evidence of opposition to Nazi anti-Semitism.[58] While there are a number of good reasons to question her results, she is right to point to the importance of these file groups. She treated all these cases as evidence of "opposition" (by assuming prima facie guilt of every accused person), but the files are far too heterogeneous to justify such treatment, and, among other things, many people were either falsely or baselessly charged. Actually, even a brief search through the Düsseldorf Gestapo case files shows not only that in that area, as everywhere else in the country, the anti-Semitic legislation was utilized for private purposes, but also that knowingly false charges were laid, on at least one occasion, with particularly tragic results.[59] That the misuse of the system was widespread becomes obvious with a systematic reading of the Gestapo dossiers, but can also be deduced from the repeatedly voiced concerns of national authorities about how to deal with the flood of false and/or careless denunciations.[60]

The Gestapo case files are excellent sources for a study of the enforcement of racial policy. They certainly reveal as much or more collaboration and accommodation as they do opposition or resistance, and are well suited for a study of political denunciations. As a group, with differentiated handling, they highlight the routine functioning of the interrelationships between the police and the people over the entire course of the Third Reich. Beyond that, moreover, there is every reason to expect that the modus operandi of the Gestapo in the area of race relations was similar to that required to enforce other policies, so that the results ought to have wider implications.

In order to illustrate the concrete way in which the enforcement process actually operated, what follows offers some conclusions based on the same kinds of files used by Gordon, but located in Würzburg. It is not surprising to find that in the private spheres of social and sexual life into which the regime sought to encroach—as when it came to policing social/sexual contacts between Jews and non-Jews (and later on, between foreign workers from the east, as well as prisoners of war, and Germans on the home front)—a greater degree of popular participation was required. Reinhard Mann concluded that nearly 30 percent of all Gestapo cases began with a denunciation. However, of the 175 cases in the Würzburg data that pertain to the social and sexual separation of Jews and non-Jews, 57 percent began with a denunciation. While Mann's figures show that something like 15 percent of all cases resulted from the Gestapo's "own observations," in Würzburg less than 1 percent of the cases of forbidden social/sexual relations across the ethnic border began that way. Without belaboring the point, it need only be added that there are no other significant differences between how proceedings were opened against persons suspected of entertaining illegal social/sexual contact with Jews and how they began in general (as shown above in Mann's figures).[61] The inescapable conclusion is that the enforcement of these racial policies might have been hampered had the Gestapo not been able to elicit assistance from the population at large. Put another way, the surveillance provided by citizens gradually eliminated the "more or less protected enclaves," the "one prerequisite" required for expressions of disobedience.[62]

The Gestapo files offer evidence that there developed among the German people an extreme scrupulousness over possible infringements of racial regulations. It became clear that only the most fastidious could avoid being denounced, because the Gestapo did not hesitate to follow up the many charges that were patently false, utterly baseless, or alleged by persons of very dubious reliability (from the certifiably insane to chronic complainers and antisocial types). Fears mounted as the authorities took the most trivial charges seriously and refrained from being overly severe with the informer even when the charge turned out to be knowingly false and/or without foundation. The Gestapo as an enforcer was also not above using "dirty" methods. Apart from coercion, intimidation, and blackmail, it employed entrapment and use of agents provocateurs, and, when all else failed, simply planted evidence.[63] While such tactics do not turn up in the Gestapo records, they must be kept in mind in any evaluation of the enforcement process. The rumors and fears of what might befall the non-compliant or merely incautious citizen at the hands of the Gestapo no doubt contributed to its effectiveness as an enforcer.

Instead of dealing with the enforcement of racial policy in its many forms, it may be useful to focus on just one case where a genuine and full-voiced rejection of Nazi anti-Semitism confronted the Gestapo and to examine how the case proceeded.

Ilse Sonja Totzke (born 1913, in Strasbourg), the daughter of upper-middle-class German parents, went to Würzburg to study music in 1932.[64] Her life went well until a motorcycle accident in 1935 put an end to any hopes of a musical career. The recurrent headaches, from which she suffered for the rest of her life, meant that even regular employment would be difficult, so that she was fortunate to inherit some 42,000 marks at the age of twenty-one. Although there were some family difficulties, she retained a generosity of spirit, even after she broke off contact with her widower father, and she helped finance the education of stepsisters from her father's new marriage. In her interrogation on 5 September 1941 by the Gestapo in Würzburg, Totzke recalled that she began making friends with Jewish people (women) in 1934–35, that is, almost at the very moment when this behavior was being actively discouraged. Her first brush with the Gestapo had come in 1936 when, for reasons unknown in her file, her mail was watched. Nothing turned up. On 3 April 1939 a more serious denunciation came to the Gestapo via a neighbor, a *Studienrat* (high school teacher), attached to the local university, who said that he "felt bound by his duty as a reserve officer" to inform on her "suspicious behavior." He believed that Totzke was a spy, a point he reiterated in a separate (later) letter (in mid-1940) as well, when he heard that she had been seen near troop movements!

Little could be done about such vague allegations, although in specific interviews her neighbors casually offered the most damning gossip. Nothing further happened until 29 July 1940, when yet another denouncer appeared at Gestapo headquarters. This time it was a clerical worker, a twenty-two-year-old woman and neighbor whose suspicions were aroused because Totzke had always avoided the "Heil Hitler!" greeting. Furthermore, Totzke was said to sympathize with Germany's enemies (the French, the Jews); while she had no job, she always had money, and obviously knew a lot about armies and such things. Totzke went out late at night and stayed home all day. As well, there sometimes appeared in her company a woman (about thirty-six years old) who "looked Jewish." Still nothing untoward resulted, even when an additional denunciation, contained in an anonymous letter "from a close neighbor" in early 1941, alleged similar "suspicions." The spelling and grammatical errors in that letter suggest that neither the teacher nor the clerical worker wrote it. Although Totzke had done little or nothing of a "criminal" nature, she had been questioned by the police, incriminated by neighbors, and denounced on at least five occasions.

For whatever reason, the Gestapo waited until August 1941 to bring her in for interrogation. Perhaps still another denunciation finally had the desired effect. That was almost certainly the case in the light of questions asked her. When it was charged that socializing with Jews might be taken to mean she did not accept the official anti-Jewish line, Totzke answered as follows:

> If it is concluded, on the basis of my Jewish acquaintances, that I do not have much use for National Socialism, I would say that I do not concern myself with politics. The action against the Jews, however, I believe is not right. I cannot declare myself in agreement with these measures. To that I would add that I am not a Communist. Every decent person is fine with me, regardless of his nationality. I chose my living quarters outside Würzburg in order

> to be by myself and to hear nothing of the world. My doctor also
> advised me to live in the open as much as possible.

Totzke was brought in again on 28 October 1941 when she was formally warned
to avoid Jews or face a spell in a concentration camp. As of 24 November 1941 it
officially became a crime for non-Jews to show friendship to Jews by appearing in
public with them.[65] At about the same time it was easier for the curious to spot
Jews, because from September on, they had been forced to wear the yellow star.
The increased sensitivity of the Würzburg Gestapo at this juncture may also have
been caused by pressures arising from the roundups and deportations of the Jews
then under way in the district.

   Totzke, for one, evidently persisted in socializing with the Jews and
refused to break off social relations, a matter once again brought to Gestapo
attention, although the means is unclear, in December 1942. At that time she
was summoned to local headquarters. Evidently she sensed more damning
information could be brought against her, and she decided to avoid the prospect
of a concentration camp sentence by fleeing to Berlin. One way or another she
kept a step ahead of the police and at times stayed with Jewish acquaintances.
Finally, she and a Jewish woman friend she met in Berlin sought refuge in
Switzerland. After a long and torturous journey they crossed the border on the
night of 26–27 February 1943 only to be caught and, eventually, turned over to
German border guards. At her hearing she put her story as follows:

> I was not ordered by anyone to bring the Jewish person Ruth Sara
> Basinsky to Switzerland. I simply had pity for the latter and wanted
> to protect her from the evacuation. I also admit that I was the one
> who convinced her to flee. For my efforts I have received compen-
> sation neither from Basinky nor from other persons. I disagree that
> I had previously helped Jews to leave illegally. The escape plan was
> totally my own, and I was supported by no one. I would like to
> mention once again that I wanted to leave Germany because I
> reject National Socialism. More than anything else, I cannot
> agree with the Nuremberg laws. I had the plan to get myself
> interned in Switzerland. I do not want to live further in Germany
> under any circumstances.

The Gestapo concluded its case by consigning Totzke to a concentration camp
because she was "beyond redemption." She never returned.

   While this woman's story is a portrait in courage, a full appreciation of
her behavior can be gathered only by keeping firmly in mind the role of the
neighbors who repeatedly denounced her. Their motives were mixed—sometimes it was "duty," sometimes resentment and envy or just antipathy. Without
the contribution of these people, enforcing the regime's measures would have
been impossible. This case, typical of the few examples of genuine opposition in

the Gestapo files, suggests that it is important to view opposition and dissent against the background of compliance, collaboration, and accommodation. Totzke's case also demonstrates the regime's largely successful effort to enforce control over the spoken word.

The most important legal basis for policing verbal expressions and "treacherous" statements was the series of decrees of early 1933, and especially the law against malicious gossip, but any number of other measures could be called on. An indication of the importance the regime attached to attaining popular compliance to the spirit of the laws, notably when it came to the broad area of the "Jewish question," may be gathered from one specific set of fifty-two Würzburg Gestapo dossiers that deal with "remarks" on the Jews or Jewish policies. These are worth examining briefly because additional features of the enforcement process are brought into sharper relief. These files reveal grumblings and complaints uttered mainly in public places, such as restaurants and pubs, by persons not infrequently under the influence of alcohol. Limited disenchantment and dissent were expressed. The delinquent statements were zealously noted by someone within earshot and reported. For innumerable incidents of verbal noncompliance, however mild, there would appear to have been a denouncer willing to inform. If the cases indicate that some people expressed solidarity with the Jews, they also contain as much or more evidence of accommodation and collaboration.

The files testify to accommodation with Nazi anti-Semitism also by what they do not say. Even at the level of verbal communication there is remarkably little outright rejection or condemnation of what was happening to the Jews. While it is true that vociferous disapproval could hardly be expected in an authoritarian regime, the persecution in Lower Franconia was particularly open to public scrutiny and virtually impossible to overlook, for the Jewish community was widely dispersed and highly visible across the district, and most communities of any size had at least a handful of Jewish citizens.[66] Apart from "individual acts" of violence aimed at the person and property of Jews, which went on relentlessly and in public view, enforcement of anti-Semitic policy was seen by the regime as part of its campaign to alter social behavior. Accordingly, there was no effort to conceal its aim to break all social bonds between Jews and non-Jews. Moreover, people in small rural communities have ways of keeping abreast of what is going on, especially when it concerns violence, property damage, and religious or political disputes.

Given the vigilance of volunteer denouncers, official and semiofficial snoopers, the extensive information-gathering and police network, the many party operatives, and so on, and, not least, the responsiveness of the Gestapo—especially on an "important" topic like the Jewish question—it would be fair to conclude that the paucity of negative remarks aimed at the regime's anti-Semitism of one kind or another may be taken as an indication of the extent to which citizens accommodated themselves to the official line and, for all intents and purposes, did not stand in the way of the persecution of the Jews. This silence is given additional significance when it is recalled that it was precisely in rural Catholic areas such as Lower Franconia "that the most vociferous condemnation of the barbarity was heard."[67] So the quiet there may lead to the suspicion that the response elsewhere was more muted.

Even in the much larger jurisdiction of the Special Court in Munich, designed especially to deal with all kinds of critical remarks, there was a total of just over seventy persons tried between 1933 and 1944 for making comments that in some, often remote way could be construed as "negative" as to anti-Jewish policy. Almost exactly half (or thirty-four) of the cases were dropped. Reading through these files, what is striking is, again, the relatively small numbers of those who were tried, and the even fewer who said that what was happening to the Jews was unjust or wrong. Once on trial, of course, no one could be expected to condemn Nazi policies; still, it was rare that anyone was even charged on such counts. It is true that the Special Courts did not handle every case of such "treacherous" remarks, and the Gestapo, regular police, or the party dealt with many more people than were sent to trial.[68]

To be sure, it must not be forgotten, as eyewitness accounts published after 1945 make clear, that not everyone who aided Jews or offered verbal sympathy was caught.[69] If there was no denunciation or if the police did not discover the matter by some other means, the aid or comfort would have gone unrecorded in the official sources, so that care must be taken not to assume that what was not picked up by the authorities did not happen. Nevertheless, taking into account such considerations, one cannot help concluding that instances of sympathy for the plight of the Jews in Lower Franconia (and elsewhere) were shockingly infrequent. Very little, negative or positive, was said even about such major turning points in the history of German Jews as the requirement to wear the yellow star (September 1941) and, not long after that, their systematic rounding up and deportation. What Ralf Dahrendorf once called the Germans' "great quiet"—their tendency not to protest, get worked up, certainly "not about the inhumanities in one's own world"[70]—is to an extent reflected in the fact that over the twelve-year history of the regime, so few errant statements on the persecution of the Jews were recorded. While there may have been a "withdrawal into the private sphere" as a kind of "mass retreat from the Nazi pressure to conform," such a "retreat" into silence was also a form of compliance, accommodation, conformity, or apathy.[71] The few instances of breaking the silence suggest the effectiveness of enforcement.

A number of conclusions can be drawn about how the Nazi dictatorship enforced policy. The regime was less dependent than one might have expected on an enthusiastic reception of the "new order" by all, or even most, citizens. A crucial factor in the enforcement process was not the "popularity" of the system, and German society as a whole did not need to become thoroughly National Socialist nor even anti-Semitic. Effective implementation of policies designed to separate Jews and non-Jews required that the regime establish the official "line," elicit cooperation, and act relentlessly on the basis of information received. There is no good reason to expect that the enforcement process, as (partially) reconstructed in this paper with respect to policies aimed at separating Jews and non-Jews, would work differently in regard to other policies. (Whether it was as successful is another matter.) The findings here, therefore, should have wider implications.

A study of policy enforcement has implications for discussions of the "police state" and "terror system" used to characterize the Nazi system. The results of this paper are consistent with a number of recent accounts. Michael Geyer, for example, suggests that all "bonds of solidarity" were destroyed "by fostering the egotism of both individuals and institutions, and by applauding as strong and healthy those 'who have no sympathy for any but themselves,'" and that "a State and society" emerged "which 'placed men side by side, unconnected by any common ties.'"[72] One can witness the competition that Geyer sees as a characteristic feature of the system with particular poignancy by examining the enforcement of racial policy. However, the "competition" that centered "around terror and force, the capacity to impose one's will on others" was conducted not only, and not primarily, "by means of physical coercion," as Geyer suggests, but rather less heroically and in more mundane fashions by exploiting the system's need for information.[73]

This paper suggests that social historians should deal more systematically with the structures of everyday life, while those who are concerned with "high politics" should consider a shift of emphasis away from decision making and an institutional orientation characteristic of many studies of the era to one that entails as well the implementation and enforcement of policy in the context of society at large. Far from any "trivialization," which some might charge results from moving away from preoccupation with Nazi leaders in order to incorporate social historical findings, such research indicates that responsibility for the criminal features of the regime cannot be dismissed as simply the work of a handful at the top.[74] Until now, few historians of Hitler's Germany have been prepared to focus on enforcement, even though this is the sphere in which official "intentions" run up against "structures." Any reevaluation of political policing will have relevance for studies of popular accommodation and has obvious implications for accounts of dissent, opposition, and resistance, because popular participation in policing had the effect of reducing the relatively "safe enclaves" that are the prerequisite of disobedience of all kinds. It cannot be forgotten that citizens played a crucial role in their own policing and helped make possible the murderous deeds of the regime.

Notes

Research was supported by the Alexander von Humboldt Foundation and the Social Sciences and Humanities Research Council of Canada.

1. Michael Kunze, *The Highroad to the Stake: A Tale of Witchcraft,* trans. W. E. Yuill (Chicago, 1987), pp. 79–80. Kunze comments that the duke "was imbued with an idea of the state which did not come into its own until the present century. He envisaged total surveillance of every citizen, supreme authority over the citizen's conscience, and control of his life. Had the duke possessed the technical facilities of our own day, he would not have needed the crude device of a show trial. So the comforting reflection that such things could not happen now is hardly justified" (p. xii).

2. These social processes led to the "nationalization of the masses." The phrase is from George L. Mosse, *The Nationalization of the Masses: Political Symbolism and Mass Movements in Germany from the Napoleonic Wars through the Third Reich* (New York, 1975).

3. For a detailed examination of these and other issues, see my *The Gestapo and German Society: Enforcing Racial Policy, 1933–1945,* (Oxford, 1990). This investigation concentrates on Bavaria and utilizes in particular some of the 19,000 Gestapo case files that survive in Würzburg. The Gestapo post in that city was responsible, ultimately, for all of the Bavarian district of Lower Franconia, a largely rural, very Catholic area, one most reluctant to vote Nazi before 1933 or to jump on the bandwagon thereafter.

4. See Robert Gellately, "The Gestapo and German Society: Political Denunciation in the Gestapo Case Files," *Journal of Modern History* 60 (December 1988): 654–94.

5. Cf. G. R. Elton, *Policy and Police: The Enforcement of the Reformation in the Age of Thomas Cromwell* (Cambridge, 1972).

6. For party policing in eastern Germany, see the Eisenach Kreisleitung files (the "Myers Collection") at the University of Michigan, Ann Arbor, Michigan.

7. Cf. Fred Hahn, *Lieber Stürmer! Leserbriefe an das NS-Kampfblatt 1924 bis 1945* (Stuttgart, 1978), pp. 228ff.

8. A recent example of this approach is Christoph Graf, *Politische Polizei zwischen Demokratie und Diktatur* (Berlin, 1983).

9. Literature is cited in Gellately, "Political Denunciation."

10. For examples of local source collections, see Robert Thevoz et al., *Pommern 1934/35 im Spiegel von Gestapo-Lageberichten und Sachakten.* Vol. 1, *Darstellung;* vol. 2, *Quellen* (Cologne, 1974); Thomas Klein, *Die Lageberichte der Geheimen Staatspolizei über die Provinz Hessen-Nassau, 1933–1936,* 2 vols. (Cologne, 1986); Jörg Schadt, *Verfolgung und Widerstand unter dem Nationalsozialismus in Baden: Die Lageberichte der Gestapo und des Generalstaat-*

sanwalts Karlsruhe, 1933–1940 (Stuttgart, 1976).

11. David Schoenbaum, *Hitler's Social Revolution: Class and Status in Nazi Germany, 1933–1939* (London, 1967) pp. 202ff. Police and political police are each mentioned once and are not cited in the index.

12. An exception here is Detlev Peukert, *Volksgenossen und Gemeinschaftsfremde: Anpassung, Ausmerze und Aufbegehren unter dem Nationalsozialismus* (Cologne, 1982), pp. 55ff. More attention might have been devoted to policing in the otherwise extensive project on Bavaria. See Martin Broszat et al., eds., *Bayern in der NS-Zeit*, 6 vols. (Munich, 1977ff.).

13. The theme is hardly touched on, for example, in Lutz Niethammer, ed., *"Die Jahre weiss man nicht, so man die heute hinsetzen soll"*: Faschismus-*Erfahrungen im Ruhrgebiet* (Berlin, 1983).

14. On the policing function of the NSDAP, see Michael Kater, *The Nazi Party: A Social Profile of Members and Leaders, 1919–1945* (Cambridge, Mass., 1983), pp. 190ff. Kater quotes Hermann Rauschning's remark that the Nazi system worked as it did because "everyone is the other man's devil, everyone supervises everybody" (p. 208). With the outbreak of war in September 1939, "the block and cell leaders intensified their control over every German man, woman, and child at all levels of everyday existence" (p. 222). Cf. Aryeh L. Unger, *The Totalitarian Party: Party and People in Nazi Germany and the Soviet Union* (Cambridge, 1974), pp. 83ff. See the quantitative analysis of the Gestapo in Düsseldorf by Reinhard Mann, *Protest und Kontrolle im Dritten Reich: Nationalsozialistische Herrschaft im Alltag einer rheinischen Grossstadt* (Frankfurt a.M., 1987), pp. 287ff.

15. A classic example of the emphasis on numbers is Eugen Kogon, *Der SS-Staat: Das System der deutschen Konzentrationslager* (1946) (Munich 1974), p. 28. Franz Dröge, *Der zerredete Widerstand: Zur Soziologie und Publizistik des Gerüchts im 2. Weltkrieg* (Düsseldorf, 1970), pp. 54ff. suggests that for every 2,500 citizens there was one SD worker. An emphasis on numbers tends to underplay the importance of factors that cannot be quantified. In fact, at the local level "the Gestapo became extraordinarily efficient by reason of rumors and fears," as small towns like Northeim, especially in the early days, "were inundated by amateur 'Gestapo' operatives." See William Sheridan Allen, *The Nazi Seizure of Power: The Experience of a Single German Town, 1922–1945*, rev. ed. (New York, 1984), p. 189. For an examination of enforcement limitations in the United States today, see Hans Zeisel, *The Limits of Law Enforcement* (Chicago, 1982), pp. 15ff.

16. These remarks are based on the files in the Berlin Document Center and the Bunsdesarchiv Koblenz (BAK). Of the twenty-one men who have been identified as having served at one time or another in Würzburg, only two were in the NSDAP before 1933. A full account of the local organization is given in Gellately, *The Gestapo and German Society*.

17. From Franz Vogt, "Die Lage der deutschen Bergarbeiter (August 1936)," in Detlev J. K. Peukert and Frank Bajohr, *Spuren des Widerstands: Die Bergarbeiterbewegung im Dritten Reich und im Exil* (Munich, 1987), p. 140. Vogt was certainly correct to claim that the denouncers represented "the most serious impediment to systematic illegal activity" (ibid.).

18. Elton, *Policy and Police*, p. 331, suggests that enforcement had relied on "amateurs" earlier as well.

19. Franz Neumann, *Behemoth: The Structure and Practice of National Socialism* (New York, 1966, orig. ed. 1942), p. 540.

20. E. K. Bramstedt, *Dictatorship and Political Police: The Technique of Control by Fear* (New York, 1976, orig. ed. 1945), pp. 137ff.

21. Martin Broszat, *Der Staat Hitlers: Grundlegung und Entwicklung seiner inneren Verfassung* (Munich, 1971, orig. ed. 1969), chap. 10.

22. In Helmut Krausnick et al., eds., *Anatomy of the SS State*, trans. R. Barry et al. (London, 1968), see Hans Buchheim, "The SS—Instrument of Domination," pp. 127ff.

23. Hannah Arendt, *The Origins of Totalitarianism* (New York, 1966, orig. ed. 1951), p. 430.

24. Ibid., p. 431.

25. Ibid. Cf. Allen, *The Nazi Seizure of Power*, pp. 189–90.

26. For the notion of "thought police," see Buchheim, "The SS," p. 202.

27. See *Trial of the Major War Criminals before the International Military Tribunal* (Nuremberg, 1948), vol. 20, p. 127. Best also remarked that "only relatively few" men from the SS, SA, or Nazi Party were taken into the Gestapo, not least because service in "police agencies was not highly paid and therefore was not very much sought after" (p. 126).

28. See, for example, Rudolf Diels, *Lucifer Ante Portas . . . es spricht der erste Chef der Gestapo* (Stuttgart, 1950), p. 222. Cf. comments of August Moritz, chief of section VI (collaboration) in Lyons, who claimed there were queues that formed at kiosks for denunciations: "We had so many that we couldn't even check most of them." Quoted in Tom Bower, *Klaus Barbie: Butcher of Lyons* (London, 1984), p. 53. See also Bertram M. Gordon, *Collaborationism in France during the Second World War* (Ithaca, N.Y., 1980), p. 316ff.

29. See Mann, *Protest*, p. 292.

30. Cf. Dieter Rebentisch, "Die 'politische Beurteilung' als Herrschaftsinstrument," in Detlev Peukert and Jürgen Reulecke, eds., *Die Reihen fast geschlossen: Beiträge zur Geschichte des Alltags unterm Nationalsozialismus* (Wuppertal, 1981), pp. 107ff.

31. See Reinhard Mann, "Was wissen wir vom Widerstand? Datenqualität, Dunkelfeld und Forschungsartefakte" (1978), unpublished paper in IfZ.

32. Mann, *Protest*, p. 246.

33. Ibid., p. 295.

34. Cf. Barrington Moore, Jr., *Terror and Progress, USSR*, (Cambridge, Mass., 1954), p. 154ff. Cf. China under the Cultural Revolution as represented by Nien Cheng, *Life and Death in Shanghai* (Glasgow, 1986).

35. On the belief in the regime's need to plant spies, see the *Deutsch-land-Berichte der Sozialdemokratischen Partei Deutschlands (Sopade)* (Nörd-lingen, 1980ff.), for example, vol. 2, the entry for 2 September 1935, pp. 1057ff. An interpretation of the Left's misperceptions is contained in Detlev Peukert's remark (in his *Die KPD im Widerstand: Verfolgung und Untergrundarbeit an Rhein und Ruhr 1933 bis 1945* (Wuppertal, 1980), p. 121) that the KPD (like the SPD?) interpreted National Socialism primarily as an instrument of large cap-italist interests, and only secondarily as a popular mass movement, with the result that they "underestimated in their conception of resistance the role of spontaneous, massive denunciation out of agreement with Nazism or from personal vindictiveness."

36. This is suggested by Walter Otto Weyrauch, "Gestapo Informants: Facts and Theory of Undercover Operations," *Columbia Journal of Transnational Law* 24 (1986): 554ff. This issue is discussed in Gellately, "Political Denunciation."

37. An exception is Martin Broszat, "Politische Denunziationen in der NS-Zeit: Aus Forschungserfahrungen im Staatsarchiv München," *Archivalische Zeitschrift* 73 (1977): 221ff.

38. Detlev Peukert, "Widerstand und 'Resistenz.' Zu den Bänden V and VI der Publikation 'Bayern in der NS-Zeit,'" *Archiv für Sozialgeschichte* 24 (1984): 665.

39. Peukert, *Volksgenossen und Gemeinschaftsfremde*.

40. For the enforcing of policy on foreign workers, see Gellately, *The Gestapo and German Society*, chap. 8. See also Ulrich Herbert, *Fremdarbeiter: Politik und Praxis des 'Ausländer—Einsatzes' in der Kriegswirtschaft des Dritten Reiches* (Berlin, 1986), pp. 124ff.

41. See the examples in nn. 27 and 28.

42. BAK R58/264 Frick to Reichsstatthalter, 10 January 1939.

43. BAK R 58/275, Berlin, 3 September 1939; Chef der Sipo to Stapo(leit)stellen. On the radio restrictions see C. F. Latour, "Goebbels' Ausser-ordentliche Rundfunkmassnahmen, 1939–1942" *VfZ* 2 (1963): 418ff. For sev-eral examples of denunciations of listening in, see William L. Shirer, *Berlin Diary* (New York, 1941), pp. 214ff., entry for 4 February 1940.

44. Hans Boberach, ed., *Richterbriefe: Dokumente zur Beeinflussung der deutschen Rechtsprechung, 1942—1944* (Boppard am Rhein, 1975), pp. 171–72.

45. See Moore, *Terror and Progress*, p. 159.

46. Cf. Broszat, "Politische Denunziationen," p. 221. Although Richard Grunberger, A *Social History of the Third Reich* (Harmondsworth, 1974, orig. ed. 1971), pp. 145ff., asserts that the regime "harnessed a vast reservoir of personal resentment and spite" of those people who aimed the weapon of the denunciation at their "social superiors," it would appear even from the examples he gives that people usually informed on others in their own social class.

47. Mann, *Protest*, p. 295.

48. Ian Kershaw, *Popular Opinion and Political Dissent in the Third Reich: Bavaria, 1933–1945* (Oxford, 1983), and idem, *The "Hitler Myth": Image and Reality in the Third Reich* (Oxford, 1987).

49. Ian Kershaw, "German Popular Opinion and the 'Jewish Question,' 1939–1943: Some Further Reflections," in Arnold Paucker, ed., *Die Juden im Nationalsozialistischen Deutschland/The Jews in Nazi Germany, 1933–1945* (Tübingen, 1986), pp. 384–85.

50. Ibid., p. 367, quoting Otto Dov Kulka and Aron Rodrigue.

51. Allen, *Nazi Seizure of Power*, p. 189.

52. Ibid., p. 157.

53. See Mathilde Jamin, quoted in Richard Bessel, *Political Violence and the Rise of Nazism: The Storm Troopers in Eastern Germany, 1925–1934* (New Haven, Conn., 1984) p. 140.

54. Hans Bernd Gisevius, *To the Bitter End*, trans. R. and C. Winstone (London, 1945), pp. 101–2.

55. Ibid., p. 105.

56. The article is in his *Dreams and Delusions: The Drama of German History* (New York, 1987), pp. 169–70.

57. See Michel Foucault, *Discipline and Punish: The Birth of the Prison*, trans. A. Sheridan (New York, 1979, orig. ed. 1975), esp. pp. 293ff. See also his "The Subject and Power" in Hubert L. Dreyfus and Paul Rabinow, *Michel Foucault: Beyond Structuralism and Hermeneutics* (Chicago, 1982), pp. 208ff. Another aspect of the surveillance system is introduced by Götz Aly and Karl Heinz Roth, *Die restlose Erfassung: Volkszählen, Identifizieren, Aussondern im Nationalsozialismus* (Berlin, 1984), pp. 13ff.

58. Sarah Gordon, *Hitler, Germans, and the "Jewish Question"* (Princeton, N.J., 1984), pp. 210ff.

59. See, for example, Hauptstaatsarchiv Düsseldorf, Gestapo case 65053. In mid-1935 a man accused his estranged wife of consummating a sexual relationship with a Jewish man; both were arrested, whereupon the Jew committed suicide. An investigation established "no basis since the national rising" for the allegation, the Gestapo released the woman, and placed her husband in custody (17 August 1935) "for having caused the arrest of his wife and the Jew . . . by way of false accusation." This case landed on the desk of the Gestapo and

in the middle of Gordon's sample. Note also the remarks on false charges in the Düsseldorf Gestapo files mentioned in Mann, *Protest*, pp. 300–301.

60. Cf. the numbers of those found not guilty when brought to trial in Hans Robinsohn, *Justiz als politische Verfolgung: Die Rechtsprechung in "Rassenschandefällen" beim Landgerlicht Hamburg, 1936–1943* (Stuttgart, 1977), pp. 78ff. In Würzburg, 46 percent of the 91 persons accused of "friendship to the Jews" appear, on the basis of an evaluation of their cases, to be falsely or baselessly charged; 36 percent of the 85 accused of "race defilement" seem also charged without foundation. See Gellately, "Political Denunciation." Other reasons for doubting that everyone charged was guilty ("but were able to cover their tracks," as Gordon [*Hitler, Germans, and the Jewish Question*, p. 213] would have it) are also discussed. For a discussion of offical reactions to the flood of anonymous, false, and/or careless charges see Gellately, *The Gestapo and German Society*, chap. 6.

61. These figures are computed from a study of the Würzburg Gestapo case files in the Staatsarchiv Würzburg (StA W); the tables are printed in Gellately, "Political Denunciation."

62. This notion is from Barrington Moore, Jr., *Injustice: The Social Bases of Obedience and Revolt* (White Plains, N.Y., 1978), p. 482.

63. Cf. Klaus Moritz and Ernst Noam, *NS-Verbrechen vor Gericht, 1945–1955: Dokumente aus hessischen Justizakten* (Wiesbaden, 1978), pp. 271ff.; and Helene Moszkiewiez, *Inside the Gestapo* (Toronto, 1985), pp. 107ff. Guidelines and hints at subsequent action may be found, for example, in StA W 425/432: Gestapo-Frankfurt to local authorities, 21 August 1942.

64. The data for what follows are in StA W: Gestapo 16015. For more on "women who said no," see Claudia Koonz, *Mothers in the Fatherland: Women, the Family and Nazi Politics* (New York, 1986), pp. 307ff.

65. See the letter of that date from Gestapo Nuremberg to the Administration in Würzburg: StA W NSDAP GL MF XII/4.

66. For an overview, see Baruch Z. Ophir and Falk Wiesemann, *Die jüdischen Gemeinden in Bayern, 1918–1945* (Munich, 1979), pp. 247ff.

67. Kershaw, *Popular Opinion*, p. 265.

68. See StA Munich: Sondergericht Munich; the remarks pertained to the Jews and Jewish policies. For an overview, see Peter Hüttenberger, "Heimtückefälle vor dem Sondergericht München, 1933—1939," in Martin Broszat et al., eds., *Bayern in der NS-Zeit*, vol. 4 (Munich, 1981), pp. 435ff.

69. Cf. Inge Deutschkron, *Ich trug den gelben Stern*, 4th ed., (Cologne, 1983, orig. ed. 1978), and the evidence in Koonz, *Mothers in the Fatherland*, pp. 345ff.

70. Ralf Dahrendorf, *Society and Democracy in Germany* (London, 1967), pp. 363–64. One of his conclusions is that "National Socialism was not

merely an episode. It was not a work of seduction by a small clique, but, by its toleration, a German phenomenon" (p. 416).

71. Peukert, *Volksgenossen und Gemeinschaftsfremde*, p. 90.

72. Michael Geyer, "The Nazi State Reconsidered," in Richard Bessel, ed., *Life in the Third Reich* (Oxford, 1987), pp. 59–60; he quotes Alexis de Tocqueville, *Democracy in America*.

73. Ibid., p. 60. Cf. Geyer's "National Socialist Germany: The Politics of Information" in Ernest R. May, ed., *Knowing One's Enemies: Intelligence Assessment before the Two World Wars* (Princeton, N.J., 1986), pp. 310ff.

74. See the examination of the "trivialization" charge in Tim Mason, "Intention and Explanation: A Current Controversy about the Interpretation of National Socialism," in Gerhard Hirschfeld and Lothar Kettenacker, eds., *Der "Führerstaat": Mythos und Realität: Studien zur Struktur und Politik des Dritten Reiches* (Stuttgart, 1981), pp. 23ff.

3

Eugenics, Gender, and Ethics in Nazi Germany: The Debate about Involuntary Sterilization 1933–1936

CLAUDIA KOONZ

Adolf Hitler once summarized his solution to the "woman question" with a simple formula: no conflict between the sexes can occur as long as each party performs the function prescribed for it by nature. Such statements, combined with the fulsome praise of motherhood in official propaganda, have led many to see the National Socialists' solution to the "woman question" as merely one variation on a ubiquitous conservative desire to expel women from politics and return them to their homes. In fact, Nazi plans for "racial revolution" created a new model of womanhood that built on both conservative and liberal antecedents. Like conservatives, Nazis insisted on women's removal from formal politics and leading positions in the economy and administration. Like advocates of women's rights, Nazi social planners believed in a distinctive feminine nature that qualified women for special tasks in public life. Thus, while official ideology dispensed the apparently timeless shibboleths about *Kinder, Küche*, and *Kirche*, social policy expelled women from formal politics, while simultaneously mobilizing them out of their homes and into a vast sphere of public life as educators, community organizers, consumers, health workers, social workers, and volunteers in dozens of National Socialist initiatives. Although such activities had for several decades characterized women's activities under religious and local civic sponsorship, they had not previously been linked so strongly to the state. Ironically, the Nazi mobilization of wives, mothers, and daughters undercut masculine prerogatives and empowered some women by allying them with the state.

To be sure, Nazi planners did not see women's mobilization into the public sphere as a goal in itself, but rather came to understand it as the prerequisite for victory in their schemes for a massive racial revolution. At the same time, the effort to mobilize women challenged religious institutions that had until 1933 formed the major organizational center of women's public activities. Although we sometimes speak about the Nazi invasion of the "private" sphere, Nazi policies did not so much invade "private" life as challenge religious hegemony over values and customs. Nowhere was the challenge sharper than in the issues related to birth and death. In this essay I will examine the reactions of leading Catholic and Protestant women to eugenics policies that contradicted normal moral maxims. I have drawn my conclusions from a small sample of correspondence written by people in the occupations most affected by the eugenic laws—women employees of religiously affiliated hospitals, schools, welfare centers, and institutions for people with disabilities. These letters (now in church archives) reveal how the new eugenic rhetoric transformed deeply felt moral values about life and death. How did women, as mothers and health-care workers, react to the radical shift in gender prescription that replaced the traditional vision of woman as life-giving with a new image of woman as the heartless pruner of "unwanted" life?

Nazi eugenics "experts" immediately recognized women's central importance in their schemes. The chief of racial politics, Walter Gross, astutely observed that, when it came to matters related to "Blood and Race," "the German woman participates more fully than the man, [who is busy] with his state, and his fighting units."[1] "Aryan" women had to bear more children, select "racially fit" mates, indoctrinate their children, and volunteer to help the "racially worthy," deserving poor. More ominously, they were expected to target clients for forced abortion, sterilization, or euthanasia, to report on "suspicious" activities in the neighborhood, to boycott Jewish shops, and to refuse shelter to fugitives.

Although fear of arrest certainly reinforced compliance, Nazi leaders realized early that only enthusiastic cooperation could accomplish the massive racial revolution they had in mind. In 1922 Hitler had explained why conversion worked better than coercion: "In the construction of a propaganda organization lies the most effective preparation for future success. When we can win with paper [*Papierkugeln*] does not need to be coerced by steel later on"[2] From the earliest days of the Nazi Party, its leaders also proclaimed the drastic implications of their eugenics notions. The major goal of any state, Hitler often proclaimed, was to pull the race of its people up to greatness.[3] Admitting no earthly predecessor, he likened himself to another hero: "Two thousand years ago another man was also denounced by the same race that today everywhere slanders and shames."[4] As prophet, messiah, Führer, reformer, and revolutionary, Hitler often gave warning of an *Angriff* (attack) against racial "defectives."[5] The impact, he predicted, would be massive. Behind the bombastic rhetoric, however, the numerical predictions varied. At the 1929 party rally Hitler had suggested that 700,000 children would be affected by the racial measures he planned. On becoming chancellor, Hitler used words like "cleansing and regeneration," but avoided mentioning "eugenics." Frick, in 1934, predicted that as many as 20 percent of all Germans would be prevented from bearing children.

A Swiss eugenicist in 1934 concluded that "only" about six million (or 10 percent) of all Germans would be deemed physically or mentally to have less than full value *(nicht vollwert)*.[6] Even though the experts' numerical calculations varied widely, propagandists prepared Germans for a radical offensive against the "racial body" *(Volkskörper)*. Long before the proclamation of the Nuremburg Racial Laws, legislation to purify the "Aryan" race was put into effect, and a massive publicity campaign popularized eugenic measures.

Although the extent of this drive remains unparalleled in any other nation, its intellectual underpinnings were ubiquitous in the interwar period. From California to Leningrad, eugenicists argued that applied genetic science could eliminate serious disabilities from the human race. In *Mein Kampf* Hitler deplored the fact that hopelessly ill people could permanently threaten the healthy majority. "It is a half measure to allow incurably ill people the permanent possibility of contaminating the other healthy ones. . . . The demand that for defective people the propagation of an equally defective offspring be made impossible is a demand of clearest reason and . . . the most human act of mankind."[7] At about the same time, Justice Oliver Wendell Holmes wrote the majority decision that upheld forced sterilization laws in the United States:

> We have seen more than once that the public welfare may call upon the best citizens for their lives. It would be strange if it could not call upon those who already sap the strength of the state for these lesser sacrifics, often not felt to be such by those concerned, in order to prevent our being swamped with incompetence. It is better for all the world, if instead of waiting to execute the degenerate offspring for crime, or to let them starve for their imbecility, society can prevent those who are manifestly unfit from continuing their kind. . . . Three generations of imbeciles are enough.[8]

In Germany as elsewhere, crusaders for eugenics reform came from progressive secular and religious circles. Conservatives, when they thought about race at all, became obsessed with anti-Semitism, but the eugenics component of Nazi ideology emerged from liberal milieus populated by sex reformers, genetic researchers, religious social workers, and physicians.

Throughout the 1920s, the National Working Committee for National Health *(Volksgesundung)* amassed data on inherited traits and lobbied for compulsory sterilization laws. Hermann Muckermann, a Catholic, worked closely in it with Hans Harmsen, a Protestant. Because the committee defined national health in physiological and social terms, it also campaigned against tobacco and alcohol consumption, pornography, premarital sexual activity, sex education, and "degenerate" culture. With the papal denunciation of sterilization and abortion in *Casti Connubii* in 1931, however, Muckermann and the Catholic members of the committee retracted their support for eugenic intervention into individual lives.[9]

Because Nazi eugenics measures clearly violated the papal decree, Catholics had no choice but to oppose them. Progressive Protestants, however, had long endorsed such measures and therefore had no hesitation in endorsing Nazi laws. This religious contrast provides us with an excellent opportunity to examine the role of non-Nazi support in the implementation of Nazi social policy. Since Nazi law contradicted Catholic principles, we would expect lower compliance in Catholic regions, and because Protestant clergy welcomed eugenics, we would expect higher compliance rates in Protestant areas. In both cases, women's reactions document the debate because, ultimately, enforcement depended on health workers, teachers, mothers, and social workers to report the "genetically damaged" individuals in their care to local officials. Women from the lower echelons of religious institutions carried out directives from the men at the top. This gendered difference in bureaucratic position correlated with a contrast in attitudes toward the eugenics legislation. In this essay, I will examine Catholic and Protestant men's and women's, leaders' and followers', responses to the early stages of the eugenic campaign that aimed at severing the racially fit from the unfit.

Early Nazi Eugenic Legislation

Barely six months after the Nazi takeover, new programs encouraged marriage and fertility only among those Germans certified by physicians as genetically healthy and of non-Jewish descent. To guide couples, the state established genetic counseling centers throughout the nation. In July 1933, legislation legalized the involuntary sterilization of "genetically deficient" people. Anticipating Catholic objections, the media did not announce the law until several weeks after the Concordat with the Vatican, and its implementation did not begin until 1 January 1934. The law mandated employees in social work, health, and educational institutions to report *(anzeigen)* to local health officials clients with the following illnesses: feeblemindedness, schizophrenia, manic-depressive syndrome, St. Vitus's Dance (Huntington's Chorea), epilepsy, blindness, deafness, dumbness, severe alcoholism, and marked physical handicaps. In only two circumstances did "inferior racial ancestry" justify reporting: the offspring of Polish parents in Silesia and the children of black French soldiers who had served in the occupation forces in the Ruhr. Jewish ancestry, in other words, did not rank as grounds for eugenic control. Once reported, an individual would be investigated by a three-physician panel. In most cases the experts decided for eugenic action: vasectomy for men and tubal ligation for women. Although the law provided for some right of appeal, the physicians' application *(Antrag)* to sterilize was rarely retracted. Conversely, the physicians rarely accepted a request from an individual to be voluntarily sterilized.[10] In November 1933 the category "dangerous moral criminal" was added to the list of genetically dangerous qualities. Morally depraved men (women were not considered) could be investigated by a medical team empowered to order castration.

To process the deluge of cases, over 250 local medical tribunals for hereditary health were established. A Department of Genetic and Racial Care in the Reich Ministry of the Interior, with over a hundred offices, began to collect information for a genetic data bank on every citizen. By the end of 1934, the government had increased penalties for abortion and the sale of birth control devices, and had made voluntary sterilization illegal. The newly created Office to Fight Homosexuality and Abortion combated the two major "unnatural" causes of low fertility. Simultaneously, health officials received orders to investigate everyone suspected of having venereal diseases (probably abut 750,000 people). Starting in late 1935, all applicants for marriage licenses (not just marriage loans) had to receive a clean bill of genetic health. Finally, in July 1936 legislation empowered local health authorities to compel "genetically unfit" pregnant women to have abortions.

In addition to sweeping coercive measures, the Reich Health Office launched a campaign to popularize the new laws. One film, *Ich Klage An* (I Accuse) made in 1940, presented a dramatic plot in a fictionalized form. Far more powerful were the ubiquitous "shorts," documentaries like *Das Erbe* (Inheritance), *Opfer der Vergangenheit* (Sacrifice to the Past) and *Mutterliebe* (Mother Love) shown with newsreels prior to feature films.[11] Popular magazines like *Neues Volk* and *Volk und Rasse* were flanked by a host of scholarly publications to spread the eugenic message. Biology textbooks were rewritten, and "crash" courses instructed adults in the fundamentals of racial science. This material, of course, was written in somber, scientific tones. But eugenics publicity borrowed heavily from religious rhetoric. The "Ten Commandments for Selecting a Mate," for example, told young people to:

1. Remember you are a German.
2. If you are genetically healthy, you shall not remain unmarried.
3. Keep your body pure!
4. Keep your soul and mind pure!
5. As a German, select as a mate only someone with Nordic blood.
6. When you select a mate, ask about ancestry.
7. Health is the precondition for external beauty.
8. Marry only for love.
9. Don't select a playmate. Choose a partner for life.
10. Hope for as many children as possible. [12]

The pledge from the marriage ceremony became an injunction not to marry a "racially inferior" partner: "What God has created separate, let no man unite." In *Mein Kampf* Hitler had written." In the diseases of the children, the vices of the parents are revealed."[13] An article in the popular press promised "Aryans" that the Jewish saying about the "sins of the fathers" would be overcome with the New Testament commandment to overcome the bad with the good. " 'Let no evil triumph, but triumph over evil with good.' "[14]

Propaganda elided the difference between the messages of conventional religious precepts and Nazi law. The loyal Nazi, by definition, placed the commandments of the state above mandates to act mercifully and to love thy neighbor. Protestant advocates of eugenics saw no contradiction between secular and religious law, but Catholics faced a crisis of conscience. Why, one wonders, did the secular state invest so heavily in winning Catholics to policies that so clearly contravened Vatican pronouncements? First, Catholic and Protestant churches both sponsored vast networks of educational, health-care, and social work institutions. Rather than bypassing this network, it made sense for Nazi administrators to operate through it. Second, after 1933, state-sponsored social institutions took into their own care individuals who they believed had the potential to become "valuable" citizens. The "hopeless" cases were increasingly shunted off to religious institutions. This two-track system would ultimately prevent religious institutions from working with individuals the state deemed to be potentially "valuable" citizens. As a consequence, most of the expense and care of the "least valuable" was borne by the churches. In other words, the largest percentage of people who would fall under the "unworthy" category fell into the custody of religious institutions. But while health officials believed they could count on Protestants, they anticipated difficulties with Catholics.

Further complicating the situation was the fact that the major diagnostic responsibility rested not on the male "experts" but on lower-ranking women. Behind the facade of the "experts'" confident prose, they knew how fluid and vague their "scientific" categories were. Since health officials and institution directors did not see clients on a regular basis, the responsibility for reporting rested with the teachers and nurses who cared for society's "misfits." They alone could determine, for example, whether environment or inheritance caused depression. Only they could judge to what extent epilepsy impaired a patient's functioning. In the complete absence of scientific knowledge about chromosomes, DNA, or genes, subjective observation became all-important. And diagnosis for the putatively most advanced scientific laws fell to the least educated caretakers of Germans in schools, institutions, hospitals, and community centers.

Catholic Reactions

Whenever important issues arose in Germany that might affect religious life, the German bishops met in the town of Fulda. On learning of eugenic laws, the bishops conferred. The prelates faced a dilemma. Whatever their reservations about eugenics, they found themselves in agreement with many aspects of Nazi social policy. Like Nazis, Catholics described the family as the "germ cell" of the social order. They praised new National Socialist family protection programs because they believed such initiatives offered financial support without government intervention.[15] Equally important, Catholic prelates welcomed the assault against abortion, venereal disease, pornography, and godless Bolshevism. Perhaps most important, Catholic leaders had for decades worked for an official agreement between their nation and the Pope. The Concordat (signed in July 1933) fulfilled that dream and lifted the stigma of second-class citizenship from Catholic Germans. Church leaders worried that if they vigorously opposed so crucial a program as racial purification, the state would retaliate by annulling the Concordat.

The Fulda Conference hoped that negotiations would allow for exceptions. Initial discussions produced no resolution. Lengthy disputes with representatives from the Ministry of the Interior failed to produce accord. On 3 November 1933 one Catholic representative noted, "No progress. The total state insists on its rights and on the purifying, strengthening effect of the law on the race [Volk]."[16] In January 1934, when the sterilization measures went into effect, Catholic priests throughout Germany reminded their congregations of Casti connubii: "It is not permitted to request sterilization for oneself or to submit others to sterilization. That is Catholic teaching."[17] Although priests did not warn their congregations about specific consequences or threaten damnation, Nazi officials found even these statements too strong. Within a week Frick threatened reprisals if such statements did not stop, but also added conciliatory hope that "friendly" negotiations would obviate further friction. At the same time, Nazi ridicule of Catholic scruples did not augur well for compromise. Nazi propaganda, for example, charged the Church with hypocrisy because popes had for centuries approved of the castration of choirboys. Recriminations continued. In April Vice Chancellor von Papen (a Catholic), having failed to change opinion at high levels, assured Cardinal Adolf Bertram, "In my opinion, a moderate judgment already prevails."[18] On 27 June 1934 (virtually on the eve of the SA purge) Hitler and Interior Minister Frick discussed eugenics legislation, as did Bishop Berning. No compromise appeared—except on one issue. Even though the obligation to report "defective" people applied to all Catholic health professionals, a Catholic physician (provided he or she did not serve on a public commission) could be released from the obligation to sign a sterilization order or to perform a eugenics-related operation.

Were Catholics charged to obey or to circumvent the law? Negotiations won a further concession of sorts. Individuals selected for sterilization could be exempted on the condition that they remained forever in the custody of privately funded single-sex institutions. The cost of such care rendered this exception meaningless to most people.

The acrimony did not abate. The Fulda bishops, in deciding not to oppose the laws head-on, placed their hopes on winning exemptions, not repeal. But their strategy increased the confusion among the faithful. Some priests openly supported the motivation behind eugenic law, and criticized only its application; if only sterilization were voluntary, they argued, Catholics could support it without reservation. "The PURPOSE of the law against genetically defective offspring is, in itself, praiseworthy from a moral theological standpoint and therefore to be supported."[19]

The implications of this formula of asking for exceptions while paying lip service to the goal have been analyzed here within the broader context of church-state relations. From the perspective of eugenics the logic held as well. "If we fundamentally refuse, we will run the risk that the Nazis will accuse us of not being staunch Nazis. We might not receive any more clients," noted one agency director."[20] Elisabeth Zillken, national chair of the Board for Catholic Charity for Women, Girls, and Children, realistically predicted that National Socialist Welfare (NSV) workers would assign only cases they deemed hopeless to Catholic welfare institutions if Catholics did not cooperate.[21] While the religious associations expressed a commitment to their traditional concern with helping the neediest (as opposed to the racially "fit" claimed by the NSV), such a division would have placed a large burden on Caritas and Innere Mission resources and personnel, while depriving these organizations of potentially useful members.

From other institutions came theological and moral questions. The Sisters of Mercy begged for guidance from ecclesiastical superiors. "Our sisters hope through prayer, sacrifice, and penance to be guided by the Holy Spirit and the grace of God's leadership in these times when decisions are so difficult."[22] When no assurance arrived, they wrote directly to the interior minister and received exemption from cooperating with the operation. But what constituted "cooperation" and how did one define the "operation?" This only pushed their questions back:

> Our concern now is to give to the sisters who come to me with questions practical guidance that agrees with the official position on these matters, and yet at the same time avoids possible disturbances in hospital administration that would endanger the positions of the nurses who are also nuns.[23]

It was all very well to exempt physicians, but actually that eliminated only a small part of the team that cooperated in any medical treatment. Nurses and nuns prepared the patient, cooked the food, filled out the initial forms, healed the wounds, sterilized the instruments. Where, they asked, does one draw the line?

Confronting this problem, Archbishop Gröber, advised by theologians, hit on a compromise that shifted the decision away from the clergy and onto the inividuals involved. He distinguished between "formal" and "material" cooperation, and applied it to the difference between filling out the initial papers *(Anzeige)* and signing the final contract recommending sterilization *(Antrag)*. Gröber assured the nuns

> that the obligation for directors of hospitals and institutions to file reports on their inmates as laid out by administrative directives of 5 December 1933 for the [sterilization] law . . . in no way contradicts Catholic doctrine. This obligation can be met by the devout Catholic without conflicts of conscience. The bishop requests that Catholic nuns in public institutions not be required to carry out the duty of carrying out the [sterilization] law of 14 July 1933. . . . In various instances the bishop agreed to the speedy transfer of overburdened priests.[24]

The *Anzeigepflicht*, said Gröber, does not constitute cooperation, but "issuing orders for sterilization is not permitted for Catholics." Of course, only physicians could actually issue the order for sterilization, and negotiations had already freed them from the obligation to order operations that contradicted their faith. The director of Catholic charities, Kreutz, explained his rationale for avoiding any confrontation with the state (which he believed the Church would inevitably lose): "In my opinion we must achieve a modus vivendi that on the one hand makes it clear that only the secular power can force obedience but on the other that unnecessary application of physical force must be avoided."[25]

Some theologians even asserted that filling out an *Antrag* might be justified in preserving the common or individual welfare:

> Considerations of common welfare are, for example, avoidance of significantly worse evil, possible amelioriation of the objective loss

> of rights suffered by all those who are affected by the law, preven-
> tion of Catholics' exclusion from public offices and positions,
> etc., etc. Individual considerations include: loss of job, loss of
> means of support for self and family, considerable damage to
> property, elimination of personal freedom, endangerment of indi-
> vidual physical integrity due to anyone's arbitrary actions.[26]

Theologians apparently found it easy to advise Catholic workers charged with
protecting their clients to submit them to sterilization in the interest of the
greater Catholic community.

The subtle theological distinction between "material" and "formal"
cooperation may have salved prelates' consciences, but it did nothing to quiet
confusion among the people (usually women) who confronted the law in their
work. Because Catholic physicians were exempted and Catholic prelates did not
face the implications of eugenic laws in their daily lives, male Catholics involved
with the eugenics issue made their peace with the Nazi state. But women
typically staffed the lower echelons of Catholic service organizations. They won
no exemptions. Nor did they receive clear guidance from their religious superiors. Thousands of letters from concerned Catholics (mostly women) to secular
and religious authorities present an astonishing picture of candid spiritual an-
guish as well as cunning delaying tactics. The letter-writers appreciated how
fluid and ambiguous the eugenic diagnostic categories were. Reading these
letters I could not judge when the writers deliberately obfuscated administrative
directives in order to impede their enforcement and when they actually did have
serious questions about the fine points of diagnostic procedures.

How, many asked, is one to gauge the impact of a "damaged" environment on a child's performance at school? How can one measure an infant's
intelligence? Another line of inquiry highlighted an ecclesiastical double standard as it applied to the stages between identification of a client through
postoperative care. Which could be considered "formal" and which "material"?
What about, for example, accompanying a client to the hospital? Elisabeth
Zillken asked her superior about the case of a nun or social worker going with a
child to the sterilization operation: did that constitute delivery of a victim to a
sinful operation, or pastoral care *(Seelsorge)* for a helpless and handicapped
individual? Supervisors needed "clear-cut directives."[27] They received equivocations.

The director of a course for health administrators in Dortmund observed
that participants reported "great confusion" at their institutions, but that most
favored outright opposition to an immoral law:

> The nuns here face difficult conflicts of conscience when they
> receive orders to deliver the girls to forced sterilization. On the one
> hand, such a girl has been entrusted to the sisters for protection.

> The sisters see the whole point of their work in their responsibility
> for individual girls. But on the other hand, judicially they have no
> custody over the girls. If the Home resists then eventually the
> authorities will proceed with force and fetch the girls with the help
> of the *Überfallkkommando* [the roundup squad]. If the Home does
> not resist, then people will assume that we have given our ap-
> proval. The questions become worse if the girl herself objects. [28]

While most institutions floundered in doubt, a few directors spoke out
clearly. Luise, Countess von Roeder und Diersburg, trustee and director of a
school in Mannheim, wrote boldly on 30 May 1936: "If we resist fundamentally
we do not fear being put at a disadvantage. In any case we will maintain our
refusal."[29] Confident of her public relations skills, she concluded that they
would neither encourage nor allow a sister to accompany patients to the hospital.

But other institutions drew the opposite conclusion: that if they did not
accompany victims to the operation, the Nazi "brown nurses" surely would.
This would produce even more dismay among their clients. Maria Matheis of
Karlsruhe said, "We have always assumed that a sister would, like a mother,
stand at the side of the girls as they tread the difficult path. The girls are
grateful."[30]

The passage of time exacerbated the confusion and dampened morale.
The spirit of opposition was undercut as theologians rationalized where they
might have stood firm. An anonymous circular letter to the Fulda bishops
communicated widespread alarm. Catholics, the author said, wanted strong
guidance; instead they had received the same sort of equivocal statements as the
Church gave out on the issue of divorced persons' right to remarry. In a seven-
page letter the author described the case of a physician on a local health board
who had resigned his post despite assurance from his confessor that such a step
was not necessary. The physician won his neighbors' respect; the priest only
scorn. People want, the letter-writer said, "authoritative instructions" not "subtle
distinctions."[31] In the summer of 1935 Cardinal Adolf Bertram himself admitted
that "the strong publicity for eugenics has unleashed the greatest confusion in
Catholic circles."[32]

All Catholics shared a desire for clarity. But the elegant theological
arguments that satisfied the prelates did not bring certainty to the members of
their flock who personally faced the options of collaboration or noncooperation.
Where the Catholic community might have stood firm, confusion at the top
brought fissure. The internal debate within the Church about how to react to
eugenics laws provides yet another case study of institutional confusion in the
face of a concerted National Socialist policy. In addition, it shows a division that
split theologians and Catholic personnel in institutions affected by eugenics
programs.

Protestant Responses

The Nazi regime in early 1933 made it plain that it would rely heavily on Protestant eugenicists and welfare institutions. Whereas Catholics (like Hermann Muckermann) lost their research and teaching positions, Protestants (like Hans Harmsen) flourished.[33] Centuries of close cooperation between the Lutheran Church and the Prussian state gave Protestants an assurance that Catholics did not feel. In addition, as James Zabel has noted, Protestant support for nationalism and political reaction eased the transition to the Third Reich.[34] Under the leadership of Reich Bishop Müller (who, it was said, wore his swastika on his heart and his cross on his breast), the majority church stood behind its Nazi state on social as well as political issues. Even after dissenters had criticized outright cooperation, Nazi administrators entrusted this important task to Protestant clergy. Interior Minister Wilhelm Frick, for example, encouraged the Protestant Committee on Sexual Ethics to continue its cooperation with the state.[35] Protestant ministers, after all, visited inmates of Ravensbrück concentration camp in an effort to improve morale. Still, within the pattern of general cooperation, motivations ranged from cynical calculation to fervent belief in eugenic principles. Some leaders (male and female) anticipated that early collaboration would yield rewards in the form of favors or autonomy.

Other Protestant supporters of eugenics defended the new laws but firmly insisted on their specifically Protestant (not Nazi) rationales and goals. These individuals saw the racial purification laws as "signs of deep necessity," not progressive and desirable in themselves.[36] They said, in effect: Obey Nazi law for Protestant reasons. When, in 1934, the Confessing Church broke away from the collaborationist German Evangelical Church, its leaders did not question eugenics legislation.

Protestants charged with implementing sterilization laws did not have to reconcile religous faith and patriotic fervor because they had lobbied for such laws for years.[37] Only their rationales differed. A Protestant social worker's report from March 1935 highlights the contrast between progressive health workers in the Inner Mission and Catholics in similar occupations:

> Our *Land* and *Volk* stand at a turning-point of immeasurable meaning. Our *Vaterland* needs not only eugenically superior people, but morally better people. . . . As long as sin exists in the world, we will need the blessings [*Segnungen*] of science to combat it.[38]

Protestants seldom mentioned the secular-scientific Nazi doctrines that praised the superior race. Instead, they spoke of ameliorating suffering in the world and bolstering their faltering attempts to stave off social degeneration. They blurred the division between Weimar and Nazi governments, even as they overlooked the political component of their own sterilization programs. God's will, rather than the Führer's wish, inspired their rationalizations. The author of the 1935 report sympathized not with the handicapped clients but with social workers who faced the daily "agony of watching the suffering and misery in hospitals, asylums, and nursing homes," and welcomed sterilization. "As Christians we take the eugenic laws seriously as God's decrees [Ordnungen], which place us under an obligation." The children, therefore, the report implied, ought never to suffer for the sins of the fathers. No offspring. No suffering. With no sense of irony (or pathos), the author noted that

> it is extremely difficult for our poor, simple-minded girls to grasp that despite the propaganda for bearing many children [including support for unmarried motherhood], at the same time sterilization can be desirable for some. A few years ago, when the desire for abortions was widespread, the readiness for sterilization would have probably been more common."[39]

The author described the "great upheaval" when children in an institution realized they were being examined for sterilization and deplored "her" girls' tendency to gossip among themselves about the operation. And, too, she noted that depression and sometimes suicide resulted. Nevertheless, she persevered: "We realize that each person lives in the chain of inherited guilt and fate, and that we work with the victims of social guilt, of our collective guilt. We have to make good that guilt and care for the victims." Guilt, while frequently mentioned in this passage, was deflected away from the perpetrators and onto patients' parents. Rather than speaking of the impact on sterilized people's lives, social workers stressed the importance of preventing "genetically damaged" offspring in the future.

Even as Protestants emphasized that their clients were being "protected, not punished," they admitted that sterilization left patients miserable. In the saddest cases, sterilized individuals had no family left and fell into suicidal depression. Gisela Bock quotes pleas made to the health officials, but overlooks the ruthless Protestant professionals who collaborated.[40]

The case of Rosa typified a whole range of young women. She told the local eugenic health administrators:

> I do not agree to undergo sterilization. I insist that I can bring healthy children into the world and raise them respectably. If I could not, then I don't know what in the world I would do. I will begin a respectable life, so that later when I marry I can be an energetic and just housewife. I await your answer.[41]

None came. Rosa, it seemed, had a strong moral sense, but she possessed a weak intellect. When clients expressed perfectly reasonable objections to sterilization, their arguments supposedly demonstrated their lack of understanding of the issues involved (i.e., the national *Erbgut,* or genetic inheritance); when they requested sterilization, they demonstrated their lack of morality. Protestant health-care workers tended to demonstrate the same lack of empathy with victims as their Nazi counterparts.

How are we to interpret such stubborn adhesion to a belief system, especially among health-care professionals? Part of the answer lies in the tradition from which Protestant social work developed. The Protestant eugenics consensus developed within the Inner Mission among people concerned about social disintegration and moral degeneration. Initially, in the nineteenth century, a few brave Protestants had set out to rescue "endangered" girls from social and economic exploitation by establishing homes for unmarried mothers, employment services, railway station hospitality centers, educational projects, and dormitories. The Depression, however, underscored their failure to eradicate (or deflect) moral decline. Overwhelmed by the task, social workers began to reverse subject and object in their discussions about "endangered" entities. Increasingly, they perceived the vulnerable social order as "endangered" by unrepentant women—who came to be seen as less than fully "worthy" human beings. Reading social workers' reports and minutes from Inner Mission meetings, I was reminded of the Calvinist language of predestination. Protestant eugenicists perceived a world divided between "unregenerates" (characterized by visible signs and spiritual scars) and the "elect." Biological sin placed these unfortunates beyond the reach of social workers' tasks in the urban wilderness.

The rhetoric of Christian and Nazi eugenicists evoked the dread of unseen sources of evil and hidden pollution. Secular eugenicists made war against recessive genes; Protestants fought hidden vice. For both, unseen pollution attacked the *Erbgut* and, like the Jewish conspiracy, fed anxiety about the modern world. This *Angst,* in turn, rationalized the attack by the strong against the weak. The respectability of such eugenic thinking, albeit with Christian underpinnings, ultimately enhanced the acceptability of a more virulent brand of biological thinking—anti-Semitism.

Conclusions

In much of our research, we assume that continuities between earlier belief systems and Nazi policies enhanced compliance with Nazi measures. Where nonpolitical institutions opposed a particular program or ideal, we anticipate more opposition. However, although the sterilization statistics announced between 1933 and 1936 reveal wide regional diversity, no correlation between compliance and religion emerges.[42] Archbishop Gröber in Freiburg read a government report on sterilization with great alarm because he saw that com-

Volkszählen, Identifizieren, Aussondern im Nationalsozialismus (Berlin, 1984).
    7. Adolf Hitler, *Mein Kampf*, ed. John Chamberlain et al. (Boston, 1939), p. 439.
    8. Jacob H. Landman, *Human Sterilization: The History of the Sexual Sterilization Movement* (New York, 1932), pp. 57–60. Cf. Allan Chase, *The Legacy of Malthus: The Social Costs of the New Scientific Racism* (New York, 1977); Kurt Nowak, *"Euthanasie" und Sterilisierung im "dritten Reich": Die Konfrontation der evangelischen und katholischen Kirche mit dem "Gesetz zur Verhütung erbkranken Nachwuchses" und der "Euthanasie"-Aktion* (Göttingen, 1980).
    9. Hermann Muckermann, "Denkschrift über eugenische Vorschläge zur Erhaltung der erbgesunden Familie," Sonderabdruck, *Eugenik* 2, no. 4 (1932). For a more personal account, cf. a lecture by Muckermann to a special meeting of marriage counselors held on 3–6 May 1932. Erzbischöfliches Archiv Freiburg (hereafter abbreviated as EAF), Eheberatung und Vermittlung, 1927–56, Generalia B2/18/108.
    10. For the religious background, cf. Cornelia Usborne, "The Christian Churches and the Regulation of Sexuality in Weimar Germany," in J. Obelkevich, L. Roper, and R. Samuel, eds., *Disciplines of Faith: Studies in Politics and Patriarchy* (London, 1987), p. 111; Gisela Bock, *Zwangssterilisation im Nationalsozialismus* (Opladen, 1986): Ernst Klee, *Was sie taten—Was sie wurden: Ärzte, Juristen und andere Beteiligte am Kranken- oder Judenmord* (Frankfurt a.M., 1986), pp. 28–77. For a detailed history of Nazi eugenics, see the excellent study by Robert N. Proctor, *Racial Hygiene: Medicine under the Nazis* (Cambridge, Mass., 1988), pp. 1–94.
    11. Friedrich Zipfel, *Macht ohne Moral: Eine Dokumentation über Heinrich Himmler und die SS* (Recording, Ariola, 1962). Dr. Hermann Vellguth, *Blut und Rasse: Ausstellung des Deutsches Hygiene-Museums* (Dresden, 1936). Staatsarchiv München (hereafter StAM) Gesundheitsämter 498a. Hitler throughout his life spoke of the "Zauberkraft des gesprochenen Wortes," Domarus, *Hitler: Reden*, vol. 1, Introduction, p. 45.
    12. Arthur Gütt and Herbert Linden, *Blutschutz und Ehegesundheitsgesetz* (Munich, 1937), pp. 12–14.
    13. Hitler, *Mein Kampf.* Hitler commented in the same section, "The sin against the blood and the degradation of the race are the hereditary sins of this world," pp. 338–39.
    14. Cf. two essays in *Neues Volk* 1 January 1934, 2, no. 1, "Verstösst das Gesetz zur Verhütung erbkranken Nachwuchses gegen das Gebot der Nächstenliebe?"; and A. V. Rohden, "'Wer da weiss, Gutes zu tun, und tut's nicht, dem ist's Sünde': Staatsethik und christliche Ethik decken sich in diesem Punkt vollkommen."
    15. The Marriage Loan program offered substantial grants to young

couples planning marriage provided (1) they met eugenic requirements (2) the woman agreed not to work for wages, (3) neither partner was "non-Aryan," and (4) both were of childbearing age. The loans came in the form of coupons for the purchase of household items. For each child born, the total debt was reduced by 25 percent. A new tax on unmarried people financed the scheme. See Michael Phayer, *Protestant and Catholic Women in Nazi Germany* (Detroit, 1990), pp. 100–109.

16. "Bericht über Verhandlungen in Berlin," Bishop of Osnabrück, report of meeting on 21 November 1934. Cardinal Bertram forwarded the report on conversations with Minister-Director D. Buttmann. Cf. also the report from the 7 November 1934 meeting in Berlin, EAF Gröber Nachlass Nb8/46.

17. Friedrich Zipfel, *Kirchenkampf in Deutschland, 1933–1945: Religionsverfolgung und Selbstbehauptung der Kirchen in der nationalsozialistischen Zeit* (Berlin, 1965), doc. no. 10, p. 179. For an excellent study of the theological and political negotiation between the bishops and the Nazi state see Klaus Scholder, *The Churches and the Third Reich*, London, 1987, 2 vols. Scholder, like most historians of church-state strife, overlooks Nachlass Nb8/46.

18. EAF, Grober Nachlass, Nb8/47. Katholische Vereine. Verhandlungen. This file contains a wealth of information about the Concordat.

19. EAF, Generalia B2/48/20, Sterilisation. A twenty-five-page unsigned mimeographed report on the "moral theological implications" of sterilization, n.d. [Spring 1934].

20. Sr. M. Clementina. St. Franziskusheim, Schwarzach/Bühl. 25 May 1934. EAF Generalia, B2/48/19.

21. Kreutz (but not signed or noted) to Bishop Wilhelm Berning of Osnabrück, 26 June 1934. Zillken to Kreutz, 3 June 1935 r-Deutsche. Caritas Verein-Archiv, Freiburg (hereafter DCV-A), R 218 iv.

22. E. R. Schlattern, Ordenssuperiorat der barmherzigen Schwestern vom hl. Vinzenz von Paul to Gröber, Freiburg, 10 January 1934. EAF, Generalia, B2/48/19, Sittlichkeit/Sterilisation.

23. Barmherzige Schwestern, 5 February 1934, to Erz. Ord. Freiburg. EAF Generalia, B2/48/19.

24. Gröber, public lecture, "Aussprache," quoted in a letter from the Erz. Ord., dated 26 January 1934. EAF Generalia, B2/48/19, Sittlichkeit/ Sterilisation.

25. Letter from the president of Caritasverband, Berlin, 26 June 1934. DCV-A, R 567.

26. See n. 19, above.

27. E. Zillken, 7 May 1934. Dortmund, Caritasdirektor (B. Kreutz) in Freiburg. For a stunning example of the impact of nuns on patients about to be sterilized, cf. the excerpt in Ernst Klee, *"Euthanasie" im NS-Staat: Die "Ver-*

nichtung lebensunwerten Lebens" (Frankfurt, 1983), p. 49.

28. G. v. Mann (signature unclear) Caritasverband, Freiburg, 17 July 1933, written to Rudolf Geis, Erzbischöfliches Konvikt. EAF Generalia, B2/48/20.

29. Kath. Frauenfürsorge-Verein, Mannheim, letter dated 30 May 1934, signed Luise Frfr. Roeder & Diersburg, Vorsitzende. EAF Generalia, B/2/48/19, Sittlichkeit/Sterilisation.

30. Letter to the archbishop of Freiburg, 26 May 1934. EAF Generalia, B2/48/19, Sittlichkeit/Sterilisation.

31. Breslau, 23 January 1935. "Rundfrage an die hochwürdigsten Herrn Oberhirten," mimeographed letter, unsigned. Ibid.

32. *Abschrift*, accompanying a letter from Bertram to Orsengingo, 13 July 1935. Here Bertram notes that Frick accuses Catholics of creating a climate of opposition *(Hetze)* in defiance of the Concordat. Sadly and presciently, Bertram concluded that if the state always had the last word, then the Concordat had no meaning anyway. EAF Generalia, B2/48/19.

33. Nevertheless, moderate eugenicists like those in the *Arbeitsgemeinschaft*, which initially strongly supported Hitler and included Gütt as a member, broke with the regime. In 1935 Catholics dissented, Harmsen left shortly thereafter, representatives from the government resigned, and the organization (which lost half its membership) added "Christian" to its name. Cf. the correspondence between Kreutz and the organization, 1935–42, DCV-A/241.4.1 Fasz. in A. Sterilisation, and 465.4, .065, and .024.

34. James Zabel, *Nazism and the Pastors* (Missoula, Mont., 1976).

35. Nora Hartwich, "Aktennotiz aus einer Besprechung am 17.4.1936," Archiv des diakonischen Werkes, Berlin (hereafter ADW), CA/GF 1419/9 II.

36. An excellent source on these confidential opinions is the Inner Mission file, "Gefährdetenfürsorge," vol. 1, p. 255. Correspondence between the Central Committee and D. Jeep, H. Harmsen, N. Hartwich, and Marx-Langenberg. This theological opinion predated 1933. For example, cf. Hans Harmsen, "Gegenwartsfragen der Eugenik," Sonderdruck aus "Innere Mission," which was brought to my attention by Friedrich P. Kalhenberg at BA Koblenz. For a post-1933 theological view, cf. Alfred O. Muller, *Ethik: Der evangelische Weg zur Verwirklichung des Guten*, vol. 4 (Berlin, 1937).

37. Ernst Klee, "Vorgeschichte: 'Vom Sozialdarwinismus zum Nationalsozialismus,'" in his *"Euthanasie" im NS-Staat*. For the continuity with post-1945 West German values, cf. his *Was sie taten—Was sie wurden*.

38. "Durchführung des Gesetzes zur Verhütung erbkranken Nachwuchses. Schulungslehrgänge. 1934–1935." ADW, CA/GF 2000/16.

39. Ms., "Die fürsorgerische Betreuung Sterilisierter und zu Sterilisierender," 26 March 1935, ADW, CA/GF 2000/16. Klee, *"Euthanasie,"*

brilliantly explores the Protestant response—even among supporters of the Confessing Church.

40. Bock, *Zwangssterilisation*, pp. 278–89. Klee discusses Protestant callousness and the limits of charity, *"Euthanasie,"* pp. 34–35.

41. "Die fürsorgerische Betreuung Sterilisierter und zu Sterilisierender."

42. Bock, *Zwangssterilisation*, pp. 424–27.

43. Report, "Die Auswirkung des Sterilisationsgesetzes in Baden," released by the State Health Ministry (21 June 1934). Still, Gröber threatened to transfer priests who undermined eugenics programs, proclaimed that sterilized people could not marry, not even each other, and (until rebuked) said Catholics need not worry about their support for sterilization, as long as they did not do the operation itself. In Baden, according to the 1934 report, of 3,025 cases (*Anträge*) 997 people were sterilized, and 940 were pending because legal problems had not been ironed out. Thirty-two of these cases were rejected. "Altogether in Baden (the public will be interested to know) 572 people have been sterilized—289 male and 283 female." The national statistics for 1934 were 84,526 sterilization orders and 31,002 already sterilized. Bock, *Zwangssterilisation*, pp. 230–31.

44. Circa 1935. EAF Generalia B-2 48/18 Blatt Nr. 1844.

45. Günter Lewy, *The Catholic Church and Nazi Germany* (London, 1966).

46. Nowak, *"Euthanasie" und Sterilisierung im Dritten Reich.*

4

Reflections on the Position of Hitler and Göring in the Third Reich

HANS MOMMSEN

Since the 1960s, research on contemporary history has agreed that the National Socialist ruling system was particularlly characterized by internal conflicts, a mutually contradictory political and economic strategy, and pronounced antagonisms between the individual holders of power. Opinions diverge, however, on the question to what extent, as a high civil servant of the Reich Chancellery put it in 1937, this "provisionally well-ordered chaos" was held together, and why, at the same time, it was able to release such unheard-of destructive energies, which in World War II led to the devastation of wide expanses of land and to the death of more than 40 million people. Traditional research has always referred to the central role of Adolf Hitler, who held the dissolving fabric of the National Socialist system together by the consciously applied principle of *divide et impera*. In addition, it asserted that National Socialist foreign and domestic policy was informed by step-by-step planning toward a preconceived goal, whose essential outlines were assumed to have been finalized already in Hitler's *Mein Kampf* and in his *Second Book,* and which, with tactical variations in detail, were effectively realized in the end.

This interpretation, represented in particular by Eberhard Jäckel in his book *Hitlers Weltanschauung,*[1] continues, in a way, the understanding of the "Third Reich" as a closed monocratic system, an understanding that dominated the immediate postwar period, even though it already could not be sustained in the Nuremberg trial of the major war criminals. The theory of conspiracy, on which the American prosecutors had based the proceedings, presumed, as the French judge Donnedieu de Vabres noted at the time, an inner coherence of the system that did not exist. Reasons of social psychology explain the emphasis on the central role of Adolf Hitler, which dominates to this day, and with whom, as Karl Dietrich Bracher put it, the National Socialist system stood or fell.[2] For, even before the seizure of power, the German public had accustomed itself to the idea, nourished by Goebbels's invocation of the Führer myth, that it was not Hitler himself (who was assumed to be of good will) but rather his dangerous advisers who were responsible for bringing the criminal and violent "dark side" of the regime to the fore, instead of the euphoric myth of the "national revival." After the collapse, this attitude reversed itself. Hitler now appeared as the root of all evil. Because—in contrast to the party, the SS, and the widely resented "bosses"—he had previously monopolized the resources of national identification for himself, he was now, understandably, seen as a traitor and as the destroyer of his own nation. The contemptuous comments of his so-called "Political Testament," in which he described the downfall of the German people as inevitable because of its lack of racial homogeneity, only strengthened this impression.

The one-dimensional interpretation of the history of the Third Reich that derived from this vision was reinforced by the theory of the "totalitarian dictatorship," which had originally evolved from the example of Stalinist liquidation campaigns. It asserted the virtual equation of National Socialism with Communism, and proceeded from the presumption of a more or less coherent formation of political intent within the regime. Additional support for the Hitler-centric viewpoint was derived from an unusual situation regarding primary sources. Aside from the host of contemporary memoirs, most of them written by enemies of the regime in the immediate postwar years, research relied primarily on the large number of Nuremberg documents and related materials. These had, however, been assembled from a judicial point of view, and detached from their context in the process. Comprehensive sets of documents were, for the time being, not accessible. Only in the 1960s, as they were returned to the West German Federal Archives, was it possible to use comprehensive sets of sources, insofar as they had survived the war. This meant that historical research relied extensively on a limited number of "key documents," even though these were frequently transmitted in isolation and the context of their creation could be investigated in only a limited way. This made it easier to interpret the foreign and domestic policy of the Third Reich against the background of certain ideological premises, and to impose an essentially deductive system on it, one that appeared to be consistent with the decisive processes and to provide a plausible picture of an otherwise confusing and contradictory wealth of events. At times the most fundamental rules of primary source analysis were violated, as in the case of the causes of the Reichstag fire. Since the relevant documents were usually missing, events were connected by the hypothetical inference that in some way the articulated will of the dictator underlay them, as the example of the implementation of the systematic murder of the Jews clearly shows.

Since the beginning of the 1960s, a growing number of authors have qualified the Hitler-centric interpretation of National Socialism. Based on the pioneering work of Karl Dietrich Bracher and his coauthors Wolfgang Sauer and Gerhard Schulz, all of whom still largely relied on separate documents drawn from the now accessible records, these authors proceeded to trace in detail the process by which intentions were formed and decisions made.[3] The ruling system, which previously appeared to be monolithic, now dissolved into a host of subsystems that were poorly, or not at all, coordinated. Hitler now appeared to be removed from the sphere of quotidian events, implementing his obsolete priorities only reluctantly, if at all, and, as a rule, too late. This basic pattern indicated that his actions were always guided by the priority of preserving his prestige and standing in the eyes of the public, as well as retaining his role as *arbiter supremus*, if not in reality then at least *pro forma*. Once again the question was posed of the extent to which Hitler must be considered the engine and initiator of the radicalization of domestic politics and the escalation of foreign policy aggression. Most scholarly studies simply assumed this.

The notion that important decisions are inconceivable without the conscious intervention of the dictator prevents many authors from pursuing in detail the question of how, and under what conditions, Hitler intervened in the process of formulating political decisions, and to what extent he thereby responded to prejudgments or self-created constraints on those decisions. German historians were influenced by a notion of politics ultimately derived from a Hegelian view of the state, from which not even Karl Marx was able to distance himself completely. More recent research, in contrast, has accentuated the disastrous interaction between a Hitler myth still partially dependent on this notion of politics and largely removed from the personal actions of the dictator and the initiatives of certain satraps of the regime, each pursuing his own particular interests. Working in part within a context of action indeed projected by Hitler, and in part continuing late imperialistic precepts, these satraps laid the foundations on which Hitler's visionary desire could find a means for at least partial realization, despite the fact that these wishes were, from inner necessity, condemned to utter failure and were, indeed, bound to produce precisely the opposite of the intended result.

The "orders of the Führer" (*Führerbefehle*) so common in the later phase of the regime were in fact very rarely formulated or initiated by the dictator himself. More frequently, they were demanded of him under exceptional circumstances, although in most cases they were backed up by an alleged or actual manifestation of Hitler's will. Increasingly, research interests have thus focused on the foreground of central government resolutions that were then ratified by Hitler, and that he passed off, to himself and others, as his own "unalterable decisions."

In light of Hitler's indecision, which was well known in the leading circles of the regime, and of his penchant for excess, political responsibility and initiative to a considerable degree rested with the holders of high political and military leadership positions. Only the interaction among these subsystems, which were by no means committed to common goals, and the dictator on whom they depended for political and psychological integration can adequately explain the political processes of the Third Reich. The analogy also holds true of Hitler's role as head of the party in the movement phase.

The so-called "intentionalist" interpretation of National Socialism as proceeding from Hitler's political program has been progressively weakened by numerous studies over the past fifteen years. Alfred Kube's research on Hermann Göring's political role in the Third Reich, published by the Institut für Zeitgeschichte under the revealing title *"Pour le mérite und Hakenkreuz,"* has profoundly undermined this interpretation, which has thus far dominated text-books.[4] Contrary to the prevalent opinion that Hermann Göring, the "second man" of the Third Reich, was unconditionally subservient to Hitler, Alfred Kube's study reveals that Göring not only pursued an independent policy at the beginning of the Third Reich, but continued to do so until his virtual removal from power after the summer of 1938. This policy evidently conflicted with Hitler's weltanschauung, and in many ways agreed with the train of thought of the conservative elites, a large number of whom were later to be found in the movement of 20 July 1944. The relative independence of high functionaries of the Third Reich has already been established for Joachim von Ribbentrop by Wolfgang Michalka and for Baron von Neurath by John L. Heinemann; a systematic study of Wilhelm Frick, for many years Reich minister of the interior, is expected in the near future. Unlike Ribbentrop, Neurath, and Frick, Hermann Göring must be included in the inner core of the regime. To the public he was Hitler's deputy. Therefore, an analysis of the policies he pursued provides an important indicator for a reexamination of the Hitler-centric paradigm.

During the phase of the seizure of power, Göring was indispensable to Hitler. At the end of 1932 he initiated contacts with Papen and Hindenburg, which were indispensable to a Nazi movement in the midst of a deep crisis. Similarly, he played a leading role in the formation of the "cabinet of national concentration." By applying heavy pressure on a hesitant Hitler, Göring forced the substitution of the Prussian president both for the Reich commissionership, occupied in Prussia by Papen, and for Hitler's personal powers under the Reich governor law *(Reichsstatthaltergesetz)*. The future marshal of the Reich con-sciously used his joint powers as Prussian minister president and Hitler's deputy to increase his personal power base, as well as to stabilize the authority of the state. Göring's early seizure of power in Prussia took place in part at the expense of the influence of high party functionaries. Highly placed advisors in Göring's entourage openly suggested that, with the passage of the Enabling Act, the NSDAP had become superfluous and must be reduced to an order charged with the selection of leaders, a view agreeable to Göring, whose relation to the party had been tense ever since the march on the Feldherrnhalle of November 1923.

However, Göring was not able permanently to secure his newly acquired position of power in Prussia, since he failed to ward off the *Verreichlichung* of Prussia, i.e., the fusion of most Reich and Prussian ministries, in view of Hitler's promise to the Reich minister of the interior, Wilhelm Frick, to do so. Thus, Göring's attempt to subject important public functionaries to his influence through new appointments to the Prussian council of state also failed. Moreover, his reliance on Himmler and Heydrich in securing his seizure of the Prussian police proved to be a boomerang. Instead of acceding to Göring's demand for a Reich police office *(Reichspolizeiamt)* and a Reich information center *(Reichsnachrichtenzentrale)* under his control, Hitler sided with Göring's rival Himmler and approved the establishment of an independent Gestapo apparatus that was only formally subject to the Reich ministry of the interior. In a countermove, Göring, still Prussian minister president, and now allied to the non-Prussian *Gauleiter* who led an emphatic resurgence of localism, sabotaged Frick's centralizing Reich reform. In 1935 Hitler finally prohibited all public discussion of the subject.

Göring could reconcile himself to this loss of power since he still had the highly qualified civil service apparatus of the Prussian state ministry at his disposal. He was also able to use the Prussian council of ministers, which even Reich ministers resorted to, as an informal platform of government until its prohibition by Hitler in 1939. Göring's staff office, manned with followers personally loyal to him and critically distanced from the party, together with the notorious "research division," remained subject to the Prussian Department of State and not, as used to be thought, to the Reich Aviation Ministry. In the early years of the regime Göring increasingly assumed the role of a "de facto Reich chancellor" (according to Dertinger's information service), since Hitler, increasingly unwilling to regularly attend to the business of governing, also largely abandoned his ceremonial duties (which included the tradition of diplomatic hunting parties).

Göring hoped to become Reich chancellor after the death of Hindenburg, an event generally expected in the near future. Hitler, however, cut through the Gordian knot of differences over the successions by fusing the offices of Reich president and Reich chancellor (he was to separate them again in 1945), a solution apparently suggested by the armed forces and surprising even to his most immediate entourage. In compensation, he appointed Göring as his deputy in all matters concerning Reich policy and, secretly, as his successor in the case of his death (a fact unknown until now). Göring's undiminished self-confidence was thus perforce relegated to the armaments sector, where as Reich minister for aviation he proceeded to fashion the air force, placed under his command at the same time, into a significant military factor; he was also behind the premature official acknowledgment of its existence. This earned him the ill will of the leadership of the *Wehrmacht*, who were attempting to give decisive priority to the equipping of new units that had been established even before 1935, when the introduction of the draft was announced. At the same time, Göring pursued an active foreign policy that was inadequately coordinated with either Neurath or Hitler. He promoted especially the economic and political penetration of southeastern Europe with the aim of securing, through bilateral agreements, the supply of raw materials essential to the Reich.

The insufficient provision of the Reich with crude oil and the scarcity of raw materials indispensable for the production of planes induced Göring to take over the commissionership for fuel, and later the Four-Year Plan. Hjalmar Schacht, Reich minister of economics, erroneously believed that he could control Göring, whom he welcomed as an ally against the rival NSDAP and the *Wehrmacht* office of armaments *(Wehrmachtsrüstungsamt)*. Schacht seriously underestimated Göring's competence in economic affairs, which he gained by enlisting the knowledge of advisers both competent in economic affairs and loyal to himself. The widely held belief to the contrary notwithstanding, there was no fundamental conflict between Schacht and Göring on the subject of the economic autarky of the Reich. Göring was indeed conscious of the long-term dependence of Germany on foreign trade. He disagreed with Schacht on the extent of the production of substitute materials, and underestimated the long-term impact on finance and foreign exchange policy of continuing the current rate of rearmament. However, his motivation in pursuing this policy was identical to Schacht's: to save foreign currency for the importation of indispensable raw materials.

Despite Hitler's undiminished sympathy for Schacht, he found himself unable to prevent Göring from arrogating important sectors of economic policy to himself, a policy that Göring pursued with the stalwartness so characteristic of him. Conflicting assessments of the risk to financial policy of increasing the production of armaments, which had in fact led to serious problems of supply toward the end of 1937, finally led to a breach between the two politicians. Contrary to Schacht's expectations, Hitler accepted his demonstratively proffered resignation, although with the characteristic condition that he remain in the cabinet, which he did until 1939. The motivation underlying the proclamation of the "Four-Year Plan for the Economy," a formulation still used at the Nuremberg party congress of September 1936, was entirely in agreement with Schacht's own views. It attempted to make the necessary foreign currency available by curtailing private consumption. Only the exploitation of the newly acquired authorizations by Göring, who now elevated himself to the position of dictator in economic affairs, made the conflict with Schacht irreconcilable.

It is crucially significant that the "Four-Year Plan," which many authors all too easily equate with the Stalinist Five-Year Plans, although Göring was initially only interested in the authority connected to it, was established on Göring's initiative. When Göring asked Hitler for permission to give a programmatic speech at the forthcoming Nuremberg party congress to prepare the population propagandistically for necessary further reductions in consumption, the dictator felt pressured and decided to take on the role himself. Hitler's subseqent elaboration, entitled "Memorandum on the Four-Year Plan" (Denkschrift zum Vierjahresplan), aside from the typical rhetoric of the introductory parts that was colored by his own weltanschauung, can thus be traced back to Göring's suggestions. The question of the authorship of the final draft, however, remains unresolved.

The announcement of the economic program did not, in fact, constitute a fundamental change of course and, despite remarks by Hitler to this effect, was not a step toward immediate preparation for war. The "Four-Year Plan," which Göring subsequently proceeded to implement through the bureaucracy, combined Schacht's "New Plan" with an intensified expansion of the production of substitute raw materials and a concurrent reduction of foreign currency expenditure. It did not signal a switch to a policy of autarky, although Hitler was at times prone to this illusion. The decision represented by the "Four-Year Plan," but never actually realized, to reorient the German economy toward war preparations was thus the result much more of Göring's technocrat mentality than of Hitler's desire for war. It was, however, characteristic of the latter that, in ordering Göring to prepare Germany for war within four years, he responded to an inconvenient conflict of competencies and seized the propagandistic leadership for himself, while showing little concern for the concrete division of power among the leaders in charge of the armaments industry.

In this context it is noteworthy that the conference of commanders of 5 November 1937, recorded in the so-called Hossbach memorandum, cannot be traced to Hitler's initiative. Rather, it was called by the Reich minister of defence to resolve questions of priorities in the armaments industry in light of the production bottlenecks, especially in the supply of steel, that Schacht had predicted. Hitler seems to have initiated the invitation of Neurath, since he intended, as Göring later recalled, to prod Fritsch to greater efforts in the armaments question through this reminder of the tense foreign policy situation. For practical purposes, the conference was directed against the imposition of quotas on the use of raw materials envisaged by Göring, which was finally solved in favor of the navy, and, indirectly, in favor of the army, although Hitler could not bring himself to set clear priorities.

Hitler's address occasioned by this meeting was cited in the main Nuremberg trial of war criminals as crucial evidence that he was already set on a plan for war. Hitler's exposition was based on cursory notes, and was intended as "testamentary heritage in the case of his death," and thus as a long-term plan. It dismayed not only Ludwig Beck, the chief of the general staff, but also Admiral Raeder and Fritsch, since it did not exclude a conflict with Czechoslovakia in the near future, in the case of an internal crisis in France. To be sure, Hitler more or less retracted this implication when Fritsch voiced his intention to postpone his vacation. Aside from the fact that the occasion for Hitler's speech did not come about on his initiative, and that the meeting was delayed once for lack of adequate preparation, it can hardly be construed as conclusive proof for the step-by-step planning of foreign policy imputed to Hitler.

Whereas Hitler deferred the Austrian question until a conflict with France, Göring continued to force the Republic into line through increased economic pressure, and accepted the risk of an open breach with Mussolini, a policy to which Hitler assented only reluctantly. Even the frequently disregarded remark of Hitler that 2 million inhabitants of the Czechoslovak Republic and 1 million Austrians must be forced to emigrate, a policy that for the time being was entirely impossible, shows that the dictator was once again pursuing his propagandistically colored foreign policy vision, and certainly not concrete plans of action. The schedule that he envisaged for a military confrontation agrees neither with the Memorandum on the Four-Year Plan nor with the provisional completion of rearmament planned by the *Wehrmachtsrüstungsamt* for 1940. The dictator was equally ill-informed on the subject of Italo-French relations. Impatience at the state of armament and general speculation on foreign policy, not a developed program of expansion, informed the dictator's train of thought, and he in many ways incorporated arguments of his military advisers into his speech. The first concrete step toward expansion originated with Göring, not with him.

Until the spring of 1938 the future marshal of the Reich generally appears to have been the driving force behind the aggressive foreign policy, while Hitler hesitated. The only exception is the remilitarization of the Rhineland, which was undertaken for reasons of prestige and almost called off by Hitler when he became aware of the risk involved. It is hardly surprising, therefore, that the *Anschluss* of Austria in March 1938 was largely initiated by Göring. At first, he pursued the policy of imposing a union of customs, currency, and military affairs on the neighboring state, thereby returning to Brüning's 1931 plan for a customs union. Only Schuschnigg's failed call for a plebiscite created the pretext for direct intervention, which Göring, quite contrary to Hitler's will, turned into a military occupation. In contrast to Göring, who "went to all lengths," Hitler only felt urged by the jubilation of the population of Linz to proclaim the annexation of the Alpine state. Surprisingly, the Duce reluctantly put up with the German advance, which represented a substantial loss of prestige for Italy, whereas Hitler as late as 5 November 1937 implied that the *Anschluss* could only take place after the death of the Duce, to whom he considered himself bound by a promise.

It is against this background that one must evaluate the Blomberg–Fritsch crisis, in which Göring, contrary to widespread belief, apparently did not take a major part. When it became clear that Blomberg, for whom even Hitler tried to build bridges, was untenable, Göring hoped that he himself had a serious chance to take over the Reich Ministry of Defense. Wilhelm Keitel, the head of the *Wehrmachtsrüstungsamt*, proposed him for this post instead of Fritsch (the most senior officer), apparently with the aim of curbing the controversial special status of the air force. Hitler, however, turned down Göring. With good reason, he rated Göring's military capacities as low, and was also conscious of opposition to Göring in the leadership of the navy and the general staff. However, he sweetened this bitter pill by naming him field marshal of the Reich, a position to which Göring had aspired. As in the case of the Reich presidency, Hitler avoided inconvenient decisions on personnel by taking the position of Reich minister of defense for himself.

Hitler's decision for a military conflict with Czechoslovakia originated not least in his desire for a foreign policy success entirely of his own. The dictator felt insecure on diplomatic terrain and abhorred conference diplomacy, which forced him to yield and thus, in his own view, to lose prestige. As commander in chief of the *Wehrmacht*, the former world war private first class felt in his element. Here the diplomats could not get in his way, and the generals, who tried to do so, were stripped of all influence. The days of Neurath, who pleaded for moderation, were equally numbered. But the step toward war was only possible because the over-eager OKW (*Oberkommando der Wehrmacht*: armed forces high command), against the warnings of the chief of the general staff, who resigned over this issue, changed the extant defensive plans to offensive ones, referring to the conference of November. At the same time Ribbentrop, against his own judgment, encouraged Hitler in the illusion that England would in the end stay out of a continental conflict. Hitler's shift to an aggressive foreign policy, which deliberately calculated the risk of war, did not take place before the spring of 1938.

In November 1937, Hitler had still not counted on taking any step toward expansion by war—barring an unusually favorable conjuncture—until 1943–44, that is, after the provisional completion of the rearmament process expected in 1940. One of the reasons he now abandoned that timetable was the domestic situation. While the overextension of economic resources was apparent everywhere, there was extreme dissatisfaction in party circles. The party felt pushed aside politically and had been forced to cede important functions, the supervision of public "opinion" among them, to the SS. Göring was prominently involved in orienting propaganda toward preparing the German economy and the German population for war. He failed to realize that this strategy, which he essentially conceived as part of a late imperialist revisionism, encouraged a widespread mentality of pressure for success, to which Hitler was by no means immune, especially because the advantage in armaments could only be temporarily sustained. The dictator's chimerical idea that he must make up for the defeat at Munich by a blitzkrieg against rump Czechoslovakia was important in this respect. It is not entirely clear which external occasions conditioned his change of opinion, since in the spring of 1939 France was neither incapacitated in its domestic policy nor embroiled in a Mediterranean war.

On the occasion of the developing Sudeten crisis Göring strove for a diplomatic solution, just like Weizsäcker and the growing opposition. In contrast to Hitler, he was aware from the beginning that Germany was in no way adequately prepared for a war on several fronts. Without stepping forward, he induced the Duce to suggest the conference at Munich, which prevented the military operation against Czechoslovakia that Hitler had ordered for late autumn. The "destruction of rump Czechoslovakia" in March 1939 was emphatically disapproved by Göring, although he did not muster the courage to voice his opinion openly. He reacted to the outbreak of war on 1 September 1939 with pronounced skepticism, and blamed this step that appeared so ominous to him on Joachim von Ribbentrop, since 1938 foreign minister of the Reich.

It was primarily the influence of Ribbentrop that caused Göring's power to wane continually after the summer of 1938. This development can also in part be traced to an unspoken rivalry between Hitler and Göring, whose urge for a negotiated settlement at Munich was instinctively perceived by Hitler. At the same time, Göring also failed in his attempts to reach a settlement with Great Britain, which he pursued, although with increasing resignation, even after the outbreak of the war. But the condition suggested to Hitler by Ribbentrop, that the British alliance should be achieved without any noteworthy German concessions, left him no further room for negotiations.

On questions of domestic policy, Göring was anything but radical. He disapproved of the November pogrom, although he utilized it in a most cynical manner for his Four-Year Plan policies. He was an avowed foe of Goebbels, and inwardly rejected the Führer myth propagated by him, although he formally retained a loyal attitude toward Hitler up to his final bid to take over in April 1945, which was followed by his dismissal and exclusion from the party. On the other side, Hitler was well aware of Göring's popularity. This explains why he publicly appointed him as his successor and head of the Reich defense council *(Reichsverteidigungsrat)*, an institution that was, however, never effectively established.

From the viewpoint of the intentionalists, Hitler had since the beginning of 1938 consciously pushed aside every person in office who opposed an aggressive foreign policy. Göring's loss of power was connected to this insofar as the ambitious Ribbentrop, who had Hitler's confidence, systematically excluded him from foreign policy. The step toward a conscious policy of war did not, however, come about according to any plan. Significant impetus for increases in Hitler's real power, such as the Blomberg–Fritsch crisis, derived from external sources. The multipolarity of foreign policy action (it is noteworthy that Göring seems to have been the first to conceive of an alliance with the Soviet Union, mainly for reasons of armaments policy)—led to a situation of stalemate, which, barring the massive loss of prestige for Hitler inherent in any compromise, inevitably left only the military option. The responsibility of Ribbentrop in this respect can hardly be overestimated.

On the other hand, Göring was decisively involved in the ultimate removal of the brakes on domestic policy. The utter fragmentation of responsibilities was in no small part set in motion by him. The decisive cause of this development, however, is to be located in Hitler's strategy, retained even after the seizure of power, of indecision in the face of diverging interests. In time, of course, a point was reached at which the ability of the entire system to function appeared endangered. Hitler may have instinctively realized that only the step toward war could ward off the imminent internal stagnation of the system, and maintain an integration that had largely been achieved by propaganda. Simultaneously, the progressive dissolution of the institutional framework provided the psychological latitude for action, in which Hitler was not forced to measure his visionary and varied goals against the realities of power politics. In the growing conflicts of interests, each of which threatened mutually to neutralize the others—conflicts that conjured up a crisis of foreign and domestic policy after the Munich agreement, and that also found expression in Göring's treatment as chancellor in diplomatic circles—Hitler, now commander in chief of the armed forces, also held a particular position.

From this perspective one must ask once again what were the driving forces that induced Hitler, against the opinion of most of his advisers, actively to prepare the attack on Poland for the end of August 1939. There are no doubts concerning his will to war, nor that the generals, including the departed Colonel General Beck, considered war as a legitimate means of politics and made the strategic and logistic preparations for it. One must, however, explain more precisely why, until the outbreak of the war, the idea prevailed even in the highest leadership circle of the regime that the "Führer," in the final analysis, was only bluffing; this impression critically weakened the military opposition's willingness to act. The diplomatic and military course of events immediately preceding the war has been described in detail. In the last hour the German-Soviet nonaggression pact reinforced the illusion of an isolated war against Poland. It was, however, decisive that as a result of its internal structure, the regime could not retreat without endangering its very existence. The prevention of war would in any case have discredited Hitler and his close entourage. This may explain the absence of any protests from Göring, protests he should have voiced in accordance with his knowledge on matters of foreign and armaments policy. Instead, he succumbed to a combination of boastfulness, lethargy, dependency on drugs, and hunting fever, and in the following period entangled himself increasingly in the unprecedented crimes of the regime. The external and internal moral corruption of the German leadership, which had rapidly progressed since 1933, made it a willing tool in the hands of Hitler, who sensed the catastrophic consequences of the decision for war in 1939 but did not dare to admit them. After Hjalmar Schacht, no one found the courage to force him to do so. The politics of chance had finally taken the place of Machiavellian power calculations.

Translated by Michael McGuire

Notes

1. Eberhard Jäckel, *Hitler's Weltanschauung: A Blueprint for Power* (Middletown, Conn., 1972).

2. Karl Dietrich Bracher, *Zeitgeschichtliche Betrachtungen zu Faschismus, Totalitarismus, Demokratie* (Munich, 1976), pp. 80ff.

3. Karl Dietrich Bracher, Wolfgang Sauer, and Gerhard Schulz, *Die nationalsozialistische Machtergreifung: Studien zur Errichtung des totalitären Herrschaftssystems in Deutschland, 1933–34* (Cologne/Opladen, 1960).

4. Alfred Kube, *Pour le mérite und Hakenkreuz: Hermann Göring im Dritten Reich* (Munich, 1986).

5

National Socialism and the Theory of the State

JANE CAPLAN

This essay is an attempt to situate the theory of the Nazi state in three contexts: the contemporary theory of the Nazi state; recent historical research into the structure and workings of the Nazi state; and theoretical analyses of the Nazi (or fascist) state, including what might be called the new state theorization literature.[1] By and large, Nazi political theory has not been widely studied, although among the studies that have appeared are works of outstanding interest that deserve a wider readership.[2] But both of the other fields are currently matters of keen debate in their respective circles, fueled, on the one hand, by the latest turns in the perennial argument about the historical status of National Socialism in German history, and, on the other, by the shift, via structuralist theory, from society- to state-based analyses of politics and public policy. They also involve what are by now familiar issues in the relationship between the knowledge generated both by historical and by politico-sociological research in their respective disciplines. The negotiation of this relationship has been a continuous process, and has taken place both within historical sociology and in interdisciplinary debates. A decade ago history seemed to be under permanent siege by sociology and political theory, but the present climate of scholarship and politics has become less congenial to universalizing theory, and many contributors to current debates on the state have insisted on the priority of historical specificity over theoretical generalization. For example, John Hall has issued "a plea for states to be understood in their historical contexts," while Theda Skocpol has criticized the search for a "grand theory of 'the State,'" and calls instead for "solidly grounded and analytically sharp understandings of the causal regularities that underlie the histories of states, social structures, and transnational relations."[3]

Having said this, the relationship of history and theory suggested above may be especially difficult to develop in the case of the Nazi state. The very characteristics of the Nazi polity that call most loudly for explanation—its peculiarity, its connotation of permanent crisis, and its brevity—are also the attributes that render most difficult its incorporation in any general theory of the patterns of state formation or in a typology of state forms. Indeed, some of the earliest theorists of the Nazi polity, such as Franz Neumann and Friedrich Pollock, doubted whether it made sense to call the "Third Reich" a state of any kind.[4] These problems are mitigated somewhat if National Socialism is seen as a variant of a generic ideology and practice, i.e., fascism. Fascist exceptionalism has been a stock-in-trade of both Marxist and liberal theory, and has been integrated, with greater or lesser success, into their general social and political theories; there have also, of course, been many attempts to offer a general typology of modern dictatorship, as in totalitarianism theory or the problematic of democratic crisis.[5] But recently there also seems to have been a de facto turn from general theories of fascism toward a more local debate about National Socialism.[6] This is due partly to the shift away from unifying theory noted above, which also reflects the changing status of Marxism as a political and theoretical method. It is also signaled in the recent fierce arguments among West Germans about the historicization of National Socialism.[7] This process of academic and political reassessment has raised theoretical and philosophical questions about exceptionalism and relativism as historiographical statuses, and about the conditions and consequences of the achievement of critical and comparative distance on the Nazi period. Although the nature of the Nazi state as such has not so far figured prominently in these debates—being overshadowed by more urgent questions about anti-Semitism and genocide, and the reception of National Socialism among Germans after 1933—there is no reason to exclude it in principle, especially because both questions implicate the role of the state as structure and agency. One influential, if contested, analysis of Nazi racial policies has argued that their radicalization is best understood not as the step-by-step implementation of a self-evident ideology, but as the unpredictable product of bureaucratic structures and procedures in the Nazi state itself.[8] Similarly, popular responses to National Socialism can be fully understood only in the context of its political conditions of existence after 1933—and here the state should be grasped not only in terms of its legitimation, or as a means of authority and coercion, but also as a means of representation.[9] This dual character of the state as a means of "power" and of "will" has a particular resonance in the history of National Socialism, as will be discussed below.

Theoretical Issues in the Interpretation of the Nazi State

The most recent resurgence of interest in state theory has not yet left its mark on the study of the National Socialist state, or even on the more typological concept of the fascist state. Reviewing recent literature on the state, I find scattered references to fascism, but no topical discussions.[10] In the older theoretical literature, the dominant note was, of course, the question of the class location and function of the Nazi (or fascist) state, notably as theorized in the concept of state monopoly capitalism.[11] The more recent empirical work discussed below clearly focuses on the Nazi state as agency and institution, but has not on the whole attempted to theorize it beyond its own confines.[12] However, some of the currents that have converged in the new theorization of the state themselves derived from work on the fascist state, and in general the relationship between empirical and theoretical work on fascism, and the revival of state theory, is more complex and intercalated than may at first appear. Structuralist interpretations of National Socialism, which tend to acknowledge a debt to empirical rather than to theoretical work, were in fact predicated on the 1960s revival both of left-wing analyses of fascism and of Marxist political theory, which converged in a new analysis of the fascist state, notably in the work of Poulantzas.[13] This in turn did much to reinvigorate the empirical and theoretical analysis of European fascism, by turning toward political questions the attention that previously had been concentrated on the issue of the social sources and implications of fascism. At the same time, the opening of the German archives permitted a new depth of empirical investigation, which bore fruit in the many monographic studies of the Nazi political system published in the 1960s and 1970s.

It was this conjunction that created the conditions for a potential retreat from the class analysis of fascism to a more specifically political analysis— although it cannot be said that the potential of this movement has been fulfilled. Both Tim Mason's concept of the "primacy of politics" and Nicos Poulantzas's concept of the "relative autonomy" of politics and the state bear more than a coincidental resemblance to the main tenets of the subsequent structuralist position—indeed, it is striking that it was Mason's historical reworking of older Bonapartist concepts that reintroduced this plastic notion into debates on the Nazi political system. "Neo-Marxists" and structuralists alike are critical of the notion that policy is the effect of a relatively straightforward process of transitive causation, whether this flows from a reductionist view of class or from an intentionalist concept of ideology. The turn from this kind of causal reduc- tionism was evident too in the more functionalist Marxist "state derivation" literature, which developed as a highly abstract field of analysis in West Germany in the 1970s.[14] State derivation theorists sought in essence to overcome the isolation of political from economic analysis, in Marxist no less than in bour- geois thought, by exploring how and why the economic and political spheres of the social totality come in fact to be separate categories in capitalism. In other words, instead of accepting this separation as given and reflecting it in their work, state derivation theorists tried to show how the form and function of the state were historically and logically "derived" from the contradictions of capitalist society. State derivationist theory thus problematized the internal *form* of the state, as well as its functional relation to capital as the site of class power or the source of favorable policies.[15] Nevertheless, despite its origins in debates about the crisis of capitalism, and its concern with the key question of why social relations in bourgeois society do appear separately as economic and political relations, state derivationism had little direct influence on the analysis of the fascist state as such, at any rate outside Germany. Rather, it has been the structuralist/autonomist models that have offered the most widely used tools of analysis, for they focus directly and specifically on the internal constitution of and relations among the apparatuses of the state. At the same time, as Skocpol et al. have pointed out, the Poulantzian model suggested a correlation between the autonomy of the state and its sociopolitical effectiveness that may not in fact be capable of empirical demonstration.[16]

On the whole, however, the influence of political theory has, perhaps not surprisingly, been more implicit than explicit in the current debates among (Western) historians about the nature of National Socialist rule.[17] Historians have not on the whole taken up the challenge of changes in theories of the state, whether Marxist, neo-Marxist, or non-Marxist; an unemphatic Weberianism still sponsors most discussions. There has been no direct confluence with current state theory; rather, the intentionalist-structuralist debate has tended to lean on the past twenty-five years of intense empirical research into the political history of National Socialism, its governing institutions, and its administrative processes. Indeed, with all the recent proliferation of empirical and theoretical literature on the workings of the National Socialist state, the basic issues under debate have in fact been remarkably stable over the nearly sixty years since the Nazi seizure of power. They continue to reappear, in different guises, in both the empirical and the theoretical literature.

In essence, the interpretive debates have circulated around two central problematics: on the one hand, the class identity and significance of the National Socialist regime in and for capitalism, as an economic institution and as a social formation; and, on the other, the relationship between Hitler's power and the political mechanisms of policy-making and execution. In different ways, this was true of the earliest and best contributions to the scholarly analysis of National Socialism, such as Ernst Fraenkel's *The Dual State* (1941), Franz Neumann's *Behemoth* (1942), and the essays of some of the other contemporary German theorists like Pollock or Kirchheimer, all of whom emphasized the technical rationality of at least some aspects of bureaucratic rule under National Socialism.[18] Subsequent inquiries in the 1950s into the concept of totalitarianism, notably by Arendt and Friedrich, took up many of the same basic questions, although in a broader historical context,[19] and they remain, as we have seen, central to the most recent discussions of polycracy and relative autonomy, as also to the expanding field of publications on the social history of the "Third Reich." Neumann in particular has had an enduring effect on later work, and the influence of his core propositions about the quadripartite distribution of power among competing elites in Nazi Germany can easily be detected in both structuralist and autonomist theories.

Neumann's influence is especially visible in an important essay on the Nazi state by Michael Geyer, which represents one of the few self-conscious attempts to fuse state theory with the findings of empirical research.[20] Geyer's analysis conjoins the concept of relative autonomy with terms taken from Weber and Frankfurt School theories to theorize the Nazi state as a system not of politics but of domination. According to this argument, politics under National Socialism was not about cooperation or even competition in the distribution of resources, but was a process of negotiation aimed at maintaining a structure of distances between the several producers of domination, whose power rested on their relative independence from one another. The deformation of the political process followed from the collapse of politics into crude domination, and from the simultaneous dissolution under National Socialism of the liberal boundaries between state, economy, and society: a double destruction of the mediations otherwise seen as essential to the polities associated with modern capitalism.

The National Socialist State in Current Historical Scholarship

Historical research into National Socialism is now dominated by a revisionist model that suggests that the Nazi regime was not, in practice, the totalitarian monolith that it once successfully projected as its public image.[21] Much of this research has focused directly on the internal structure and workings of the Nazi regime, investigating such questions as the organization of the institutions of central and local government, the role of the NSDAP in the new state, and the power and political personality of Hitler. This dispersal of attention into micro-studies represents in some ways a retreat from overarching interpretation, at least on the political front. It is now common among historians to regard the "monolith" interpretation of the "Third Reich" as having been superseded by a new image, one that represents it as a fragmented and disorganized parody of the German state. According to this view, Nazi Germany was not an efficient machine of political domination ruled by an omnicompetent Führer, but a system of semi-institutionalized conflict between barely coordinated locuses of rival power. The regime as a whole progressively and parasitically ate away at the inherited ideological and administrative structures on which it rested, proving incapable of generating the conditions for its own stabilization and reproduction, in terms either of institutions or of policy-making procedures; on the other hand, a superficially powerful alternative *ideology* of self-legitimation was generated, if only by repetition.

The Nazi regime thus had a shattering, if temporary, effect not only on the way that Germany was governed, but also on the *ideas* of government and the state as such. If no coherent remodeling process took place, this was not for want of programs for reform. On the contrary, the regime was rife with rival visions of how to realize the Nazis' promise of a political "new order," including, eventually, the problem of how to extract the Nazi Party from the paralysis that institutionalized power seemed to have brought on it. For if the regime as a whole appears as a monstrous concentration of dynamic and unstoppable power, to many of its representatives and contemporaries its political institutions hardly realized their original aspirations for a refounded national state. The zeal of National Socialism was concentrated, catastrophically, on the exercise of domination in the form of terror, genocide, and war; meanwhile, the state apparatus as such was managed in a way that amply bore out Hitler's insistence that the state was not an end in itself but a means to other ends.

One of the most striking paradoxes of the National Socialist political system is thus the tension between, on the one hand, the immense concentration of power it embodied and the ideological unity it espoused and, on the other, the fragmentation of its structure and processes in practice. This tension is mirrored both in the contemporary representations of the regime by its bearers and in the historiographical debate about it. The poles of unity and disorder were far from invisible to participants in the political processes of the Nazi regime itself, who repeatedly noted the gulf between the regime's ideological espousal of unity and its practical inability to develop orderly processes of policy generation and execution. The dualism between concentration and fragmentation as historical characteristics of National Socialist rule is also reflected in the current historiography of the regime. Thus the sequence of historical interpretations is commonly presented as I have just done: as an older image of concentration and unity now displaced by a new image of amorphousness and disorder. Moreover, the deep fracture between the "intentionalist" and "structuralist" interpretations of the Nazi regime, which has dominated debates among historians for the past decade, itself repeats this dualism in form, although not precisely in content. On the one hand, "structuralist" historians such as Hans Mommsen and Martin Broszat have depicted the Nazi state as a grossly decentered polycracy circulating around a "weak dictator." This interpretation argues for an active relationship between the structure and function of the state apparatus, or, in other words, for attention to the way in which the mechanisms and processes of administration contributed to the content of policy as well as to its technical implementation.[22]

Major policy choices are seen not so much as the outcome of ideological intention, far less of reasoned discussion, but as having been generated in and by the processes of government and administration themselves. Rather than representing the fulfillment of an ideological project, policy reflected, often in a distorted or displaced form, a "decisionism" occasioned by momentary power constellations and calculations. In this context, Hitler appears less as the direct author of policy than as a source of legitimacy, whether for the political authority of individual actors or for specific policy options. Against this, Klaus Hildebrand, among others, has argued that despite the polycratic nature of administration at a secondary level, Nazi Germany was essentially a *Führerdiktatur* in which ultimately, if not evenly or universally, it was Hitler's intentions and authority that determined the distribution and uses of power.[23] For intentionalists, policy originated, in the last analysis, in the ideology and will of Hitler and perhaps of other leading Nazis; the power of subordinate agencies was strategically distributed according to Hitler's policy of divide and rule, and they were primarily the executants of political decisions external to their own operations.

Despite their differences, both the structuralist and intentionalist interpretations concur in seeing the Nazi state as relatively amorphous and chaotic, and both, moreover, rest on a similarly close reading of documentary sources. One might even want to note the extent to which these current representations of Nazi Germany as a political system may themselves be seen as an artifact of the research process itself, rather than as contestants for a progressively revealed truth about its essential nature. In this view, one reason for the shift in the prevailing imagery of the Nazi regime from monolith to fragmentation is the relatively recent availability of the massive archival resources on which the construction of polycracy depends. The new density of research has certainly had the effect of revising or deepening older interpretations, and not only about the political structure of the regime. Yet it is hard to believe that there is a single unified and coherent history of National Socialism that cumulative empirical research can voice more and more adequately; far less that there is a simple additive relationship between the density of empirical reconstruction and the theorization of the Nazi state as a political institution. Although documentation is crucial for the legitimation of accounts of specific events or processes, the familiar tension between reconstruction and interpretation resists resolution, at the level of such macro-institutions as the state itself, simply through the attestation of additional primary sources. Nevertheless, as I have argued elsewhere, empirical coherence is a necessary condition of theoretical analysis, even if it is neither sufficient to the theoretical project nor entirely self-legitimating as an end in itself.[24]

The complexities of these relationships between representation and interpretation are well illustrated by the history of the bureaucracy in Nazi Germany, a history that also links these issues to the problem of the conformation of the state itself. I do not propose to rehearse the evidence I have presented in detail elsewhere for the intricacies of the Nazi state, or for the extent to which its structural and functional complexity cannot be grasped simply as the product of a collision between a dynamic party and a rational state.[25] A close analysis of this aspect of the National Socialist political system illustrates the explanatory limitations of its dualist division into the "state" as anterior, rational, structural, and bureaucratic, and the "party" as posterior, irrational, dynamically unstable, and charismatic. Rather, both institutions were implicated in a struggle for the control of the means or resources of power, directed at their own institutional assertion and reproduction, as well as at the deployment of power for external purposes. Fear of deprofessionalization was one issue for the bureaucracy, but this was only part of a broader crisis of politics as a legitimate practice (which predated the Nazi Reich). The critique of bureaucracy that so clearly marked Nazi Party writing was also an auto-critique, and a displaced critique of political practice as such.

National Socialist Political Theory

The institutional conflict over the means of authority and representation was paralleled by the theoretical debate about the nature of the Nazi state after 1933. Nazi ideology was hostile to the concept of the state as well as to its practices, a fact that left political theory under National Socialism largely in the hands of conservative jurists and political scientists, rather than party ideologues as such. But only a few of these, including Carl Schmitt, and perhaps Reinhard Höhn and Ernst Forsthoff, had any claim to be original political or legal theorists.[26] Most of the rest of the academics and practitioners who continued to write on political or constitutional theory after 1933 took on the secondary task of accommodating what they believed to be National Socialist ideology into their lectures and textbooks. In these they attempted to legitimate not only the Nazi regime, but also their own professional right as theorists to speak authoritatively about the new dispensation.

The greatest problems they faced were, first, to distance themselves from the traditions of both positivism and the state as an end in itself; second, to conceptualize the relationship among *Volk*, Führer, NSDAP, and state; and third, to make sense of the fact that the rule of law itself was so shaky in the new Germany. The result was a series of largely formulaic representations, in which the concepts of the *Volk* and Führer took rhetorical and explanatory primacy. Thus, Walter Sommer characterized the new state as neither a "state without a people," nor a "civil service state," nor a "state as end in itself," but "the state of the German people, of the German people embodied in the NSDAP."[27] Otto Koellreutter, a leading law professor and prolific writer on constitutional politics, argued in a lecture to the Kant Society in Halle that "For a *völkisch* system of thought, the state as an independent value falls into the background," and cited the Nazi ideologue Alfred Rosenberg as his authority for this: "We do not want the total state, but the totality of the National Socialist movement in the state; we do not want a corporative state, but a political power structure of corporative construction."[28] For Ernst Huber, another widely published constitutional lawyer, the state was to be seen neither as an end in itself nor as a mere instrument: "precisely by being permeated by the essence and spirit of the people [Volk] the state has obtained a new dignity and authority. . . . [T]his state is the people itself in its political form."[29]

What these and many similar formulas share is the effort to capture the total character of the Nazi polity without falling into the trap of identifying this with the state as such. Before the seizure of power, the party had claimed to represent the totality and universality of the (racial) nation in a period of extreme decomposition; after the seizure of power, it was faced with the challenge of translating this proposition from the realm of ideology into that of politics. This proved virtually impossible, however, for it was based on the false premise of a straightforward correspondence between representational and real unity, one that would also efface conflict. It was one thing to propose Hitler as the representation of unity—a symbolic function that is attached to every head of state—but National Socialism went well beyond this.[30] In a banal form, this confusion was captured by Hans Frank's proposition that Hitler would perform every task if he could, but that since one man could not actually do this in practice, a corps of subsidiaries was necessary;[31] or by the "categorical imperative" he addressed to bureaucrats: "Act in such a way that if the Führer knew of your action, he would approve the action."[32] More sophisticated but no less misleading versions of the premise that this symbol of unity could in fact be made concrete pervaded the political and legal ideology of the Nazi regime, and helped to obstruct the development of any effective theory of the state. Typically, these formulations took the shape of a declaratory sentence in which subject and object—Führer and constitution, justice and law, Volk and state—confront each other barely segregated by a copula. As Huber put it, for example: "The basis of a constitution's authority is the type and idea of the people, and through this unity there is to be sure no difference, and also no division, between law and reality, between norm and existence."[33] Or, to quote Frank again: "The constitutional law of the Third Reich is the legal formulation of the historic intentions of the Führer."[34] As Dietrich Kirschenmann has observed, "The National Socialist concept of law inserts the word Führer wherever the reality of rule threatens to come into contradiction with the basic unit of ideology [Ideologeme]. . . . In short, it bonds deed and theory in the last instance to a Führer removed from reality and at the same de-realized: it makes use of a Führer-formula."[35]

The representation of the as yet unknown unity of the National Socialist system replicated the problem of realizing it in practice. Irresolution and mediocrity marked both, and the problem of what "really" constituted the Nazi state was displaced to an unspecified future.[36] What had been achieved so far was regarded as provisional and subject to later substantiation or revision, yet it was also commonly treated as if it constituted the logical first steps in a deliberate refoundation of the German state. But, as Walter Sommer put it in 1937, it was also "futile to write learned treatises about the nature of the new state, here our pens will scratch in vain," because only Hitler knew what the state would look like ten years from now, and he would not be influenced by what academics had to say.[37] However, what was never realized was the simplistic division of labor between the party cadre as "leadership" and the state apparatus as "administration" (*Führung* and *Verwaltung*). Instead of this dualism, there was a contest over the ground itself. Hess and Bormann maintained their pressure to "Nazify" civil service personnel while Interior Minister Frick's policies tended toward the creation of a strong state on the authoritarian model, in which the *Berufsbeamtentum* would enjoy a clearly legitimated primacy in a well-defined but extensive sphere of competence. To use Michael Geyer's terms, these strategies threatened the structure of distances between the "producers of domination" by asserting the overriding claims of one of these over the others.[38] Moreover, on a more abstract level, Interior Minister Frick's administrative strategy also threatened to expose the fallacy at the heart of the Nazi claim to represent a real unity or conflict-free totality. Not only did the civil service constitute a historically legitimated rival in this field, but Frick's relentless insistence on the achievement of administrative unity, centralization, and concentration was intolerable to Nazi ideologues, and to political leaders like Hitler or Goebbels, precisely because it exposed the fact that unity was open only to partial and symbolic representation, not to total and concrete realization.

It may perhaps be stated as a general rule that the identification of the bureaucracy's interests with "the general interest" operates most effectively in a context of silent affirmation; it falls apart when the bureaucracy has to enter an open and vocal competition for this role. (This may be seen as a local version of the generic problem identified by Claus Offe of legitimation by concealment.) At any event, in the Nazi polity, totality had to be either everywhere or only in Hitler, but it could not be shared, far less fixed, in the intermediate structures required by a hierarchical administration. This was the circle that Hans Frank kept trying to square in his copious writings on administration; and institutionally it was reflected in the persistent strife that arose from the structure and staffing of the administrative *Mittelinstanz*.[39] Similarly, individuals rather than offices were repeatedly charged with the performance of new tasks, culminating in the appointment of Goebbels as plenipotentiary for total war. Yet, ultimately, Frick's claims on behalf of the civil service also rested on the assertion that it, too, embodied a representational totality. To be sure, the civil service's claim was more firmly rooted in German political history, and, partly for this reason, it also relied on an elaborate code of substantive and procedural rules as well as a real division of labor. But the ultimate clash was not between the administrative rationality of the state and the dynamic parasitism of the party, but between two political concepts that were equally dynamic and irrational in terms of the realities of political representation and mediation in the modern state. If National Socialism sought to achieve a system of government without administration, the civil service ideal was an administration that effaced government as a political process.

The central problem here was the reproduction of the state as a political and administrative apparatus, in a form capable of representing "the nation" as this was construed in a given historical and ideological context. Historically, the Nazi state can be seen as a dual process of centralization and concentration, marked by both deficiency and excess. On the one hand, the Nazi ideological project was to eliminate what Charles Maier has called the historic insufficiency of the German state as a centralized polity—yet to accomplish this *not* by enhancing the power of the inherited institutions of the state, but by substituting the more amorphous proto-institutional claims of the party to a monopoly of social as well as political organization. On the other hand, the civil service— itself a powerful social institution—aimed to retain and reauthorize the excessive power of bureaucratized over political and social structures. In the short period of the existence of the "Third Reich," the results of this twin struggle over the control of the state apparatuses and over their relationship to a recomposed civil society were massively dislocating. The Nazis may have wanted "pure" politics in theory, but what they got in practice was a series of adulterated and corrupted bureaucracies.

As I have suggested, analyses of Nazi Germany that otherwise differ markedly in their approaches and emphases have tended to concur in seeing the Nazi state as a relatively unintegrated power structure that also exerted a virtually unprecedented degree of terroristic violence inside Germany and beyond its borders. For Nazi Germany presented a situation in which competition for the resources of state power (the means of reproduction, coercion, et cetera) was lodged *within* an expanded and amorphous state apparatus itself, while simultaneousy the state was engaged in a massive double effort of political self-assertion: the reconstruction of society by terroristic means, and the extension, rather than simply defense, of its territorial sovereignty by military and imperialist means. At the same time, the predominant ideology rejected the concept of a distinction between state and civil society. Using Michael Mann's terminology, we could say that the National Socialist period was one of violent upheaval in both the infrastructural and the despotic deployment of state power, in a polity whose territorial and political boundaries were both in flux.[40] In this sense, the Nazi state was one in which the structural relationship between the means of despotic and of infrastructural power was dissolved: these powers became institutionally separated and thrown into conflict, while at the same time, of course, the state was detached both from democratic controls and from a legitimation that could be revoked. Yet the state stood neither "above" society nor alongside it as a site of internal compromise and external coercion; rather, civil society experienced in violent form the consequences of this endemically fragmented political system.

Notes

1. This paper draws on material from the introduction and chapter 9 of Jane Caplan, *Government Without Administration: State and Civil Service in Weimar and Nazi Germany* (Oxford, 1988), which is reprinted with the permission of the publisher. I am also grateful to participants in the conference "Re-Evaluating the 'Third Reich', " and the colloquium on "State, Revolution, and Social Development" at the UCLA Center for Social Theory and Comparative History, especially Perry Anderson, Saul Friedländer, Ian Kershaw, and Charles Maier.

2. See especially Michael Stolleis, *Gemeinwohlformeln im national-sozialistischen Recht* (Berlin, 1974), and Dietrich Kirschenmann, *"Gesetz" im Staatsrecht und in der Staatsrechtslehre des Nationalsozialismus* (Berlin, 1970); also Bernd Rüthers, *Die unbegrenzte Auslegung: Zum Wandel der Privatrechtsordnung im Nationalsozialismus* (Frankfurt, 1973), and Jürgen Meinck, *Weimarer Staatslehre und Nationalsozialismus: Eine Studie zum Problem der Kontinuität im staatsrechtlichen Denken in Deutschland 1928 bis 1936* (Frankfurt, 1978). Ernst Fraenkel, *The Dual State: A Contribution to the Theory of Dictatorship* (Oxford, 1941), was the forerunner of these studies.

3. John A. Hall, ed., *States in History* (Oxford, 1986), "Introduction," p. 18; Theda Skocpol, "Introduction," in Theda Skocpol et al., eds., *Bringing the State Back In* (Cambridge, 1985), p. 28.

4. Frederick Pollock, "Is National Socialism a New Order?" *Studies in Philosophy and Social Science* 9 (1941): 440–55; Franz Neumann, *Behemoth: The Structure and Practice of National Socialism* (London, 1942), pp. 382–84.

5. See for example the studies edited by Juan J. Linz and Alfred Stepan, *The Breakdown of Democratic Regimes* (Baltimore, Md., 1978).

6. Michael Geyer has argued against the comparative study of fascism in "The State in National Socialist Germany," in Charles Bright and Susan Harding, eds., *Statemaking and Social Movements* (Ann Arbor, Mich., 1984), p. 228, n. 12. For a counterargument in favor of fascism as a concept and of comparative studies of Nazi Germany and fascist Italy, see Tim Mason, "Whatever Happened to Fascism?", in this volume.

7. From the growing literature on the *Historikerstreit*, see principally *"Historikerstreit": Die Dokumentation der Kontroverse um die Einzigartigkeit der*

nationalsozialistischen Judenvernichtung (Munich, 1987); also Richard Evans, *In Hitler's Shadow: West German Historians and the Attempt to Escape from the Nazi Past* (New York, 1989); Roderick Stackelberg, "1986 vs. 1968: The Turn to the Right in German Historiography," *Radical History Review* 40 (1988): 50–63; Geoff Eley, "Nazism, Politics and Public Memory: Thoughts on the West German *Historikerstreit*, 1986–1987," *Past and Present* 121 (November 1988): 171–208; and Charles Maier, *The Unmasterable Past: History, Holocaust, and German National Identity* (Cambrige, Mass., 1988).

8. Hans Mommsen, "The Realization of the Unthinkable: The 'Final Solution of the Jewish Question' in the Third Reich," in Gerhard Hirschfeld, ed., *The Policies of Genocide: Jews and Soviet Prisoners of War in Germany* (London, 1986), pp. 93–144; see also Martin Broszat, *The Hitler State* (London, 1981).

9. On the relationship between politics and *Alltag* in Nazi Germany, see Detlev Peukert, *Inside Nazi Germany* (New Haven, Conn., 1986); and Alf Lüdtke, "Einleitung," in idem, ed., *Alltagsgeschichte: Zur Rekonstruktion historischer Erfahrungen und Lebensweisen* (Frankfurt, 1989).

10. For example, the collection edited by Gregor McLennan, David Held, and Stuart Hall, *The Idea of the Modern State* (Milton Keynes, Philadelphia, 1984), includes chapters on imperialism, communism, etc., but nothing on fascism. The same is true of Hall, ed., *States in History*, and Evans et al., *Bringing the State Back In*.

11. This is discussed in Bob Jessop, *The Capitalist State: Marxist Theories and Methods* (New York, London, 1982), chap. 2.

12. See Peter Hüttenberger, "Nationalsozialistische Polykratie," *Geschichte und Gesellschaft* 2 (1976): 417–42.

13. The starting point for the revival of the left analysis of fascism was the exchange of articles on the theory of fascism in the West German left-wing periodical *Das Argument* in 1964–66: *Das Argument*, 'Faschismus-Theorien' 1 (no. 3, 1964), 2 (no. 1, 1965), 3 (no. 2, May 1965), and 4 (no. 6, December 1966). For Poulantzas, see his *Fascism and Dictatorship: The Third International and the Problem of Fascism* (London, 1974). Discussion here is confined to the Western literature; for a recent East German contribution, see Ernst Gottschling, "Der faschistische Staat: Das deutsche Beispiel," in Dietrich Eichholtz, ed., *Faschismusforschung: Positionen, Probleme, Polemik* (Berlin, 1980), pp. 73–98.

14. Tim Mason, "Der Primat der Politik—Politik und Wirtschaft im Nationalsozialismus," *Das Argument* 8, no. 6 (December 1966): 473–94; reprinted as "The Primacy of Politics—Politics and Economics in National Socialist Germany," in S. J. Woolf, ed., *The Nature of Fascism* (New York, 1968), pp. 165–95; Nicos Poulantzas, *Fascism and Dictatorship*; also Jane Caplan,

"Theories of Fascism: Nicos Poulantzas as Historian," *History Workshop Journal* 3 (1977): 83–100.

15. See John Holloway and Sol Picciotto, eds., *State and Capital: A Marxist Debate* (London, 1978); also Jessop, *The Capitalist State*, chap. 3; Martin Carnoy, *The State and Political Theory* (Princeton, N.J., 1984), chap. 5.

16. Evans et al., eds., *Bringing the State Back In*, p. 353.

17. The outstanding attempt to apply Poulantzian categories to modern German history is David Abraham's *The Collapse of the Weimar Republic: Political Economy and Crisis* (New York, 1986), which by intention stops short of an analysis of the Nazi regime. Geyer, "The State in National Socialist Germany," and Ian Kershaw, "The Nazi State: An Exceptional State?" *New Left Review* 176 (July–August 1989): 47–67, are the best historical theorizations; Kershaw's essay was not available to me for this essay.

18. Fraenkel, *The Dual State*: Neumann, *Behemoth*; Otto Kirchheimer, "The Legal Order of National Socialism," *Studies in Philosophy and Social Science* 9 (1941): 456–75; Pollock, "Is National Socialism a New Order?" Mason's use of the term "primacy of politics is anticipated by Pollock's discussion of this concept, p. 453.

19. Hannah Arendt, *The Origins of Totalitarianism* (New York, 1951); Carl J. Friedrich and Zbigniew K. Brzezinski, *Totalitarian Dictatorship and Autocracy* (Cambridge, Mass., 1956). See also Anthony Giddens, *The Nation-State and Violence* (Berkeley, Calif., 1987), chap. 11.

20. Geyer, "The State in National Socialist Germany."

21. In place of exhaustive references, I refer readers to two comprehensive recent surveys of historical work: Ian Kershaw, *The Nazi Dictatorship: Problems and Perspectives of Interpretation* (London, 1989); and John Hiden and John Farquharson, *Explaining Hitler's Germany: Historians and the Third Reich* (London, 1989).

22. See Broszat, *The Hitler State*, and the essays by Hans Mommsen and Tim Mason in Gerhard Hirschfeld and Lothar Kettenacker, eds., *The "Führer State": Myth and Reality: Studies on the Structure and Politics of the Third Reich* (Stuttgart, 1981), pt. 1. For general discussion of the structuralist/intentionalist debate, see Hiden and Farquharson, *Explaining Hitler's Germany*, chap. 3, and Kershaw, *The Nazi Dictatorship*, chap. 4. The term "Polykratie" appears to have first been introduced into the literature by Gerhard Schulz in 1960; see Karl Dietrich Bracher, Wolfgang Sauer, and Gerhard Schulz, *Die nationalsozialistische Machtergreifung: Studien zur Errichtung des totalitären Herrschaftssystems in Deutschland, 1933/34* (Cologne, Opladen, 1962), p. 599. For a detailed example of structuralist explanation in action see Mommsen, "The Realization of the Unthinkable."

23. See Klaus Hildebrand's essay in Hirschfeld and Kettenacker, eds.,

The "Führer State", pp. 73–97; also Gerald Fleming, Hitler and the Final Solution (Oxford, 1986).

24. Caplan, "Theories of Fascism."

25. See Caplan, Government Without Administration.

26. On Schmitt and his problems under National Socialism, see Joseph W. Bendersky, Carl Schmitt: Theorist for the Reich (Princeton, N.J., 1983), chaps. 9–12.

27. Walter Sommer, "Die NSDAP als Verwaltungsträger," in Hans Frank, ed., Deutsches Verwaltungsrecht (Munich, 1937), p. 169. Sommer was a career civil servant (and doctor of law) who held a leading post on Rudolf Hess's political staff.

28. Otto Koellreutter, Volk und Staat in der Weltanschauung des Nationalsozialismus (Berlin, 1935), quoting Rosenberg from Völkischer Beobachter, 9 January 1934. This lecture was a critique of Carl Schmitt.

29. Ernst Huber, Neue Grundbegriffe des hoheitlichen Rechts (Berlin, 1935).

30. Cf. Geyer's concept of "ideological politics" in "The State in National Socialist Germany," p. 208.

31. Hans Frank, Recht und Verwaltung (Munich, 1939), p. 14. This was Frank's justification for the existence of a hierarchical bureaucracy, to which he was strongly committed.

32. Hans Frank, Die Technik des Staates (Berlin, Leipzig, Vienna, 1938), pp. 15–16.

33. Ernst Huber, Wesen und Inhalt der politischen Verfassung (Hamburg, 1935), p. 51. Huber was a professor of constitutional law who published frequently after 1933.

34. Hans Frank, Rechtsgrundlegung des nationalsozialistichen Führerstaates (Munich, 1938), p. 39.

35. Kirschenmann, "Gesetz" im Staatsrecht und in der Staatsrechtslehre, p. 17. See also Tim Mason, "Intention and Explanation: A Current Controversy about the Interpretation of National Socialism," in Hirschfeld and Kettenacker, eds., The "Führer State," p. 35.

36. The best discussion of this at the level of political and legal theory is Stolleis, Gemeinwohlformeln im nationalsozialistischen Recht.

37. Quoted in Kirschenmann, "Gesetz", p. 198.

38. Geyer, "The State in National Socialist Germany."

39. The Mittelinstanz was the intermediate level of the field administration. Friction between party and state offices was particularly intense at this level; in addition, the Reich Interior Ministry's plans for administrative rationalization envisaged far-reaching reconstruction at this level, and this too became a persistent bone of contention.

40. Michael Mann, "The Autonomous Power of the State: Its Origins,

Mechanisms and Results," in Hall, ed., *States in History*, pp. 113–16. As Mann defines his terms, "[Despotic power] denotes power by the state elite *over* civil society. [Infrastructural power] denotes the power of the state to penetrate and centrally co-ordinate the activities of civil society through its own infrastructure" (p. 114). Structurally, this dualism parallels Skocpol's distinction between the state as (a) a set of institutions and activities that determine public life, and (b) a goal-oriented collectivity of agents.

6 _____

Innovation and Conservatism in Economic Recovery: The Alleged "Nazi Recovery" of the 1930s

HAROLD JAMES

How different was Nazi economic policy from the strategies adopted by the presidential governments of the Weimar Republic? Often we make over-convenient assumptions about the 1930s: that in a system in which economics had become highly politicized, a new political system translated simply into a new economics; or that because Hitler said he was doing something new he really did innovate; or that political totalitarianism solved an economic problem.

The myth of a peculiarly Nazi "economic recovery" had already been generated in the 1930s, and since then has served a wide diversity of political interests. At the time, it was termed the *Wirtschaftswunder.*[1] The Nazis themselves needed to boast about their economic success. Weimar governments had, they claimed, failed to deal with the problems of an over-indebted and bankrupt countryside or with the crisis phenomenon of mass unemployment. A struggle for the survival of the German peasantry and a "battle for work" became key ingredients in a Nazi propaganda campaign of considerable effectiveness.

Other observers had a different political argument, but reached the same conclusion: Nazi economics was working. Keynes saw the Nazi "success" as evidence that market capitalism, unless regulated and managed through the actions of a politically liberal state, would succumb to the superior power of totalitarian economies. To him, the successes of Hitler and Stalin constituted a proof that the world needed economic management if democracy was to survive. Economic liberals drew the opposite conclusion. During the 1930s, and also after World War II, Wilhelm Röpke and Walther Eucken attacked the interventionist economy as inherently totalitarian. What more convenient way of discrediting economic interventionism than to show that it had been created by Nazi Germany? In international economics, Harry Dexter White made the same argument: at Bretton Woods in 1944 he tried to discredit the management of trade and financial flows, and Keynes's proposals for a new international economic order, by describing all this as "the Schachtian system."

Uncovering and exposing myth is an important part of the historians' task. The surprising conclusion provided by a study of the development of fiscal policy, of trade and currency strategy, and of views of the appropriate mix between public and private is that 30 January 1933 did not mark a major turning point in Germany's interwar economic history. Rather, there existed substantial continuities between the course taken by Weimar's presidential governments and that of the Nationalist-Nazi coalition under Hitler's chancellorship.

Fiscal Conservatism and Work Creation

Part of the confusion about the nature of Nazi economic policy stems from the ambiguity of the Nazi program before 30 January. The party was pulled in opposite directions, partly because of its socially highly heterogeneous support, and partly for the simple logical reason that promoting economic recovery conflicted with the goal of not appearing irresponsibly and dangerously adventurist. In the course of 1932, the party's platform shifted frequently and dramatically. It often simply assumed that the party would be able to overcome the existing "system." Hitler and his movement had pledged themselves to conduct a "battle for work" (*Arbeitsschlacht*). In the electoral campaigns of 1932, the most explicit Nazi statement on work creation came from Gregor Strasser in his Reichstag speech of May 1932, which promised 10 billion RM to be spent on roads, agricultural improvements, and the resettlement of urban workers in the countryside. These measures were supposed to generate up to two million jobs; but the program was soon attacked as being too inflationary, and in October 1932 a new program only specified a spending of 3 billion RM.

The Nazi dilemma—of how to be expansionary without being inflationary—was by no means unique to that party. Almost every political actor in Depression Germany—political parties, labor unions, civil servants, and ministers—faced a similar problem. Some kind of action in the face of the economic crisis seemed a political necessity: merely saying that nothing could be done, that the world depression or Allied reparations bore the blame for an insoluble

predicament, looked like political ineffectiveness. Political actors were expected
to "do something." At the same time, political action was perceived to run the
risk of endangering established interests, or of threatening a new expropriation of
workers and the middle classes through inflation.

The discussion about job creation in these terms went back to 1931.
Already before the banking crisis of July 1931, which immediately weakened the
economy further, employment projects looked like a way of dealing at least with
the political consequences of economic crisis. In the course of 1932, discussion
of job creation schemes had become a political commonplace. The trade unions
in April 1932 drew up a major reflationary proposal at an Extraordinary Congress in order to be able to demonstrate to their members that they had adopted
an activist approach. The Weimar governments, and even the fiscally highly
orthodox Brüning regime, also believed that it was desirable politically to "do
something"—although the actual outcome of that action might be uncertain.

In 1931 the Brüning government had instituted a commission to study
unemployment as well as possible measures to reduce its extent and impact.
Some of the Brüning ministers—especially Labor Minister Adam Stegerwald
and Finance Minister Hermann Dietrich—pushed hard for work creation measures. In April 1932 the cabinet agreed to "economic pump priming"
(Wirtschaftsankurbelung) to the extent of (a rather modest) 135 million RM. In
the last months of the Brüning government unemployment policy acquired a
major political significance. However, before the Brüning schemes could begin
to operate, the government had been dismissed by von Hindenburg who appointed Franz Papen in Brüning's place. Papen's larger-scale approach developed
on the foundations laid by his predecessor. The chief element was an indirect
stimulus to job creation: the payment of tax credits as a subsidy to employers who
would hire new workers (linked with permission to pay wage rates below the
negotiated level). Only a relatively small sum—167 million RM—was devoted to
direct job creation.

The Papen package led to 15,169 new jobs in textiles and 12,638 in
mining: in other words, the immediately visible impact was slight in a country
with over six million registered as jobless.[2] Papen's successor, Schleicher, turned
to direct job creation in place of the subsidization of private business, with 500
million RM allocated.

The link between political popularity and the ability to create jobs
through government action had been established already before 30 January
1933. From 1933, the Nazi regime tried to make a propaganda success out of
work creation measures. Support for house construction and renovation (extending a scheme already introduced by Papen) involved 332 million RM in subsidies
and 667 million RM in loans. Tax concessions for motor vehicles (10 April)
encouraged a rapid recovery for automobile production. In July 1933 a general
reduction of the corporation tax load followed. Direct work creation measures

(chiefly in the so-called Reinhardt Program) amounted between 1932 and 1935 to a total of over 5 billion RM—although it should be borne in mind that this represents only around 1 percent of GNP for this period: in other words, at least in quantitative terms, not a substantial stimulus.[3]

The schemes for work creation were supplemented by direct administrative regulation of the labor market: from 1933, young males were sent to work in agriculture, and if they refused they lost their entitlement to unemployment benefit. Females were encouraged to leave the work force through marriage loans (but even though the Depression had increased the share of women in employment the number of women employed—although not the proportion—still rose after 1933). A voluntary labor service *(Arbeitsdienst)* had already been established by Brüning in the Emergency Decree of 5 June 1931 as a way of supporting "unemployed workers" through land improvement, the creation of rural settlements and small allotments, local road works, and sewer construction. This scheme remained in operation after 1933, even though Hitler had written to Papen that it had "no value either economically or in any other way."[4] In June 1935 labor service became compulsory.

The Nazi work creation program bore a similarity to conservative proposals during the Depression, advocated by figures such as the lord mayor of Leipzig, Carl Goerdeler. This vision saw economic policy primarily in terms of socially corrective policy—bringing workers back to the land and away from the trouble spots of the big cities. It had little in common with the schemes proposed during the course of 1932 by the Left and the labor movement—in which an important part of the policy had been the expansionary effect of creating employment with public funds *at the current wage rate.*

The period of voluntary labor service under Nazi rule could hardly be reckoned as a large-scale experiment or a radical innovation. The *Arbeitsdienst* paid low rates for highly labor-intensive projects of the ditch-digging or road-building kind. Between 1932 and 1935 the number of men working in the *Arbeitsdienst* actually fell. Another category of workers taken into state-run projects—"emergency workers"—had a similarly limited effect on the labor market. The number of workers employed in this way reached a peak in 1934, but the scheme was then cut back, and in the winter 1934–35 only a trivial 6 million RM out of the Reich budget was spent on the project.[5]

The relatively meager resources directed toward work creation contrasted oddly with the propaganda image of a regime that would get Germany to work. Two contrasting political pulls operated: on the one hand, the need to demonstrate success in the battle for work; on the other, the widespread fear of budgetary expansion and inflation. The traumatic effects of the postwar inflation produced a deep scar on the German collective memory, one that influenced both decision making and popular debate. During the Depression, accusations of being inflationary formed a stock-in-trade of almost every political movement.

At the Harzburg rally of the National Opposition (October 1931), as the Nazis and the old Right moved closer together, the former president of the central bank (Reichsbank) Hjalmar Schacht accused the Brüning government of preparing a new inflation. Hitler in April 1932 explained that inflation would be produced by the parties currently ruling: "The specialists in inflation are sitting in the parties which now rule the state."[6] On the other hand, the parties of the Left—SPD as well as KPD—charged that the Right wanted a repeat of 1918–23 in order to strengthen the position of the big farms and trusts, and to wipe out their debt at the expense of Germany's small savers. This charge led to the swings and shifts in the Nazi economic program in 1932. Hitler felt that the Strasser reemployment program offered ammunition to the Left in the mutually reciprocated propaganda war of inflation smear stories, and forced the withdrawal of this platform. Fear of doing anything that might be considered inflationary remained a powerful motive in 1933—in the election campaign, and in announcing the success of work creation. In 1934, when claiming successes in the battle for work, Hitler still needed simultaneously to explain with emphasis that "the German Mark has remained stable."[7]

Another argument for fiscal conservatism came from the German bureaucracy. Among officials in the Finance Ministry and the Reichsbank, a widely held interpretation suggested, first, that the major government anticyclical program of 1925–26 had not been very effective in generating employment, and, second, that the Depression was a consequence of the high level of government deficits in the mid- and late 1920s. In consequence, tackling the Depression required fiscal constraint rather than relaxation. But this was an interpretation not confined simply to Treasury civil servants. Otto Wagener claimed that in 1931 Hitler objected to big work creation schemes on these grounds—and because of the inflation argument as well. He attacked the Nazi economic specialist Bernhard Köhler who had been arguing that the state should print money to deal with the slump: "That's exactly what previous governments have done. *They* pour money for unemployment relief down the drain."[8] "Keynesianism," or expansionary fiscal policies, might endanger the propaganda image of a party espousing respectability and stability.

This caution presented problems within the National Socialist movement. The Nazis—as a catchall protest party that purported to offer patent solutions to any and every problem Germany might face—certainly attracted a generous sprinkling of fanatics who saw currency experimentation as a cure-all for economic difficulties. Köhler or Gottfried Feder (who had a scheme for disappearing money), or even the highly eccentric pair Max Roosen and Werner Kertscher (who tried to assassinate the central bank president in 1932 in order to call attention to their currency views), found in the NSDAP a suitable vehicle for their proposals: but they remained marginal, and in the course of 1933–34 the party and the government redefined themselves in an increasingly conservative way.

For a time, the economy's future lay open and discussion blossomed as the Nazi theorists attempted to make their point. The great opportunity for a fundamental restructuring of the economy along lines of state socialism, corporatism, or monetary experiment was the great Bank Inquiry of 1933–34. This presented the chance many would-be experimenters were so eagerly awaiting. The inquiry had the task of investigating reforms for a financial sector that in 1931 had broken down completely: it would be easy to implement any proposals since the bank crisis had left a considerable part of the financial system in the hands of the state. Already on 13 July 1931, the day the Darmstädter Bank's collapse became public knowledge, the Ministry of Justice began to investigate legislation to limit the purchase and ownership by a company of its own shares— a manipulation that had contributed to the outbreak of the bank crisis.[9] The Brüning government then started to intervene systematically in the banking sector: removing bank directors responsible for mistaken policies, appointing a state commissar for banking as the price for public aid, imposing audit requirements for banks, and regulating interest rates. The inquiry's purpose was to systematize, and perhaps extend, the Brüning measures concerning Germany's banks.

At the inquiry, the Nazi "experts" at first set the tone: Wilhelm Keppler, for instance, explained that in a proper order, banks and "capital" were supposed to "serve" the people and the economy, but that finance had made itself into the "master of the economy," not its servant. He wanted municipally owned savings banks to expand their activity at the expense of the private banks. Yet these views were quickly set aside.[10]

The Nazi theorists were allowed to state their theories, which were then ignored. Indeed, Reichsbank president Hjalmar Schacht was quite keen to boast that this was precisely his plan:

> Dr. Schacht replied that the whole object of the inquiry in his view was to let all the people with new theories talk themselves out, and to bring them face to face with competent experts, who would give the real answers to their theories. Dr. Schacht would confine himself in the main to asking questions. The chancellor [Hitler] seemed to him absolutely sound and was always prepared to take good advice. Dr. Schacht believed in fact the party theorists would have no great influence in this affair.

"My strong point," conceded Schacht in speaking of the Bank inquiry, "is my modesty. You see, I shall let the others do all the discussion and take all credit, and I shall see myself that all the right measures are put through."[11]

Schacht's account corresponded to the actual conduct of the inquiry. In one of the sessions, the chairman, Vice President Dreyse of the Reichsbank, noted: "I can establish that the discussion has ended with a complete victory of the bankers and bank directors." Another banker expressed his delight that "the tasks of bankers were recognized in the new Reich."[12]

The "right measures" that Schacht spoke of were indeed implemented by the new Bank Law of 5 December 1934, which regulated the ad hoc bank supervision erected under the terms of the Emergency Decree of 19 September 1931 and laid down reserve provisions for major loans. The limitation of dividends to 6 percent (Law of 29 March 1934) was intended to bring down interest rates (and make bonds and state paper relatively more attractive than shares—rendering the public financing of the state debt easier). It was a more sophisticated and well-thought-out version of the interest reduction laid down in the Brüning emergency decree of 8 December 1931. Whereas the Brüning decree had increased the confusion and uncertainty of Germany's financial markets, the March 1934 law did indeed stabilize—and then increase—bond prices (and cut interest rates). It hardly needs to be pointed out that the new measure could not seen as the outcome of a Nazi war on capitalism.

The same fear of dangerous experimentation also marked the initial Nazi approach to fiscal policy: the result was pragmatic, cautious, and surprisingly orthodox. The Brüning government had increased the general deflationary pressure by putting up taxes—and had in the process made itself great enemies. Yet the Nazis on the whole left taxes at the high levels set during the Depression, with the exception of the tax reductions provided in the work creation program (for house construction) and for automobiles. State Secretary Reinhardt of the Reich Finance Ministry actually argued that there should be no major tax reform until the first Nazi priority—the reduction of unemployment—had been accomplished.[13] There would be no large-scale bonfire of Brüning's tax decrees. From a modern, or a Keynesian, perspective this appears a bizarre order of priorities: but there existed among Nazi policy-makers no concept of providing an economic stimulus through a general reduction in tax burdens (as opposed to specific fiscal stimuli).

Conservatism prevailed when it came to the issue of how to fund public deficits. Once more the legacy of the past left a suspicion of unsound finance—with the public, with the financial community, and with the civil service. Such government deficits as did emerge after 1933 were carefully camouflaged. Deficits appeared as "anticipations of future revenue" in the accounts. The work creation program, for instance, was largely funded through tax certificates (*Steuergutscheine*)—paper that might be used at a future date to settle Reich tax liabilities, and that in the meantime could be discounted by the banking system. These certificates had been used in Papen's September 1932 program as a subsidy to employers who hired extra workers. Schleicher used them to raise the 500 million RM for public works. After 1934 a new concealment device was employed—the subsequently notorious bills drawn on the Metallurgische Forschungsgesellschaft (Mefo-bills)—again as a consequence of the regime's obsession with avoiding any appearance of strain on the budget, as well as in order to keep secret the extent of rearmament.

Even allowing for all these concealment devices, the fiscal expansion of the early years of Nazi rule was initially rather limited. Work creation measures had accounted for just over 1 percent of GNP. The macroeconomic picture of the budget is equally unexciting. Government deficits altogether represented 2.2 percent of GNP in 1933–34, 3.6 percent in 1934–35, and then 5.2 percent in 1935–36. As Arthur Lewis already pointed out in 1949, this rise of the public-sector borrowing requirement from a relatively modest level to increasingly inflated proportions over the course of the 1930s means that Nazi economics cannot be taken as an experiment in Keynesianism.

> Unfortunately the German experiment ceased to be helpful just as it was becoming interesting. What interests economists in this sort of situation is whether, after heavy government expenditure has set recovery in motion in this way, private investment will start to grow cumulatively, and so make it possible for government expenditure to be curtailed without the system collapsing once more. . . . From 1935 the German economy . . . becomes only an illustration of the workings of a war economy, detailed examination of which, now that we have all had the same kind of experience, is tedious for any but the specialist.[14]

When large deficits appeared, they followed as a consequence of rearmament—rather than from the intention of giving a fiscal stimulus. In 1936, military spending more than doubled (on the army and navy, it rose from 1735.7 million RM to 3596.4 million RM, and for the air force from 1035.7 million to 2224.7 million).[15] Already before 1936, military spending (some of which was camouflaged as work creation) had been a substantial element in recovery. From 1934, rearmament had had some impact on employment—so that, for instance, by 1936 the German air industry employed more workers than did automobile manufacture.[16] After 1936 the political restraints on military spending were lifted entirely.

But even after the swelling of the fiscal stimulus in 1935–36, and the turn toward a war economy in 1936, the deficits were financed in a relatively orthodox and anti-inflationary way. The pressures exerted by a public worried about the security of savings bank deposits continued to influence the government. It treated the purchase of state paper as a sort of daily financial plebiscite about the regime, recalling the events of 1916, when German citizens had suddenly refused to buy Reich loans. Until the end of 1938, in fact, private purchases of government loans continued, and only after this did the share of government debt held by the banking system rise dramatically.

This interpretation of Nazi fiscal policy as substantially orthodox—even as carrying over many of the deflationary dogmas of the Depression Era—may seem surprising to those weaned on a historical literature that emphasizes concealment devices, semisecret spending, and rearmament in Nazi policy. It was, however, an interpretation of the Schacht period (1933–36) that was widely held at the time. Contemporary observers found it hard to say precisely what was innovative about Nazi approaches to economic policy. For instance, in March 1935 a Bank of England memorandum stated that Schacht was contemplating an 18 percent budget cut: "Is he in fact contemplating a form of deflation which seems quite beyond the imagination of all postwar democratic politicians, yet which is well within the scope of National Socialist thought, which is in fact in complete harmony with their economic ideology, namely budget deflation on a large scale?" In fact, of course, the Nazi regime never came near to enacting such a dramatic austerity campaign—not least because it was frightened of the social and political destabilization that such a step would entail. But later that year, Pinsent, the financial secretary of the British Embassy in Berlin, was still quoting Schacht as saying that "under present conditions the standard of living in Germany must fall"; and Schacht's attempts in late 1935 and 1936 to restrict the import of consumer foodstuffs (and especially fats) did amount to a squeezing of general living standards.[17]

How do we account for economic recovery in the face of all this conservatism in policy? Part of the recovery was doubtless an illusion, one created in 1933 by an imaginative use of statistics. The unemployment figures were cut at a stroke in July 1933 by 619,000 by the elimination from the count of emergency relief workers, members of the Labor Service, and those employed in Land Help or in public relief. Even the manipulation of employment figures can, however, account for no more than around 200,000 additions to the employment series.[18]

By now historians and economists, who have for over fifty years wrestled with the problem of accounting for the "Nazi economic recovery," have concluded that there can be no single explanation, and that a large number of causes played a role.

The price-control mechanism for agriculture by means of the Reich Food Estate (*Rechsnährstand*) in 1933 helped to halt a price decline that had threatened to plunge Germany's farmers into bankruptcy and also to bring down the credit system. But the institution of price support coincided with the low point and then a recovery in world food prices, with the result that a Nazi political apparatus reaped some of the acclaim that might more properly have gone to the international commodity market. From 1935, price controls in agriculture had an opposite effect: prices were held down, increasing the disposable income available to urban workers.

Motorization was a deliberate National Socialist strategy; it was fostered by the abolition of the tax on new automobiles (10 April 1933), and, most famously, by the public construction of highways *(Autobahnen)*. The Nazis undoubtedly exaggerated the employment creation effects of this. In 1933 the maximum figure employed in constructing *Autobahnen* was 3,900, in 1934 8,863, in 1935 115,675, and in 1936 124,483. Including all those employed in supplying the construction sites (the secondary work creation effect) as well as the administrative machinery organizing the building drive, no more than 250,000 people were estimated to have been employed on the *Autobahnen* at any one time. [19]

How far the "motorization" of Germany in the 1930s, and in particular the indisputable rise in car production and sales, was a consequence of government policy is also debatable. Relative to Britain or France, Germany was underdeveloped as a market for automobiles in the 1920s; this was partly because of the excellent railway system, which made alternative transport less attractive. Tax policy in the 1920s had curbed automobile sales, in part because such sales entered into the computation of Germany's capacity to pay reparations under the "prosperity index" provided in the Dawes Plan. The growth of the 1930s may have been in part simply a making up of a deficit in automobiles incurred in the previous decade, although the catching-up process clearly benefited from sympathetic government policy.

The most convincing case that government action led to recovery has been made for building and construction. Public spending on housing, one of the major investments of Weimar governments, had been cut back in response to the fiscal crisis that afflicted all levels—communal, state, and central. The new regime reversed these cuts and gave tax concessions for house renovation and the breaking up of old large apartments into smaller units. According to one calculation, employment in building (including road building, also a favorite for Nazi spending) increased by 276 percent from February 1933 to February 1934, while in iron and steel the corresponding rise was only 20 percent. [20] The combination of government spending, altered taxes, and an existing housing shortage (in marked contrast to the position in the United States) allowed a rapid rise in the German building industry. By 1936, spending on construction had overtaken that of any year in the 1920s. [21]

On the other hand, it is difficult to account adequately for the early stages of recovery with this explanation. In 1934, when the recovery was already underway, building was at 74.8 percent of the 1928 level, while textiles stood at 99.7 percent and foodstuffs at 97.1 percent. Producer goods output was 76.1 percent of 1928, consumer goods 93.0 percent. The most dramatic rise of all was in automobiles (136.3 percent). [22] The figures of producer goods recovery look very much more impressive, it is true, if presented as recovery figures, from the Depression low, since the collapse in output had been most severe there.

Of course, if the Nazis had cared less about building, recovery would have been slower: but it looks implausible to take construction as the driving force on the road out of depression. In addition, retrospective critics of the Brüning government who claim that the large sums spent on agricultural support would have been more wisely spent on building[23] miss both a political and an economic point. Such a diversion of funds would have been unacceptable to the farming lobby, whose political influence extended over all the major parties, and over Reich President von Hindenburg, as well. It would have also been detrimental to the economy as a whole, since bankruptcies, defaults, and an endangering of the whole credit system would have been the consequence.

The most plausible view of the early stages of recovery—the first two years, 1933 and 1934—would be as a relatively spontaneous cyclical recovery: a rise in consumption (benefiting all consumer goods, but especially automobiles) and an increase in inventories (which had been run down to unusually low levels during the Depression, in large part as a consequence of the 1931 financial crisis). Inventories increased in 1933 for the first time since 1928: this is largely accounted for by artisan business, and by trade and commerce; in industry there was still a very small net disinvestment. By 1934, all inventories were increasing.[24] The prospering consumer economy suffered a major shock in 1934 when a new currency shortage led to a reordering of Germany's trade and a cutback in imports. By allocating raw materials, the supply of consumer goods was curtailed. There were also signs of quality deterioration in consumer goods. Finally, after 1934 the maintenance of high (and un-Keynesian) rates of taxation further deterred consumption. From 1935, public investments and rearmament took over from where the consumer boom of the early Nazi period had left off, and the Nazi *Wirtschaftswunder* turned into a display of producer goods dynamism.

Public investment had already reached 1928 levels by 1934, and in 1936 private industrial investment also passed the 1928 mark.[25] By 1938 producer goods had reached 135.9 percent of their 1928 value, while consumer goods remained at a lowly 107.8 percent.

Until 1934–35, then, we are dealing with a rather different phenomenon than that usually associated with the Nazi era. At first there was a surprisingly dynamic "normal" recovery, and after that a transition to a *Staatskonjunktur* (state-led recovery), though one that preserved many aspects of the old fiscal conservatism. The change in policy occurred while recovery was already well under way, and it took place within the framework of rather orthodox policies. The use of administrative measures to tackle unemployment, coupled with an initially highly conservative fiscal policy, remained as a legacy of the Depression Era. It would be hard to find here a Nazi revolution.

Trade Policy and Debt

Trade policy on the other hand appeared—according to the choice of perspective—either as innovative, or else as unscrupulous and devious. The related issues of trade and international debts had presented the central international economic difficulty of the world economic crisis. They were bound together in the following way. Debtors attributed their defaults to the cession of capital flows, the worsening of their terms of trade, and the international spread of protectionism. Tariff protection offered a way of halting the deterioration of trade balances and could be defended as a measure calculated to allow the prompt—or at least the continuing—servicing of debt. Finally, measures designed to control currency movements could be used to disguise trade measures and thus reduce the probability and extent of retaliatory measures.

A tightly controlled exchange policy, regulation and restriction of debt repayment, and a push toward the bilateralization of trade—these were the hallmarks of 1930s economies, and of the flight away from a liberal international order throughout the whole world. But all these features were particularly pronounced in the German case. Indeed, they were generally referred to—and later condemned as—"Schachtian economics." Such controls of foreign transactions allowed greater room for domestic maneuver—by providing a framework within which domestic controls could be applied—controls of investment, capital movements, and even (through the allocation of scarce raw materials) production levels.

"Schachtianism" is a misnomer for all this. In fact, Germany had started to apply all the major elements of the "Schachtian system" before the chancellorship of Hitler and before Schacht had been reappointed as president of the German central bank. Its progenitor was not Schacht but Reichsbank president Hans Luther. The new system began as a response to the bank and credit collapse of July 1931. Foreign currency had to be registered. Foreign loans were frozen in Germany. A law on payments abroad (1 August 1931) stopped the free operation of capital markets. The law also inaugurated a novel approach to trade issues: imports were divided into three categories (essential; necessary "to a certain extent"; and unnecessary), and the classifications were used to issue permits.[26] This early form of "Schachtianism" lasted only a few months, although it appears to have struck a favorable response with some industrial leaders. Later, in March 1932, a memorandum produced by the Reichsverband der Deutschen Industrie (RDI) on currency control argued strongly against the launching of a tariff war (which would hurt relations with the Netherlands and the Scandinavian countries, which were major importers of German manufacturing goods). But it also stated that "the principle of not using currency policy in the service of trade policy has been exaggerated."[27]

The method of running trade policy through semisecret lists of undesirable imports had in fact produced initially too much bureaucratic complication, and in October 1931 foreign exchange was instead allocated to German importers as a share of the previous year's requirements: 50 percent from May 1932 to February 1934. After February 1934, because of a growing shortage of foreign exchange, the proportions had to be reduced. By the summer of 1934, the old scheme was in collapse. Exchange was simply allocated each day at the Reichsbank between 5 and 7 P.M. according to what happened to be available.[28] Between January and September 1934 the German balance of trade was negative (deficit: 247 million RM), and the Reichsbank lost almost all its gold and foreign currency reserves (they dropped from 317 million to a trivial 79 million RM: at the beginning of 1933 they had still been 964 million RM and in December 1930 they had stood at 2,907 million).

In September 1934 a plan based on an openly explicit acknowledgment of the bilateral principle (New Plan) was adopted in order to restrict German purchases requiring foreign exchange. The trade balance of course reflected the extent of recovery in 1933–34: as the German economy grew, it sucked in more imports. In 1935–36 further expansion threatened the New Plan in turn and obliged Schacht to cut back further on imports—which led him into a major political struggle with Robert Ley of the Deutsche Arbeitsfront and Walter Darré of the Reich Agricultural Estate.

At these moments of conflict over policy—in 1934, and again in 1936— there existed a choice only in a very fundamental sense: between a continuing and incremental process of detachment from the world economy, on the one hand, and reintegration in the international economy, on the other. The latter course would mean the end of bilateralization, the repayment of debts, and the devaluation of the mark to a realistic rate. The terms of the debate, and the nature of the choice, had already been laid down in 1931. What were the costs and benefits of these alternative courses?

THE GAINS FROM ISOLATION

Integration into the world economy would bring no benefits to Germany if other countries were unwilling to reverse their own drives to *protectionism and economic nationalism*. Why should Germany be expected to give a lead? Central and Eastern European states waited for the traditional centers of the world economy to show the way. In consequence, the first moment when German devaluation looked possible was 1936, after the British-French-American tripartite pact on currency stabilization. Germany alone could not bring the world back to multilateralism.

Some German economists and businessmen looked favorably at the prospect of *a time away from the world economy*—as if it were a "time out," a spell when they might be protected by the combination of artificial exchange rates and currency control. Businessmen from the traditionally protectionist coal and steel industries were not enthusiastic about agricultural protection—partly because of its effects on the cost of living and thus on wage demands, and partly because of the hostile reactions from exporters of agricultural goods to Germany. A very comprehensive list of the aims German businessmen hoped to achieve before their economy was reintegrated into the world is provided by the steel and engineering industrialist Paul Reusch in July 1932 in a letter to Max Warburg (Reusch had an influential voice in these matters: he was one of the German representatives on the board of the Basel Bank for International Settlements):

> As I have already told you in person, I agree with your view that at present currency experiments cannot be contemplated. But once the German public budgets are set in order, once the internal situation is clarified and stabilized, once England has stabilized her currency, and, above all, once the reparations issue is settled, we should devalue as soon as possible to the same extent as sterling is devalued against gold. Only so will industry be capable of exporting again. [29]

This letter states very powerfully the case that devaluation could only be beneficial if undertaken with a balanced budget. The prerequisite for an economic recovery on conservative lines—fiscal rectitude and a destruction of the labor movement—were in place by 1933, but even after this there were few industrial voices raised in favor of devaluing. A visiting British banker in October 1933 found only one German openly in favor of devaluation—the export manager of the Vereinigte Stahlwerke. [30]

Domestic political considerations were paramount in keeping Germany on the isolationist tack. Here there was little change from Brüning to Hitler: both were highly sensitive to popular fears of inflation. A devaluation might mark the beginning of a new inflation. Inflation trauma not only obstructed fiscal expansion—it stood in the way of currency devaluation.

Hitler drew from World War I the lesson that inflation had a socially destructive effect: "the last war was lost because of a limitless lack of understanding for the susceptibilities of the masses of small savers and housewives." "I have pledged my word. I will not make inflation. The people would not understand it." [31] One of the key indicators as to whether a new inflation was taking place was the exchange rate: in 1922–23 the daily dollar quotation acquired immense significance as the chief guide to the mark's loss of value. Rumors about devaluation and inflation did indeed circulate in 1935–36: the Gestapo reports, for example, give instances of Schacht's speeches being cited as evidence that the German currency "was without real backing, only a fiction." [32] Popular fears as well as Hitler's obsession made devaluation a highly precarious choice in domestic political terms.

There were also *foreign political calculations*. The large volume of foreign debt frozen in Germany after 1931 gave German policy-makers a valuable negotiating weapon. In 1932 fear for the security of commercial debt in Germany played a major part in softening up Britain and the United States for a reparations solution at Lausanne. After July 1932 and the end of reparations, foreign debt was still used in the same way—to secure, for instance, more favorable treatment of German fish exporters by the British, or—more politically—in the case of the Special Agreement of 4 July 1934 to reassure Britain about German intentions after the bloody purge of the army and the SA on 30 June 1934 (the so-called Night of the Long Knives).

While political issues—concern about the pace of German rearmament, about the nature of German goals in southeast Europe, or about the treatment of German Jews—might pull the Western powers together and create alliances such as the Stresa Front of 1935, economic themes had the reverse effect. Von Neurath explained in 1933 how economic measures might be used

> in order to avoid under all circumstances warlike complications, which at the present time we cannot cope with. . . . By means of a statement that the objectives of our policy are exclusively economic and financial we can succeed in breaking up the front that has now been formed against us because of concern about the possibility of surprise actions on the part of Germany.[33]

Debt frozen in Germany, and the wish of foreigners to unfreeze it, formed the key element in a strategy of encouraging "economic appeasement." All participants in the game of currency control and debt blocking knew that Germany's foreign exchange resources were limited, and that the creditors stood in a competitive relationship with each other. The British hoped for preferential treatment of their commercial debt; Schacht held out the possibility of exporting more cotton to the United States; the Swiss were promised more German tourism and repayment on short term debt. "Debt divides" and "Bilateralism breaks apart" might be taken as the slogans for German economic diplomacy during the 1930s.

THE COSTS OF AUTARKY

Servicing loans in an orderly way may often be the best way to *obtain new money.* Although the Nazi leaders sometimes expressed the hope that Germany might find new international credits, they never undertook serious steps to obtain them. Indeed, in the conditions prevailing on the international capital market in the 1930s, the prospect for fresh inflows of capital into Germany looked bleak. As a result, an argument based on credit as a reason for moving back into the world economy carried little conviction and played a small role in German calculations.

German exporters were immediately affected by *the overvaluation of the mark.* After the British (1931) and then the U.S. (1933) devaluation, German prices were 30 to 40 percent above the world level. Part of the German response to September 1931 involved the intensification of deflation in an attempt to drive German prices down to British levels—in the December 1931 Emergency

Decree. But there were also other ways of making good the German disadvantages. Exporters received some compensation through a diversity of schemes to subsidize "additional exports" (by taking payments in blocked marks, or in scrips, or by repurchasing foreign domiciled German bonds at a discount and then reselling them at the higher prices prevailing on the German domestic market). In the case of the bond repurchases, Germany's frozen debt actually provided one way out of the problems caused by the German failure to abandon exchange control.

The amount of the export subsidy varied wildly—depending on the firm concerned, the commodity, and the country to which the export was being made. Gerhard Knoll states that the subsidy lay anywhere between 10 and 90 percent of the value.[34] This was a highly bureaucratic process, which famously produced enormous amounts of paperwork. The scheme operated through twenty-five "Price Examination Centers for Exports" *(Preisprüfungsstellen für die Ausfuhr)*; by the time of the New Plan, forty forms were required for each export transaction. This bureaucratism undoubtedly irked German exporters: Göring was even able to play with the dissatisfaction of German exporters when he began his campaign to succeed Schacht as economic dictator. On the other hand, it did offer the government a gigantic element of control—there was the advantage for the state of being able to regulate, very carefully, business contacts with foreigners. And the defenders of the scheme could also argue that after 1933 German exports grew at a faster rate than did the general level of international trade.

Some German *manufactures dependent on imported goods* suffered. The industry most affected was textiles: already in March 1934 imports of raw materials for textile producers had been severely cut back in response to the worsening situation for foreign exchange. The New Plan made a further cut. An index of textile production (1928 = 100) reached 105.1 in May 1934—a reflection of the staggeringly quick recovery in some consumer goods. But it then fell—to 93.8 in October 1934 and 88.6 by August 1935. Whereas in April 1934 German wool-weaving employment was 88.4 percent of capacity, by the end of the year the equivalent figure was 73.4 percent.[35] It was not only textiles that were hit by the foreign exchange control bottleneck: it was politically highly significant that by 1935 there were even signs that armaments producers were unable to get the raw materials they needed.

After 1933, Schacht toyed off and on with the idea of a devaluation that would solve all the problems of German exporters and manufacturers, and reverse the road to autarky. By 1936, he had surprised foreign observers by making himself into the public champion of the world economy. If a devaluation did not mean abandoning a fixed parity, but merely shifting from one fixed rate to another, the danger of inflation could be reduced. Thus in 1933 "he had pledged himself not to go off gold, but had never pledged himself not to lower the parity. . . . He thought on the other hand that merely to depart from the gold standard in Germany would almost certainly cause a panic in the German population." In 1934 he complained to U.S. Ambassador Dodd about the economic nationalism of the 1930s:

> The whole modern world is crazy. The system of closed national barriers is suicidal and we must all collapse here and the standard of living everywhere be reduced. Everybody here is crazy. And so am I. Five years ago I would have said that it would be impossible to make me so crazy. But I am compelled to be crazy.

In November 1935 the British ambassador in Berlin reported: "I learn from a reliable source that Dr. Schacht would seize a favorable opportunity to devalue the Mark to sterling level."[36] In September 1936, once the Tripartite Stabilization Pact had been concluded, the issue of devaluing became acute. Should Germany join the Western countries? Schacht was apparently in favor, but any move was blocked by Walter Funk, the state secretary in the Propaganda Ministry (and Schacht's eventual successor as economics minister). Goebbels's diary entry records: "Spoke with Funk. He prevented a German inflation. Schacht wanted to devalue as well. But Funk went straight to the Führer. And he intervened."[37]

Schacht's change of mind to pursue the path of rejoining the world economy scarcely reflected the political calculation of costs and benefits. In general, in the 1930s, only one state that had embarked on exchange and trade control and debt freezing reversed its policy (Austria in 1936, but the 1938 *Anschluss* took it back into the world of the controlled economy). For Germany, not devaluing, but remaining at the old mark parity was the logical outcome of the decision to make the popular fear of inflation the foundation of policy. The calculation that the political gains of not devaluing and not reintegrating in the world economy outweighed the economic gains from such a course was a choice that had already been made in 1931.

The Mixture of Public and Private

How far did the public/private mix reflect Nazi ideology? It is not hard to find in Nazi writings statements calling for a state socialism. Hitler personally believed that private business had failed. "The role of the bourgeoisie is played out," he claimed. The captains of industry were "gullible fools."[38] In 1936, the Four-Year Plan was accompanied by a threat that if private business failed to accomplish the national task, the state might easily step into its place.

In the course of 1933, the institutional framework of German business life was completely reordered: the old interest organization the Reichsverband der Deutschen Industrie was dissolved and replaced by a *Reichsstand* (Reich estate). The new professional organizations excluded Jews—and thus marked the first step in the driving of Jews out of German business life.

At the same time, labor politics were completely transformed by the destruction of the free (Socialist) trade unions on 2 May 1933, and the subsequent surrender of the Christian and liberal unions. The economic consequences of these political steps ruled out a repeat of the wage push that had occurred in the later 1920s, and had then severely reduced the profitability of enterprise and in general weakened Weimar's economy. For instance, as late as 1935–36, when parts of the economy showed signs of overheating, real gross hourly earnings for the iron and steel industry actually fell.[39]

As the old professional organizations, and the labor unions, collapsed, it seemed inevitable that the state should move into the vacuum and that the state's power should grow. Yet, until 1936, the Nazi state made little use of its new-found strength.

The first problem as to the legitimate scope of political activity in the economy concerned the banking industry. As a consequence of the collapse of 1931 and the rescue attempts of the Brüning government, a large part of the capital of German banks was owned by the state: 91 percent of the Dresdner (merged with the Danat Bank), 70 percent of the Commerzbank, and 35 percent of the Deutsche Bank. The Conservative (DNVP) economics minister Hugenberg suggested placing both the Dresdner Bank and the Gelsenkirchen steel works (another Depression victim that had been rescued by the state) under the management of the Central Reich Cooperative Bank (Reichszentralgenossenschaftskasse) so that both institutions could be used to support bankrupt agricultural enterprises. Hitler refused: "He feared that such a foundation would be criticized either as concealed state socialism or as an attempt of big capital to assert itself." Reforms would "take time": nothing could be done at the moment. Hitler's response captures the tentative nature of Nazi policy in the recovery phase.[40]

The Bank Inquiry of 1933–34 produced, as we have seen, few fundamental changes: it merely established limitations on the size of loans, and limited the number of Supervisory Board seats that any one banker might occupy. Instead of using the banks as a base for the creation of a socialized credit sector, the financial institutions were turned back to the private sector. The Deutsche Bank bought out the Reich already in 1933 by selling off an empty building. In 1936, the Commerzbank used the bourse to secure a privatization, and in October 1937 the Dresdner Bank had completed the process of ridding itself of Reich ownership.[41]

The second major clash as to the place of private business did not occur until 1936–37—it involved the Four-Year Plan, the extent of German autarky, and in particular the use of German iron ore. Here the conflict was settled in a very different—and much more radical—way. It was a political tug-of-war between business and the state, one that German industry lost humiliatingly. Schacht attempted, rather late in the day, to form an alliance with the steel industry of Rhine-Ruhr in his struggle with the other Nazi leaders—Darré, Ley, and now particularly Göring. Schacht believed that business would attempt to resist Göring's plans for autarky and—in particular—the schemes for the creation of a steel works, the Reichswerke "Hermann Göring," with capital raised from the private steel works, and the plans for the development of German iron ores. On 5 August 1937 Schacht sent Göring an ultimatum to stop the slide to autarky: an increase in the domestic production of raw materials would strain industrial capacity, result in a collapse of exports, and make it impossible for Germany to undertake strategically necessary imports. "I am unable," he concluded, "to raise the means for projects whose extent and duration are as difficult to ascertain as their effectiveness. The provision of banknotes and book money does not mean the provision of raw materials and food. It is impossible either to bake bread with money or to cast cannons with it."[42] Schacht also drafted a memorandum that was presented by Albert Vögler of the Vestag to other steel industrialists. But in a dramatic meeting on 24 August 1937, and after very obvious pressure had been applied by Göring, the united front of Rhine-Ruhr business crumbled. Business gave in, Schacht's policy was abandoned, and he had little choice except to give up the Economics Ministry.[43] At this stage it was clear that the conservative phase of Nazi policy-making had come to an end.

Conclusion

The verdict on the early period remains surprising. Until 1936, the evidence supports the conclusion that Nazi policy-makers had—in Knut Borchardt's phrase—limited *Handlungsspielraum* ("room for maneuver"). A rather unadventurous and conservative policy, following the lines laid down by previous governments' responses to the world depression, coincided with a staggering economic recovery. From January 1933 to July 1935, recorded employment rose from 11.7 million to 16.9 million.[44] It is remarkable that a return to virtual full employment should occur within the confines of a policy still dominated by the preconceptions and prejudices of the Depression Era. The implication is that any government could have reaped the rewards that the Nazis harvested with such propagandistic insistence, or that—as regards economic policy—"it did not have to be Hitler" to produce recovery.

Yet Nazism made very powerful claims to have inserted its ideology into everything, including the economy. At the beginning of 1935, the *Völkischer Beobachter* boasted: "All these capitalist institutions have received a new foundation. The system is an instrument in the hands of the politicians. Where capitalism still believes itself untouched, it has already been harnessed to politics."[45] How do we reconcile radical claims of this kind with other observations on how little had changed? In 1939, C. W. Guillebaud concluded:

> It would not appear that, in adopting this policy, the Germans were governed by considerations based on economic theory and analysis, but rather by the necessities of the situation in which Germany found herself in 1933. . . . [T]here is no evidence to show that the original policy was influenced at all by abstract theories. Insofar as there could be said to have been an economic theorist of early National Socialism, Herr Gottfried Feder, who belonged to the extreme left-wing of the Party and subsequently fell into disfavour and obscurity, would seem to have the best claim to the title. Dr. Schacht has been the financial genius of the new economic system, but the agricultural and industrial controls have mainly been worked out empirically by the civil servants and administrators, with some regard to war-time methods, e.g., those developed in England in 1917–18.[46]

Nazi economics may initially be described as the extension of something rather nonideological: a reaction to the Depression in the context of a controlled trade economy. As a consequence of the world economic crisis, Germany was isolated from the problems it had encountered when it had, in the 1920s, attempted to integrate itself into the world economy. After 1935–36, this gave way to a rearmament economy in which the room for political influence was much greater. Under the Four-Year Plan, the scope for state direction of investment increased, and Germany became a state-planned economy.

Governments in depression have less room for maneuver, and less space for the intrusion of political ideology, than governments wrestling with recovery and economic success, when more options become available. At the beginning of the Nazi dictatorship, the scope for the application of ideology in economics was severely limited. It may be that the "primacy of politics" (Tim Mason's phrase) can only be established in favorable economic circumstances. On the other hand, a movement as intensely ideological as National Socialism could not bear to admit the extent of the limitations it faced, and so dressed up conservative policies in populist and lurid propagandistic guises.

Historians have wondered how to assess the workings of economic policy in the Third Reich. In a remarkable passage, Peter Hayes presents a graphic and vivid analogy:

> It is perhaps accurate to say that, to German industry, the emergent economic system was still capitalism, but only in the same sense that for a professional gambler poker remains poker, even when the house shuffles, deals, determines the ante and the wild

cards, and can change them at will, even when there is a ceiling on winnings, which may be spent only as the casino permits and for the most part only on the premises.[47]

Yet by 1933 this was already a familiar scene. Weimar's economy had already been highly politicized. Furthermore, the politicization of the economy, and the association of successful politics with economic triumph, represent one of the reasons for the Nazi response, and for the insistence with which it pushed its propaganda image.

At the London Conference (July 1931), which recommended a voluntary freezing of credits to Germany in the wake of the financial crash, the prominent German banker Carl Melchior spoke to the state secretary in the Finance Ministry, Hans Schäffer, in the tranquil setting of St. James's Park:

> What I have just experienced means the end of a way of life, certainly for Germany, perhaps also for other people. Today we have renounced the rules on which rest economic relations between peoples. That means that in the future common values are no longer in force. These disturbances will extend to other areas and I fear that those who experience this will see things of which today no one has any idea. Even the actors who will be called to play in this drama today still know nothing of it.[48]

What more perspicacious interpretation of 1931 could have been made?

The German economy as it emerged out of the economic crisis and the breakdown of 1931 was susceptible to a great deal of political and bureaucratic pressure. The Nazis did not—it hardly needs to be pointed out—inherit a well-running market economy and then proceed to turn it into state-dominated command system. Instead they added layers of regulation and regimentation onto an already extensively regulated and regimented system.

The contrast between Nazi economics and Weimar control during the 1920s can be reduced to two major breaks in continuity. The two structural changes that molded the shape of the "Nazi economic recovery" (which was in fact already underway in 1932) are, first, the control of wages and the destruction of the labor movement, which removed the wage pressure experienced by the 1920s economy whenever output expanded; and, second, the dedication to cutting Germany off from the world economy through the instruments of frozen debts, trade regulation, and an overvalued exchange rate. Both of these "innovations" can hardly be said to have come from Nazi ideology: they had been elaborated as a bureaucratic/governmental response by the Brüning government in the second half of 1931. It was then that the rules of the capitalist game were fundamentally altered.

Notes

1. For instance, H. Priester, *Das deutsche Wirtschaftswunder* (Amsterdam, 1936).

2. M. Wolffsohn, *Industrie und Handwerk im Konflikt mit staatlicher Wirtschaftspolitik? Studien zur Politik der Arbeitsbeschaffung in Deutschland, 1930–1934* (Berlin, 1977), pp. 62 and 101.

3. See L. Grebler, "Work-Creation Policy in Germany, 1932–35," *International Labour Review* 35 (1937): 329–51 and 505–27; K. Schiller, *Arbeitsbeschaffung und Finanzordnung in Deutschland* (Berlin, 1936); R. J. Overy, *The Nazi Economic Recovery* (London, 1982); and R. J. Overy, "Heavy Industry and the State in Nazi Germany: The Reichswerke Crisis," *European History Quarterly* 15 (1985): 313–40.

4. H. Köhler, *Arbeitsdienst in Deutschland: Pläne und Verwirklichungsformen bis zur Einführung der Arbeitsdienstpflicht im Jahre 1935* (Berlin, 1967), p. 250.

5. Overy, *The Nazi Economic Recovery*, p. 261; Wolffsohn, *Industrie und Handwerk*, p. 48.

6. *Völkischer Beobachter*, 6 April 1932. On the fear of inflation in general, see K. Borchardt, "Das Gewicht der Inflationsangst in den wirtschaftspolitischen Entscheidungsprozessen während der Weltwirtschaftskrise," in G. Feldman, ed., *Die Nachwirkungen der Inflation auf die deutsche Geschichte* (Munich, 1985).

7. Proclamation of 5 September 1934 in M. Domarus, *Hitler: Reden und Proklamationen, 1932–1945: Kommentiert von einem deutschen Zeitgenossen* (Munich, 1965), p. 448.

8. H. A. Turner, Jr., ed., *Hitler aus nächster Nähe: Aufzeichnungen eines Vertrauten, 1929–1932* (Frankfurt, 1978) pp. 332–33.

9. K. E. Born, *Die deutsche Bankenkrise: Finanzen und Politik* (Munich, 1967), p. 152.

10. Bundesarchiv Koblenz (BAK) R2/13682. Proceedings of Bank-Enquete, 6 September 1932 session.

11. Bank of England (BoE) OV34/5, 6 October 1933 and 17 November 1933. G. H. Pinsent's notes on interviews with Schacht.

12. BAK R2/13683, Dreyse on 24 November 1933, Kauffmann on 29 November 1933.

13. *Die deutsche Volkswirtschaft 1933*, p. 554. F. Blaich, "Die 'Grundsätze nationalsozialistischer Steuerpolitik' und ihre Verwirklichung im Dritten Reich," in F. W. Henning, ed., *Probleme der nationalsozialistischen Wirtschaftspolitik* (Berlin, 1976), pp. 99–100.

14. W. A. Lewis, *Economic Survey, 1919–1939* (London, 1949), p. 96.

15. BAK R2/21781, July 1939, "Entwicklung der Ausgaben in den Rechnungsjahren 1934–1939." See also Overy, *The Nazi Economic Recovery.*

16. R. J. Overy, "Unemployment in the Third Reich," *Business History* 29 (1987): 272.

17. BoE OV34/6, 11 March 1935, Overseas and Foreign Debt Memorandum: "The Export Problem"; Pinsent's account of 22 July 1935 interview with Schacht.

18. D. P. Silverman, "National Socialist Economics: The Wirtschaftswunder Reconsidered," in B. Eichengreen and T. Hatten, eds., *Interwar Unemployment in Historical Perspective* (The Hague, 1988).

19. R. J. Overy, "Cars, Roads and Economic Recovery in Germany, 1932–1938," *Economic History Review* 28 (1975): 466–83. K.-M. Ludwig, *Technik und Ingenieure im Dritten Reich* (Düsseldorf, 1974), p. 333.

20. J. J. Lee, "Policy and Performance in the German Economy, 1925–1935: A Comment on the Borchardt Thesis," in M. Laffan, ed., *The Burden of German History, 1919–1945* (London, 1988), p. 141. See also S. Lurie, *Private Investment in a Controlled Economy: Germany, 1933–1939* (New York, 1947); G. Spenceley, "R. J. Overy and the Motorisierung: A Comment," *Economic History Review* 32 (1979): 100–106; and C. S. Maier, "The Economics of Fascism and Nazism," in idem, *In Search of Political Stability: Explorations of Historical Political Economy* (Cambridge, 1987).

21. Overy, *The Nazi Economic Recovery*, p. 49. There is a general issue involving how statistical material on recovery should be presented. Some commentators claim that "the significant variable is not whether 1935 investment and employment had reached 1929 levels; it is the increase over Depression levels." Maier, "The Economics of Fascism and Nazism," p. 99. If we are concerned with demonstrating ways in which policy contributed to structural economic change, a comparison of the economy *at equivalent levels of employment* is unavoidable. Any depression will show a large drop in producer goods (usually including construction), and in the recovery phase there is a correspondingly larger percentage increase in such industries even if only to return to the *status quo ante*. Such figures illuminate neither the intention (if any) behind government policy nor its impact on economic structure.

22. E. Wagemann, *Konjunkturstatistisches Jahrbuch 1936* (Berlin, 1935), pp. 49–50.

23. Lee, "Policy and Performance," following the interpretation of Peter-Christian Witt, "Finanzpolitik als Verfassungs-und Gesellschaftspolitik: "Überlegungen zur Finanzpolitik des Deutschen Reiches in den Jahren 1930 bis 1932," *Geschichte und Gesellschaft* 8 (1982): 400–401.

24. "Die volkswirtschaftlichen Investitionen, 1924–1934," in *Statistisches Handbuch von Deutschland, 1928–1946* (Munich, 1949), p. 604.

25. Ibid., p. 605, and Lurie, *Private Investment*, p. 23. Lurie shows

rather lower figures for private investment, and they affect his argument. He apparently did not have available the Länderrat figures that are published in the *Statistisches Handbuch*.

26. H. James, *The Reichsbank and Public Finance in Germany, 1924–1933* (Frankfurt, 1985), pp. 215–18.

27. BAK R11/1365, 23 March 1932. RDI Handelspolitische Kommission, and 11 March 1932, RDI memorandum.

28. BoE OV34/6, C. Rogers 3 August 1934, "memorandum on a visit to Berlin."

29. Historisches Archiv der Gutehoffnungshütte 400101251/Ob, 3 July 1932, Reusch to Warburg.

30. Midland Bank Archive, 30/207, 13 October 1933, W. F. Crick, "Report on a Visit to Germany."

31. H. Rauschning, *Gespräche mit Hitler* (Zürich and New York, 1940), pp. 195–96; and Turner, ed., *Hitler aus nächster Nähe*, p. 401.

32. BAK R58/1127, 5 March 1935, Düsseldorf Gestapo Report.

33. G. Schmidt, *England in der Krise: Grundzüge und Grundlagen der britischen Appeasement-Politik* (Opladen, 1981), p. 223.

34. G. Kroll, *Von der Weltwirtschaftskrise zur Staatskonjunktur* (Berlin, 1958), p. 492.

35. Wagemann, *Konjunkturstatistisches Jahrbuch 1936*, pp. 283 and 289.

36. BoE OV34/5, 17 November 1933, Pinsent's memo on interview with Schacht; OV34/7, 8 November 1935, Phipps report. W. E. Dodd, Jr., and M. Dodd, *Ambassador Dodd's Diary* (London, 1941), p. 185.

37. Institut für Zeitgeschichte, ED 172/72, 30 September 1936, Goebbels diary entry (note that the printed version edited by Elke Fröhlich contains a misprint in this entry: *abwarten* in place of the correct *abwerten*).

38. Rauschning, *Gespräche mit Hitler*, pp. 26 and 44.

39. BAK R43II/541, Lohnerhebungen. For example: from the summer of 1935 to the summer of 1936, effective gross hourly earnings for skilled metalworkers rose from 95.6 Pf to 98.3 Pf, but fell for pharmaceutical workers from 101.7 Pf to 100.5 Pf; effective hourly wages for the iron and steel industry fell from the winter of 1935 to the summer of 1936 from 92.0 PF to 91.8 Pf.

40. BAK R43II/244, 2 February 1933, Wirtschaftspolitischer Ausschuss.

41. M. Pohl, *Konzentration im deutschen Bankwesen, 1848–1980* (Frankfurt, 1982), pp. 398–403.

42. Text in Kroll, *Von der Wirtschaftskrise*, p. 521.

43. M. Riedel, *Eisen und Kohl für das Dritte Reich* (Göttingen, 1973), pp. 208–26; Overy, "Heavy Industry and the State in Nazi Germany," pp. 313–40.

44. Wagemann, *Konjunkturstatistisches Jahrbuch 1936*, pp. 12 and 16.

45. Quoted in A. Barkai, *Das Wirtschaftssystem des Nationalsozialismus: Der historische und ideologische Hintergrund, 1933–1936* (Cologne, 1977), p. 109.

46. G. W. Guillebaud, *The Economic Recovery of Germany* (Cambridge, 1939), pp. 215–16.

47. P. Hayes, *Industry and Ideology: IG Farben in the Nazi Era* (Cambridge, 1987), p. 79.

48. Hans Schaffer, "Carl Melchior," manuscript.

7

Rationalizing Industrial Relations: A Debate on the Control of Labor in German Shipyards in 1941

TILLA SIEGEL

If industrial relations are defined as relations between the organizations that represent the interests of capital and labor, it is actually a contradiction to speak of industrial relations in Nazi Germany. The Labor Front, which was created in May 1933 after trade unions had been destroyed, developed into an organization that was far from resembling a trade union. While it did try to influence government labor policy and infringe on managerial autonomy within the plant, the role allotted to the Labor Front in the Nazi labor order was neither that of a collective bargaining institution nor that of an authority that regulated working conditions.

Though there was no autonomous organization of labor, such organizations did exist for capital, notably the Reichsgruppe Industrie (Reich Group Industry—RGI), which represented specific business interests. However, the Nazi labor order prescribed by the "Gesetz zur Ordnung der Nationalen Arbeit" (Law for the Ordering of National Labor—AOG) in January 1934 stipulated that there was to be no form of collective bargaining over working conditions, and thus also no employers' organizations. Instead, within the plant working conditions were to be regulated according to the leader-follower principle, the employer being the "leader of the plant." The more general regulation of working conditions fell into the province of the Ministry of Labor.

This institutional setup left no room for industrial relations in the organizational sense. In fact, it aimed at eliminating them in order to "finally overcome the class struggle." However, industrial relations in the loose, unorganized sense of the term persisted as a conflict-ridden problem in Nazi Germany. As Timothy Mason and many in his wake have shown, the mere act of authoritarian will—accompanied by repression and propaganda—was not enough to ensure industrial peace or, viewed from the other side, to contain the working class to the extent the Nazi regime hoped when destroying trade unions. Labor policy on the part of the government, the Labor Front, and management remained a process of muddling through by any available means.

The more recent debate on the history of the working class in Nazi Germany has concentrated primarily on the specific Nazi use of terror, ideology, and propaganda to integrate workers into the *Volksgemeinschaft*, and on how the regime was at times compelled to improve working conditions in order to prevent social unrest from threatening rearmament and war production. This debate has largely been shaped by the idea that the irrationality of Nazi ideology and of the party often collided with the rationality of big business and the military. This essay, on the other hand, aims to show that, on all fronts—government, Labor Front, and management—the politics of "industrial peace" in Nazi Germany increasingly resorted to very "rational" managerial concepts that had already been well developed in the "rationalization movement" of the Weimar Republic, and that were well known in the United States. These concepts were also later to become important features in industrial relations in the Federal Republic of Germany. They are comprehended by the more general and fashionable term "Fordism."

Instead of tracing the development of labor policies throughout the existence of the Nazi regime, this essay will focus on a debate that took place within the regime in 1940–41, in which several means of increasing the efficiency of labor in the shipbuilding industry were discussed. A practical reason for using this debate as an illustration is that it is extremely well documented. This alone, of course, is not sufficient reason, especially since it was not in itself a spectacular debate. However, it also illustrates well the way in which labor policy in Nazi Germany was conducted. Further, it inaugurated new strategies for increasing the efficiency of labor that, little more than a year later, were prescribed for the entire armament industry. Thus, the "Investigation of the Wage and Working Conditions of the Shipbuilding Industry" of early 1941 is taken here as a starting point for reinterpreting some central features of labor policy in Nazi Germany, namely: the decision-making process within the regime; the problems of wage and price control, of labor deployment, and of increasing the efficiency of labor; and, finally, the measures adopted to cope with these problems. Of course, one significant feature of labor policy at that time, and of the debate under review, was that although it was motivated by some unrest among workers, it was conducted behind the scenes. All letters, minutes, and reports cited below were classified as secret or at least confidential. [1]

Like other armament industries in Germany by the end of the 1930s, the shipyards had little problem in "marketing" their products: the state (here the Navy) was an excellent and insatiable customer. On the other hand, armament industries did compete with each other as far as their supply of labor and raw material was concerned. In our case, it was competition with the aircraft industry that triggered the debate in question. The aircraft industry enjoyed the special protection of Göring, who, in his wide collection of high-ranking offices, served as head of the Ministry for Aviation and, in the early war years, was chief of the Council for the Defense of the Reich *(Vorsitzender des Reichsver- teidigungsrates)*; he was also commissioner for the Four-Year Plan *(Beauftragter für den Vierjahresplan)*. In this capacity Göring saw to it that the aircraft- producing industry was privileged, not only in the allocation of raw materials, but also with respect to permission to pay relatively high wages and special bonuses in order to attract sufficient workers from other plants. From a Septem- ber 1939 Hitler order *(Führerbefehl)*, which considerably stepped up the demand for submarines and which was followed by preparations for operation "Sea Lion" (the invasion of England), it might be thought that the shipbuilding industry was privileged in a similar way. However, in 1939 and 1940, Admiral Raeder repeatedly asked Hitler for permission to increase the country's submarine- producing capacity and "replenish" the deficit of labor that was already hamper- ing the production of submarines. [2] Hitler, while giving this permission in July 1940, regarded operation "Sea Lion" as no more than a last resort in case England was not "willing to be peaceful." He decided to wait to see what effects an intensive air war would have on England. [3] While the shipbuilding, and especially the submarine-building, industries were left to work with what they had, the intensification of the air war against England led to a "crash program" to step up production in the aircraft industry.

The features of this "crash program" were described in a report on the Heinkel aircraft plant in Rostock: in place of forty-five airplanes per month before the program, in September 1940 the Heinkel plant produced ninety-two aircraft. The output in October was similar. This impressive increase in produc- tion was said to have been achieved by the existing work force working overtime. Whereas previous overtime amounted to 5 to 10 percent of all hours worked, in September and October it reached 22 percent—fourteen to eighteen hours at a stretch—and this without any decline in efficiency. During the "crash program," workers received special rations, including the much-coveted coffee and a free dinner with a glass of apple juice. Weekly incomes also rose considerably because of the longer workdays and extra pay for overtime. In addition, the Ministry of

Aviation offered special bonuses, which for the Heinkel plant amounted to a total of a half million RM per month. In September, Heinkel set this sum aside for the construction of recreation facilities. (The fact that two other aircraft-producing plants in the vicinity, Arado and Bachmann, had paid out the bonus in cash is reported to have caused "considerable disgruntlement" among workers at Heinkel. Thus, "it was inevitable" for Heinkel to distribute the bonus in cash: 35 RM for unmarried workers, and 50 RM for married workers, with an additional 10 RM for each minor in the family.[4])

While the Ministry of Aviation and the managers of the aircraft plants seem to have been pleased with the results of the "crash program,"[5] it made their counterparts in the Navy and in some shipyards quite unhappy. On 22 November 1940, the Armament Inspectorate (Rüstungsinspektion) for Rostock reported that the "crash program" at Heinkel and Arado had led to "disaffection and grievances" at the Neptun shipbuilding plant which was also located in Rostock. The bonuses, on top of already relatively high wages and good working conditions in the aircraft industry, were said to have "naturally" resulted in workers quitting their jobs at Neptun. Although workers were forbidden to change employment, "a man who is really set on quitting will almost always find ways and means to do so." Those who stayed compared their working conditions with those in other area plants, which, in face of the relatively unfavorable conditions at Neptun, had "a very negative effect on the willingness to work and on the mood" of the workforce. On 19 December 1940, the Armament Inspectorate service again warned of the increasing disgruntlement of workers and decreasing efficiency of labor at the Neptun plant. As a solution to the problem, it suggested that special bonuses be paid at Neptun as well—to be allotted hierarchically according to skill, gender, age, and marital status—and that "in the long run untenable wage conditions" be completely revised. The reaction of the High Command of the Armed Forces to these reports was at first rather reserved. The only advice it gave was to contact the Trustee of Labor responsible for that industry.[6]

Admiral Raeder, however, was more active. In the last days of December 1940 he requested that the Ministry of Labor permit a wage increase in the shipbuilding industry, arguing that Hitler had, on 30 December 1940, "ordered that wages in the shipyards be adjusted immediately to those in the aircraft industry." Instead of complying with this request, the Ministry of Labor initiated a discussion of what the Führer order was really about. On 2 January 1941, State Secretary Syrup of the Labor Ministry wrote to the chief of the Reich Chancellery, Lammers, asking what exactly the contents of the Führer order were. Without further information, Syrup added, he saw himself unable to assume the responsibility of adjusting wages in the shipyards to those in the aircraft industry, since this would imply a wage hike of 50 to 100 percent. The wage structure that, according to Syrup, had been upheld with "utmost difficulties" would be disrupted, and the entire wage system would be seriously impaired. In Syrup's opinion, the problem was not that wages in the shipyards were too low, but rather that wages in the aircraft industry were too high.[7]

On the next day, 3 January, representatives of the Navy, the Labor Ministry, the Reich Commissar for Price Control, and the shipyards Blohm & Voss (Hamburg) and Deschimag (Bremen), together with the Special Trustee of Labor for the shipbuilding industry, Völtzer, met in Berlin to discuss "in general the form in which this Führer order is to be executed." At this meeting, Völtzer countered the 30 December 1940 order by quoting a "guideline" issued by Hitler, according to which "any increase in wages that did not result from better performance was nothing but a piece of inflationary paper." Völtzer emphatically opposed any wage increase. He pointed out that in July 1939 most wages in the shipyards had been increased by 10 percent, which in turn had led to wage increases in other industries. On the other hand, Völtzer declared himself unable to lower wages in the aircraft industry without being explicitly ordered to do so by Göring. Obviously, Völtzer did not believe that such an order could be obtained from Göring.[8]

On 7 January 1941, high-ranking representatives of the Army, the Navy, and the Ministry of Labor arrived at an agreement that amounted to a considerable modification of the Führer order of 30 December. While a general increase of wages in the shipyards was to be avoided, extra pay for work on Sundays was to be doubled, and, if possible, some fringe benefits were to be increased. The Navy was to see if it could furnish additional food and coffee from its supplies. The major shipyards were to be privileged in the deployment of labor. Trustee of Labor Völtzer was to investigate the conditions in particular shipyards. It was decided to await the effects of all these measures and to meet again after four weeks to discuss further action.[9]

The procedure described so far, as well as that which followed the meeting of 7 January give occasion to reconsider the role of these Führer orders, which are frequently taken, in accounts of the social history of Nazi Germany, as a decisive factor in the shaping of specific social policies. Considering the dictatorial powers Hitler enjoyed, this line of interpretation is understandable. However, in many particular cases it seems advisable to look more closely behind the scenes of the decision-making process. In our case, one could view the agreement reached on 7 January 1941 as a result of the Führer order in three different ways. Marie-Luise Recker, for example, takes the following stand: "Since Hitler insisted on better wages in the shipyards, a compromise was finally arrived at: A wage raise was rejected, but fringe benefits . . . were considerably improved."[10] While Recker maintains that Hitler requested an improvement in working conditions in the shipbuilding industry in order to secure sufficient labor for the building of submarines, one might also argue that the main objective of Hitler's order, and of the compromise reached afterward, was to appease the unrest reported among workers in the shipyards. On the other hand, in the meeting of 7 January State Secretary Syrup referred to a different "statement by the Führer," to the effect that there should be no wage raise unless it was tied to better performance. It could thus be argued that it was this more general Führer order that led to the decision not to raise wages in the shipbuilding industry.

The point of listing three views of one and the same event is to show that basing an interpretation of actual labor policies on one or another Führer order is a very tricky business, indeed. The debate on working conditions in the shipyards (like, for example, the better-known debate of May–June 1940 over whether women who were not gainfully employed should be conscripted to work in industry) illustrates the point that it was the practice of regime members to support their argument by referring to some Führer order. Sometimes, as was the case with Admiral Raeder, these were obtained ad hoc, specifically to achieve a particular end.

The contention here is that the Führer orders were often treated as merely one of many arguments in a debate, and were rarely the decisive, final factor in the decision-making process. The agreement reached on 7 January 1941 was *not* final; fringe benefits were *not* to be "improved considerably (as Recker assumes), but only "improved if possible." State Secretary Syrup clarified this position in a letter of 12 January 1941 to Trustee of Labor Völtzer, stating that the only improvement to be actually implemented was the doubling of overtime pay for Sunday work, from 50 to 100 percent of regular wages (an improvement that was rescinded soon afterward). As far as other fringe benefits were concerned, Völtzer was ordered to "study" them and to permit improvements only "if necessary," "if need be," and "in the case of possible disaffection."[11] What is more, at the root of the agreement was not merely the regime's tightrope walk between the economic and the social prerequisites of the war economy, i.e., between keeping labor costs low by proclaiming and upholding a wage freeze, on the one hand, and preempting worker opposition by granting better fringe benefits or (in particular cases) increased wages, on the other hand. The *main* task set for Völtzer in the wake of the 7 January meeting was not to study the possibility of wage increases or the improvement of working and living conditions in order to prevent unrest. Rather, it was to investigate working conditions, in cooperation with representatives of the main Labor Front offices, with the "leaders of the plant" (meaning the employers), and with the Labor Front stewards (who were the main functionaries of the Labor Front within the plant), in order to find ways and means to increase the productivity of the "followers," i.e., the work force.[12]

Although the debate had been triggered by wage discrepancies between the Neptun shipyard and the Heinkel aircraft-producing plant in Rostock, Völtzer investigated more than these two plants alone. He held six hearings of "expert councils" in Kiel, Hamburg, Bremen, Stettin, Danzig, and Königsberg, where managers as well as Labor Front stewards of all the major shipbuilding plants were present. Besides the Heinkel and Neptun plants, the Schichau shipyard at Königsberg and the Navy shipyards at Wilhelmshaven and Kiel were inspected. Völtzer's investigation reflected the fact that the creation of a host of new, and often competing, offices under Nazi rule required extensive consultations when labor-policy decisions for a whole industry were being formulated. A whole array of officials was present at the various consultations: senior Labor Front functionaries, representatives of the Navy, the Commissars for the Defense of the Reich, the NSDAP and Labor Front leaders of the provinces concerned, as well as the regional armament inspectors, Trustees of Labor, and presidents of the Labor Exchanges. While the unrest among workers at some shipyards was obviously behind Völtzer's herding together of all these "experts," he insisted that workers should have no knowledge of the proceedings. At all meetings, Völtzer asked the participants to keep the discussions confidential, so that no unrest and unfounded hopes be provoked among workers.[13]

The main question discussed in all of Völtzer's consultations was "whether and how the wage could be used to increase efficiency at the major German shipyards." However, all additional factors that might conceivably better productivity were also thoroughly discussed, i.e., all forms of fringe benefits, transport, housing, recreational facilities, food, clothing, medical services, and even such incentives as awarding the Distinguished Service Cross to especially industrious workers.[14] According to the minutes of the inspections and hearings of the "expert councils," working and living conditions differed from plant to plant and from region to region. The general verdict, however, was that housing could be "described without exaggeration as being in a catastrophic state," that transport was "at times extremely bad," and that the supply of food and clothing was rather unsatisfactory.[15] While all this did not apply to the living conditions of shipyard workers alone, it was recognized as detrimental to their efficiency as well as to their discipline. The insufficient—and in Wilhelmshaven, Kiel, Lübeck, Stettin, and Gotenhafen even catastrophic—state of the transport systems, for example, was considered by Völtzer a "convenient ruse" for "irresponsible elements" to justify their coming to work late or not at all.[16]

Völtzer was well aware that under wartime conditions the state of housing and transport, as well as the supply of food and clothing, could not be improved in the short run, and the remedial measures he proposed in his final report were rather vague. He asked that more housing be built and that the Navy provide some of the required materials—obviously without expecting that his requests would be fulfilled. In addition, he mentioned that the Labor Front had promised to include the shipyards in its distribution of vitamin pills. But while living conditions were thoroughly studied, although not improved, it was the "hidden reserves of efficiency" within the plants that claimed paramount attention. The discussions prompted by Völtzer's investigation, as well as the remedial measures proposed, centered ultimately on how the performance of workers could be increased.

The simplest way to get more work out of each worker is to increase the hours of work. Since more hours worked also means more paid out in wages, such measures, within certain limits, meet with relatively little opposition on the part of wage earners. This consideration lay at the bottom of the decision of the Ministry of Labor to double overtime pay for Sunday work. With this measure it had hoped on the one hand to increase production, and, on the other hand, to quiet the dissatisfaction caused by the discrepancy between the income of these workers and that of workers in the aircraft plants. In his summation of expert opinions in his final report, Völtzer pointed out, however, that the effect of doubling overtime pay for Sunday work was counterproductive: instead of working more hours altogether, workers would come on a Sunday only to be absent on a weekday when their remuneration would be smaller. [17]

As it was, working hours in the shipyards already amounted to sixty hours per week, and often two or three Sundays per month. Exceptions to the rule were the result of inclement weather conditions and blackout regulations. [18] In Völtzer's consultations, shipyard managers and Labor Front stewards expected "no additional output worth mentioning in any way" from more overtime work. [19] One manager of the Howald shipyard in Hamburg supported the leading Labor Front functionary of that region, who argued that the performance of workers "decreases sharply with an increase in hours worked, the borderline being fifty hours per week." [20] In his final report, Völtzer stated that in the major shipyards the work week was "fully utilized. A considerable increase seems to be impossible without hazarding performance." [21]

Undoubtedly, the reluctance to lengthen the working week was partly due to the general policy of the regime in the early war years, when the mobilization of the economy was tuned to the concept of a blitzkrieg. The final report of the United States Strategic Bombing Surveys after the war came to the "inescapable conclusion" that in those early years "Germany's war production was not limited by her war potential—by the resources at her disposal—but by demand; in other words, by the notions of the German war leaders as to what was required for achieving their aim." [22] However, those war leaders who were more directly concerned with intensifying the utilization of labor seem to have been aware that lengthening the working week is not a very reliable remedy for a shortage of manpower. Not only did workers vote with their feet—that is, stay away from work in spite of increasingly draconian disciplinary measures—but on the job their productivity generally decreased with increased overtime. This applied especially to modern production processes. For example, the fact that the average working week in metal industries was shorter in September 1942 than in 1913–

14 was explained by the Reich Bureau of Statistics *(Statistisches Reichsamt)* as an effect of the shift to industrial production and the concomitant intensification of work. [23]

An inquiry conducted at the end of 1942 by the Army High Command among its Armament Inspections seems to have arrived at the same conclusion. The Armament Inspectorate had reported that lengthening the work week to sixty hours and more had not resulted in a corresponding increase in output. The Army High Command referred in its findings to the experiences of two major industrial plants. One of them, in Saxony, was reported to have introduced a so-called "relaxation week" of forty-eight working hours every fourth week, during which productivity was said to have been "as high as if fifty-nine to sixty hours had been worked as usual." The other plant, in Berlin, had reduced the workday from ten to eight hours in 1941, and thereby achieved a considerable reduction of hours lost through sick leave. [24]

It is interesting to note that the report on this inquiry was mentioned by a high-ranking functionary of the Labor Front, Theodor Hupfauer, [25] in March 1943, when under Albert Speer, the minister for armament and munitions, the war effort of German industry was stepped up considerably. Hupfauer referred to the inquiry conducted by the Army in 1942 in a speech given at the Subcommittee "Man and Performance," which was part of the Labor Front's Reich Chamber of Labor (a platform where leading representatives of industry and of the Labor Front discussed strategies to increase workers' performance). In his speech of March 1943, Hupfauer discussed the advantages and disadvantages of lengthening the work week in view of the increase in output required by the war. Although such a measure seemed tempting, its eventual success was in his opinion "more than uncertain." He mentioned not only the findings of the Army inquiry, but also those of earlier studies made in the United States (by Frederick W. Taylor) and in Great Britain, according to which more was achieved in a workday of eight hours than in one of ten to twelve hours. In view of these findings, Hupfauer pleaded, as the report of the Army had done before, for 54 working hours per week for men and 48 for women. At the same time, he insisted that the final decision on working time must rest with the "leaders of the plants." One reason why uniform regulation of working time for all of industry was not feasible was that only "industrious" workers worked more intensively when their working hours were reduced. Although Hupfauer again referred here to earlier studies made in the United States, his statement also points at the racism inherent in Nazi labor policy. In contrast to "German" workers, i.e., German nationals who were not Jews or racially discriminated against for some other reason, foreign forced labor was considered to be "less efficient." The regime and its organizations, as well as management, therefore did not hesitate to lengthen the working week for foreign workers to the limits of total exhaustion.

Even in the case of "German" workers, considerations of the relation between efficiency and the length of the work week only in exceptional cases led to a reduction of the latter. The average weekly hours worked in German industry reached their highest point, at 49.5 hours, in September 1941, and remained near 49 hours in the years 1940 to 1943. This statistical average is not equal to the scheduled work week, since it excludes the hours lost through sick leave and absenteeism. Furthermore, it conceals divergent tendencies for individual industries and for particular groups of workers. The average for women was generally lower, mainly because many of them worked part-time. The average in many consumption goods industries was lower, too, because, typically, a high percentage of women was employed in them, and because their production and supply of raw materials was restricted. A statistical average of 60 hours worked can be assumed to have been the rule in key armament industries. [26]

In its attempts to strike a balance between the need to make up for the scarcity of labor and the fact that the modern production process, as a rule, requires fit and to some extent willing workers, the regime frequently resorted to "crash programs" such as the one described for Heinkel. In one sector or another of the armament industries, workers always worked extraordinarily long hours during the brief periods of such programs. Especially then the regime relied heavily on "educational measures," since, to quote Hupfauer's 1943 speech, "mentally, the knowledge of how necessary the longer hours are will without doubt have a favorable influence on the total efficiency of a plant. This has been proven by the tremendous performance of the model war plants." To give one example: in March 1943, the "model war plant" of the aircraft producer Messerschmitt in Regensburg had introduced "voluntary" shifts in addition to already long working hours. The workers of that plant were "persuaded" to work more hours not by the inducement of higher incomes, but rather by coercion and propaganda. The extra pay for the additional shifts was given to Robert Ley, the leader of the Labor Front. In April 1944, "regular" weekly working hours at that plant were set at 72 hours for all workers, including women and minors. [27]

It should be noted that "educational measures" for holding the balance between working hours and efficiency at a high level were more than merely propaganda. In 1943, the Labor Front devised an "absentee file," which was meant to help industry register not only the difference between scheduled and actual working hours, but also the particular reasons for workers not coming to work. This file seems to have met with an eager demand on the part of industry. In devising it, the Labor Front was also in tune with the Plenipotentiary for Labor, Fritz Sauckel, then responsible for the Labor policy of the Nazi regime, who had issued several decrees penalizing slowpoking and absenteeism. [28]

Complaints about the poor discipline of workers were frequent throughout the war. The shipbuilding industry was no exception to this rule. In Völtzer's 1941 investigation, shipyard workers "dedication to work" was not considered to be very high. It was especially the conscripted workers who bore the brunt of the critique. Since they were hit hardest by the shortage of housing and frequently suffered a loss of income in comparison to their former jobs, many of them tried to get away from the factory to which they were allocated by staying away from work or by showing poor discipline on the job.[29] Even more than the impaired discipline of conscripted workers, it was the general "tempo of work" that gave Völtzer and his experts quite a headache. In his final report, Völtzer stated that the "low productivity" and "calmer tempo of work" must be seen as specific to shipyards. Their production was spread over a large area and was thus harder to supervise than in other sectors, where workers were confined in buildings. In particular, the long journeys to work sites in the open air offered many "possibilities to sidle off." The remedies proposed were permanent rationalization of the plant and increased supervision, control, and "education." With respect to supervision and control, the shipyard managers were confronted with difficulties common to Germany industry in general. The scarcity of labor resulted, too, in a scarcity of supervisory personnel, and the control and "education" of workers was made especially difficult by the fact that "nowadays followers were a motley mix."[30]

The strategies proposed by Völtzer were influenced by still another difficulty in increasing disciplinary control over the "followers," even if it was not explicitly mentioned. This was the difficulty of getting the utmost productivity out of workers without alienating them too much. It was not only the regime that had a political interest in balancing the economic and social demands of the war, i.e., efficient armaments production *and* a contained level of dissatisfaction. Employers, too, knew very well that with regard to actual output, coercion was a very dubious alternative to other means of inducing "dedication to work" in the "followers." Thus, as much as coercion was indeed intensified by governmental authorities, employers, and the Labor Front alike in the course of the war, more subtle means for increasing labor efficiency were applied as well. Here again, the remedy proposed by Völtzer to combat the allegedly poor performance of workers in the shipyards mirrored a general trend observed in the entire armament industry. As a result of his consultations, Völtzer doubted whether increased control over workers and a longer work week would be feasible or effective in raising output. Instead, he strongly advocated a rationalization of the wage system, meaning that the manner in which piece-rate wages were calculated should be modernized and job evaluation introduced. From the former measure he expected an increase of 10 to 20 percent in the efficiency of labor.[31]

In the major shipyards, 80 to 90 percent of the wages were based on piecework. According to Völtzer, the methods used to calculate them were very "obscure."[32] In other words, the time in which a worker was expected to produce a certain number of finished or semifinished pieces in order to receive the base rate was merely estimated. This crude method of determining the relation between wages and "pieces" had always been a point of contention in industrial relations. Piece-rate wages are meant as an incentive for workers to improve their performance. In Germany, as a rule, remuneration rose in accordance with the percentage of pieces produced over the base rate. However, when extra performance exceeded a certain percentage, management took this as an indication that the piece rate was incorrect, and frequently applied the so-called piece-rate scissors, demanding that more pieces be produced for the same base rate. Workers, on the other hand, tended to anticipate the "piece-rate scissors" and took care not to be too effective—or, to put it in their terms, not to raise the degree of their exploitation. They "held back in their performance,"[33] it was alleged, and management felt cheated out of the fruits that might otherwise have been reaped, in the form of increased productivity, as a result of modernizing the production process.

The scarcity of labor, together with the wage freeze promulgated by the September 1939 "war economy decree," had changed the lines of conflict to a certain extent. In the light of the high demand induced by the war, managers had almost no problem in marketing their products, but considerable problems in finding sufficient personnel. Since it was only the base rate, and not extra pay for extra performance, that was subject to the wage freeze, managers could circumvent the freeze by not adapting piece-rate standards to rising productivity—thereby allowing workers to earn more—in the hope that this would keep them from grumbling or, worse, from quitting their jobs.[34] It was the Labor Ministry and its Trustees of Labor who at times ordered managers to cut base rates, in an attempt to increase the efficiency of labor. One often-cited example was a joint action, undertaken for this purpose, by the Labor Front and the Trustee of Labor for Thuringia in 1938–39, which reportedly improved performance in the industries concerned by 25 percent.[35]

In his proposals, Völtzer envisioned not only cutting base rates in German shipyards, but also the introduction of a more modern method of determining piece-rate wages, namely, the REFA method. REFA is the abbreviation for *Reichsausschuss für Arbeitsstudien* (Reich Committee for Work Studies), which had been founded in 1924 under the guiding hand of the Berlin metal industry and had cooperated with the Labor Front since 1935. REFA had been an early advocate of German versions of the Taylorist concepts of scientific management and the premium wage. The REFA piece-rate wage was based on time studies. The number of pieces to be finished in a certain period (usually one hour) for a certain wage rate was calculated by studying the labor process in detail, measuring the time particular workers needed to perform a particular operation, and then relating their performance to an assumed "standard performance," which was defined as being valid "for human labor in general, irrespective of the labor process and individual capacity."[36] This method increased managerial control over workers, who for this reason frequently opposed it. In contrast, however, to the former "obscure" methods of determining piece-rate wages, the REFA method could claim to be more scientific and objective, and thus to produce "fairer" wages. Frederick W. Taylor had already claimed these two characteristics for "scientific management" when he wrote in 1911: "What constitutes a fair day's work will be a question for scientific investigation, instead of a subject to be bargained and haggled over. Soldiering will cease because the object of soldiering will no longer exist." Later, representatives of REFA and even publications of the Labor Front repeated Taylor's ideas almost word for word. [37]

In the debate of 1941 on wages in German shipyards, the Janus face of the time-study piece-rate wage found expression in divergent opinions. Some managers and Labor Front stewards feared the workers' distrust of REFA" and the "resistance of workers to the stopwatch," knowing just as well as Labor Minister Seldte that "nothing decreases efficiency more than unruly workers." On the other hand, representatives of those shipyards that had already introduced the REFA method pointed out that discussions among the personnel had ceased. "Where true times are given, there is no need to discuss." And: "At first, the followers were extraordinarily distrustful when the new calculation of piece rates was introduced. However, since the REFA system is built on an absolutely fair basis, it has been accepted quickly by the followers; some of them now even ask for a calculation of their piece rate according to the REFA system." When, at the end of February 1941, the minister of labor ordered that the REFA method be applied in all major German shipyards, he asked the Labor Front to start a campaign in order to "educate" the workers, or in other words, to convince them that the new method was objective and made for fairer wages. [38]

Also in February 1941, and at the suggestion of Völtzer, the minister of labor ordered that new wage categories be introduced at the Schichau shipyard at Königsberg. As a relatively new shipyard, it had few "regular" workers, and it had therefore experienced great difficulties in bringing the job ratings of conscripted "German" and "non-German" workers, such as Kaschubes, Ukrainians, and Poles, as well as prisoners of war, into accordance with the traditional wage groups. The traditional wage system counted four groups, categorized according to skill and gender. In its place, eight wage grups were introduced and defined—more "scientifically"—on the basis of job evaluation. [39] There was to be no special wage group for women, but their wage rate was set at 75 percent of the rate of male workers in each group. At the same time, the differentials between wage groups were increased in order to give more incentive to the highest-skilled (male) workers. [40]

While the management of the shipyard at Königsberg and the Labor Front stewards wholeheartedly endorsed the new wage system, the top management of the Schichau company only reluctantly agreed to its adoption, fearing negative repercussions in their shipyards at Elbing and Danzig. Equally, managers of the shipyards in the west of Germany entered "a general protest against this innovation . . . because during the war too much unrest among workers might be caused by the new ratings." And, finally, a representative of the Labor Front office "Iron and Metal" stressed that "the Labor Front would not permit such a change in the wage system during the war."[41] In stating this, he spoke not *in principle* against job evaluation. Rather, he followed the general policy of the Labor Front, which at that time was working on a job evaluation system of its own and was trying to prevent the official introduction of the wage systems developed by industrial organizations.

Little more than a year later, in September 1942, Fritz Sauckel, the Plenipotentiary for Labor, ordered a revision of piece rates for the entire armament industry on the basis of the REFA method, and the introduction of the "Lohngruppenkatalog Eisen und Metall" (Wage Group Catalog Iron and Metal—LKEM) that, except for even larger differentials, was identical to the system introduced earlier in the Schichau shipyard in Königsberg. The LKEM was based on a job evaluation system that the Reich Group Industry had published in 1941, and that was subsequently modified to simplify its practical application and to meet certain requests of the Labor Front. It is not necessary to explain again the aims of Sauckel's 1942 "measures to bring order into wages"; they were the same as those described above for the shipyards: maximum efficiency. "Scientific" methods to determine wages were applied in order to improve government control of wage movements and managerial control of workers' performance, and in order to put an end to the "bargaining and haggling" that was rife in the industry even under the oppressive conditions of the Nazi regime.[42]

The purpose of this paper is to discuss not the material results of those measures,[43] but rather how these measures contributed to a rationalization of industrial relations. First of all, it must be noted that the rationalization of wage-setting and intrafirm wage structures probably received its greatest single impetus from government wage stabilization policies during World War II—not only in Germany, but also, for example, in the United States.[44] But job evaluation and, to an even greater extent, time studies had been developed much earlier as managerial strategies to eliminate "waste": waste of material, waste of time, and waste of labor. As to the latter, time studies give management a better knowledge of the labor process and thus reduce the possibilities of workers "holding back in their performance." Job evaluation presupposes a thorough analysis of the task in question, making it easier to put the right worker in the right place. And finally, since both methods make a claim to "science" and "objectivity," they contribute to a rationalization of industrial relations in the sense that wage grievances can be handled, to a certain extent, in a formalized fashion. This statement requires some explanation.

In the eyes of management, wage grievances lead to a waste of labor in many ways. Dissatisfied workers may not work as well; they may waste their time in discussions; they may quit their jobs, which would entail a costly retraining of their replacements; or—even worse and more costly—they may organize and go on strike. Time studies and job evaluation treat grievances over wages, which have always been a major cause of industrial conflict, as if they were a purely "technical" problem. Their underlying assumption is that the competitive mechanisms of the labor market, with or without collective bargaining, or—as in the case of Nazi Germany—even in the presence of state intervention, provide an objective control over the general wage level. The task is therefore to determine scientifically what is a "fair day's work" for a certain wage rate and how the wage rates of individual workers relate to one another within the firm. If a worker is dissatisfied with his or her wage, the complaint now appears not as a matter of conflicting interests between labor and management, but as a matter of whether the wage-setting methods have been applied correctly. Thus there seems to be no reason for intrafirm conflicts over the wage. Time studies hold out to workers the promise of freedom from arbitrary "rushing" by superiors. The promise of job evaluation is that of "equity," an equally powerful argument in the attempts to assure "industrial peace." As two contemporary experts, Samuel L. H. Burk and Eugene J. Benge, claim: "Experience has shown that employees are usually more concerned with equitable comparison of their individual *job rates* with those of fellow workers than they are with the absolute amounts of their salaries and wages."[45]

What remains to be discussed is whether unrest among workers in Nazi Germany was reduced by the argument that scientific methods result in fairer wages. Since very little is known at present about workers' reactions to Sauckel's "measures to bring order into wages," such a discussion has to remain largely speculative. However, the activities of the Nazi regime provide some indication. Although the regime itself was far from being efficient, given its corruption and perennial internal power struggles, it obviously believed that the propaganda of efficiency was a powerful factor in integrating workers into its *Volksgemeinschaft*. Especially the Labor Front, itself an overblown and corrupt organization, increasingly tried to pound into workers' heads that an efficient "follower" was a good "follower." From the second half of the 1930s on, the Labor Front openly professed its intention to turn the *Volksgemeinschaft* into a *Leistungsgemeinschaft*, or "community of achievement." Its social master plan for the period after the "final victory" aimed at a totalitarian rationalization of the entire German society. Even more important, in its practical activities the Labor Front very soon concentrated on increasing the efficiency of labor. It did this not only by strongly advocating "scientific" methods of wage determination and by contributing to a rationalization of the workplace through its "Beauty of Work" office, but also by trying to "rationalize" labor power itself through such Labor Front offices as the office "Vocational Training and Shop Management" and the "Office for Women," as well as through the associated organization "Strength through Joy."[46]

The way in which Sauckel's wage measures were propagated also indicates how strongly the regime relied on the catchwords "efficiency" and "equity" in the later years of its rule. The many newspaper articles, as well as the "education" campaign of the Labor Front, concentrated on explaining in detail the technicalities of the new wage measures and how they would produce fair wages. And, for once, the promise of "equity"—only in the restricted sense of how the rate of one worker related to that of the others—was not meant as a false promise. Even though in practice the lack of trained personnel often led to unjust revisions of incentive wages,[47] the institutions involved in the reform in fact did what they could to have the revisions carried out as correctly as possible. Thus, a manual for managers advised against cutting wage rates by a uniform percentage, even when the "followers" voluntarily agreed to it. Obviously, the authors of the manual, namely the REFA, felt that in the long run the propaganda that workers should sacrifice some of their income for the good of the Volksgemeinschaft was less convincing and more harmful to efficiency than the argument that now—at last—wages were determined on a scientific and objective basis.[48]

On the other hand, the fact that in 1942 "equity" meant that only a small group of skilled workers would be better off, and that most others would have to work harder to earn the same income as before, did not escape the workers' attention. The Secret Service (Sicherheitsdienst—SD) of the SS reported in January 1943 that many workers saw the new wage measure as an attempt to lower their wages and had spoken "according to their different attitudes and special conditions more or less harshly against them." The following statement was said to characterize accurately the attitude of workers:

> Workers have received the announcement of the new incentive wages with great skepticism and distrust. Although most workers still have no knowledge of the size and importance of those wages, they do scent in the whole *new wage system a kind of sweat and Stakhanov system*. They are afraid that now the last remaining drop of energy will be squeezed out of them.

In order to pacify the "extraordinarily deep distrust" among workers, the SD concluded that propaganda should be intensified even more, "to make workers understand that the present measures were not tantamount to the application of the 'piece-rate scissors' but were rather a correction that resulted from technical improvements, and that were meant to increase the efficiency of the war economy."[49] It would be mistaken to infer from this last statement that the regime or even the SD had become any more lenient by 1943. Quite the contrary was true. But it does illustrate that in internal debates on how to fashion propaganda to bolster outright coercion, the "propaganda drums" were not considered to be very effective any longer. As the SD reported in May 1943, even one of the famous all-out appeals for efficiency issued by Robert Ley, leader of the Labor Front, had shown that "it was hard to reach and enthuse the mass of the hard-working followers, because they are extraordinarily sober-minded in the everyday conditions of wartime life, and in their assessment of the situation they accept only downright facts."[50]

Judging by the immediate postwar years, the idea that the incentive wages introduced during the war were "Stakhanov systems" seems to have carried the day among workers. This was not true, however, for many officials of the newly created trade unions. They made considerable, and successful, efforts to overcome the distrust workers felt, especially about the REFA-method. When the REFA was reestablished again in 1950, it was with the participation of the trade unions. The job-evaluation system of the LKEM remained predominant in the metal industry, to be superseded only by more sophisticated job-evaluation systems. Trade unions cooperated in the development of those systems, as well as in the introduction of similar ones in other industries. The argument of the unions was that scientific and formalized wage structures and rate settings in incentive wages ensured equity and protected workers against arbitrary wage cuts, especially in times of crisis. If somebody had asked their opinion about the fact that those systems had been strongly favored by the Nazi regime, trade union officials and soon most workers would probably have replied that this constituted a critique of the way those systems had been applied, but not of their underlying principles. The principle of reducing the main focus of industrial relations—the wage—to the status of a technical problem, of making efficiency the major yardstick for one's income, and, indeed, of making it the major yardstick for measuring individual achivements as well as those of the society, remained largely unquestioned for a long time.[51] Although a similar development can be observed, for example, in the United States, it appears that the Nazi regime, rather than casting doubt on the beneficial effects of these principles, gave a strong impetus to the tendency to seek in technocracy the solution to social conflicts of interest.

Notes

1. The several hundred pages documenting this debate can be found in the archive of the Institut für Zeitgeschichte (IfZ) in Munich: MA 190/I. My article is based on research carried out for a history of governmental and managerial labor and wage policy in Germany from 1933 to 1945. Tilla Siegel, *Leistung und Lohn in der nationalsozialistischen "Ordnung der Arbeit"* (Opladen, 1989).

2. Raeder applied to Hitler for better production conditions in submarine production on 10 October, 1 and 22 November, 8 December 1939, and on 26 January, 20 June and 31 July 1940. IfZ Munich, MA 10/I fol. 11ff., 33, 41, 50, 93, 150, 153, and 196.

3. Ibid., fol. 199 (of 13 August 1940).

4. Investigation of wages and working conditions at the Heinkel plant, Rostock; IfZ Munich, MA 190/I, fol. 720160f.

5. Workers at Heinkel were possibly not quite as happy. In October 1938 the "Deutschland-Berichte" of the Social Democratic Party in Exile reported that the "mood" in the plant was not very good—in spite of relatively favorable wages and bonuses. Almost every day people were arrested and imprisoned by the commander of the company police and firemen. Some were released after one or two days, others were given to the Gestapo. The plant was said to be riddled with spies of all kinds. "The whole atmosphere under which one has to work here is oppressing." Deutschland-Berichte der Sozialdemokratischen Partei Deutschlands (Sopade) (1938. Repr. Frankfurt a.M., 1980), p. 1093.

6. Letters of the Armament Inspectorate for Rostock to the High Command of the Navy, 22 November and 19 December 1940; IfZ Munich, MA 190/I, fol. 720354f. and fol. 720351. Letter of the High Command of the Army to the Armament Inspectorate for Rostock, 30 December 1940; ibid., fol. 720341.

7. Letter written by Syrup to Lammers on 2 January 1941, IfZ Munich, MA 190/I, fol. 720316ff.

8. Note on the meeting at the Headquarters of the Navy in Berlin, 3 January 1941. From the end of 1938 until September 1939, the Trustee of Labor had already ordered that piece-rate wages in the aircraft-producing industry be investigated. In some cases they were lowered considerably—at Heinkel, for example, by about 20 percent. IfZ Munich, MA 190/I, fol. 720111ff. and 720117f., respectively.

9. Note on the meeting in the Labor Ministry, 7 January 1941. IfZ Munich, MA 190/I, fol. 720340. See also note on a meeting in the Office for Economic Armament of the Army, 9 January 1941; ibid., fol. 720338.

10. Marie-Luise Recker, Nationalsozialistische Sozialpolitik im Zweiten Weltkrieg (Munich 1985), p. 197.

11. Letter of 12 January 1941, Labor Ministry to Völtzer; IfZ Munich, MA 190/I, fol. 720335ff.

12. Ibid., fol. 720335. It is rather difficult to translate the titles of Labor Front functionaries. The choice of the term "steward" (Betriebsobmann) to designate the main representative of the Labor Front within the plant should not imply that Labor Front stewards played the role of trade union representatives.

13. For example, at the hearing on 23 January 1941 in Hamburg; IfZ Munich, MA 190/I, fol. 720182.

14. Final Report of Völtzer's investigation, dated 15 February 1941; ibid., fol. 720122f. and 720108.

15. Ibid., fol. 720071, 720129, and 720128.

16. Ibid., fol. 720154.

17. Ibid., fol. 720124. Free days were not always tantamount to leisure. Many workers used those days to work in their gardens or little farming plots, an activity that was very important in view of the shortage of food.

18. Ibid., fol. 720071, 720152, 720176, 720192, 720208, and 720270.

19. Ibid., fol. 702208 and 720228.

20. Ibid., fol. 720192.

21. Ibid., fol. 720125.

22. "The Effects of Strategic Bombing on the German War Economy," The United States Strategic Bombing Survey, Overall Economic Effects Division, 31 October 1945, p. 6.

23. Statistisches Reichsamt, "Ergebnisse der amtlichen Lohnerhebungen für März 1943," German Central Archives (DZA) Potsdam, 31.02, Sign. 2890, fol. 98.

24. Inquiry of the Army High Command, 1942, on the question "Equal or better performance after a reduction of working hours"; quoted after a speech given by Theodor Hupfauer at the meeting of the "Reich Chamber of Labor" (Reichsarbeitskammer), "Sub-Committee 'Man and Performance,'" 11 March 1943, pp. 6, 8, and 9; Bundesarchiv Koblenz (BAK), NS 5 I/21.

25. For reference see note 24, above. Hupfauer was the head of the "Office of Social Responsibility" (Amt Soziale Selbstverantwortung), which in the Labor Front was the main office concerned with matters of labor policy. Hupfauer also held an important position among the men who helped Minister Speer increase the efficiency of the German armament industry. In Hitler's will, Hupfauer was designated as future minister of labor.

26. See the U.S. Strategic Bombing Survey, "The Effects of Strategic Bombing," pp. 35 and 215. See also Statistisches Reichsamt, "Ergebnisse," fol. 97f.

27. BAK, NS 5 I/74, Bekanntmachung des Betriebsführers (Announcement of the Plant Manager), 1 April 1943 and 25 April 1944.

28. Hupfauer's speech of March 1943, p. 15. At the same meeting, there was mention of a study conducted at a major company in the electrical equipment industry. Hours lost in that company were reported to have amounted to 20 to 25 percent of scheduled working time. About 10 to 12 percent could be "retrieved" by "appropriate measures" (p. 21). See also Betriebs-Information (published by the Labor Front), no. 2 of 1943; and Tilla Siegel, "Wage Policy in Nazi Germany," Politics and Society 14, no. 1 (1985): 31f.

29. IfZ Munich, MA 190/I (files of Völtzer's investigation), fol. 720152, 720286, and 720180. For other years and industries see also Recker, Sozialpolitik, p. 43 (fn. 100); Timothy Mason, Arbeiterklasse und Volksgemeinschaft (Opladen 1975), pp. 1182, 1204, and 1210; Siegel, "Wage Policy," pp. 31 and 32.

30. IfZ Munich, MA 190/I, fol. 720125 and 720193. In the winter of

1939–40, the Armament Inspectorates for Hamburg and Wilhelmshaven complained that in the local shipyards the performance of young workers (between
twenty and twenty-five years) was "50 percent below the normal level." See
Mason, *Arbeiterklasse*, p. 170.

31. IfZ Munich, MA 190/I, fol. 720129.

32. Ibid., fol. 720125.

33. According to a study conducted in late 1940 by the "Wehrwirtschaft-
und Rüstungsamt" of the High Command of the Armed Forces, this was exactly
what workers in the shipyards did. They were reported to be adjusting their work
speed in order to earn no more than about 135 percent of the base rate. Ibid., fol.
720323.

34. In spite of price controls it was still relatively easy to increase prices
when wage costs rose. Therefore managers were less interested "in achieving the
utmost labor intensity," said a manager of the Howald shipyards in Hamburg.
Ibid., fol. 720190.

35. In 1939–40, piece rates at Heinkel were revised "against the wishes
of the followers, indeed even those of management." This revision was reported
to have led to a considerable increase in output. Ibid, 720323 and 720162f. For
further instances see Recker, *Sozialpolitik*, p. 46; Mason, *Arbeiterklasse*, documents nos. 203 to 212; Siegel, "Wage Policy," p. 20f. For protests by managers
against a cutting of base rates see Recker, *Sozialpolitik*, p. 39.

36. That was the definition of 1943; *Leitfaden für die Lohngestaltung
Eisen und Metall* (published by REFA) (Gera, 1943), p. 107. Today the REFA
admits that a "standard performance" cannot be quantified. Nonetheless, it has
remained the basis for the time-study rate that is still used today in the Federal
Republic. See REFA, *Methodenlehre des Arbeitsstudiums*, pt. 2 (Munich, 1971),
p. 135.

37. Frederick W. Taylor, *The Principles of Scientific Management* (New
York, 1967), p. 142f. See also *Das REFA-Buch* (Berlin, 1928), p. 7; *Jahrbuch
1937* of the Institute for Labor Science *(Arbeitswissenschaftliches Institut)* of the
Labor Front, pp. 183 and 189. For an analysis of the REFA piece-rate wage, see
Siegel, *Leistung und Lohn*, chap. 5.

38. IfZ Munich, MA 190/I, fol. 720223, 720027, 720221f., 720186,
and 720090.

39. Beginning no later than 1939, the Ministry of Labor had initiated
preparations for such a new wage system. DZA Potsdam, 62.01, DAF/Handakte
Hupfauer, Sign. 194, fol. 108. BAK, R 41/57, fol. 4. See Recker, *Sozialpolitik*,
pp. 223ff.

40. IfZ Munich, MA 190/I, fol. 720285 and 720303. For men, the base
rate of the highest wage group in the old system was 119 percent of that of the
lowest. In the new system, the base rate of the top wage group was 132 percent of
that of the third group from the top, and 158 percent of the lowest wage group.

Ibid., fol. 720132f. Usually there was a special wage group for women, which ranged below that for unskilled men.

41. Ibid., fol. 720131f., 720175, and 720300.

42. DZA Potsdam, 31.02, Sign. 3676: "Richtlinien über lohnpolitische Massnahmen zur Herstellung der Lohn- und Akkordgerechtigkeit und zur Leistungssteigerung in deutschen Rüstungsbetrieben" (i.e., the official guidelines to Sauckel's decree of September 1942).

43. They were, to state it briefly, not quite as impressive as Sauckel and representatives of the Labor Front tried to make the public believe. For a more detailed account of Sauckel's "measures to bring order into wages" and their results, see Tilla Siegel, *Leistung und Lohn*, chap. 4.

44. For an account of wage policy in the United States during World War II see *Problems and Policies of Dispute Settlements and Wage Stabilization during World War II*, Bulletin No. 1009, U.S. Department of Labor (Washington, D.C., 1950), esp. chaps. 3 and 4. For a brief account of general trends in wage structures, see Mark W. Leiserson," Wage Decisions and Wage Structures in the U.S.A.," in *Wage Structure in Theory and Practice*, ed. E. M. Hugh-Jones (Amsterdam, 1966), p. 13f.

45. *The Encyclopaedia of Management*, Carl Heyel, ed. (3d ed., New York, 1980), p. 510. For comparison a quotation from an article published in 1937 by the Labor Front: "Every human being has a certain sense of what is just. Everybody will be most likely to be content when, comparing his performance and remuneration to that of others, he can see that he is being treated fairly" (see Siegel, *Leistung und Lohn*, p. 220).

46. See Carola Sachse, *Betriebliche Sozialpolitik als Familienpolitik in der Weimarer Republik und im Nationalsozialismus: Mit einer Fallstudie über die Firma Siemens Berlin*. Forschungsberichte des Hamburger Instituts für Sozialforschung (Hamburg, 1987), vol. 1, esp. chap. 4, section 4; idem, "Industrial Housewives: Women's Social Work in the Factories of Nazi Germany," *Women and History* 11–12 (1987); Tilla Siegel, "Welfare Capitalism, Nazi Style," *International Journal of Political Economy* 18, no. 1 (1988): 82–116; Siegel, *Leistung und Lohn*, chap. 3.

47. This was pointed out in a report of February 1944 by the Secret Service of the SS. See Heinz Boberach, ed., *Meldungen aus dem Reich. Die geheimen Lageberichte des Sicherheitsdienstes der SS, 1938–1945* (Herrsching, 1984), pp. 6356ff.

48. REFA, ed., *Leitfaden für die Lohngestaltung Eisen und Metall* (Gera, 1943), p. 50.

49. Boberach, ed., *Meldungen*, pp. 4730f.

50. Ibid., pp. 5218f.

51. This principle is based on a specific, technocratically defined concept of rationality inherent in the idea of rationalization. In Max Weber's terms,

it is formal rationality, which aims at optimizing the means-ends relationship, without questioning the means or ends themselves. As early as the 1920s, the German "rationalization movement" declared formal rationality to be the norm for rational behavior per se, in industry as well as in public and private life. See Tilla Siegel and Thomas von Freyberg, *Industrielle Rationalisierung unter dem Nationalsozialismus* (Frankfurt a.M. and New York, 1991), esp. chap. 2, section 1 and chap. 5, section 4.

8

The Domestic Dynamics of Nazi Conquests: A Response to Critics

TIM MASON

There is widespread agreement that the war that began in September 1939 was a disaster for Nazi Germany. This was Hitler's own view, clearly expressed at the time.[1] Contrary to the foreign policy axioms laid out in *Mein Kampf* and frequently repeated by Hitler thereafter, the Third Reich found itself at war with Great Britain and the British Empire. Contrary to the "timetable" for military expansion that Hitler elaborated in November 1937, the Third Reich found itself involved in a major European war already in 1939, rather than in the years 1943–45, the period that Hitler seemed to believe would be optimal for large-scale imperial expansion. Hitler's own erratic, confused, and increasingly unrealistic conduct of policy in the ten weeks that followed the British and French declarations of war is but one proof of the extreme seriousness of the new international situation brought about by the German invasion of Poland. The Nazi-Soviet Pact was an expedient that did not make good this damage. The invasion had consequences of an irreversibly damaging nature to the interests of the Third Reich (for example, the future intervention of the United States), which Hitler's prior calculations had ruled out as to be avoided at all costs.

What went wrong? I think it is important to put the question in this way because it is quite conceivable that Nazi domination of Europe and of adjacent subcontinents could easily have been wider, longer, and even more destructive than it actually was. The Third Reich's opportunities to consolidate and extend

its regime of racial imperialism in the late 1930s were very great; these opportunities were put at extreme risk, and soon (December 1941) destroyed, by the
war that Hitler had wanted in 1938, and actually began in September 1939. Why
did Hitler force the pace in this way, disregard his own "timetable," undermine
his own continental and world strategy with respect to the British Empire? Since
my argument is much concerned with the timing of events and decisions, it is
important to note that he was already willing to take this huge risk in September
1938, and would clearly have preferred a war to the Munich settlement.[2]

In the 1970s I put forward, in various forms, the hypothesis that the
accelerating dynamic of Nazi aggression in 1938 and 1939 was strongly conditioned by the *internal* problems of the regime, problems that progressively
narrowed the margins for foreign policy choices and made it increasingly difficult for the regime to wait for the right moment to launch its wars of conquest.[3]
These internal problems appeared as consequences of forced rearmament after
1936—of a rearmament drive that required resources far in excess of those
available in Germany, given the way in which the regime distributed economic
resources. (By 1939 the rearmament targets were far in excess of any conceivable
available supplies, but that is a slightly different argument.) I concentrated
special attention on the labor market and the working class. By the end of 1938
the overheating of the economy had led to a situation in which there were one
million unfilled jobs. This had a wide variety of consequences: new workplace
wage-bargaining; clear signs of a decline in work-discipline and industrial productivity; a growing drift of workers away from poorly paid into better-paid jobs;
and a degree of wage inflation that led to an increased demand for consumer
goods. All of these developments impeded the progress of rearmament—just *how*
seriously they impeded rearmament is one of the questions under discussion. I
originally maintained that these developments did considerable quantitative
damage to the rearmament programs of the later 1930s.[4] I still believe this to be
true, although Michael Geyer has pointed to other, different constraints during
1937.[5]

The Nazi regime responded to these new threats and difficulties in a very
distinctive way. It *did* enact countermeasures to control wages and to direct labor,
but these measures came a good deal later and were applied with less rigor than
was considered necessary by many employers and most experts with practical
responsibilities in these areas. The regime used much less dictatorial power than
it seemed to have at its command. The main reasons for this tentativeness and
uncertainty lay clearly in political fears of a hostile, possibly mass, collective
reaction on the part of the working class. Much impressed by the strike movements and by the alleged collapse of the home front at the end of World War I,
the Nazi leaders felt it necessary to purchase at least the passive acquiescence of
the much-abused German working class. It was for this reason, I argued, that the
labor regimentation of mid-1938 was so late and incomplete, for this reason that

there were very few increases in basic tax rates and food prices, and so on. The main new burden imposed on German workers was a lengthening of the working week, which resulted in substantial increases in weekly earnings (overtime bonuses). But at the same time, in June 1938 and then again in the winter of 1938–39, the regime vastly expanded its armament programs, thus making much more acute all of the contradictions inherent in the situation. These were real contradictions, not just technical problems that could be resolved by more sophisticated organizational and administrative interventions (although there were some of these too). In their essence they raised a fundamental problem of the dichotomy between *means* (the regimentation of people and resources) and *ends* (further rearmament), and thus tended to develop into a deep crisis of the power and legitimacy of the whole regime.

The labor market and relations between the regime and the working class were not the only spheres in which signs of acute economic overstrain appeared during 1938 and 1939. Budgetary problems and the threat of inflation became drastic at the end of 1938. Foreign trade and agriculture also came under heavy pressure, the first as a result of the worldwide recession of late 1937, which restricted Germany's capacity to export (and thus to import vital raw materials), the second, agriculture, as a result of a massive labor shortage and of strict price controls on foodstuffs. In both these sectors too, the government did not intervene in a consistent and rigorous manner in order to allocate resources to the armaments industries and to farmers. In both cases such interventions would have meant heavy sacrifices for the mass of the urban consumers. It is vital to observe that all of these four acute new social and economic problems came to a head at the same time—during 1938. They posed a major new set of simultaneous challenges to a regime that, in political, economic, and administrative terms, was not well prepared to meet them.

As far as we can tell (the sources are not very good, given the verbal conduct of government affairs), Hitler was quite well informed of these new and deepening problems—informed above all by Göring, also by the military leaders, and by the head of the Reich Chancellery to whom many reports on the shortages and economic conflicts were addressed. Hitler's advisers did not speak with one voice. Some suggested slowing down the pace of rearmament and of the rush toward war (Schacht, Darré, and sometimes Göring), others favored forcing through tougher domestic policies (Price Commissar Wagner), and some proposed both of these things at the same time (General Thomas, Göring). Hitler, it seems to me—and this is the crux of my case—stood all of these arguments on their head: to judge from admittedly few recorded statements, he concluded that if the economic and internal political situation really was so strained, this was *in fact* a strong reason for launching military aggression *sooner rather than later.* He began to speak in this sense in November 1937, and half a dozen of his official and informal policy statements between then and November 1939 contain clear allusions to this logic of risking war on account of domestic/economic weakness. There is no space to reproduce all of these statements here.[6] What is striking is their correspondence to the actual situation inside Germany. This reading of Hitler's reasoning fits in with the generally accepted picture of him as a politician for whom defiance and risk-taking were ultimate virtues. The documentation is neither ample nor unequivocal, but Hitler seems to have believed that military conquest would enable the regime to break the chains of immediate domestic bottlenecks and conflicts, and would result in plunder, that is, in the forcible short-term acquisition of resources and manpower that were either not available in Germany, or could be redistributed in favor of the armaments sector only at the risk of great unpopularity for the regime.[7] There is a vital difference between this kind of short-term logic and the long-term goal of *Lebensraum*, to which Hitler was clearly committed.

There was in Hitler's mind a second connection between the urgency of war and the state of domestic affairs, a connection that I did not emphasize enough in my original work: he was constantly worried by the fear that if the period of peace and relative prosperity of the late 1930s were to continue for too long, the German people would lose what he imagined to be their sense of aggressive discipline, militarism, and ideological fervor. People could easily forget, he feared, what the true heroic goals of Nazism were and how many sacrifices they entailed.[8] Ministers, generals, and senior civil servants gave concrete meaning to this piece of Hitlerian logic in that they saw the beginning of war as the crucial opportunity to put the whole economy in order: to cut wages, lengthen working hours, raise taxes, ration foodstuffs and consumer goods, move workers from one factory or city to another by administrative decree, intensify police terror, and so on. In short, they hoped that the emergency of war would make acceptable to the German people a mass of repressive legislation that had long been necessary anyway; that it would restore discipline, sacrifice, and the Nazi sense of communal struggle—for which Hitler yearned but which he feared to impose—to the everyday conduct of economic life. And, in fact, a large number of decrees of this kind were issued in September 1939. Short of total mobilization, the government made a major effort to use the start of the war in this way.[9]

Thus far, in very rough summary, my argument: in 1938–39 either peace alone or war alone could stabilize (or temporarily save) the politico-economic system. Indefinite further forced rearmament within Germany's existing boundaries was not a practical policy option. And war entailed a wild gamble concerning the response of Great Britain and France. I want to stress that it is a domestic, social and economic argument about the timing, and thus about the international constellation, of the start of World War II that leaves Hitler at the center of the stage, personally taking the crucial initiatives and decisions. In this sense it differs a lot from orthodox Marxist-Leninist interpretations, which attach great weight to the economic imperialism of Germany's big financial and industrial combines.[10] In my view it was, rather, the perceived possible breakdown of the whole system of Nazified, militarized capitalism that precipitated events.

Most other historians working in this field have more or less rejected my hypotheses.[11] Direct or, more usually, indirect support for the line of inquiry that I have pursued has come from the research and interpretations of Hans-Erich Volkmann,[12] David E. Kaiser,[13] and Michael Geyer.[14] One part of my argument revolves around the connections that existed between what was going on in German society and what was going on in Hitler's mind, and the importance of these connections for the acceleration of Nazi foreign policy toward war. Most historians, obviously, have focused on Hitler's intentions and calculations, and have argued that not labor shortages, economic bottlenecks, and the risks of mass discontent, but quite other things, were at the forefront of his mind in these years. Three such interpretations call for brief discussion at this point.

I do not want to consider here the school of historiography that sees Hitler as immersed in the relationshp between the week-by-week tactics of diplomacy and his final goals, and that thus tends to suggest that the "wrong" war of September 1939 was in some sense the outcome of a series of diplomatic errors; I simply do not believe that the foreign policy of the major powers, least of all that of Nazi Germany, was "foreign" policy in this narrow meaning of the term. Much more persuasive is the fundamental foreign policy argument that Hitler *never* understood Britain and the British Empire, that his idea of some kind of a division of world power between a Germanized continent of Europe and a sea-based British Empire grew out of a total misconception of British interests, and that the British government (even that of Chamberlain) was bound to become involved in war with Nazi Germany as soon as that power entered on wars of aggression. This line of argument emphasizes not the faulty application in the 1930s of the strategy that Hitler had elaborated so clearly in *Mein Kampf,* but the fact that that strategy was itself founded upon a deep misunderstanding of the basic British need for some kind of balance of power on the continent of Europe. This did not rule out the semi-peaceful revision of some of Germany's frontiers, but it did rule out expansionist wars.

This case, that Hitler fundamentally misconceived British interests, seems to be a strong one. What remains difficult to explain, however, is his failure to read the increasingly clear signs from March 1939 on (at the latest) that he was in fact heading for an immediate war with Britain and the British Empire. The British Parliament ratified the military guarantee to Poland immediately after the signing of the Nazi-Soviet Pact. For reasons that remain open to further discussion, Hitler was quite unable to recognize and to adjust to very clear evidence of the collapse of one of the central axioms of his foreign policy. This blindness and inflexibility in the summer of 1939 are hard to account for. It is difficult to accept that he simply did not believe that the Chamberlain government would go to war—at least, any such belief on his part requires a lot of explanation, given all of the evidence to the contrary that was so easily available. There are some hints in the documentation that a concern with domestic and economic problems played a role in producing this inflexibility.

Two further alternative interpretations of "what was on Hitler's mind" in 1938–39 both stress his sense that the factor of *time* was turning against him. For his biographer Fest, this had the quality of an existential change in Hitler: the collapse within him of the controlled calculating politician, capable of waiting for the right opportunity, and a regression to the impatient, millenarian, and above all violent mob leader of before 1923. The description is sensitive and convincing, but Fest gives no reasons why this change should have occurred in 1938, not earlier, not later.[15] Dülffer at least offers a reason: Hitler, he argues, was increasingly concerned that Nazi Germany was losing its lead in the international arms race, losing its advantage especially from late 1938 on to Britain and the Soviet Union (and he was already casting an eye toward the United States).[16] This trend, it follows, strongly induced Hitler to take great military and diplomatic risks in 1939, to launch a war of conquest before it was too late. (This argument, it should be noted, has less purchase for 1938, when Hitler was already set on war.) That Hitler was preoccupied by the problem of the arms race is beyond doubt, but it brings us back to the question that I posed at the outset: Why was Nazi Germany unable to accelerate further the pace of its own rearmament in 1938 and 1939? This had to do, in part, I would insist, with the regime's inability to allocate its resources consistently and effectively in favor of the armaments sector of the economy, with its efforts to produce both guns and butter, with its need to produce the biggest army in the world *and* to placate its working population with high real wages. These goals had become incompatible by 1938–39.[17] In my view, Nazi Germany needed war and conquest *in order* to go on rearming at a high rate; the evolution of the international arms race and the changing balance of power cannot possibly be dissociated from the basic conditions of production inside Germany. Thus Dülffer's point adds an important dimension to my interpretation, but does not contradict it.

A different criticism calls for extended consideration: that is that my documentary sources, and the way in which I have used them, tend to exaggerate the acuteness of the social and economic crisis in 1938–39. It has been said that I take the documents that describe the details and symptoms of this crisis too much at face value, and that the real situation on the domestic front was less tense, less fragile than I have portrayed it to be.[18] This is not one single criticism, but an argument that contains a series of different points that must be discussed in sequence.

The first such point is perhaps the easiest to identify and the most difficult to assess. It was always obvious that some employers and some procurement agencies deliberately overstated their needs for resources, in the hope that, by "making concessions," they would finally end up with roughly the amounts of raw materials and workers that they could actually use. This was a transparent technique in the struggles over shortages, and the decision-making bodies frequently recognized it as such, but the real problems of urgent bottlenecks remained, and indeed grew, even when these inflated demands had been discounted. Less easy to judge is the possibility that those officials in the economic, labor, and military administrations who advocated more austere policies *may* have used their regular reports to the government in order to draw an especially black picture of the situation, which was one way to get the government to change policies. Similarly, special reports, like Darré's long letters to Hitler, may have given a particularly dramatic picture of those sectors of agriculture in which the loss of labor and the decline of production were most severe.[19] The authors of official memoranda without doubt used selective emphasis as a regular technique of representing interests and of trying to influence policy-making—this is a basic fact of life in bureaucratic infighting. It is very hard to say, however, by how much, quantitatively speaking, the reports really did exaggerate. Industrialists probably tended to exaggerate most of all, but my general impression is that the sources did not overstate the problems by a great deal, and this for three reasons. First, the German civil service and the Army had strong traditions of factual accuracy in their paperwork. Second, by 1938 there were a large number of different agencies, some of them purely Nazi, making reports on the same problems and in some degree in competition with each other—serious distortions by one agency could easily be identified by another.[20] If, lastly, there is no way that this issue can be resolved in general terms and in a final manner, the actual breakdown of the accelerated armaments drive of June—October 1938 strongly suggests that pessimistic reports were accurate. Michael Geyer's highly technical investigation of this episode shows in detail the shambles that ensued when constraints on armaments production were lifted at the end of May 1938. Within five months there were insuperable shortages of iron, steel, nonferrous metals, building material workers, and cash for the new running programs of the armed forces. Major cutbacks were then ordered and implemented with Hitler's assent.[21] This is the evidence of real events, not of routine or special reports.

More subtle, and occasionally more telling, is the argument that the reports on the developing crisis were influenced by the ideologies, by the conservative prejudices and fears of their authors; that army officers, civil servants, and industrialists were naturally inclined always to blame the working class for economic problems, and too often to go in fear of its possible subversive action. For this reason, it has been said, they actually misunderstood some of the realities that they observed. While this was not always the case (officials of the Ministry of Labor and of the War Economy Staff showed some verbal sympathy for the growing exhaustion of the industrial workers), two of my critics have pointed to a good example of such a distortion. I gave some prominence to reports, among others, to one from the managing director of a large mining firm, that the per capita productivity of coal miners was falling considerably in the later 1930s. This was attributed at the time simply to diminishing effort, to a decline in working morale, absenteeism, "the human factor"; and I accepted this upper-class interpretation of working-class behavior. It was at least partly wrong. One main cause of the fall in output in the mines was the failure of employers to recruit young miners and the growing dependence of the industry on older workers who were objectively less capable of great physical exertion.[22]

The fears, repeatedly expressed by conservatives and Nazis, that there might be another 1917–18, another mass movement against exploitation and war, were, clearly, fixated memories and ideological distortions that were not appropriate to the new situation of the late 1930s.[23] The memories and invocations were certainly dramatic and persistent.[24] While I never thought that they were appropriate in a literal sense to the years after 1938, the issue certainly calls for much more careful analysis than I actually gave it. There was obviously a great deal of discontent and economic ambition among the working population, but the leaders of the class had been killed, imprisoned, or exiled, its organizations smashed. Thus the real danger was not that of mass protest movements or open revolts, but rather, as I originally suggested and as Herbst argues systematically, that of the steady disaggregation, disintegration, of the social order and of the fascist disciplines on which it rested: obedience, sacrifice, the work ethic, intense labor on behalf of a Greater Germany.[25] The real danger was that markets and plans would fall apart under the pressures of economic overstrain, labor shortages, and the manifold noncooperation of the working population. Thus it can be argued that, insofar as they fixed their minds on the open class conflicts of 1917–18, the Nazi elite misrepresented to themselves the problems that they actually faced twenty years later. This is no doubt a helpful addition to and revision of my argument, one that gives greater precision to an important issue. The fact remains, however, that the *outcomes*—in terms of tentative social and economic policies and inadequate rearmament—remained the same, *whatever* the reasons or motivations may have been.

But from this point of criticism there follows a further one. If it is true that the real danger facing the regime was that of a disintegration of the social and economic order, then it must be asked: What was the position of other social groups and classes? Is it correct to define the problem as above all one of the conflictual relationship between the regime and the working class?[26] Much research remains to be done on these questions, but it seems fairly clear that many sections of the middle class were also *not* called on to make heavy sacrifices in the interests of the rearmament drive of the late 1930s. Industrial salaries in the private sector (not in the civil service) probably rose faster than wages at this time,[27] and there was a boom in middle-class consumption. On the fate of small entrepreneurs both before and after the beginning of the war the evaluations of the experts seem to diverge somewhat, but the government's attempts to close down small and inefficient workshops and factories in order to release capacities and workers for the big armaments firms were something less than draconian.[28] The upper middle class's most important item of conspicuous consumption, gasoline, remained unrationed before the war, although all the armed services suffered from continuing and serious shortages of fuel. And well-to-do young women found it notoriously easy to get around a decree that required them to perform a year of "duty" in agriculture or in domestic service before entering regular employment or study.[29] It is true that income taxes for the middle classes were raised twice in 1939, and that the corporation tax was steadily increased; and it is true that Germany's farmers were squeezed very hard during 1938 and 1939. But overall it *cannot* be said that the regime paid a special regard to the economic interests of the working class, trying to bribe it alone into passive acquiescence to the drive toward war. Rather, there was a flourishing civilian economy at all levels of society, which put limits to the expansion of rearmament in a whole variety of different ways. In this account the working class was a special case in an overall strategy of political pacification through the means of relative economic well-being. It was a special case because industrial wage earners were so numerous, because they were in such desperately short supply, and because only they were well placed to take collective disruptive action, but the problem was indeed a general one that encompassed the whole society in its relations with the regime. I accept the need to redescribe the domestic situation in Germany in these terms. But it must be noted that to do so involves listing additional types of intervention (against middle-class interests) that the regime did *not* make in favor of the armaments sector of the economy. In altering it, the point actually broadens my argument, does not negate it.

Building on this observation that the problems of administering the Nazi economy were in fact diffuse and heterogeneous, Ludolf Herbst went on to challenge in a fundamental way my proposition that Nazi Germany was indeed "in crisis" in 1938–39. Other historians have cast doubt on the appropriateness of the word "crisis" in general terms, but Herbst threw the whole apparatus of systems theory at the question, demanding that the concept of crisis have a precise, theoretically and empirically verifiable definition. He concluded that the position in Germany did not conform to any such definition, and that my whole argument was thus mistaken. The demand for precise definitions obviously gives rise to a worthwhile, although complex, discussion. I want to confine myself here to four of the component arguments.

First, Herbst insists that the economy was just one of the "subsystems" of the whole system of power, and that it is necessary to examine all the other subsystems in order to assess the extent of crisis. This point can be granted, but I wish to argue for the overriding importance of the economic subsystem. A regime that was about to send its armed forces into war had to be able to equip them properly, and the Nazi regime was not in this position. (See the remarks below on the conflict over strategy in November 1939.) Furthermore, the economy was the arena in which most Germans came into most constant and continuous contact with the demands of the government in these years. But Herbst has in fact very little to say either about the real economy or about economic policy at this time. He denies that the relevant problems were basically social and economic in origin, and he evades the vital question of whether the regime was unable to rearm, or rather chose not to rearm, more intensively.[30] The central fact in my analysis is the *reality* of the massive labor shortage, and of its economic, social, and political consequences. Herbst's approach reduces this, and all the other realities of extreme tensions in the economy, to very general problems of social justice and, above all, of politico-economic management *(Steuerung)*.[31] Management, however, must be measured against actual problems, as Geyer, Kaiser, and I have tried to do. Geyer leaves no doubt that the real economy was in immediate crisis late in 1938. Based on a detailed analysis of the precipitous developments in industry and finance after the allocations to the armed forces were suddenly doubled in June 1938, he concludes that there arose an "economic, armaments, and financial chaos." This took the form of chronic shortages of all the factors of production and of rises in unit costs, as the armed forces competed with each other for nonexistent capacities; this then led to a sudden policy reversal in November, one that gave priority once more to exports and cut the armed forces' demands for steel for 1939 by half. The Reich Treasury was temporarily empty; existing contracts were left hanging in the air.[32] Geyer is unambiguous that in May 1938 "the leadership of the Third Reich quite consciously risked a crisis": "the precarious armaments boom was transformed into an open economic and financial crisis," and there were no administrative solutions to "the short-term and deliberate overburdening of German industry."[33] This was especially acute in the building sector; new munitions and armaments plants remained on the drawing board, and for 1939 the armed forces demanded more building capacity than existed in the whole German economy.[34] Geyer concludes his detailed inquiry thus: "It was a reproduction crisis [of the economic system] under the conditions of Nazi rule. . . . [The] state was not capable of achieving the rearmament of the nation . . . while at the same time guaranteeing private capital formation."[35] This is in economic and military terms a more comprehensive analysis of the same real developments and actual policy decisions that I have tried to document for the labor market and for class relations. Geyer's repeated and precisely documented use of the term "crisis" is notable. On Herbst's own chosen ground of systems analysis the term does not seem inappropriate for this "subsystem" of the Third Reich in the period under discussion.

Second, Herbst strongly advances the view that the regime in 1939 still had unused reserves of power, unused capacities to steer developments and manage problems, and power to intervene with particular new measures or programs in order to alleviate the most pressing difficulties and to stabilize the system. This was true of budgetary policies and credit creation, a point of actual crisis late in 1938.[36] But in the field of armaments the position in 1939 was characterized by a combination of restraints that were dangerous to the actual military (big delays in programs, no stockpiling), and the launching of new mythomaniac programs for the air force and the Navy that could only accentuate the basic problems. This creation of new contradictions does not look like successful *Steuerung* through the successful deployment of unused reserves of power.

Arthur Schweitzer has argued that the government did succeed in reimposing some rudiments of administrative order in parts of the economy during the first half of 1939.[37] Administrative order was an important source of power for the system, as the redeployment of manpower on the occasion of mobilization was to show in September 1939.[38] But the state of the real economy mattered more. Although in this respect a detailed analysis of the months prior to Hitler's decision to invade Poland has still to be done, there is no doubt that the yawning gap between strategic needs and mobilizable resources became greater as Germany's international position worsened. To say this is *not* to underestimate the regime's actual achievements in rearmament, but rather to point to the high degree of economic and political instability that this effort generated. Hans-Erich Volkmann's overall picture of 1939 is one of an economy and of the key economic agencies working in highly straitened circumstances; aside from public finance, the one new measure of stabilizing management that could be deployed was the important increase in trade with the Soviet Union.[39]

With respect to social and labor policies the actual events that took place on the outbreak of war *in no way* bear out the view that the regime possessed unused reserves of power (see below). Finally, any attempt to assess the Nazi regime's latent capacities to draw on new powers every time the crisis worsened must come to terms with Göring's exasperated comment in July 1938: the "Führer wants to take as few decisions as possible."[40] Hitler, the ultimate source of managerial power, was notoriously indecisive in social and economic matters; he usually preferred the soft, less unpopular options, while at the same time demanding more and more weapons. On this central issue, Hitler contradicted himself all the time, leaving his immediate subordinates in confusion. This was a very important element of "system destabilization." The argument, like many in systems theory, must to some degree remain hypothetical, but, contrary to Herbst, I would maintain that the regime had come very near to exhausting its capacities for self-stabilizing interventions, short of war, given the extreme pace of war preparations. It seems to me more likely that the system needed war in order to create new sources of power for itself.

A third point concerning the definition of "crisis" perhaps carries more weight. Is open confrontation an essential component of a true crisis? Herbst seems to insist that the real lines of potential confrontation in Germany on the eve of war were in fact not very clear-cut, that class conflict was too muffled to justify use of the term.[41] As examples of the blurring of these lines there can be quoted many cases of employers who gave in to wage pressure from below, improved fringe benefits and the like, and passed on the costs to the consumer who was usually, directly or indirectly, the state; also cases of employers who engaged in open acts of piracy in the labor market, taking over workers from their competitors with offers of higher pay and better working conditions. In such ways industrial conflict was temporarily forestalled. To this evidence of sporadic collusion between the two classes in industry, Herbst adds the correct observation that parts of the Nazi mass organizations (of the party and the DAF) were not at all happy about rigorous policies of reallocating resources from the civilian to the military sectors of the economy and imposing heavy sacrifices on the working population. The latter were thus faced with employers, some of whom might from time to time appear as allies on specific matters, and with a political regime of which different sections spoke with different voices.

Where was the real enemy? This degree of muddle and confusion, which was to become greater from September 1939 on,[42] acted, it is argued, as a kind of buffer between victims and oppressors, making the victims' sense of injustice less sharp, less well-focused. This historical description is basically accurate in respect of part of the developments in Germany. Concessions to workers, however, did not always lead to satisfaction and greater cooperation; they sometimes made workers more aware of their market power and whetted their appetites for further concessions.[43] And there were clear lines of conflict, too, especially on every occasion that the regime did actually intervene against working-class interests. The formation of clear enemy camps is perhaps too pure a model of "crisis"; much depends on the precise events that one imagines to be necessary for an actual crisis of the system to break out. In the case of Nazi Germany one must clearly think first of a "crisis" *within* the regime, such as that of September–November 1939, rather than of the kind of strike movement that took place in Italy in March 1943. At a more general level, not all historical crises manifest themselves in actual breakdown, revolution, or the clear division of society into enemy camps.[44] For all the elements of confusion, the processes of conflict and of economic and social disintegration that were taking place in 1938–39 constituted at least the preliminaries, the basic ingredients, of a crisis in class relations. And to put it in counterfactual terms, I believe that without war in 1939 the regime would have been compelled to make policy choices that would have brought such a crisis nearer.

This argument is incomplete in that it refers mainly to factory politics. Did industrial discontent indicate a wide-scale, hidden political discontent? In my original work I tended to imply that it did, thus reinforcing the notion of a general crisis. I have since revised this view,[45] which rests on the unsustainable proposition that passive loyalty to the class organizations destroyed in 1933 was still widespread in 1938–39. I greatly underestimated the disillusionment and fatalism that the policies of the parties and the trade unions caused among their supporters in 1933, and the depoliticization that followed. More recent local studies and oral history research underline the need for revision on this point. This work has brought out strongly the way in which the subjects of the Nazi dictatorship tended to isolate one sphere of experience from another, to separate in their minds that which was bad from that which was tolerable, and from that which was good. Thus it was perfectly possible that workers who showed bitter resentment against wage cuts, longer hours, or attempts to bind them to their workplace by force of law felt at the same time that Hitler was a good political leader, or that the cheap mass tourism of "Strength through Joy" was a good thing, or that the regime's foreign policy revived their national pride.[46] It was even possible, it seems, for many people in 1939 to be opposed to the war and to admire Hitler at the same time.

Rejection of Nazi social and economic policies where they hit people's immediate material interests thus did not necessarily imply a disguised rejection of the regime in general, even though partial rejections could be resilient and sustained. This consideration magnifies the importance of the economic component in my overall argument about the relationship between Nazi domestic and foreign policies.

The final question about the precise meaning of the concept of "crisis," and its applicability to prewar Germany, concerns the degree of diffusion of the consciousness of crisis as such. There is no doubt that most people in Germany did not feel that they were living in the midst of a social, economic, and domestic political crisis (as opposed to foreign policy crises). Real crises, it is argued, are always and necessarily characterized by a widespread sense or understanding of the critical nature of developments. Herbst systematically develops an (all too casual) remark of my own, that real knowledge of the crisis, consciousness of it as such, was restricted to relatively few people: to the political, military, and economic elite who were in possession of the facts about the social and economic problems *as a whole*, who knew that the Nazi rulers were set on vastly expanded armaments projects and on war, and who knew that the regime was having the greatest difficulty in finding the human and material resources for these projects.[47] These were the sort of people who wrote the strictly confidential documents on which I based my interpretation. They formed the narrow elite that experienced the collapse of the armaments drive at the end of 1938; or, to take another concrete example, those who were permitted at exactly this time to hear Göring's lengthy and desperate description of the economic situation at the first meeting of the Reich Defense Council on 18 November

1938.[48] (This speech is the clearest evidence that Herbst is mistaken in believing that the top political leadership was not worried about the structural problems of the economy. Unlike Göring, Herbst quite ignores the elite's concern for *future* perspectives and trends.)[49] Their knowledge and understanding, above all their fears of an *impossible future*—Göring used the words "appears impossible"[50]— were of course top secret.

The regime had a monopoly of all relevant information and discussion. People working at lower levels of the economy and administration experienced and knew about only particular symptoms of the general problem—managers had to deal with particular bottlenecks and deadlines; workers found that they could exploit their own scarcity value; train drivers knew that there were not enough railway wagons; farmers knew that they could not restock their farms fully; and so on—but they did not know much more. It is definitely true (unlike 1928–33) that the full dimensions of the economic problems, above all their future implications, were not common knowledge. In this sense the power of censorship in "stabilizing the system" was very great. It was not even obvious to everyone in the elite that the political leadership was reluctant to impose those austerity measures that its armaments projects demanded, that it wanted to have its cake and eat it too, that it was prepared to risk an unprepared war. Can there be such a thing as a "crisis" of which so few people were aware, a secret crisis of the system, so to speak? Herbst flatly denies this.[51] It is a serious and open argument. I think that it can indeed be true of a *latent* crisis *in a dictatorship*, of a crisis that had not yet reached an undisguisable breaking point. This crisis was narrowly averted at the end of 1938. However, September–October 1939 did mark such a breaking point insofar as a sense of crisis among industrial workers, faced with the punitive War Economy Decree, was both clear and widespread.[52]

To sum up: does this combination of ignorance and the confusion of different political outlooks, which certainly was characteristic of the mass of the population, greatly attenuate or disqualify the concept of "crisis"? I think it does only if we imagine "crisis" to entail the incipient general breakdown of the whole system of rule. I now wish to argue a more restricted case: that the refusal of most of the population to cooperate *economically* in the preparation of war, and the unwillingness or inability of the regime to cope with this refusal, was by 1938 creating an *economic* crisis. And the fact that the regime nevertheless continued with expansive armaments and foreign policies created a huge contradiction, which amounted to a fundamental crisis of policy choices, and thus to an (albeit hidden) crisis of the regime itself. That is to say, the *economic crisis* was *in itself* serious enough. And it brought in its tow political and then military problems of a basic kind that could only be disguised, but could not begin to be resolved in peacetime.

This proposition needs to be illustrated in more detail, but first there is one final objection to my general picture that has to be considered. It is argued that the yardstick against which I am measuring the equivocations and weaknesses of Nazi social and economic policy is a quite unrealistic, utopian one—that of a total war economy in peacetime.[53] What is more, this yardstick is supposed to have been taken over from the platform of the one general, Georg Thomas (responsible for the economic affairs of the armed forces), who did not share Hitler's view about the possibility of *Blitzkriege* against single smaller states, but had the different goal of preparing Germany at once for a major war against France. My yardstick, my model, for greater austerity and more comprehensive rearmament does not in fact come mainly from this source, nor is it abstractly utopian, nor is it a post hoc model based on the deficiencies that became entirely apparent in October 1939. It is based rather on a very large number of different demands and proposals for specific measures of austerity, which came from many different sources between 1936 and 1939—proposals by industrialists, the price commissar, the minister of agriculture, the Labor Administration, the armed forces, and many other agencies.[54] That is to say, it is an immanent model, composed of the kinds of legislation and intervention that were thought necessary at the time by *most* of those who held responsibility for labor, economic, and armaments policies. Most of these demarches were put into effect in part, with delays, or not at all. My idea of what was objectively necessary in order to concentrate resources on rearmament also tried to take account of the huge new demands placed on the economy by the three massive additional programs put into motion between June 1938 and January 1939: the building of the West Wall, the headlong rush for war with Czechoslovakia, and then the vastly expanded naval and air force programs. Thus the yardstick by which the Nazi regime can be said to have held back the progress of rearmament is provided by the Nazi regime itself—both in its documented acts of omission, and in the targets for rearmament that it nevertheless set for itself. No external or invented criteria are involved at all. There were consistent reasons why the regime fell far short of its targets: for one, fear of great unpopularity and discontent kept really rigorous measures off the statute book after 1936.

 With the invasion of Poland and the British and French declarations of war we move from the discussion of documents and of the concepts necessary to analyze them to a series of dramatic events that help to give weight to my general thesis about the crisis-ridden relationship between domestic affairs and war in 1938–39. I have already described in detail in print the first of these, the War Economy Decree of 4 September 1939 and the speedy withdrawal of many of its clauses, and must summarize them very briefly here.[55] Right at the start of the war the government imposed a set of draconian sacrifices on the working population: higher taxes for the best-paid wage earners, a new policy of wage cuts, longer working hours, the abolition of overtime bonuses, a freeze on holidays, the rationing of food and consumer goods, and a big program of civil conscription.[56] This legislation met with such a degree of passive resistance and manifest hostility on the part of the workers that much of it had to be repealed or revised by the end of November 1939. Hitler himself approved reducing the incidence of civil conscription on 12 November (at precisely the same time as he was demanding the immediate invasion of France!). Even the real emergency of a major war would not induce the working class, dragooned and intimidated as it was, to accept sacrifices of this kind. [57]

These events shed a very clear light upon the prewar situation. They prove that the regime could under no circumstances have imposed a policy of full austerity in peacetime. They show that the Nazi leaders who had insisted that all sorts of material concessions be made to the working population in order to keep it under control during the later 1930s—that is Ley, Kaufmann and most of the *Gauleiters*, often Göring, usually Hitler himself—had been *politically* correct. They show that the government had never had much room for maneuver on these issues; that, contrary to what Herbst says, in this sector, at least, the regime did *not* possess unused capacities or reserves of power to intervene and stabilize the situation in favor of the armaments drive, not even on the commencement of war. The events of September–November 1939 also show the regime immediately putting the pacification of the working people before the overall (if not the short-term) demands of the war economy, even though Germany was already at war with Britain and France, and was indeed about to invade France.

This domestic retreat was not accompanied by any deceleration in military strategy. On the contrary, at precisely the same time, Hitler, in a panic over the quite unexpected strategic situation, ordered the armed forces to prepare to invade France before Christmas 1939. Once again, contradictions were driven to an extreme point. [58] As late as 6 November 1939 the invasion of France was scheduled for 12 November, one week later. One of the main reasons why the whole military leadership opposed Hitler's plans on this point grew directly out of the long-term policy of guns *and* butter, which I have outlined above: that is, after the campaign against Poland the German armed forces lacked the munitions, the bombs, fuel, spare parts, trucks, cars, and some raw materials that would be necessary to undertake *any* further military campaigns in the near future. On one estimate, the Army had enough munitions to permit one-third of its divisions to fight for a further four weeks. The economic policies of the 1930s had left the Nazi *Wehrmacht* with sufficient resources only to defeat the weak Polish forces. Any immediate confrontation with France would, German generals thought, have led to Germany's defeat. This lack of military supplies then produced one of the turning points of World War II, and one of the major military/political crises in the history of the Third Reich: on the agenda was either Germany's defeat on the battlefield or a conservative military-civilian coup against Hitler.

In my original interpretation I did not attach sufficient importance to this conjuncture, for the conflict over the timing of the invasion of France contains in a dramatic manner almost all the elements of the argument. First, Hitler was trying to make good the policy disaster of August–September 1939 by means of a still more adventurous, indeed desperate, step, the invasion of France in November. Second, the armed forces were discovering that, because of past overall policies, they did not have the material resources for such a gamble (they also had no operational plans). Third, as a result, a deeply serious threat was posed to the unity and permanence of the regime. And finally, while all this was going on, the government was dismantling many of its war economy measures against the German population under the compulsion of domestic pressure and discontent.

The regime was splitting at the top and disintegrating openly at the base. If we wish to look for a "crisis" capable of impeccable definition as such, this seems to be a good place to start. (One element of publicity, thus of public consciousness, was missing, for the conflict over the invasion of France remained a top secret.) It turned out that an open internal confrontation and/or military defeat was averted, it appears, only because Göring found at the last minute a subtle way of persuading Hitler to back down on 7 November; the invasion of France was then postponed some thirty times until May 1940, by which time the German armed forces had been able to retrain, and to restock, thanks in part to supplies from the Soviet Union. Because the invasion of France was then so overwhelmingly successful, I think historians have tended to give far too little weight to the events of October–November 1939. These events shed a lot of light on the ways in which high policy, domestic and military, was made, not only in the critical weeks themselves, but also with respect to war preparations in general. Contradictions led to political-economic crises that at least fueled military aggression; and when the first act of aggression created an acute strategic danger, Hitler's immediate reaction was to try to launch a second one at once. Throughout, the social and economic situation was at odds with the strategic choices; the two spheres were not coordinated, but were connected by a conflictual relationship, in which economic overstrain could be adduced as a powerful promiscuous argument for extreme strategic gambles, and at the same time undermined these gambles, as in November 1939. In describing the drive toward war as a "flight forward" *(Flucht nach vorn)* I may have been seduced by the need to find a phrase that would put things in a nutshell; but the conflict over the invasion of France leaves no doubt that Hitler was capable of responding to crises in exactly this manner. The politico-economic system of Nazi Germany generated its own impasses, which the leadership consistently attempted to meet by means of violent improvisations.

The invasion of Poland highlighted one such relevant factor about war at this stage in the regime's history—the utility of plunder. Hundreds of thousands of Polish prisoners of war were already performing essential labor in German agriculture in October and November 1939; and to them were added civilian workers, whose recruitment by labor offices operating directly behind the advancing German lines was an early priority. Leaving on one side the conquest of raw materials, industrial plant and rolling stock, etc., here was a way in which military aggression provided immediate relief for the most severe of German economic difficulties, the supply of labor to agriculture. Hitler already formulated this as a basic point for occupation policy in Poland on 17 October 1939; there must be low living standards in Poland, he said, since the Reich must recruit labor there. Ulrich Herbert has brought out well the novelty of this policy.[59] One must insist that it did match perfectly the most urgent needs of the German economy.[60]

To sum up thus far: my argument about the domestic components in the origins and timing of the war of 1939 needs to be refined, qualified, and added to at many points. I have tried to discuss the most important of these points above. I cannot yet see the need to abandon the basic approach. Such debates are not well served by exaggerating the differences between the points of view at issue. I am in full agreement with Ludolf Herbst that the Third Reich tended to use its power and its violence to disguise and postpone the structural problems of Nazi rule, and that these problems tended therewith to become more acute, potentially more destructive, in time. I also agree that "in the interests of short-term efficiency, the system as a whole was subjected to processes of decay and dissolution."[61] In its own programmed self-destruction, the Third Reich took a substantial part of the world down in flames with it. The open question is *when* and *why* did these elements in the system actually become determinant of high policy. My own provisional answers remain: in 1938, and on account of internal contradictions that were located not only, but most importantly, in the economy.

A discussion of this kind, however, must be put into a broader historical perspective. Any specific interpretation of a particular turning point or crisis in the history of the Third Reich has to stand the test of being an adequate, or appropriate, part of an overall interpretation. If the view put forward of a small part of the story does not fit in with any plausible picture of the whole, then that view of the part is likely to be wrong, however well-documented it may appear to be. How do these vital criteria apply to my argument concerning the domestic component in the Nazi drive to war in 1938–39? A variety of different long-term perspectives could be chosen with a view to testing the hypotheses in this sense: the questions at issue are many and complex, and deserve a much fuller discussion than I have space for here. I can conclude only with some schematic remarks on four elements of a longer historical perspective, of an overall interpretation.

The first concerns the development of class relations over the whole period between 1933 and 1945. On the surface my interpretation of 1938–39 does not fit in very well with what we know of such general developments. Until

1936 mass unemployment continued to exercise the heaviest social and political discipline. In the picture I have drawn, the German working class, although deprived of its collective rights and independent organizations, then reappears in the late 1930s as a fairly vigorous historical actor, able to cause the regime perplexity and weakness of purpose, and able to secure changes in state policy. More recent research has shown that this did not continue to be the case to the same degree through the war years.[62] The power of command of the regime over the industrial workers became greater, not less, and even toward the end of the war, movements of discontent and opposition tended to be isolated and exceptional.[63] Thus the events of 1938–39 were not a good guide to the future. The main reasons for this reassertion of dictatorial control seem to me to lie in changes that were wrought in, and by, the war itself (and *not*, that is, in the actuation of preexisting forms of consent).

The Nazi regime never again challenged the working class with a single, open, and major attack on its working conditions and living standards, as it had done in September 1939. The closest it came to doing this was in cutting food rations in April 1942, a measure that provoked a rash of memories of 1917–18;[64] but, in general, the further deterioration in the condition of the working class during the war was a gradual and piecemeal process and not the result of massive measures of economic repression.

The years on which I have concentrated thus appear to be exceptional with respect to working-class behavior and with respect to relations between the class and the regime; they were novel, but, on account of war, they were not a portent of future conflicts or of future governmental weakness. There are good reasons why 1938 and 1939 were *in fact* exceptional. They were the *first* years in which the number of jobs vastly exceeded the number of available workers, with all the new opportunities this offered to workers, and with all the new challenges and disruptions it caused the employers and to the state. For the same reason, they were the *first* years in which the state had to try to regulate, comprehensively, the whole huge and complex area of the labor market, wages, and working conditions. These were exceptionally difficult administrative tasks. They pitted a dictatorial machine lacking in personnel and experience against a most uncooperative population.[65] These were also the years of transition from peace to war, to a war that was not popular. For all these reasons the years 1938–39 formed a unique conjuncture, a special period of transition in which everything was at stake. In my original work I did not sufficiently emphasize their peculiarity as two critical years of transition. To call them such does not, I think, diminish the validity of the interpretation, but rather gives these problems their precise place in a long-term chronology.

On two other counts, however, the picture of a domestic crisis helping to propel Germany into war in 1939 does fit in more simply with long-term perspectives on the history of the Third Reich. I have argued that war became necessary in order for rearmament to be continued at a high level. Following from this, and subsequently in time, war became in every sense an end in itself for the regime. This seems to me to be the overriding fact about the Nazi conduct of World War II, including its resistance to the bitter end. It was not just a matter of Hitler extolling the virtues of martial combat. In a material sense, in the invasion of the Soviet Union the *means* (armed force) and the *goal* (living space) were collapsed into each other and, in the barbaric German policies of occupation, became indistinguishable from one another. It was clear in advance that the German armies would have to live off the land.[66] This war of racial destruction and economic imperialism became an end in itself, and that is one reason why Nazi Germany lost the war in Russia. If we try to imagine some kind of German victory, it was only to be a prelude to further military expansion in the Middle East and North Africa. And so on. If, for Nazism, wars basically served the prosecution of further wars, this decisive logic first broke through in Hitler's policy-making in 1938–39, when the limits of rearmament within Germany's existing boundaries and within its existing "constitution" were reached. Hitler's basic choice in 1938–39 was, perhaps, to get war started, *so that it could be continued*—whatever the immediate strategic risks, and whatever basic strategic goals he may have had. It is not my intention in any way to belittle detailed investigations of the development of Hitler's strategy, but there may be some risk of overlooking the fact that this was based on a categorical and continuing option for *war as such*, an option that made a perverse kind of sense in domestic and economic terms at the time at which it first became manifestly clear. After that, conquests were to provide the space and the resources for further conquests. To put it another way, a Third Reich "at peace" is an unimaginable contradiction in terms.[67]

Plunder provides the last long-term perspective that tends to validate this approach to Nazi policy-making in 1938–39—above all, the plunder of people. This was not a long-nurtured goal of policy, but rather an ineluctable necessity, given Nazi economic policy and aims. Some eight million foreigners worked in Germany during the war, most of them as prisoners of war or deportees. This points to a basic fact that was already becoming visible in 1938: there were simply not enough German people to permit the fulfilment of Nazi ambitions, hence the need to conquer other people. But foreign workers were also used during the war in a very precise way: to keep to a minimum the sacrifices imposed upon German women. This protection of many German women from long hours in munitions factories, etc., was not only direct protection of the women them- selves; quite as important, it was a protection of the regime's reputation among men, among the women's husbands and fathers, who were themselves mostly soldiers or armaments workers (and whose morale, or prejudices, the regime had to respect). The conscription of German women into industrial wage labor in large numbers would have been intensely unpopular among men; the regime knew this, and there is much evidence for that fact. [68] But on two occasions when this step had to be seriously considered the German armed forces conquered new populations that could be brought to work in Germany. This was the case with the French in the summer of 1940, and with the Russians in the winter of 1941–42. In each case the regime had been just about to take the bitter risk of conscripting German women, and then stopped, because conquered labor could be used to fill the gaps. The level of mobilization of German women for war work remained low through to 1945. [69] In this vital sphere the policies of guns and butter, so distinctive of the later 1930s, were continued throughout the war by means of the conquest and plunder of foreign workers. War, that is, was essential to the maintenance of this very important piece of civilian economy in wartime Nazi Germany.

Finally, there is perhaps a basic dilemma of perception. At the level of one's deepest historical intuitions there must remain a great sense of incompatibility between the Third Reich that, on the one hand, we know to have mobilized such terrifying destructive energies, to have unfolded such sustained and violent bureaucratic and military power, to have resisted until the very end of the war; and, on the other hand, the Third Reich depicted above: a regime whose leadership was increasingly entrapped in economic and political contradictions largely of its own making and that sought escape or resolution or maintenance of its distinctive identity through a series of sudden lurches in policy and through ever more explosive risk-taking. Instinctively we feel the crises and confusions, the desperate improvisations and the brutal irrationalities that so consistently characterized affairs at the apex of the politico-economic system, to be out of key with the evidence of the sweeping march of conquest and genocide and with the tenacious defense of the Greater German Reich in 1944–45. How can the latter possibly have been the outcome of policy-making procedures that were demonstrably so incoherent and crisis-ridden, of a political and economic system so riven with conflict and contradiction? Something *seems* not to add up.

I believe that one must insist on the truth and the compatibility of both of these faces of Nazi Germany. The historiographical problem is less that of reconciling the two realities, which may be attempted, for example, by emphasizing the manner in which Hitler himself personified both elements simultaneously. The problem is rather that of working out, in all spheres and at all levels, a set of dynamic and dialectical relationships between the strong centripetal pressures at work at the top of the regime and the efficacy of particular sectors of it—of the army, the police/SS, of much of the civil administration, of industry—in the years 1942–44. These relationships may well have been positive rather than negative, at least in the short run. That is, crisis, violent irrationality, and institutional decomposition at the top may in fact have furthered, for a time, the actual effectiveness of the component parts of the dictatorship. Competition among these component parts, their having to act perpetually under conditions of great pressure and often independently of each other, drew out potentials of power that might otherwise have lain dormant. (The price of this was the growing fragmentation of the regime into a series of incompatible racial, economic, and strategic projects, a process that was virtually complete by 1942.) These schematic remarks can do no more than suggest in a rough and ready manner how what I have called the basic dilemma of perception may be resolved—or, better, one possible approach to its resolution.

In one sense, the particular example that I have tried to analyze does not illustrate this general argument very well, for the preparation and mobilization for the war of 1939 was in many respects a failure: at every level (diplomatic, economic, domestic-political) the elements of overstrain were too great, and the Third Reich was saved in the crisis of October–November 1939 more by sheer good fortune than by anything else. But this was not true of earlier and later turning-points, from the Röhm Purge to the invasion of the Soviet Union, all of which illustrate the strict compatibility between crisis-ridden policy-making and the development and deployment of vast political and military power. The example of 1938–39 remains of value, however, not only because of its intrinsic historical importance, but also on account of the multiplicity and clarity of those elements in the situation which made Hitler's option for war such an explosive gamble. Violent lurches of this kind were no less essential parts of the history of Nazi Germany than such manifestations of power as the extermination of the European Jews or the occupation of Italy in September 1943.

Analyses need to emphasize both elements in the system, and to explore their interdependence in a concrete manner. Versions that give exclusive emphasis to the Nazi regime's growing output of a military and economic power inevitably create the impression that the steps that led in this direction were relatively smooth.[70] These steps were, on the contrary, highly discontinuous, decisionistic, risk-laden, increasingly blind to economic and strategic realities, and thus increasingly violent. It is a central part of my argument that such policy-making was not only willful, but also emerged with a high degree of necessity from the economic and political system of Nazi Germany itself. It is no paradox, still less a contradiction, that policy-making of this kind could unleash phases, or sectoral blocks, of great power, especially of destructive power; in ways that still need to be understood in detail, the two in fact went hand in hand. What the system, and the policy-making that it engendered, could *not* do was construct a coherent, imperial, and stable Third Reich. That possibility had already begun to fall apart in 1938–39—an observation that in no way belittles the immense efforts necessary on the part of the Allied Powers finally to defeat Nazi Germany.

Notes

1. See Joachim C. Fest, *Hitler: Eine Biographie*, (Frankfurt a.M., Berlin, Vienna, 1973), p. 827, n.295.

2. The evidence is well summarized by Fest, *Hitler*, pp. 763ff. and 776.

3. See my *Arbeiterklasse und Volksgemeinschaft: Dokumente und Materialien zur deutschen Arbeiterpolitik, 1936–1939* (Opladen, 1975), esp. Chaps. 13–21; "Innere Krise und Angriffskrieg 1938/1939," in Friedrich Forstmeier and Hans-Erich Volkmann, eds., *Wirtschaft und Rüstung am Vorabend des Zweiten Weltkrieges* (Düsseldorf, 1975); Tim Mason, *Sozialpolitik im Dritten Reich* (Opladen, 1977), esp. Chap. 6; "The Workers' Opposition in Nazi Germany," *History Workshop Journal* 11 (1981), pp. 120–37. The following paragraphs draw in a highly condensed manner on this work.

4. Without giving evidence or arguments, Ludolf Herbst denies that the developments did quantitative damage: "Die Krise des nationalsozialistischen Regimes am Vorabend des Zweiten Weltkrieges und die forcierte Ausrüstung," *Vierteljahreshefte für Zeitgeschichte (VfZ)* 26, no. 3 (1978): 390. It is not possible to give precise numerical values to the phenomena under discussion, but those in positions of economic and administrative authority clearly had the impression that the damage done was considerable. They may have been exaggerating a little—see below.

5. See Michael Geyer, "Rüstungsbeschleunigung und Inflation: Zur Inflationsdenkschrift des Oberkommandos der Wehrmacht vom November 1938," *Militärgeschichtliche Mitteilungen*, no. 2 (1981): 135, n.105. Geyer points out that during 1937 Germany heavy industry was limiting output to optimum levels in terms of plant economics and was giving priority to the temporarily flourishing export market.

6. I have laid out the evidence in Mason, *Sozialpolitik im Dritten Reich*, pp. 307ff. See also Ludolf Herbst, *Der totale Krieg und die Ordnung der Wirtschaft* (Stuttgart, 1982), p. 72.

7. For early evidence of Hitler's enthusiasm for plunder, see his reaction to the occupation of Prague in March 1939; Mason, *Sozialpolitik im Dritten Reich*, p. 308f.

8. Fest rightly gives emphasis to this point; see Fest, *Hitler*, pp. 738ff., 831f., 840, and 924f. Andreas Hillgruber also quotes two striking examples of Hitler's worries on this account: *Hitlers Strategie: Politik und Kriegführung, 1940–1941* (Frankfurt a.M., 1965), pp. 219 and 365.

9. It has been interestingly argued that there was a close link between Nazi racial thought and Nazi social policies, on the grounds that the quality of the German "racial stock" depended on a decent level of civilian prosperity, good nutrition, good working conditions, etc. Ludolf Herbst first put forward this interpretation in his contribution to Wolfgang Benz and Hermann Graml, eds.,

Sommer 1939: Die Grossmächte und der europäische Krieg, (Stuttgart, 1979), p. 82; see now Herbst, *Der totale Krieg,* pp. 71, 89, 150, and 163. On the basis of the evidence of the above paragraph, this looks like a typical piece of propaganda or wishful thinking as far as the top leadership was concerned, with the exception of measures that directly affected the birth rate (marriage loans, child allowances, etc.). The housing conditions of the working class, a key factor in "racial progress," were badly neglected by the regime throughout. There is certainly no evidence that the regime deliberately tolerated increased living standards in the late 1930s out of eugenic considerations.

10. I cannot accept this part of the careful critique of my work by Lotte Zumpe, *Jahrbuch für Wirtschaftsgeschichte,* no. 4 (1979).

11. For a clear summary with a full bibliography of the first stages of the discussion see Andreas Hillgruber, in Benz and Graml, eds., *Sommer 1939,* pp. 340ff. For some of the later negative judgments (I am sure that this list is not complete), see Alan S. Milward, *War, Economy and Society, 1939–1945* (London, 1977), p. 14; Ian Kershaw, *The Nazi Dictatorship* (London, 1985), pp. 78ff. (with many useful references); and, above all, Herbst, "Die Krise des nationalsozialistischen Regimes." Since I believe that Richard Overy's critique, "Germany, 'Domestic Crisis' and War in 1939," *Past and Present,* no. 116 (1987), rests on a fundamental misunderstanding of what constitutes evidence for the existence of a crisis, I shall make few references to his original arguments. I have replied separately to Overy in *Past and Present,* no. 122 (1989).

12. "Die N-S Wirtschaft in Vorbereitung des Krieges," in *Das Deutsche Reich und der Zweite Weltkrieg,* vol. 1, publication of the Militärgeschichtliches Forschungsamt (Stuttgart, 1979), esp. pp. 327ff. and 364ff.

13. David E. Kaiser, *Economic Diplomacy and the Origins of the Second World War* (Princeton, N.J., 1980), esp. pp. 268 and 282. See also his "Comment" on Overy's work in *Past and Present,* no. 122.

14. Geyer, "Rüstungsbeschleunigung und Inflation."

15. See Fest, *Hitler,* pp. 788 and 832–42.

16. Jost Dülffer, "Der Beginn des Krieges 1939: Hitler, die innere Krise und das Mächtesystem," *Geschichte und Gesellschaft,* no. 4 (1976): esp. pp. 461ff.

17. Dülffer, ibid., p. 469, allows that they would have become incompatible in time, but his own full evidence of the massive state civilian and military projects of 1938–39 suggests that that time would come sooner rather than later.

18. See Herbst, "Die Krise des nationalsozialistischen Regimes," p. 351f. Without taking account of the contrary evidence, Overy, "Germany, 'Domestic Crisis' and War," asserts that there were no serious problems, just "frictions"—see esp. p. 148.

19. For Darré's closely argued demarches, which Hitler refused to discuss, see Bundesarchiv Koblenz (BAK), R 43 II, vol. 213b.

20. There are examples of this happening in the excellent article by Klaus Wisotzky, "Der Ruhrbergbau am Vorabend des Zweiten Weltkriegs," *VfZ* 30, no. 3 (1982): 423ff.

21. Geyer, "Rüstungsbeschleunigung und Inflation."

22. Wisotzky, "Der Ruhrbergbau," pp. 427ff., discusses this problem in a differentiated way. Wolfgang Franz Werner, *"Bleib übrig": Deutsche Arbeiter in der nationalsozialistischen Kriegswirtschaft* (Düsseldorf, 1983), makes the point more bluntly, and polemically attributes the official figures to me, p. 25f.

23. Werner, *"Bleib übrig"*, pp. 12 and 31.

24. The theme runs like a red thread through Fest's biography of Hitler. See the cathartic conclusion of Hitler's Sportpalast speech of September 1938, p. 766; also esp. pp. 849 and 924.

25. Mason, *Sozialpolitik im Dritten Reich*, pp. 312–16; Herbst, "Die Krise des nationalsozialistischen Regimes," pp. 365f, 373, and 376, makes this point in a particularly convincing manner. He sees "disintegration" as a possible prelude to open conflict within Germany, and seems to argue that only the latter would have constituted evidence of a real crisis.

26. See Herbst, "Die Krise des nationalsozialistischen Regimes," p. 373.

27. See Michael Prinz, *Vom neuen Mittelstand zum Volksgenossen*, (Munich, 1986), pp. 165ff.; Geyer, "Rüstungsbeschleunigung und Inflation," pp. 157 and 183 n.204; Werner, *"Bleib übrig"*, pp. 98 and 108.

28. Two contributors to Benz and Graml, eds., *Sommer 1939*, seem to differ a little in their assessments: Fritz Blaich, p. 41, and Ludolf Herbst, pp. 96ff. See also Herbst, *Der totale Krieg*, p. 120f., who points out that the trade sector got off more lightly than small producers *(Handwerk)*. Winkler, "Der entbehrliche Stand," *Archiv für Sozialgeschichte* 18 (1977): 32ff., argues that *Handwerk* was indeed being pushed to the wall. On the early war measures, see Werner, *"Bleib übrig"*, pp. 61f. and 82ff.

29. Dörte Winkler, *Frauenarbeit im "Dritten Reich,"* Hamburg, 1977, pp. 57ff.

30. Herbst, "Die Krise des nationalsozialistischen Regimes," pp. 365 and 388.

31. Ibid., pp. 375 and 365ff.

32. Geyer, "Rüstungsbeschleunigung und Inflation," pp. 129f. and 143f.

33. Ibid., pp. 136, 143, and 146.

34. Ibid., p. 179.

35. Ibid., p. 146.

36. See Fritz Federau, *Der Zweite Weltkrieg: Seine Finanzierung in*

Deutschland (Tübingen, 1962). Richard J. Overy has recently added some important points on this question: "'Blitzkriegswirtschaft'?" *VfZ* 13 (1988): esp. pp. 391ff.

37. See "Plans and Markets: Nazi Style," *Kyklos: International Review for Social Sciences*, fasc. 1 (1977).

38. I agree with Herbst ("Die Krise des nationalsozialistischen Regimes," p. 369), that the civil service played a very important role in holding the Third Reich together at this juncture.

39. See Hans-Erich Volkmann, *Das Deutsche Reich und der Zweite Weltkrieg*, vol. 1, pp. 177–368.

40. See Mason, "Innere Krise," p. 173.

41. Herbst, "Die Krise des nationalsozialistischen Regimes," pp. 376 and 383.

42. This is one of the main themes in the material collected by Werner, *"Bleib übrig."*

43. For examples that contradict Herbst's notion that concessions pacified class conflict, see Mason, "The Workers' Opposition in Nazi Germany," pp. 125f.

44. Italy in the later 1970s furnishes a good example of this point; by any definition the country was in crisis in these years.

45. See my introduction, "Die Bändigung der Arbeiterklasse im nationalsozialistischen Deutschland," to the volume by Carola Sachse et al., *Angst, Belohnung, Zucht und Ordnung* (Opladen, 1982).

46. For me, by far the most illuminating work on these themes has been the inquiries by Lutz Niethammer and his colleagues into working peoples' memories of their experiences in the Ruhr area. See Lutz Niethammer, ed., *"Die Jahre weiss man nicht, wo man die heute hinsetzen soll"* (Berlin, Bonn, 1983), vol. 1; Lutz Niethammer, ed., *"Hinterher merkt man, dass es richtig war, dass es schiefgegangen ist"* (Berlin, Bonn, 1983), vol. 2; Lutz Niethammer and Alexander von Plato, eds., *"Wir kriegen jetzt andere Zeiten"* (Berlin, Bonn, 1985), vol. 3. For sensitive discussions of workers' opposition, see the editor's introduction to vol. 1, esp. pp. 23ff., and the evidence presented by Ulrich Herbert in vol. 1, p. 94f., and vol. 3, p. 26. The theme of the compartmentalization of people's consciousness runs like a red thread through all three volumes: see, for example, the cases documented by Bernd Parisius in vol. 2, pp. 115, 127, and 131; and the general discussion by Ulrich Herbert in vol. 3, esp. p. 29, also pp. 24, 26, and 32. See further Reinhard Mann, *Protest und Kontrolle im Dritten Reich* (Frankfurt, New York, 1987), p. 42f. This work underlines the correctness of the criticism in Herbst, "Die Krise des nationalsozialistischen Regimes," p. 382f., and cf. the earlier critique by Alf Lüdtke in *Gesellschaft: Beiträge zur Marxschen Theorie*, vol. 6 (Frankfurt a.M., 1976).

47. See Herbst, "Die Krise des nationalsozialistischen Regimes," p. 378f.

48. See Mason, *Arbeiterklasse und Volksgemeinschaft*, doc. 152.

49. Herbst, "Die Krise des nationalsozialistischen Regimes," p. 381.

50. Mason, *Arbeiterklasse und Volksgemeinschaft*, p. 917.

51. See Herbst, "Die Krise des nationalsozialistischen Regimes," p. 390. He also denies that elite consciousness of crisis is evidence of its real existence. Even as a general proposition I find this unacceptable; the point seems totally out of place in this particular context.

52. Herbst bypasses these crucial events in his discussion of the extent of the awareness of crisis.

53. See Herbst, "Die Krise des nationalsozialistischen Regimes," p. 385ff.

54. I published a substantial number of such demands and proposals. See, for example, *Arbeiterklasse und Volksgemeinschaft*, doc. 71ff., doc. 128; and doc. 151; also Darré's interventions on agriculture—see n.19 above.

55. See in brief my "Labour in the Third Reich 1933–1939," *Past and Present*, no. 33 (1966); in detail, *Arbeiterklasse und Volksgemeinschaft*, chaps. 19–21. Werner, *"Bleib übrig"*, pp. 35–43, 48, 51–54, 66ff., and 72–79, provides a much more comprehensive picture of this crisis, in that he covers fully the initial response to rationing measures; this response was especially hostile. For additional striking evidence of absenteeism, see Stephen Salter, "The Mobilisation of German Labour, 1939–1945," D.Phil. thesis (Oxford, 1983), pp. 193f. and 210. Werner is clearly mistaken in arguing that the core of regular industrial workers stood aside from these protests during *these* months (p. 80). Later in the war it is true that women and young workers seem to have been more inclined to protest, take days off, etc.

56. See Mason, *Arbeiterklasse und Volksgemeinschaft*, chaps. 19 and 20. Overy, "'Blitzkriegswirtschaft'?" p. 383, is mistaken in describing these measures as "total economic mobilization." The mobilization of September 1939 was partial, deliberately incomplete. See Mason, *Arbeiterklasse und Volksgemeinschaft*, chap. 18, and Georg Thomas, *Geschichte der deutschen Wehr- und Rüstungswirtschaft (1918–1943/45)*, ed. Wolfgang Birkenfeld (Boppard am Rhein, 1966), pp. 129, 154–57, 172ff., 499f., and 510f.

57. Herbst, "Die Krise des nationalsozialistischen Regimes," p. 381, and idem, *Der totale Krieg*, p. 109f., cites the retreat by the regime on the domestic front merely as evidence of the shrewd psychological intuition of the leadership. He greatly underplays the element of real conflict that was present in the situation.

58. For summaries of these events, see Hillgruber, *Hitlers Strategie*, pp. 34–38; and Mason, "Innere Krise", p. 180f. Detailed accounts are furnished by

Hans-Adolf Jacobsen, ed., *Dokumente zur Vorgeschichte des Westfeldzuges, 1939–1940* (Göttingen, 1956), vol. 1; and idem, *Fall "Gelb"* (Wiesbaden), 1957. On the military opposition and resistance to Hitler, see H. Deutsch, *The Conspiracy against Hitler in the Twilight War* (Minneapolis, Minn., 1968).

59. See Ulrich Herbert, *Fremdarbeiter: Politik und Praxis des Ausländer-Einsatzes" in der Kriegswirtschaft des Dritten Reiches*, (Berlin, Bonn, 1985), esp. pp. 11, 36, and 67ff. This is among the most important recent studies of the history of Nazi Germany.

60. In addition to Herbert, see Ian Kershaw, *Popular Opinion and Political Dissent in the Third Reich* (Oxford, 1983), chaps. 1 and 7, for the situation of farmers in Bavaria.

61. Herbst, "Die Krise des nationalsozialistischen Regimes," p. 391.

62. For an excellent summary, see Herbert, *Fremdarbeiter*, p. 17. Salter, "The Mobilisation of German Labour," covers the whole topic fully, and with great lucidity and subtlety. Werner, *"Bleib übrig"*, furnishes much more detail, but his study is less well organized and his interpretation less differentiated.

63. For some of these exceptions, see Werner, *"Bleib übrig,"* pp. 155–59 (air raids and hours of work in 1941), 193 (wage demands during 1942), and 268–74 (opposition to evacuations from autumn 1943 on).

64. Ibid., pp. 194–97, gives a good account of the problems over food rations during 1942.

65. On the administrative weakness of the machinery of the Trustees of Labor, see Rüdiger Hachtmann, "Von der Klassenharmonie zum regulierten Klassenkampf," *Soziale Bewegungen, Jahrbuch 1: Arbeiterbewegung und Faschismus* (Frankfurt, New York, 1984), p. 163f. Schweitzer, "Plans and Markets," contains hints in a similar direction for 1938.

66. See Hillgruber, *Hitlers Strategie*, pp. 264ff.; O. Bartov, *The Eastern Front, 1941–1945: German Troops and the Barbarization of Warfare* (London, 1985).

67. I do not wish with this argument to fall back toward earlier interpretations by Rauschning or Bullock of Hitler as a cynical nihilist. It is possible to accept fully that he had an ideological commitment to the destruction of the Soviet Union and to the conquest of living space there, while maintaining the strongest possible doubts that the Nazi war would have ended, or even been greatly reduced in intensity, in the case of military victory in Russia.

68. For some particularly striking evidence, see Niethammer, *"Die Jahre weiss man nicht,"* pp. 126f., 267, and 270.

69. See Mason, "Women in Germany, 1925–1940: Family, Welfare and Work," *History Workshop Journal*, no. 2 (1976): 20; Herbert, *Fremdarbeiter*, pp. 96ff., 142, and 175. Overy, " 'Blitzkriegswirtschaft'?" pp. 425ff., is mistaken on this general issue; if the mobilization of female labor in Germany really were as

thorough as he presents it, the repeated, agonized debates in the political leadership about whether to conscript women or not become incomprehensible. The problem was the shortage of women for factory labor. Overy obtains his high figure for *economically active* women *(Erwerbspersonen)* by including all those who worked as family assistants, often for no wage, on farms, in shops, etc. It is true that their contribution to the war economy, especially in agriculture, should not be underestimated, but the problem that the regime repeatedly faced, and ducked, was that of finding sufficient women for factory labor.

    70. This point constitutes my greatest disagreement with the recent work of Richard Overy on these questions. See Overy, "Hitler's War and the German Economy—A Reinterpretation," *Economic History Review* (2d ser.) 35 (1982): 272–91; "Germany, 'Domestic Crisis' and War"; and " 'Blitzkriegswirtschaft'?"

9

Polycracy and Policy in the Third Reich: The Case of the Economy

PETER HAYES

In December 1945—and not for the last time in his career—John Kenneth Galbraith popularized an overstatement that soon became an orthodoxy. Fresh from examining the German war economy for the U.S. Strategic Bombing Survey and from interviewing numerous captured Nazi policy-makers, he announced to the readers of *Fortune* magazine that "Germany Was Badly Run." "The myth of ruthless Nazi competence," as he later summarized his case, was just that—a myth. Instead of an almost invincibly disciplined despotism, the Third Reich turned out on close inspection to have been a demonstration of "the inherent inefficiencies of dictatorship." Its leaders had proved not only technically and intellectually inadequate, but also remarkably susceptible to the corruptions of power. Their internecine squabbling and "unabashed hedonism" had dispersed Germany's resources, squandered its opportunities, and snatched defeat from the jaws of victory. Somewhat belatedly, in spite of both themselves and heavy air raids, they had managed to generate ever-increasing military production from 1942 to 1945. There remained, nonetheless, said Galbraith, "the simple fact . . . that Germany should never have lost the war," and the explanation lay in "undermobilization." To be sure, he later conceded,

> No defeated government looks good. Had the Germans or the
> Japanese come to Washington, they would have been appalled by

the inept nontalent that had been unloaded on the wartime administration or that had found shelter there. But after all al-
lowance, the story of defective planning, bad judgment, and
incoherent administration [in Nazi Germany] . . . was impressive.

For a time, the story was also iconoclastic. *Fortune* had "misgivings"
about publishing Galbraith's essay, he recalls in his memoirs, since "the thesis
seemed . . . too drastically at odds with accepted truth."[1] Presumably too many
Americans had been taken in by the serried ranks and marauding tanks displayed
in Nazi newsreels or by the goading image of a well-oiled and single-minded
enemy juggernaut portrayed in our own. But whatever the grounds for disbelief,
it rapidly collapsed under the weight of postwar revelations. The Nuremberg trial
records, the published recollections of high-ranking German officials and officers, and the initial studies of professional historians like Hugh Trevor-Roper
and Alan Bullock—all seemed to confirm the prescience of Franz Neumann,
who in 1942 had dubbed the Nazi regime "a non-state, a chaos, a rule of
lawlessness and anarchy," in short, a monster of indeterminate shape, a Behemoth.[2] Of course, Neumann's was not the only reigning metaphor. Some
scholars preferred to depict Nazism as a form of gangland rule; others saw it as a
kind of feudalism, complete with warring barons united only by personal loyalty
to the Führer from whom they derived their fiefdoms.[3] Regardless of the image
adopted, however, students of the Third Reich proceeded by the 1950s from two
generally accepted but not quite harmonious facts: on the one hand, the Nazi
system had been characterized by a high incidence of infighting and inefficiency;
on the other hand, it still had conquered nearly all of Europe, systematically
massacred millions of people, maintained its grip on Germany until the bitter
end, and succumbed only to the combined exertions of much of the globe.
Galbraith's discovery, reinforced by Burton Klein's famous findings, perhaps
clarified why Germany lost the Second World War, but also posed new puzzles.[4]
        Over the past thirty years, historians have responded by gravitating toward
either of two formulations of the nature of Nazi rule: one calls it a monocracy,
the other a polycracy.[5] The monocratic viewpoint finds method in the Reich's
madness. Its advocates reconcile dictatorship with disorder by positing a divide-
and-rule strategy on Hitler's part. The proliferating organizations, overlapping
competencies, contradictory objectives, and uncoordinated administration characteristic of the Nazi regime were, on this showing, intentional. Like everything
else in the Third Reich, they embodied the Führer's will, they served as chosen
means to ideological ends. If he tolerated, even encouraged, empire-building
and rivalry among his subordinates, he did so to preserve his position as supreme
arbiter. If confusion and fragmentation resulted, they never impeded him from
pursuing his twin central and long-fixed goals: the conquest of living space and
the eradication of the Jews.[6] If he did not act out *Mein Kampf* immediately or
unhesitatingly, his foreign policy still followed "a logical (though not a predeter-

mined) course."[7] If competing objectives forced deviations from stated principle, these were merely a function of recognizing the need to attend to first things first.[8] Finally, if Germany went to war underarmed for a long conflict, that, too, was purposeful. It reflected the conscious adoption of a "blitzkrieg strategy" that envisioned a series of brief, devastating concentrations of the Reich's restricted resources at the point of impact and thus relieved the regime of undertaking more stringent, stressful preparations.[9] In short, the Third Reich was *both* messy and totalitarian; indeed, it remained the latter in part *because* it was the former.

Obviously, Hitler takes center stage in this analysis, which is precisely the problem, according to its critics. Their objections are simultaneously political and epistemological—political because, as A. J. P. Taylor once protested, "With Hitler guilty, every other German could claim innocence,"[10] epistemological because, in Tim Mason's words, "Unless virtually the whole of modern social science constitutes an epochal blind alley, 'Hitler' *cannot* be a full and adequate explanation, not even of himself."[11] Concerned to lay bare the complicity of others and to penetrate to deeper structures of causation, these critics have advanced a different model of how the Third Reich worked.

This polycratic school of thought sees the inconsistencies of Nazi policy as imposed, rather than intentional. They were expressions, not of the Führer's desires, but of the limits on his power established by his image and temperament, by relations and forces in German society, and by political constraints within and outside his movement, such as the strength of big business and the army, the variegated nature of his following, and the need to retain popular allegiance.[12] Far from being free to make policy in Germany single-handedly, Hitler had to enter into largely implicit "pacts" with the representatives of these given conditions.[13] While semicongruent interests and loyalty to him held the contracting parties together, their incessant attempts to encroach on each other's turfs and to obtain his favor became an autonomous force. Disunity in the Third Reich was not a device, but a dynamic, not a method, but a kind of ghost in the machine. Bidding wars for the reactive Führer's patronage ratcheted up the march toward real war, aggravated domestic tensions, and even finally produced the decision to murder the Jews.[14] Nazi Germany was driven less by Hitler's ambitions than by an unruly power structure in which relentless rivalry begat a cumulative radicalization of policy that could have no other outcome but self-destruction.

Interestingly, the debate between these two conceptions has taken place without much reference to Galbraith's point of departure in 1945: the German economy. Perhaps the time has come to return our attention to that sphere, take note of recent research, and see whether it lends weight to either or both interpretations. Doing so may lead to the sort of intellectual integration of apparent opposites that seems characteristic of much of the best recent work on other issues in the history of the Third Reich.[15] One can at least begin this process of reevaluation by addressing three questions. How inefficient was the Nazi economy? How polycratic were the policies that governed it? What difference did the resulting situations make to the fate of the Third Reich?

Inefficiency, of course, is in the eye of the beholder, and the initial question perhaps amounts, at first glance, to asking whether the bottle is half full or half empty. One needs to consider the multiple possible angles of vision and standards of measurement. The usual ones, those of Galbraith and Klein, are obvious: from the vantage point of 1945, one assesses the German economy according to its failure to produce enough to win the war that took shape from 1939 to 1941. An equally adverse appraisal results if one rates the Nazi record with reference to the postwar German "economic miracle," since gains in industrial productivity during the Third Reich were quite unexceptional.[16] Still a third negative judgment emerges from a recent study that diagnoses the increasingly sclerotic condition of the Weimar economy and concludes that Hitlerian economics aggravated rather than arrested it.[17] But these three tests, although they lead to informative conclusions, are somewhat artificial. Arguably, after December 1941 an optimally organized German economy was neither conceivable nor capable of bringing the Third Reich to victory. Moreover, to focus on productivity or international competitiveness is to judge by objectives that were of far less interest to the Nazi regime than changing the volume and content of the nation's output.[18] It is, in fact, possible to argue that from the perspectives of 1933, 1938, 1943, and even in a sense 1941, the German economy under the Nazis performed rather effectively given the prevailing circumstances, that it fulfilled the realistic demands made on it, and that where it fell short, responsibility lay more with the personal defects of Hermann Göring, its sometime leader, and the overwhelming scope of its assignments than with the means of their execution.

To begin with, the Nazi state did carry out the most rapid recovery from the Depression among major industrial nations. By 1938–39, joblessness had virtually disappeared, stock prices had rebounded from the crash, and real wages had reached their earlier peaks. The nation's nominal and real external debt and the domestic interest rate had roughly halved since 1932; the gross national product had risen over the same period by 81 percent, the money supply by 60 percent, and total tax revenues by 100 percent.[19] Aggregate industrial investment, employment, and output had surpassed their levels of 1928, and within each category a net transfer from consumer to producer goods had occurred.[20] An armaments industry had been built almost from scratch, and a large, modestly mechanized army, supported by a military budget exceeding all civilian state expenditure, had been created, without meaningful growth in the cumulative government deficit.[21] Domestic production and per capita consumption of nearly all basic foodstuffs also increased between 1932 and 1938, bringing with them small but perceptible improvements in the general standard of living and the degree of German agricultural self-sufficiency.[22]

Of course, no social or political group or sector felt thoroughly satisfied with the trend of events by 1938, but every interest felt partially so. Labor had found work and wages at the price of liberty and influence. Management had obtained the subordination of the work force and the restoration of admittedly restricted profits in return for operating within an ever more burdensome network of official controls. Farmers, the problem children of every industrial economy, continued to suffer from low incomes and a flight from the land, but also benefited from appreciable state assistance in the form of several hundred thousand conscripted househelpers and harvesters, funds to purchase machinery, and forced reductions in the prices of fertilizers, which therefore nearly doubled in use during the first half of the Twelve-Year Reich.[23] Above all, Hitler had acquired, although rather more slowly than he wished, a firm enough political, industrial, and financial base to intimidate other nations and to pursue his external ambitions. In short, the German economy accomplished during the 1930s the task he had set for it, as for all public policy, in 1927: "to secure the inner strength of [the] people so that it can assert itself in the sphere of foreign policy."[24]

Even before all these economic returns were in, the Führer could dare to make the economy's assignment more concrete. In 1936, his famous memorandum on the Four-Year Plan called for an economy "capable of war" by 1940.[25] Here, too, historians often forget, he largely succeeded, however narrowly. Neither the Four-Year Plan nor the rearmament drive ever met on time most of the spiraling targets set for them. Nevertheless, by 1939, Hitler had an operational air force, a massive army, an almost complete *Westwall* of fortifications facing France, and a domestic food supply that appeared (and proved) nearly immune to blockade.[26] Although sizable shares of the nation's needs for fats, fibers, iron ore, and other vital metals and minerals still had to be imported, the Reich's planners could feel reasonably confident of making up foreseeable wartime shortfalls from stockpiles and restrictions on nonmilitary uses.[27] That such vital materials as rubber or munitions turned out to be in short supply in September 1939 should not blind us to the fact that by mid-1940 their monthly production in Germany had come to equal consumption.[28] In almost every calculable respect, the Hitlerian Reich enjoyed a much more favorable starting point for hostilities in 1939–40 than had the Wilhelmian Reich twenty-five years earlier, and the same advantage prevailed in less calculable regards. Between 1937 and 1939, ever-tighter restrictions on the availability of consumer goods and raw materials accustomed the populace to saving and austerity, and businessmen to central direction, even before the fighting began.[29] This time, preparations had already been made, down to detailed plans regarding barracks and guards, for the deployment of prisoners of war as agricultural laborers.[30]

Naturally, all was not well with the German economy in 1939. Clearly, key, eventually fatal bottlenecks existed, notably in coal and steel production. But it is hard to ascribe the presence of these to administrative chaos—the former rested on faulty estimates by the mining industry of the adequacy of current capacities to wartime needs; the latter had led to the formation of the Reichswerke Hermann Göring and seemed in the process of solution.[31] Of course, the regime owed much of what it had achieved to a policy of, in effect, "strip-mining the economy"—that is, to having laid waste its productive future for short-run gains in output—and this could not go on forever. Hitler not only increasingly remarked on this, however; he had also foreseen it from the day he took power and planned on repairing the damage through plunder.[32] Admittedly, the escalation of military demands coalesced in 1938 with certain other domestic and international economic trends to overload Germany's labor market, foreign exchange reserves, and supplies of iron and steel. This conjunction set off a wild free-for-all within the German economy for several months and enabled already worried planners to push back the fulfillment dates of numerous production targets by two years.[33] It also contributed to twin moves that had disastrous diplomatic consequences; the despoiling of Germany's Jews in late 1938 and the occupation of Prague in March 1939. The spectacles of impoverished Jewish refugees and tearful Czechs did much to make further appeasement of Hitler over Poland politically unacceptable in Britain.[34] Germany's economic difficulties thus played a role in dictating the *timing* of the Second World War by altering Allied calculations while hardening German ones.[35]

Otherwise, however, to say that an economic "crisis" afflicted the Reich in 1939 appears somewhat exaggerated. Shortages of foreign exchange remained the crucial problem, as in every year since 1934, but, try as they would, the Balkan purveyors of primary products to Germany could find no escape from continuing to trade largely on its terms.[36] Rapid growth in state spending was beginning to pose financial difficulties, but the regime headed them off by inaugurating a system of partially paying for government contracts with delayed tax rebates and by surreptitiously covering the gap between expenditures and revenues with bank savings deposits. As for the tight labor supply, it was being alleviated by the importation of foreign workers, one-half million of whom worked in the Reich in 1939, by the "combing out" of uncompetitive little shops and enterprises, the number of which fell by 190,000 between 1936 and 1939, by the shortening of apprenticeship periods, and by an enormous retraining program.[37] The German economy was not unmanageable in 1939, not threatened by bankruptcy, inflation, and proletarian dissatisfaction, and not falling between the two stools of guns and butter, but more or less on course and only somewhat behind the schedule Hitler had laid down in 1936 and then amended at the Hossbach Conference in November 1937.[38] *Die Wirtschaft* was, however, bumping up against its structural limitations, namely a work force and resource base too small and inelastic for Hitler's purposes. The key gulf in 1939—both in Hitler's mind and in retrospect—was not between what what Germany *was* doing and what he wanted, but between what Germany *could* do and his growing requirements.

Much the same can be said regarding 1941, even though the victories of the intervening years seemed to have loosened the economic contraints on the Reich. To be sure, luck had a lot to do with the situation. Hitler was fortunate that the Allies did not attack him in 1939–40.[39] He was even luckier that interwar developments in German army doctrine combined with his own free-spending on rearmament to permit the motorization of about 10 percent of the *Wehrmacht*, largely on an experimental basis. That, in turn, permitted his generals to *rediscover* in Poland the blitzkrieg strategy that had been conceived in the 1920s and that not only won the victories of 1939–41, but also coincidentally suited the economic capacities of Nazi Germany.[40] Finally, Hitler was favored most of all by Britain's actions in 1938–39. By ignoring the Soviets during the Munich crisis, then guaranteeing Poland's territorial integrity the following March, the British successively gave Stalin the reason and the possibility to make a deal with the Reich, from which flowed the indispensable access to Russian raw materials that sustained Nazi Germany in 1940–41.[41]

But if fortune smiled on the Führer, his regime also made use of the purely European phase of World War II. It is not accurate to depict this period as so much lost time until Albert Speer appeared to clean out the Augean stables, as his writings would have us believe. In particular, one can no longer credit the hoary notions that German war production made few inroads on civilian consumption prior to 1942 and that Hitler scaled back military output and strength in 1940. Between 1938 and 1941, the regime forced down per capita civilian consumption within Germany by 20 percent and per capita consumer goods output by 22 percent and raised the output of producer goods by 28 percent; by the end of the period, a substantial share of nominally consumer goods was already being allotted to the *Wehrmacht*; meanwhile, the proportion of the German work force thought to be engaged in the economic war effort increased from 20 percent in 1939 to 60 percent; and, considered either in raw terms or as a fraction of total national income, German military expenditure rose at a virtually steady rate from 1938–39 to 1943–44.[42] In truth, the productive achievements of 1942–44 associated with Speer's name depended heavily on the groundwork laid by his predecessors, including Fritz Todt, and occurred even though the number of agencies and persons contending for control of the German economy remained fully as large as in previous years.[43] Above all, in this connection, it now appears that the Third Reich succeeded in mobilizing a larger share of its net national product for war than did any of the other belligerent powers from 1939 to 1943, and that it did so virtually *throughout* the period (see Table 9.1).[44]

Table 9.1
Value of Resources Supplied to the War Effort as % of National Income
(Net National Product)

	UTILIZED DOMESTICALLY				FINANCED DOMESTICALLY			
	US	UK	USSR	Ger	US	UK	USSR	Ger
1939	1	16	—	25	2	8	—	24
1940	1	48	20	44	3	31	20	36
1941	13	55	—	56	14	41	—	44
1942	36	54	75	69	40	43	66	52
1943	47	57	76	76	53	47	58	60
1944	47	56	69	—	54	47	52	—

The columns on the left include resources acquired from abroad, e.g., American aid and net imports, but exclude supplies sent to other belligerents; the figures on the right count war goods exported but not those received.

None of this evidence suffices to elevate the Nazis to the status of first-rate economic managers. Certainly, enough was left undone during Hermann Göring's tenure at the head of the German economy from 1937 to 1942 to justify Richard Overy's reference to an "era of incompetence." But Overy's analysis also suggests that the central problem was personal more than systemic. Göring was both greedy for power and swamped by the task of applying what he amassed. The combination impeded the development of real coordination and strengthened "the reluctance on the part of much of industry to convert the war." Besides, he faced a formidable problem in the first years of fighting: the need not only to supply the materials required by the military effort, but also to finish the as yet incomplete industrial infrastructure that produced them.[45] Finally, there was the disincentive of overconfidence, born of Dunkirk, Compiègne, Stalin's purges, and the influx of almost three million new foreign workers during 1940.[46]

Historians, thus, may go too far when they explain the insufficiency of German war production by noting that "neither fascist ideology nor the institutional procedures that came in its wake indicated how to make necessary choices," or that the nature of the regime entailed an "inability to allocate its resources consistently in favor of the armaments sector."[47] Infighting in the German economy took place within definite, designed confines. It had both invigorating and inhibiting effects. And it was, at bottom, as much an expression as a cause of Germany's inadequacies. Recognizing these points has important implications for our understanding of the workings of so-called fascist economies and for the debate detween the proponents of either monocracy or polycracy. Demonstrating them requires turning to the second and third questions raised earlier in this essay and beginning with a compressed examination of why the Nazi economy accomplished what it did.

The usual explanations are terror and popular enthusiasm, and they are not so much wrong as incomplete. The Führer himself appreciated the value of fear, boasting once to Hjalmar Schacht that "the primary cause of the stabilization of our currency is the concentration camp."[48] And, as Jack Gillingham has shown, even the Ruhr coal miners, among whom were few fanatical Nazis, produced prodigiously under severe circumstances during the war, largely out of patriotism.[49] But, while the Gestapo, *Gleichschaltung*, Hitler's charisma, resurgent national pride, large doses of official flattery, improved living standards, and assorted social innovations designed to signal the onset of a classless society all did their work with the populace, the Nazi regime applied something else, which was the key to its success. This was the National Socialist Party's own, distinct, coherent, if rather hybrid economic doctrine, one that centered on the bridling and spurring of capitalist competition.

Hitler and the Nazi faithful always took a purely instrumental view of economics—it was a means to win the victory of the German race in the unremitting historical struggle among peoples for their "daily bread."[50] Since that victory depended, the party taught, on the creation of a vast, contiguous, agriculturally self-sufficient, and ethnically pure empire, the question was how to make the German economy serve this objective. Ideological reeducation, by itself, would take too long; simply bludgeoning the economy into submission would, sooner or later, kill the goose that laid the golden eggs; far better, then, to restructure the economic reward-system and let individual ambition do the rest. That was the plan outlined in the two principal economic programs the party prepared prior to the seizure of power in 1933 and that the regime enacted over the next three years. It amounted to increasing government control over the factors of production, detaching the German economy from foreign influences, and making the rights of ownership contingent on their exercise as the state sanctioned—in other words, to creating an environment in which the institution of private property was never abandoned, but the disposition and possession of it were always in question.

Consequently, in the Third Reich official regulations soon policed imports and exports, costs and prices, wages and working conditions, raw material supplies, investments, and the flow of foreign exchange. Along with changes in the tax structure and limits on dividends, these measures channeled capital almost exclusively into those industries identified as vital by Berlin, since only here did the possibilities of profits and growth continue to exist.[51] To be sure, this system did not take shape overnight. One of its decisive and by historians least-noticed components was not published until 30 January 1937—namely, a new German Corporation Law that reduced the influence of shareholders over management and removed obligation to them as grounds for a firm to refuse to allocate funds as the regime wished.[52] By and large, however, the mechanism was in place by 1936, even before the Four-Year Plan was unveiled and the rearmament drive really took off. Thus, the economics editor of the *Völkischer Beobachter* could claim in that year, without great exaggeration, that "where capitalism considers itself still untouched, it is, in fact, already harnessed to politics. . . . National Socialist economic policy corresponds to the technical age. It lets capitalism run as the motor, uses its dynamic energies, but shifts the gears."[53] And, he might have added, "does the steering."

That this was so resulted, as well, from another tool of Nazi economic policy that was forged between 1933 and 1936, but that had been more implicit than explicit in the party's Darwinian ideology. Such incentive as controls alone could not provide, policy-makers learned, conscription and/or the stimulation of competition could. Prototypical of this process was the way, beginning in 1935, in which Hans Kehrl, a leading economic planner, overcame the opposition of German business to increased production of synthetic fibers. Balked by IG Farben, the giant chemicals combine, and by most textile manufacturers, Kehrl simply set up five regional fibers companies with loans from the public treasury, forced nearby textile firms to purchase the stock in the new enterprises, and required a 20 percent admixture of artificial thread in all clothing for German consumption, thus creating the preconditions of profitability and driving the giant Farben concern into expansion in order to cash in on the new situation and preserve at least a part of its market share.[54] Similar maneuvers induced IG in 1935 to increase its output of aluminum and magnesium faster than it desired; blunter ones simultaneously prompted Farben to furnish technical information to a new company instigated by the state to make poison gas. Such actions already had compelled ten brown coal producers a year earlier to form a new synthetic fuel maker, Brabag AG.[55] All these developments turned out to be mere dress rehearsals for the most intimidating instance of state dragooning of private enterprise in the Third Reich: the foundation in 1937–38 of the

Reichswerke Hermann Göring to mine and smelt low-grade German iron ore and convert it into steel.[56] In sum, between 1934 and 1938 the Nazis learned how to lure and lash, tempt and threaten, coax and corner German business into serving their regime's desires.[57]

This combination of controls, compulsion, and competition helps explain why Hitler was able to press autarky and armament far beyond the levels most German big businessmen anticipated in 1933 or regarded as economically and politically sound in 1938.[58] It also largely accounts for the participation of German executives in takeovers of Jewish-owned property, the spoliation of enterprises in occupied lands, and the exploitation of slave labor—all of which important segments of the corporate world considered misconceived.[59] The genius of the Nazi regime lay in its installation of a "road race of organizations" backed by "the threat in cases of recalcitrance to entrust doing the dirty work to another."[60] By mobilizing individual initiative in this manner, the Nazi economy, despite all the confusion and contentiousness it contained, performed so formidably from 1933 to 1944. Thus, if polycracy characterized the execution of German economic policy, it did so to productive as well as destructive effect.[61]

Moreover, polycracy did not determine the fate of that policy. Of course, an answer to the third question raised earlier—What difference did administrative confusion and inefficiency make?—is difficult to formulate with precision. As Charles Maier has remarked, inefficiency is both too vague a descriptive term and too universal a feature of war production to permit confident comparisons among the belligerents in World War II.[62] At most, one can say that the British record with regard to the optimal employment of resources hardly set a model for the German, that the Soviet one may have been notably better, and that planners in every nation had stories like Walter Rohland's of chrome that could have built tanks being diverted to flatware for the officers' messes of the *Luftwaffe*.[63] To be sure, Hitler did not make good his accumulated economic deficiencies after 1941 and failed to exploit the economic advantages provided by the conquest of western Europe. But, when all is said and done, can one contend that economic misallocations caused Germany's defeat? Bad military decisions perhaps did, notably during the first months of the invasion of Russia, or later when the Führer fiddled with the designs of powerful weapons.[64] Perfectionism bedeviled the civilian production and the military procurement processes and thus made German war supplies relatively costly.[65] But these circumstances proved fatal precisely because Germany's economic limits gave the Nazi regime so little margin for error in comparison to the Allies.[66] As one contemporary said, the Reich's producers were in the position "of people who had to cover themselves with too short a blanket: the more one succeeds in his attempts to be well covered, the more the other must suffer."[67] A better-coordinated Third Reich, it seems likely, would have been more murderous, but not, in the end, more victorious.

Even Nazi labor policy, generally regarded as the most spectacular example of the regime's allocative timidity and ineptitude, takes on a different hue when seen in light of Germany's structural disadvantages. After all, *Kinder, Küche, und Kirche* was not only an ideological fixation, but also a biological strategy for overcoming the numerical insufficiency of the *Volk* to Hitler's objectives for it. Moreover, it is vital to bear in mind that, in 1939, 36 percent of the married German women, 88 percent of the unmarried ones between fifteen and sixty years of age, and 52 percent of all German females over fifteen were already employed. Even before forced laborers began to replace men called to arms in Germany, women over fourteen already composed a higher share of the native work force in the Reich than they ever attained during wartime in the United States or Britain.[68] Although foreign laborers, even enslaved ones, later proved less productive on average and probably more expensive than additional German women would have been, hiring an equivalent number of new female German workers (some 7 million) was scarcely possible between 1941 and 1945, let alone likely to yield more in net material output than it would have cost in morale. The regime, in effect, chose to shore up one weakness attendant on the inadequacy of German resources to their task (popular discomfort) at the expense of another (production).

Nazi labor policy was reprehensible from the outset of the war and increasingly repulsive, brutal, and counterproductive as time went on, but from the perspective of Berlin, *all* the choices available in this sphere had potentially high costs. Similarly, it may be true that, from the point of view of maximizing output, the Third Reich kept too large a share of its able-bodied men under arms compared to the other belligerent nations, but given the smallness of the German population relative to that which stood behind its enemies on any front after 1941, this pattern would have been hard to avoid.[69] Whether one is talking of labor or some other central resource, after 1941 (and perhaps even after 1938) too many essential claimants chased too few supplies. Everything—tanks, guns, U-boats, coastal fortifications, airplanes, fuel and rubber factories, the transfer of key productive installations underground, etc., *ad infinitum*—seemed vital in some way to the Herculean war effort, and every conceivable distributional system had to neglect something indispensable.

The key Nazi failings were ones of conception, not coordination. Germany simply could not marshal the wherewithal to "arm in depth" and defeat a coalition of Britain, the United States, and the Soviet Union. The Third Reich was, in the end, no more equal than the Second to the demands of fighting on multiple fronts and on the sea, not to mention, this time, in the air. Better budgeting of men, money, and material would not, in all probability, have overcome this fact.[70] Consider the data in Table 9.2 concerning the relative strength of the powers engaged in the Second World War.[71] While these figures suggest that Germany enjoyed material superiority over its opposition in 1939 (providing we exclude the resources of the British and French empires and dominions), they also indicate the Reich's substantial disadvantages against the enemies it feared as of 1938, let alone the ones that coalesced in 1941. A table showing relative access to key raw materials (and thus including data for the various empires) would be even more devastating in its implications.[72]

Table 9.2
Coalitions

Category	1939–40 (1938)			1941–45	
	G/It	Br/Fr (with USSR)		G/It/Fr/J	Br/US/USSR
Population	112.3	89.5	(270.1)	226.4	366.5
Percentage world manufacturing production	15.5	15.1	(24.1)	25.1	51.1
Iron and Steel production (millions of tons)	25.5	16.6	(34.6)	38.6	57.3
Energy consumption (in millions of metric tons of coal	255.8	280	(457)	436.3	1070
Total Industrial potential (UK/1900 = 100)	260	255	(407)	422	861

Even allowing for the fact that such quantitative indices beg a host of important historical questions, these statistical relationships imply something vital. For Nazi Germany, the Second World War was virtually bound to occur and to spread "prematurely." Given the nation's narrow resource base, the regime's bid for world power inevitably became a vicious circle in which the attempt to free the Reich of reliance on foreign raw materials merely increased the nation's appetite for and dependence on them.[73] Given the degree of rearmament required to compensate for the country's population disadvantage, its vulnerability to attack on several sides, and its needs to overcome the English Channel and the expanse of Russia, even Chamberlain's government had been alerted by 1939 to the fact that Britain could no more stand pat while Göring amassed the means to intimidate it than when Tirpitz had tried to do the same. To Hitler, by 1938–39 superior German preparedness was an ever-receding prospect, like the horizon.

The Nazi Führer's mounting tendency to command the economy to do everything at once, in particular his succumbing in 1938–39 to an economic "activism that ignored all limits," reflected his growing appreciation of this situation.[74] That he even hazarded the attempt seems to have had more to do with his fatalism concerning Germany's capacities than with any sense of specific economic problems. In 1939, concerned about his indispensability and mortality, fearing that his current military advantages would not last, and hoping that Britain would back down once more but having at least neutralized the Russians, he gambled over Poland—and got a larger war than he bargained for.[75] In June 1941, frustrated by his inability to defeat Britain, perhaps uncomfortable with his dependence on Stalin's shipments, and alarmed at Soviet claims to his Balkan preserve, he rolled the dice in Russia, expecting to remove the pressure from the east and to break Britain's resolve.[76] Six months later, he declared war on the United States, perhaps as a matter of honor but probably in order to show solidarity with Japan and thus to ensure that it would not make an early peace that would free the United States to concentrate even indirectly on the Reich.[77] In each of these instances, Hitler struggled to avoid the overpowering constellation that his actions, in fact, created. On none of these occasions was he impelled by internal infighting or any economic imperative other than the one he had recognized consistently—the insufficiency of Germany's resources to achieving world power within the prevailing context. But at all three turning points, he overreached.

In these words lies the resolution of the debate between monocrats and polycrats and the basis for an appropriate assessment of the importance of administrative shortcomings and economic mismanagement in the Third Reich. Hitler, not someone else, overreached, and he did so in response to fundamental and almost intractable material deficiencies, not in passive acceptance of such epiphenomena as courses of action presented him by the nature of the power structure over which he presided. That his actions had such devastating effects resulted, not least, from the way his Darwinian economic system tapped and channeled the energy and ingenuity of his *Volk*. Thus, an emphasis on the confused and competitive nature of policy in Nazi Germany can tell us much about *how* it wrought what it did and then failed, but not about *why*. To explain that, historians have to focus on the futility of Hitler's bid to make Germany a *Weltmacht* at a time when the prerequisites for that status had outstripped the nation's capacities.[78]

Such conclusions do not, contrary to A. J. P. Taylor, give every other German of Hitler's day a claim to innocence. Neither, however, do they allow us to draw Galbraith's comforting inference about "the inherent inefficiencies of dictatorship."

Notes

1. For this quotation and those in the preceding paragraph, see John Kenneth Galbraith, *A Life in Our Times* (New York, 1981), pp. 210–11 and 229.

2. Franz Neumann, *Behemoth* (New York, 1944), p. xii.

3. Alan Bullock, *Hitler: A Study in Tyranny,* (London, 1952); Robert Koehl, "Feudal Aspects of National Socialism," *American Political Science Review* 54 (1960): 921–33. Koehl's analogy was anticipated by Kurt Lachmann, "The Herman Göring Works," *Social Research* 8 (1941): 224–40.

4. Burton Klein, *Germany's Economic Preparations for War* (Cambridge, Mass., 1959).

5. Of course, the lines of argument emerged before these terms entered general usage. "Monocracy" surfaces in Eberhard Jäckel, *Hitler in History* (Hanover, N.H., 1984), pp. 28–30. "Polycracy" acquired currency via Martin Broszat, *Der Staat Hitlers* (Munich, 1969), pp. 363–403, and Peter Hüttenberger's essay, "Nationalsozialistische Polykratie," *Geschichte und Gesellschaft* 2 (1976): 417–42.

6. This is the position of Karl Dietrich Bracher, Eberhard Jäckel, Andreas Hillgruber, and Klaus Hildebrand in their numerous publications. For a convenient summary in English, see Hildebrand's *The Third Reich* (Winchester, Mass., 1984), and for a compact, forceful, and up-to-date statement of the argument, see Hermann Graml, "Wer bestimmte die Aussenpolitik des Dritten Reiches?" in Manfred Funke et al., eds., *Demokratie und Diktatur* (Düsseldorf, 1987), pp. 223–36.

7. Alan Bullock, "Hitler and the Origins of the Second World War," in Henry A. Turner, Jr., ed., *Nazism and the Third Reich* (New York, 1972), p. 223.

8. David Schoenbaum, *Hitler's Social Revolution* (New York, 1966), especially pp. xxi–xxii.

9. Alan Milward, *The German Economy at War* (London, 1965).

10. A. J. P. Taylor, *The Origins of the Second World War* (Greenwich, Conn., 1961), p. 18.

11. Tim Mason, "Intention and Explanation: A Current Controversy about the Interpretation of National Socialism," in G. Hirschfeld and L. Kettenacker, eds., *Der "Führerstaat": Mythos und Realität* (Stuttgart, 1981), p. 30.

12. See, in particular, ibid.; Broszat's *Staat Hitlers,* Edward N. Peterson, *The Limits of Hitler's Power* (Princeton, N.J., 1969); and, in part, Ian Kershaw,

Popular Opinion and Political Dissent in the Third Reich (Oxford, 1983). Certainly the most thoroughgoing formulation of this position is Hans Mommsen's depiction of Hitler as a "weak dictator"; see Mommsen's contribution to this volume.

13. Hüttenberger, "Nationalsozialistische Polykratie," pp. 417–42. Arthur Schweitzer, "Business Power in the Nazi Regime," *Zeitschrift für Nationalökonomie* 20 (1960): 414–42, and Neumann, *Behemoth*, are the forefathers of this argument.

14. Hans Mommsen, "Die Realisierung des Utopischen: Die 'Endlösung der Judenfrage' im 'Dritten Reich,'" *Geschichte und Gesellschaft* 9 (1983): 381–420.

15. See the contributions of Ian Kershaw, Robert Gellately, and Christopher Browning to this volume.

16. R. J. Overy, *The Nazi Economic Recovery, 1932–1938* (London, 1982), pp. 37 and 62–63.

17. Harold James, *The German Slump* (Oxford, 1986).

18. Here I am taking issue somewhat with Harold James's depiction of the allegedly "conventional" nature of the Nazi recovery, both in his contribution to this volume and in his otherwise excellent *The German Slump*. It seems to me that the Nazi regime sought, from its outset, to engender a particular kind of economic revival, one that redistributed resources toward sectors vital to "arms, autarky, and aggression." For telling indications that this was so, see Fritz Blaich, *Wirtschaft und Rüstung im "Dritten Reich"* (Düsseldorf, 1987), pp. 15–16 (on tax policy *re* motor vehicles) and 27 (on prohibitions on the expansion of textile plants).

19. R. J. Overy, "Germany, 'Domestic Crisis' and War in 1939," *Past and Present*, no. 116 (1987): 149–50.

20. Williamson Murray, *The Change in the European Balance of Power, 1938–1939* (Princeton, N.J., 1984), pp. 18–19.

21. Overy, "Germany, 'Domestic Crisis' and War in 1939," p. 149; Michael Geyer, "Zum Einfluss der nationalsozialistischen Rüstungspolitik auf das Ruhrgebiet," *Rheinische Vierteljahrsblätter* 45 (1981): 207. For an example of the spectacular growth of the arms industry, see Williamson Murray, *Luftwaffe* (Baltimore, Md., 1985), pp. 8–9.

22. J. E. Farquharson, *The Plough and the Swastika* (Beverly Hills, Calif., 1976), pp. 161–81.

23. Fritz Blaich, "Wirtschaft und Rüstung in Deutschland 1933–1939," in W. Benz and H. Graml, eds., *Sommer 1939* (Stuttgart, 1979), pp. 53–54.

24. Telford Taylor, ed., *Hitler's Secret Book* (New York, 1961), p. 34.

25. See Wilhelm Treue, "Hitlers Denkschrift zum Vierjahresplan 1936," *Vierteljahrshefte für Zeitgeschichte* 3 (1955): 184–210; Dieter Petzina, *Autarkiepolitik im Dritten Reich* (Stuttgart, 1968), pp. 48–51.

26. Murray, *Luftwaffe*, pp. 13–14 and 22; Murray, *The Change in the European Balance of Power*, p. 350; and, especially, on the food supply, Lothar Burchardt, "The Impact of the War Economy on the Civilian Population of Germany during the First and Second World Wars," in Wilhelm Deist, ed., *The Germany Military in the Age of Total War* (Dover, N.H., 1985), pp. 47–49. For technical reasons related to Burchardt's failure to make his data for 1914–18 and 1939–44 comparable in key respects, I think he overstates his conclusions on p. 64.

27. Blaich in Benz and Graml, eds., *Sommer 1939*, pp. 60–61. In fact, the Reich's planners proved too confident; see Murray, *The Change in the European Balance of Power*, pp. 326–32.

28. Ibid., pp. 23–24; Peter Hayes, *Industry and Ideology: IG Farben in the Nazi Era* (New York, 1987), p. 348.

29. Blaich in Benz and Graml, eds., *Sommer 1939*, pp. 58–61; R. J. Overy, "Hitler's War and the German Economy: A Reinterpretation," *Economic History Review* 35 (1982): 283–84. In 1938, before the war began, consumption amounted to 59 percent of German national income, a decline from 81 percent in 1933 and 71 percent in 1928; R. J. Overy, *Goering, the "Iron Man"* (Boston, 1984), p. 83.

30. Ulrich Herbert, *Geschichte der Ausländerbeschäftigung in Deutschland 1880 bis 1980*, Berlin, 1986, p. 123, and *Fremdarbeiter: Politik und Praxis des "Ausländer-Einsatzes" in der Kriegswirtschaft des Dritten Reiches* (Berlin, 1985), p. 65.

31. John R. Gillingham, *Industry and Politics in the Third Reich* (London, 1985), pp. 53–54; R. J. Overy, "Heavy Industry and the State in Nazi Germany: The Reichswerke Crisis," *European History Quarterly* 15 (1985): 316–18.

32. For the quoted phrase, see Joachim Fest, *Hitler* (New York, 1975), p. 538; on Hitler's reasoning, MacGregor Knox, "Conquest, Foreign and Domestic, in Fascist Italy and Nazi Germany," *Journal of Modern History* 56 (1984): 53.

33. Geyer, "Zum Einfluss der nationalsozialistischen Rüstungspolitik," pp. 247–49; Hayes, *Industry and Ideology*, pp. 206–8.

34. On the economic reasons for the assault on the Jews, see Helmut Genschel, *Die Verdrängung der Juden aus der Wirtschaft im Dritten Reich*, (Göttingen, 1966), pp. 186–217; and Avraham Barkai, *Vom Boykott zur "Entjudung"* (Frankfurt, 1988), pp. 126–28 and 146–52; on those favoring the occupation of Prague, see Hans-Erich Volkmann, "Zur rüstungsökonomischen Bedeutung und grossraumwirtschaftlichen Motivation der Eingliederung der Sudetengebiete und Böhmen-Mährens in das Deutsche Reich," *Studia Historiae Oeconomicae* 14 (1979): 161–86. On the effects in Britain, see especially Martin Gilbert and Richard Gott, *The Appeasers* (London, 1967), pp. 308–23.

35. Cf. Tim Mason's contribution to this volume, "The Domestic Dy-

namics of Nazi Conquest."

36. See David E. Kaiser, *Economic Diplomacy and the Origins of the Second World* (Princeton, N.J., 1980), pp. 303 and 316–17; and Bernd Jürgen Wendt, "England and der deutsche 'Drang nach Südosten,'" in I. Geiss and B. Wendt, eds., *Deutschland in der Weltpolitik des 19. und 20. Jahrhunderts* (Düsseldorf, 1973), pp. 483–512. This is not to say that the Balkans could satisfy Germany's needs. By 1939, the key officials in Berlin knew better. See Alfred Kube, *Pour le Merite und Hakenkreuz: Hermann Göring im Dritten Reich* (Munich, 1986), pp. 294–99; and Hayes, *Industry and Ideology*, pp. 298–300.

37. Overy, "Germany, 'Domestic Crisis' and War in 1939," pp. 150–52; Blaich, *Wirtschaft und Rüstung*, pp. 20, 25–26, and 35; John Gillingham, "The 'Deproletarianization' of German Society: Vocational Training in the Third Reich," *Journal of Social History* 19 (1985): 428.

38. Hans Kehrl, *Zur Wirklichkeit des Dritten Reichs*, n.p., n.d. [1975], pp. 19–21. See also Richard Overy's reply in "Debate: Germany, 'Domestic Crisis' and War in 1939," *Past and Present*, no. 122 (1989), pp. 231–32.

39. Murray, *The Change in the European Balance of Power*, pp. 326–34.

40. Williamson Murray, "German Army Doctrine, 1918–1939, and the Post-1945 Theory of 'Blitzkrieg Strategy,'" in Carole Fink et al., eds., *German Nationalism and the European Response, 1890–1945* (Norman, Okla. 1985), pp. 71–94; and Matthew Cooper, *The German Army, 1933–1945* (New York, 1984), pp. 130–76.

41. Christopher Thorne, *The Approach of War, 1938–39* (New York, 1968), p. 137; Adam Ulam, *Expansion and Coexistence* (London, 1968), pp. 267–75; Vojtech Mastny, *Russia's Road to the Cold War* (New York, 1979), pp. 23–24. See also, however, Jiri Hochman, *The Soviet Union and the Failure of Collective Security, 1934–1938* (Ithaca, N.Y., 1984) for a powerful argument to the effect that Stalin consistently preferred an accommodation with Germany to an alliance with the Western powers.

42. See Overy, "Hitler's War and the German Economy," pp. 283–85, and idem, *Goering*, pp. 96–97 and 139–40. I have made a slight adjustment to the published figures pursuant to Prof. Overy's letter to me of May 19, 1989.

43. See Charles S. Maier, "The Economics of Fascism and Nazism," in his *In Search of Stability* (New York, 1987), pp. 111–12; Hayes, *Industry and Ideology*, pp. 319–20; and Blaich, *Wirtschaft und Rüstung*, pp. 44–48.

44. Mark Harrison, "Resource Mobilization for World War II: the U.S.A., U.K., U.S.S.R., and Germany, 1938–1945," *Economic History Review* 41 (1988): 171–92, especially pp. 183–84, for the table that I have reassembled here. Harrison's essay shows that the usual figures on which historians have relied in assessing relative resource mobilization, notably those of Berenice Carroll, *Design for Total War* (The Hague, 1968), are either obsolete or misleadingly constructed; see especially p. 182.

45. See Overy, "Hitler's War and the German Economy," pp. 285–91 (the quoted phrases appear respectively on pp. 287 and 291); and idem, *Göering*, pp. 138–63. Also Ludolf Herbst, *Der Totale Krieg und die Ordnung der Wirtschaft* (Stuttgart, 1982), p. 115, for the argument that Göring possessed the necessary machinery and authority to manage the economy by the end of 1939, just not the necessary leadership qualities. For more on industrialists' foot-dragging with regard to economic mobilization, see Overy, "Heavy Industry and the State in Nazi Germany," 321, 329–30, and 332, and idem, *Nazi Economic Recovery*, pp. 63 and 66.

46. Herbert, *Geschichte der Ausländerbeschäftigung*, pp. 130–32.

47. Maier, *In Search of Stability*, p. 115; Mason, "Domestic Dynamics of Nazi Conquest," above. I, too, may have succumbed to this explanatory temptation; *Industry and Ideology*, pp. 320–21.

48. Quoted in Willi A. Boelcke, *Die Deutsche Wirtschaft, 1930–1945* (Düsseldort, 1983), p. 132. Göring made the same point somewhat more delicately to a meeting of the council of ministers on 12 May 1936 when he remarked that "measures which in a state with a parliamentary government would probably bring about inflation, do not have the same results in a total-itarian state"; quoted in Overy, *Goering*, p. 55.

49. John Gillingham, "Ruhr Coal Miners and Hitler's War," *Journal of Social History* 15 (1981): 637–53.

50. The argument in this and the succeeding paragraph summarizes that of my *Industry and Ideology*, pp. 70–73 and 166–73, which relies heavily on the excellent works of Avraham Barkai: "Die Wirtschaftsauffassung der NSDAP," *Aus Politik und Zeitgeschichte*, Beilage 9 (1 March 1975), pp. 3–16; "Sozialdar-winismus und Antiliberalismus in Hitlers Wirtschaftskonzept," *Geschichte und Gesellschaft* 3 (1977): 406–17; *Das Wirtschaftssystem des Nationalsozialismus* (Cologne, 1977); and "Wirtschaftliche Grundanschauungen und Ziele der N.S.D.A.P.," *Jahrbuch des Instituts für Deutsche Geschichte* 7 (1978): 355–85.

51. Such initiatives also similarly redirected the labor market; see Blaich, *Wirtschaft und Rüstung*, pp. 18–19.

52. See F. A. Mann, "The New German Company Law and Its Back-ground," *Journal of Comparative Legislation and International Law* 19 (1937): 222–33; Hayes, *Industry and Ideology*, p. 168; and Curtis W. Bajak, "The Third Reich's Corporation Law of 1937," (Dissertation, Yale University, 1986).

53. Fritz Nonnenbruch, *Die dynamische Wirtschaft* (Munich, 1936), pp. 42–43.

54. See Hayes, *Industry and Ideology*, pp. 144–47.

55. Ibid., pp. 133–39.

56. Overy, "Heavy Industry and the State in Nazi Germany," pp. 313–40. The oft-repeated argument (most recently in Ian Kershaw, *The Nazi Dic-tatorship* (Baltimore, Md., 1985), pp. 53–54) of G. W. F. Hallgarten and

Joachim Radkau, *Deutsche Industrie und Politik* (Frankfurt, 1974), p. 255, that the formation of the Reichswerke actually benefited private steel producers by relieving them of the costs of exploiting low-grade ore and by holding up prices is valid only for the short run, and few steelmakers were impressed.

57. Here I am disputing the arguments of Hüttenberger and Schweitzer (see notes 5 and 13) and Kershaw, *Nazi Dictatorship*, p. 60. Gerhard Thomas Mollin, *Montankonzerne und "Drittes Reich"* (Göttingen, 1988), is instructive in this regard.

58. On the differences between the kind of rearmament program some businessmen hoped for and the kind they got, see the incisive comments of Michael Geyer, "Etudes in Political History," in Peter Stachura, ed., *The Nazi Machtergreifung* (Winchester, Mass., 1983), p. 114; and idem, "Zum Einfluss der nationalsozialistischen Rüstungspolitik," pp. 214–19. For indications of widespread opposition to overpursued autarky and armament, see Overy, *Economic Recovery*, p. 63, and "Hitler's War and the German Economy," pp. 279–80. For IG Farben's attempts to slow down the autarky drive, see Hayes, *Industry and Ideology*, pp. 159–61, 196, and 199.

59. For numerous examples, see Hayes, *Industry and Ideology*, chaps. 5–8.

60. Hans Mommsen, "Zur Verschränkung traditioneller und faschistischer Führungsgruppen in Deutschland beim Übergang von der Bewegungs- zur Systemphase," in W. Schieder, ed., *Faschismus als soziale Bewegung* (Hamburg, 1976), p. 176.

61. For an interesting demonstration of this point with regard to armaments, see Michael J. Neufeld, "The Guided Missile and the Third Reich," in Monika Renneberg and Mark Walker, eds., *Science, Technology and National Socialism* (New York, forthcoming).

62. Maier, *In Search of Stability*, pp. 110–11.

63. On the British, see not only Table 9.1 above, but also Noel Annan, "Gentlemen vs. Players," *The New York Review of Books*, 29 September 1988, p. 64, reporting the findings of Correlli Barnett, *The Pride and the Fall: The Dream and Illusion of Britain as a Great Nation*. On the Soviets, see Harrison, "Resource Mobilization for World War II," esp. pp. 190–91. For Rohland's anecdote, see Walter Rohland, *Bewegte Zeiten* (Stuttgart, 1978), p. 90.

64. For example, see Russel H. S. Stolfi, "Barbarossa Revisited: A Critical Appraisal of the Opening of the Russo-German Campaign (June–December 1941)," *Journal of Modern History* 54 (1982): 27–46; Albert Speer, *Inside the Third Reich* (New York, 1970), esp. pp. 362–69; and the semipopular account of Ronald Lewin, *Hitler's Mistakes* (New York, 1984), especially pp. 84–124.

65. See Overy, "Hitler's War and the German Economy," pp. 286 and 289.

66. Harrison, "Resource Mobilization for World War II," p. 181.

67. Kurt Krüger, quoted in Hayes, *Industry and Ideology*, p. 321.

68. See Overy, "Debate," pp. 239–40; idem., "'Blitzkriegswirtschaft'? Finanzpolitik, Lebensstandard und Arbeitseinsatz in Deutschland 1939–1942," *VfZ* 36 (1988): 425–28; idem, "Mobilization for Total War in Germany, 1939–1941," *English Historical Review.* 103 (1988), pp. 627–29.

69. Harrison, "Resource Mobilization for World War II," p. 186.

70. See Murray, *The Change in the European Balance of Power*, p. 27.

71. Compiled from the charts in Paul Kennedy, *The Rise and Fall of the Great Powers* (New York, 1987), pp. 199–202, and "The First World War and the International Power System," in Steven E. Miller, ed., *Military Strategy and the Origins of the First World War* (Princeton, N.J., 1985), pp. 12–14. I have used figures for France in 1941–44 as an (obviously very rough) proxy for the resources of occupied Europe.

72. See, for example, the graphs in Murray, *The Change in the European Balance of Power*, pp. 5–6.

73. For a fuller statement of this argument, see Hayes, *Industry and Ideology*, pp. 154–55.

74. Michael Geyer, "Rüstungsbeschleunigung und Inflation," *Militärgeschichtliche Mitteilungen* 28 (1981): 140 and 146.

75. See Jost Dülffer, "Der Beginn des Krieges 1939: Hitler, die innere Krise und das Mächtesystem," *Geschichte und Gesellschaft* 2 (1976): 464–65; Overy, "Hitler's War and the German Economy," p. 275, and "Germany, 'Domestic Crisis' and War in 1939," pp. 161 and 163–65; and Knox, "Conquest, Foreign and Domestic," p. 54.

76. Jäckel, *Hitler in History*, p. 69. But see also Knox, "Conquest, Foreign and Domestic," p. 56.

77. Jäckel, *Hitler in History*, p. 86; Andreas Hillgruber, "Die weltpolitischen Entscheidungen vom 22. Juni 1941 bis 11. Dezember 1941," in Karl Dietrich Bracher et al., eds., *Nationalsozialistische Diktatur, 1933–1945: Eine Bilanz* (Düsseldorf, 1983), pp. 457–60.

78. For the suggestive argument that the structure of international power relations had turned decisively against Germany by the end of the First World War, and that at least some German military planners discerned this, see Michael Geyer, *Aufrüstung oder Sicherheit* (Wiesbaden, 1980), pp. 177–88, especially the concluding paragraph.

10

Beyond "Intentionalism" and "Functionalism": A Reassessment of Nazi Jewish Policy from 1939 to 1941

CHRISTOPHER R. BROWNING

In the past two decades interpretations of National Socialism have for the most part been divided between two schools, characterized by Tim Mason as the "intentionalists" and the "functionalists."[1] The former focus on Hitler and his ideology. The course of the Third Reich, in their view, was primarily determined by the decisions of Adolf Hitler, which in turn were calculated or "intended" to realize the goals of an ideologically derived "program" to which he had clung with fanatical consistency since the 1920s. The latter focus on the structure and institutions of the Third Reich. They explain what happened in Nazi Germany as an unplanned "cumulative radicalization" produced by the chaotic decision-making process of a polycratic regime and the "negative selection" of destructive elements from the Nazis' ideological arsenal as the only ones that could perpetually mobilize the disparate and otherwise incompatible elements of the Nazi coalition.[2]

When these two approaches have been applied to Nazi Jewish policy and the origins of the Final Solution, drastically different interpretations have resulted. According to the "intentionalists," Hitler decided on the mass murder of the Jews in the 1920s and thereafter worked with consciousness and calculation toward that goal. Insofar as Nazi Jewish policy in the 1930s could be seen as conscious preparation for the mass murder, it was embraced as evidence of continuity; when it did not, it was dismissed as either temporary expediency or the irrelevant and unguided experiments of Hitler's subordinates. The ultimate decision to implement the Final Solution was tied to the invasion of Russia, for the conquest of *Lebensraum* and the total destruction of European Jewry were seen as so inextricably connected in Hitler's ideology that he inevitably sought to realize the two simultaneously. [3]

The "functionalists" eschewed this Hitler-centric, ideologically grounded interpretation. For them, the diversity and contradictions of Nazi Jewish policy in the 1930s—Karl Schleunes's "twisted road to Auschwitz"—were proof that Hitler and the Nazis were not operating programmatically toward a premeditated goal. Insofar as consensus was eventually reached in Nazi Jewish policy, it was for the expulsion of the Jews—a goal Hitler and the Nazis pursued well into the fall of 1941. Only when failure of the blitzkrieg in Russia blocked expulsion did mass murder emerge as a solution. According to Uwe Adam, the breakthrough to mass murder resulted from a belated decision by Hitler. More provocatively, Martin Broszat and Hans Mommsen argued that it occurred without any specific and comprehensive decision or order from Hitler. The system's automatic mechanisms for "cumulative radicalization," more than Hitler's ideology and leadership, explained the origins of the Final Solution. [4]

Neither of these interpretations in the extreme form that I have articulated above has been able to bear the weight of the subsequent research they have helped to stimulate. At a conference in Stuttgart in May 1984 devoted particularly to the decision-making process and Hitler's role in the crucial events of 1941, the "functionalist" position as articulated by Broszat and Mommsen did not carry the day. The consensus of the conference was that Hitler had indeed made a series of decisions in the spring and summer of 1941 for the mass murder of the European Jews. [5] While the intentionalist interpretation of the pre-1941 period did not come under the same scrutiny at Stuttgart, its linear and monocausal explanation has likewise been buffeted as research has uncovered the diversity and complexity of Nazi Jewish policy.

A number of scholars have been in the process of moderating the less tenable aspects of "intentionalism" in order to articulate a more defensible position. For example, Eberhard Jäckel admits the diversity and "planlessness" of Nazi Jewish policy before 1941; that is, the top Nazi leaders around Hitler did not know from the beginning that they were going to murder the European Jews. Moreover, he emphasizes the incremental nature of Hitler's decision making in 1941. The Final Solution, in other words, did not result from a single, comprehensive *Führerbefehl*. Many aspects of the "functionalist" image of Nazi Jewish policy are accepted but with one absolutely vital exception. Jäckel still insists that Hitler himself knew that his ultimate goal was the systematic mass murder of European Jewry, an intention he vainly tried to signal to Himmler and others ever since the autumn of 1938. With the possible exception of Heydrich, they could not or would not take the hint. The detours, delays, confusion, and incremental progress toward Hitler's goal are, in Jäckel's mind, to be explained by the difficulty Hitler faced in bringing the other top Nazis, especially Himmler, around to his own unprecedented radicalism.[6]

In a much less drastic modification of the intentionalist position, several American scholars have recently argued that by late 1938 Heinrich Himmler and Reinhard Heydrich did indeed understand that Hitler wanted to murder the European Jews as the "optimum" solution to the Jewish question, but all three knew perfectly well that they had to await the "opportune" moment to implement such a plan.[7] Meanwhile they worked to accomplish what was within the realm of possibility at the time.

Where do matters stand now? If ultrafunctionalism stands vanquished, does some form of moderate intentionalism stand triumphant? I would say no. I will argue that an examination of Nazi Jewish policy in the hitherto rather neglected period of 1939–41 not only demonstrates the inadequacy of the traditional "intentionalist" and "functionalist" positions but also raises serious doubts about the "moderate intentionalist" positions now being advanced by Jäckel and others. I shall do this first by focusing on the two major aspects of Nazi Jewish policy in this period, population resettlement plans and ghettoization, and then by considering their implications for assessing Hitler's own role.

First, let us examine Nazi resettlement policy. The Nazi invasion of Poland in September 1939 was accompanied by numerous exhortations to mass murder from Hitler and other Nazi leaders. These exhortations and orders lacked consistency and precision, as they included, at various times, Poles, Jews, priests, nobles, intelligentsia, legionnaires, teachers, the ruling class, insurgents, and "anti-German elements."[8] Polish historians estimate that within the first eight weeks, the Germans executed close to 20,000 Poles.[9] All of this makes clear that Hitler did not shy from ordering mass murder in 1939, nor did his followers shy from carrying it out.[10] Insofar as these executions became systematic, they aimed at liquidating leadership groups and the carriers of Polish nationalism. The Jews were not the priority target. Selective quotation with the aid of hindsight to imply that one of these exhortations was evidence for an intention or conception of the Final Solution is, in my opinion, a distortion.[11]

Specific plans about the fate of the Jews at this time lay in the realm of massive population transfers, not mass murder. On 14 September, Heydrich told his division heads regarding the Jews, "Proposals are being submitted to the Führer by the Reichsführer [Himmler] that only the Führer can decide."[12] The nature of the plans that Hitler approved were revealed in a series of meetings and conversations involving either Hitler or Heydrich in the last two weeks of September.[13] The western third of Poland, soon annexed to the Third Reich as the "incorporated territories," was to become purely German through the expulsion of Poles, Jews, and Gypsies, and the resettlement of ethnic Germans from the Soviet sphere. The expelled Poles were to be dumped into central Poland, and the Jews (first of all from the "incorporated territories," but eventually from all of German-occupied Poland and the Third Reich) were to be sent to the furthest extremity of the German empire—the district of Lublin.[14] At least some were to be expelled from there over the demarcation line.[15] Thus the Nazi plan envisaged a massive demographic upheaval producing three belts of population—German, Polish, and Jewish—from west to east. As Hitler told Rosenberg, only time would tell whether, "after decades," the German settlement belt would move yet further eastward. The man appointed to be in charge of this vast movement of peoples, both coming and going, was of course Heinrich Himmler.[16]

In considering the Nazis' failure to realize their resettlement plans of September 1939, it is important to remember that they had imposed upon themselves not just one but three massive population transfers: Jews, Poles, and ethnic Germans. Any one of these alone was a considerable task: the attempt by the Germans to realize all three simultaneously was beyond their capacity. Army objections to the disruption threatened by moving Jews into the cities forced Heydrich to condition such movements on not disturbing military interests. Heydrich's very unrealistic plan to "resettle" the Jews within three to four weeks was dead within ten days.[17] Even after Hans Frank's civil administration replaced army control in Poland in late October, the real logistical problems did not disappear. By mid-March 1940, some 175,000 Poles had been expelled from the incorporated territories, and close to 300,000 Jews were driven out or had fled the incorporated territories when stripped of their lodging and livelihood. But this was a mere fraction of the millions targeted for expulsion. Resettlement had bogged down, as Göring and Frank in particular united to oppose further explusions into the General Government of Poland.[18]

By this time Hitler had indicated his disenchantment with the idea of a Lublin Reservation for the Jews that he had envisaged the previous fall.[19] Himmler took the hint and on 25 May 1940 discussed with the Führer his memorandum entitled "Some Thoughts on the Treatment of Alien Populations in the East." In this memorandum he reiterated his intention to dump Poles from the incorporated territories into the General Government, where they would form a reservoir of denationalized migrant laborers. The Jews were to disappear in a different way; they were now destined for "a colony in Africa or elsewhere." Concerning this overall plan for a systematic eradication of the ethnic composition of eastern Europe, Himmler concluded: "However cruel and tragic each individual case may be, this method is still the mildest and best, if one rejects the Bolshevik method of physical extermination of a people out of inner conviction as un-German and impossible."[20] Himmler noted Hitler's response: "The Führer read the six pages through and found them very good and correct." Moreover,

Hitler told Himmler he could share both his memo and the Führer's approval of it with Göring and others.[21] Himmler had not only triumphed over Göring and Frank on the issue of Polish expulsions, but he had placed the expulsion of the Jews—now overseas—into an entirely new framework.

A concrete scheme for overseas expulsion quickly emerged from the German Foreign Office in the shape of the Madagascar Plan.[22] Hitler immediately embraced the idea, informing Mussolini on 18 June of his intention to use Madagascar as a Jewish reservation and again discussing the subject with Admiral Raeder on 20 June.[23] In Berlin Heydrich immediately moved to take jurisdiction of this project.[24] In Poland German officials also accepted the Madagascar plan as Hitler's official policy. Frank was able to stop the resumption of Jewish deportations from the incorporated territories, scheduled for August, since all the Jews would soon be expelled in the opposite direction.[25] Moreover, he ordered a halt to all ghetto-building as "illusory" in view of the "plan of the Führer" to ship the Jews to Madagascar.[26]

Realization of the Madagascar Plan required the defeat of not only France but also Great Britain. It thus faded with the fortunes of the *Luftwaffe* over England. But expulsion fever did not end there. In the fall and winter of 1940, Hitler once again let Frank know that the General Government would be the recipient of mass deportations of Poles and at least some Jews.[27] Heydrich made plans to expel over one million people into the General Government in 1941, thus dwarfing the demographic upheavals that the Nazis had already engineered.[28] This time, however, mention of a Jewish reservation was conspicuous by its absence. The new wave of expulsions had barely begun, moreover, when it was stopped abruptly on 15 March, as preparations for the invasion of Russia, Operation Barbarossa, made further rail transport unavailable.[29] Shortly before, sometime in February 1941, Hitler revealed to close associates—in this case Bormann, Keitel, Speer, and Ley—his growing frustrations over the intractability of the Jewish problem. In any case, he confided, he "was thinking of many things in a different way, that was not exactly more friendly."[30]

Such a scenario does not fit the traditional interpretations of either the "intentionalists" or "functionalists." Contrary to the "intentionalists," it indicates that the leading Nazis, with Hitler's instigation and approval, initially were quite serious about expulsion as a solution to the Jewish question. Contrary to the "functionalists," it indicates both that Hitler played an active role in shaping policy, and that solving the "Jewish question" through expulsion was an idea whose time was already past by the spring of 1941. There is simply no documentary evidence for a plan for the massive expulsion of the Jews into the conquered wastelands of the Soviet Union, as hypothesized by the "functionalists," that is commensurate with the well-documented resettlement plans of the pre-1941 period. It was not defeat in Russia but the failure of the earlier expulsion plans that helped trigger the quantum leap to mass murder.

Jäckel's modified intentionalist thesis also does not hold up. Rather than providing evidence for a fundamental misunderstanding between Hitler and Himmler, in which the former said murder while the later chose stubbornly to understand expulsion,[31] this scenario shows Himmler as extremely sensitive to Hitler's changing moods and responding with alacrity to every hint and signal from Hitler. Indeed, is it even plausible that between 1938 and 1941 Himmler emerged as the second most powerful man in Nazi Germany because he was either too stupid, too stubborn, or too morally inhibited to understand what Hitler was asking him to do? Instead, I would argue, Himmler's stock rose precisely because he, more than any of his rivals, had the capacity to interpret Hitler's signals and ideological exhortations and to cast them into concrete programs. If one wants to know what Hitler was thinking, one should look at what Himmler was doing.

A study of ghettoization in the pre-1941 period leads to similar conclusions about the inadequacy of all of these interpretive approaches. "Intentionalists" have seen ghettoization as a conscious preparatory step for the systematic mass murder that followed.[32] In contrast, the "functionalists" have argued that ghettoization played a vital role in the unplanned "cumulative radicalization" that led to the Final Solution. According to Broszat, the spectacle of overcrowded ghettos confirmed the Nazi image of the Jew as subhuman while the threat of a further deluge of deportees from the Reich led local authorities to initiate massacres that gradually took on the shape of a comprehensive program of mass murder.[33] According to Hans Mommsen, starvation in the ghettos allowed local authorities to rationalize mass murder as the "most humane" solution.[34]

In my view, ghettoization was neither a conscious preparatory step for mass murder nor part of an automatic mechanism of radicalization at the local level.[35] The initial concentration of Polish Jews in the cities was intended as a prelude to their imminent expulsion. Instead, semipermanent sealed ghettos emerged in Lodz, Warsaw, and elsewhere—just the opposite of what had been intended. Quite simply, ghettoization was an improvised response by local authorities to the failure of the expulsion plans. Stuck with Jews whom they could not move out, local authorities in the incorporated territories and the General Government—at different times and for different reasons—established sealed ghettos.[36] There was in fact no common, uniform ghettoization policy dictated by higher authorities as part of an overall plan.

Once the ghettos were sealed, local authorities everywhere faced an identical crisis within six months. Cut off from the economic life of the cities around them and not disposing of the great sums of wealth attributed to them by the common anti-Semitic stereotype, the ghettoized Jews began to starve in large numbers. In Lodz and Warsaw, the cities with the two largest ghettos, the local Nazi authorities argued among themselves over what to do next. In Lodz the ghetto was sealed at the end of April 1940, and both the impossibility of expelling the Jews in the near future as well as the looming starvation crisis were apparent by midsummer. Alexander Palfinger, deputy to the head of the ghetto admin- istration, Hans Biebow, argued, "A rapid dying out of the Jews is for us a matter of total indifference, if not to say desirable."[37] Biebow advocated a different policy; even at the cost of initial subsidies, the Germans should "facilitate the self- maintenance of the Jews through finding them work."[38] Biebow, not Palfinger, won the local policy struggle. At a meeting of 18 October 1940 on the future fate of the ghetto "it was established at the outset that the ghetto in Lodz must contnue to exist and everything must be done to make the ghetto self-sustain- ing."[39]

The disgruntled Palfinger left Lodz to join the ghetto administration in Warsaw. That ghetto had been sealed in mid-November 1940. There the district governor Ludwig Fischer had noted: "The Jews will disappear because of hunger and need, and nothing will remain of the Jewish question but a cemetery."[40] With Fischer's backing, Palfinger and his colleagues Waldemar Schön and Karl Naumann proceeded to cut off food supplies to the Warsaw ghetto. Reports of the food cut-off reached Krakow.[41] The looming demographic catastrophe in the Warsaw ghetto finally provoked intervention from the head of the Economic Division, Dr. Walter Emmerich. His expert, Rudolf Gater, composed a report that posed the alternatives starkly: one could view the ghetto either "as a means to liquidate the Jews" or as a source of labor that had to be sufficiently fed to be capable of productive work.[42]

The climactic showdown between the practitioners of starvation from Warsaw and the advocates of ghetto self-sufficiency from Krakow occurred in April 1941. Fischer sought to allay criticism by claiming that there was "no danger at all of famine" in the ghetto. Supplies were adequate and production was going forward. Emmerich brushed this fantasy aside. "One must free oneself from the notion that it is still going well in the ghetto." As the ghetto had been created for the long haul, economic planning must be done accordingly, he argued. "The starting point for all economic measures has to be the idea of maintaining the capacity of the Jews to live."[43] Noting that "[t]he responsibility that the government took on with the creation of a Jewish district of 500,000 human beings [*Menschen!*] is very great, and a failure would always be blamed on the authorities of the General Government," Frank sided with Emmerich.[44] Schön and Palfinger were transferred; Heinz Auerswald and Max Bischof were put in charge of the ghetto administration, with the specific task of achieving economic self-sufficiency.[45]

In both Lodz and Warsaw the terrible food shortages and high death rates did not end, but the ghettos did not simply disappear through what the Nazis euphemistically called "natural diminution." Without this change of policy, the ghettoized Jews would have suffered the same fate as the two million Russian prisoners of war who died of starvation and exposure in the first nine months of the Russian war.[46]

Such a course of events does not support the "functionalist" view of automatic mechanisms of radicalization at the local level. The polycratic model of the "functionalists" is confirmed, but not the predicted outcome. Left to themselves, most local authorities tended to moderate, not radicalize. Only renewed intervention from above would replace a policy of ghetto maintenance, however inadequate, with ghetto liquidation.

Likewise, the policy struggle over ghetto maintenance supports neither the "intentionalist" interpretation of ghettoization as a conscious preparatory step in the long-held plan for mass murder nor the more recent view of a tacit understanding, dating from late 1938, for mass murder as the "optimum" solution. Why the stay of execution for Polish Jewry until the spring of 1942, if this was the conscious goal since before the war? If Hitler, Himmler, and Heydrich had been impatiently waiting for the "opportune" moment to implement the mass murder of the Jews, what could have been easier and more opportune than to seal off the Polish ghettos and have two million Jews "disappear" through starvation? For a regime that had implemented the "euthanasia" murder of over 70,000 Germans, unleashed the genocidal liquidation first of the Polish intelligentsia and then of Russian Jewry, and presided over the mass death of two million Russian prisoners of war by April 1942, why the delay in embarking on the Final Solution to the Jewish question in Poland?

Finally, Jäckel's version of modified intentionalism finds no comfort here either. He has postulated that Hitler could not immediately implement his intended goal of murdering the Jews because no one, including Himmler, shared his radicalism. In fact, there was no shortage of Nazis in Poland anxious to murder the Jews through starvation, but they got no help from above. No sign came from Hitler, and the would-be murderers had to wait for a new turn of events.

If the historiographical conflict between "intentionalism" and "functionalism" has stimulated fruitful research that has ultimately exposed the inadequacy of both models in explaining the origins of the Final Solution, has it also demonstrated the bankruptcy of any kind of "decision-making" model? I would argue that this is not the case. In fact, a brief review of the decision-making process in 1941 confirms a pattern of decision making emerging from the earlier discussion of resettlement policy that is vital to any understanding of the origins of the Final Solution.

Hitler's hint of February 1941 that he was viewing the Jewish question in a "different" and "not exactly more friendly" way followed the failure of the earlier resettlement schemes and preceded the invasion of the Soviet Union. The Jewish problem, which had already proved intractable, now threatened to reach immense proportions, for more conquered territory once again meant more Jews. The mirage of a *judenfrei* German empire receded with every military and diplomatic triumph. The time was ripe to break this vicious circle through the quantum leap to mass murder as a solution to the Jewish question.

Such a quantum leap was unquestionably facilitated and fueled by the fundamental position of the "Jewish-Bolshevik" identity in Nazi ideology. When Hitler decided to destroy Poland, the fate of the Polish Jews could wait, but the fate of the Polish leadership classes could not; the Nazis pursued a genocidal elimination of all potential carriers of the Polish national idea. As the Nazis prepared to confront and destroy Bolshevism in 1941, neither the Russian Communists nor Russian Jews could wait; both would have to be eliminated, for ultimately they were one—the political and biological manifestations of the same "Jewish-Bolshevik" conspiracy.

On four occasions between 26 February and 30 March 1941, Hitler insisted that the Bolshevik leadership and intelligentsia would have to be murdered. On only one of these occasions (to Jodl on 3 March) did he refer explicitly to a "Jewish-Bolshevik intelligentsia."[47] But he consistently referred to the coming conflict as a struggle between two incompatible worldviews that required not a conventional war but a "war of extermination."

Between early March and early June 1941, military, SS, and other planners sought to cast Hitler's ideological pronouncements into specific policies—to make the "war of extermination" a reality. The economic experts agreed that "millions of people will doubtless starve to death when we extract what is necessary for us from the country."[48] An edict on the jurisdiction of military courts and the guidelines for troop behavior incited summary execution and collective reprisal and stripped the civilian population of any shred of legal protection. The *Kommissarbefehl* ordained the execution of all Communist functionaries. Most fateful of all, the military reached agreement with the SS, according to which the Special Commando units *(Einsatzgruppen)* of the Sipo-SD were independently to carry out "special tasks" resulting from the final struggle between two incompatible political systems.[49]

The reaction of the old elites, particularly the military, to Hitler's pronouncements and their preparations for Operation Barbarossa revealed a growing overlap in ideological outlook with the axioms of National Socialism. They shared the geopolitical, social Darwinist postulate that Germany must seize *Lebensraum* to secure its position in the world. They embraced the anticommunist crusade. And above all, they accepted the identity of communism and the Jews. But more than just an overlap of national-conservative and Nazi ideologies was at work here. Recent military and political events had had their cumulative impact. Hitler's astounding string of victories had swept away previous reservations and criticisms and persuaded the old elites that he was indeed a man of destiny. Moreover, participation in the policies of destruction seemed the best means to assure their own position in the "New Order." They were no longer willing to leave the "devil's work" to the SS, as in Poland.[50]

The quantum leap to mass murder as a solution to the Nazis' self-imposed Jewish question initially took place, therefore, in the context of a war of extermination against Bolshevik Russia, not yet in that of a "Final Solution" to the Jewish question in Europe. The pervasive predisposition among the German elites, party and nonparty alike, to perpetrate mass murder in Russia under the guise of anticommunism and military necessity, as well as anti-Semitism, was crucial. But the mass murder campaign against the Jews soon broke loose from this context and gained an autonomy, indeed a priority, in its own right.

This crucial escalation occurred in mid-July 1941, when Hitler once again provided the impetus through a series of pronouncements. On 10 July he proclaimed himself the Robert Koch of politics, who had discovered the Jews as the fermenting agent of social decomposition.[51] On 16 July Hitler observed that Stalin's call for partisan resistance "had its advantages: it gives us the opportunity to exterminate whatever stands in our way."[52] And on 17 July he told visiting Croatian Marshal Kvaternik of his intention to approach every European country with the demand for the removal of every last Jew from Europe.[53]

Hitler's new signals brought immediate results. The hesitant and overburdened *Einsatzgruppen*, already reinforced in early July by six commando units from Eberhard Schöngarth's Sipo-SD in the General Government, were now significantly augmented by the assignment of two full SS brigades from Himmler's personal *Kommandostab*, one each to the higher SS and police leaders Erich von dem Bach Zelewski and Friedrich Jeckeln. These units were immediately engaged in the massacre of Russian Jews. For two weeks Himmler toured the Russian front, personally urging his killers on.[54] By mid-August the murderous assault on Russian Jewry had hit full stride.

Hitler's mid-July exhortations, in the euphoria of his seeming victory over Russia, had even greater significance, however. Judging by Himmler's and Heydrich's actions, it is most probable that Hitler's final decisive intervention in mid-July in the murder of Russian Jewry was also the point at which he instigated the initial preparations to extend the mass murder to the rest of European Jewry. On 20 and 21 July, Himmler was in Lublin visiting Odilo Globocnik, who was subsequently in charge of the three death camps of Operation Reinhardt.[55] On 31 July, Heydrich visited Göring and obtained his signature on a document authorizing Heydrich to prepare and submit an "overall plan" for a "total solution" of the Jewish question in the territories of Europe under German influence.[56] These, I would argue, were the initial actions of Himmler and Heydrich in implementing the mass murder of European Jewry. Thus they must have received the unmistakable signal from Hitler of what was expected from them in this regard as well.

Hitler rejected pleas by Heydrich and Goebbels in August to begin immediate deportations from Germany. They were to take place after the Russian campaign.[57] Nothing shows more clearly that Hitler himself conceived of the murder of Russian Jewry and the Final Solution to the Jewish question in

Europe as two different operations than his insistence that the first be done under the guise of war and the second be commenced only after the end of the Russian campaign (which was, of course, to end soon).

The last cluster of decisions culminating in the Final Solution occurred in late September and early October. On 14 September Rosenberg urged Hitler to approve the immediate deportation of German Jews in retaliation for the Russian deportation of Volga Germans to Siberia. This time Hitler agreed, for four days later Himmler informed Greiser in the Warthegau of interim deportations to Lodz of 60,000 Jews, because the Führer wished to make the Old Reich and Protectorate *judenfrei* as soon as possible, hopefully by the end of the year.[58] After meetings on 23 and 24 September that involved Hitler, Himmler, Heydrich, and Goebbels, the propaganda minister noted that Berlin, Vienna, and Prague were the first cities to be cleared of Jews, once again hopefully by the end of the year.[59] However, the overfilled ghettos in Poland had no room for these Jews, and by early October the decision had been made to send many of the deported Jews directly to Russian territory. At a meeting with Hitler, Heydrich, Keitel, and Jodl, Himmler reported on the deportation of the Jews and mentioned Riga, Reval, and Minsk in particular.[60] Hitler clearly took a keen interest in the points of both departure and arrival of the deportations, as well as the difficulties involved, for he discussed these matters again on 6 October.[61] Action quickly followed words, for deportations to Lodz began on 15 October and to Minsk, Riga, and Kowno on 8 November.

As Hitler hesitantly moved toward approving fall deportations from the Third Reich, those charged with implementing the Final Solution searched for ways to accomplish their unprecedented task. The death camp emerged as the technological and organizational solution. On 3 September 1941 Russian prisoners of war were gassed in Bunker 11 of the Auschwitz *Stammlager* in the first test of Cyclon B. In October small numbers of Jews were trucked into Auschwitz and gassed in the old crematory. Likewise, in early October three SS officers arrived in Belzec and were visited there by Eichmann. A draft of Polish workers began constructing the future barracks and gas chambers on 1 November. Also in October the future commandant of Chelmno, Herbert Lange, searched the countryside of the Warthegau for an appropriate site, traveled to Berlin, and then returned no later than early November to begin construction work on that camp.[62] If Hitler was directly involved in discussions in late September and early October concerning rather specific details of the initial deportations, it is difficult to believe that he was not simultaneously briefed on and did not give his blessing to the plans for the death camps. Certainly, by late October, many middle and low echelon officials were beginning to learn what was in store for European Jewry.[63]

What can we conclude about the decision-making process that led to the Final Solution? First, Adolf Hitler was an active and continuing participant.

From September 1939 to October 1941 the evidence indicates that Hitler instigated and approved every major change in Nazi Jewish policy. Second, while we do not know the details in all cases, Hitler's participation was usually indirect. He would give signals in the form of relatively vague and inexplicit statements or exhortations. Others, especially Himmler, responded to these signals with extraordinary alacrity and sensitivity, bringing to Hitler more specific guidelines for his approval. On occasion, not only guidelines but quite concrete proposals—such as those for marking German Jews or commencing deportations from particular cities in the Reich to particular destinations in the east—were submitted to Hitler as well. If one continuity above all others emerges from this study, it is the close and sympathetic relationship between Hitler and Himmler. Interpretations that see either Himmler forcing a reluctant Hitler to live up to his rhetoric or Hitler coaxing a reluctant Himmler to mass murder do not, in my opinion, fit the evidence.[64]

Third, the chronology suggests a rather consistent pattern between victory and radicalization, indicating that the emergence of the Final Solution may have been induced as much by Hitler's fluctuating moods as by a fanatically consistent adherence to a fixed program. In September 1939, in the flush of victory over Poland, Hitler approved the initial plan for the demographic reorganization of eastern Europe, including the Lublin Reservation. In May and June 1940, with the astonishing victory over France, he approved Himmler's memorandum on the treatment of the eastern populations and the Madagascar Plan. In July 1941, with the stupendous early victories in the Russian campaign, he accelerated the *Einsatzgruppen* campaign and instigated the Final Solution. And in late September and early October, with the resumption of the drive on Moscow and the great encirclement victory of Vyazma and Bryansk, he approved the deportations from the Third Reich. At the same time, death camp construction commenced. It would appear that the euphoria of victory emboldened and tempted an elated Hitler to dare ever more drastic policies. The one exception to this pattern was the March decision for the *Einsatzgruppen* assault on Russian Jewry. Here the frustration and disappointment over the failure of the earlier resettlement plans, together with the looming confrontation with "Jewish Bolshevism," moved Hitler to the quantum leap to mass murder.

Such a scenario, in my opinion, breaks the old "intentionalist" and "functionalist" molds and helps to clarify the roles of Hitler and Himmler as well as the timing of the decisions for the Final Solution. However, it also raises a very serious question of another kind. If the Final Solution was not the product either of a long-term plan or an inherent and automatic mechanism of radicalization, and if the decision-making process was as amorphous and unstructured as I have portrayed, how does the historian account for the broad and almost uniform receptivity to the signals emanating from Hitler and his inner circle? If the Final Solution was the product of successive German victories, why was it pursued so doggedly in the years of German defeat? In short, what sort of consensus about the Jews existed in German society that enabled such a haphazard process for making and disseminating decisions to harness an entire society to the task of mass murder, and furthermore to the continuing pursuit of that policy of mass murder even when the conditions that gave birth to it had drastically altered?

At least three "consensus models" for explaining the Holocaust have been advocated in recent years—what I would suggest calling the anti-Bolshevik, eugenics, and bureaucratic/technocratic interpretations. Many historians have emphasized the vital importance of anti-Bolshevism, but none so emphatically or sweepingly as Arno Mayer. In his recent book *Why Did the Heavens Not Darken? The "Final Solution" in History,* Mayer portrays the Final Solution as a by-product of or companion piece to the anti-Bolshevik "crusade." This crusade was based on a broad consensus of old and new elites as well as the lower middle classes in Germany. All agreed on the need to extirpate "Judeobolshevism" as well as gain *Lebensraum* in the east. When the "crusade" began to falter, the abstract notion of extirpating "Judeobolshevism" was transformed by rising German fury and fear into the concrete and intensifying mass murder of East European Jewry. The economic exigencies of total war and the desperate attempts to stave off defeat only added extermination through forced labor (now encompassing West European Jewry as well) to the vengeful massacres to which Jews were already subjected. In Mayer's view, therefore, the Final Solution was not an autonomous and conscious program to kill all European Jews because they were Jews. Rather it was "grafted" onto other murderous programs, above all onto the anti-Bolshevik crusade, that enjoyed broad consensus support in the Third Reich. [65]

The eugenics model argues for a second kind of consensus in German society for the Final Solution. Professor Henry Friedlander has summed up this viewpoint quite succinctly: namely, broad sectors of German society, not just party ideologues, shared the common vision of a *Volksgemeinschaft* healthy in mind and body. There was no place in this vision for three alien groups: the mentally and physically handicapped, so-called "asocials" (habitual criminals, homosexuals, vagabonds, Gypsies, prostitutes, etc.), and so-called "racial inferiors," above all, the Jews. The realization of a homogeneous and healthy society—a major element of Nazi appeal—required the exclusion of these alien groups. The same party ideologues and traditional social planners worked together to achieve this desired exclusion of all three groups, and in each case it evolved to mass murder—euthanasia, *Aktion* 14f13, and the Final Solution. In each case the perpetrators could utilize the pervasive negative stereotype of the respective victim group. [66]

In his pathbreaking and still classic work *The Destruction of the European Jews,* first published in 1961, Raul Hilberg portrayed the Final Solution as an bureaucratic-administrative process, in which—out of a Faustian temptation to accomplish the unprecedented—the German bureaucracy destroyed the European Jews. In the revised and expanded 1985 edition, Hilberg even more emphatically emphasized the aspect of bureaucratic consensus—"shared comprehension" and "synchronization"—behind the mass murder.[67] Quite recently, Götz Aly and Susanne Heim have argued for a more mundane basis for this bureaucratic consensus, namely the utilitarian calculations of lower-echelon technocrats and social planners that in overpopulated and underdeveloped eastern Europe the mass elimination of surplus population, particularly primitive preindustrial workers, would best lead to the rapid economic rationalization and modernization of the conquered territories. The mass murder of the Jews was, in the view of Aly and Heim, therefore, the means chosen by technocrats and social planners to facilitate the demographic and economic restructuring and modernization of the Nazis' east European colonial empire. These virtually anonymous lower-echelon social planners did not make the key decisions themselves, but they articulated the vision and presented the alternatives that shaped the decisions of those above them.[68]

Each of these models contains too much of value to be dismissed out of hand, but each still leaves explanatory gaps. While for Hitler Bolshevism may have been merely the latest manifestation of the eternal Jewish conspiracy, it would seem that the Jew as Bolshevik—the latest addition to the multifaceted anti-Jewish stereotype—was the key to energizing the latent anti-Semitism in German society.[69] Clearly the crusade against Bolshevism and war of destruction in Russia provided both the occasion for the quantum leap to mass murder and the ideological bridge that the old elites crossed over to become active accomplices in the Final Solution.[70] The origins of the Final Solution simply cannot be explained without reference to Barbarossa and the pervasive ideological tenet of the Jewish-Bolshevik identity. But does the anti-Bolshevik crusade explain Hitler's mid-July decision, in the euphoria of victory and clear expectation that soon he would have a free hand on the entire continent, to murder the Jews of Europe *after* the Russian campaign was over? Can it explain the growing conviction among Germans—even during the period of the Nazi-Soviet Nonaggression Pact—that the Jewish question had to be solved one way or another? Can it explain the vast plans for a demographic reorganization of Europe (of which getting rid of all Jews was an integral part) that were being made both *before* the Russian campaign and for *after* the destruction of the "Judeo-bolshevik" regime, plans that involved the uprooting and removal of over 30 million people strictly on racial grounds? Anti-Bolshevism is a vital component of any explanation of the factors that enabled the Nazis to carry out the Final Solution, but it must not be taken so far as to obfuscate or deny the reality of the fact that Hitler and the Nazis took their racism seriously. It was precisely their understanding of history as racial struggle (in which the Jews played the most nefarious role) that imbued the Final Solution with the comprehensive commitment to kill every last Jew in Europe. It is precisely this total commitment that is absent from Mayer's concept of the Final Solution.

Clearly, euthanasia was "a conceptual as well as technological and administrative prefiguration" of the Final Solution.[71] And eugenics provided one more route to the Final Solution for the "respectable elements" of German society, especially those in the medical profession (to say nothing of the actual personnel of the death camps of Operation Reinhardt). But many Germans opposed the euthanasia program, and it was for the most part halted even at the height of Hitler's power and popularity. In contrast, the murder of the Jews was pursued even into the years of obvious defeat and aroused no similar dissent in German society. Can they really be seen as two parts of a common consensus?

Clearly, the German bureaucracy was the key means by which the Final Solution was implemented, but was this "machinery of destruction" self-propelled, as Hilberg implies? Was it driven primarily by its own Faustian sense of mission or, as Heim and Aly argue, by the technocratic visions of its virtually anonymous lower-echelon social planners? As we have seen in the case of ghettoization in Poland, it required intervention from above to reverse the victory of local officials advocating ghetto maintenance over those advocating starvation. If the officials actually in charge of the largest concentration of Jews within the German empire were not part of the "shared comprehension" or common technocratic vision for murdering the Jews until they received un-equivocal signals from above, a model of bureaucratic consensus seems dubious.

Where does this leave the historian seeking a consensus-model for the Final Solution? I would suggest, at least as a *tentative* starting point, that the Nazi campaign to murder the European Jews had gained a great deal more "autonomy" and "priority" in its own right by late 1941 than these other models indicate. A commitment to "solve the Jewish question" no longer needed to be part of some other program. Clearly, the Nazis did not come to power primarily because of their anti-Semitic message, nor did anti-Jewish policy have a priority in Nazi actions until 1941. Anti-Bolshevism, eugenics, and the bureaucratic momentum created by cadres of so-called Jewish experts were all tributaries to the growing consensus that the "Jewish question" was real, and it had to be solved. But above all, the war itself created the fateful atmosphere. Through the war the Nazis were increasingly able to impose their own image of the enemy, or *Feindbild*, on the German nation. By 1941 Germans accepted that the Jews were "the enemy," who—in line with what Hitler had advocated since 1919—had to be removed entirely *one way or another.* Ghettoization was temporary; resettlement proved unrealizable. When Hitler gave the signals that he alone could give to legitimize mass murder as the necessary solution, all the anticipation, receptivity, and initiative on the local level that were needed to implement such a mass murder campaign were forthcoming. Most Germans were "indifferent" to the mass murder campaign, if they were fortunate enough not to be directly involved.[72] But randomly entangled Germans from all strata of society conscientiously—indeed often zealously—carried out the myriad tasks expected of them, without which the murder campaign would not have functioned. If Germans followed many paths to the Final Solution, ultimately they killed Jews not just because Jews were communists, or alien bodies polluting the healthy *Volksgemeinschaft*, or obstacles to modernization, but because they were Jews and, as such in wartime, the enemy.

Notes

1. Tim Mason, "Intention and Explanation: A Current Controversy about the Interpretation of National Socialism," Gerhard Hirschfeld and Lothar Kettenacker, eds., *Der "Führerstaat": Mythos und Realität* (Stuttgart, 1981), pp. 21–40.

2. See the starkly contrasting articles of Hans Mommsen, "Hitlers Stellung im nationalsozialistischen Herrschaftssystem," and Klaus Hildebrand, "Monokratie oder Polykratie? Hitlers Herrschaft und das Dritte Reich," Hirschfeld and Kettenacker, eds., *Der "Führerstaat"*, pp. 43–97.

3. Andreas Hillgruber, "Die 'Endlösung' und das deutsche Ostimperium als Kernstück des rassenideologischen Programms des Nationalsozialismus," Manfred Funke, ed., *Hitler, Deutschland und die Mächte* (Düsseldorf, 1978), pp. 94–114, and "Die ideologisch-dogmatische Grundlagen der nationalsozialistischen Politik der Ausrottung der Juden in den besetzten Gebieten der Sowjetunion und ihre Durchführung 1941–1944," *German Studies Review* 2, no. 2 (1979): 263–96; Eberhard Jäckel, *Hitler's Weltanschauung: A Blueprint for Power* (Middletown, Conn., 1972); Lucy Dawidowicz, *The War Against the Jews* (New York, 1975); Helmut Krausnick, "The Persecution of the Jews," in Hans Buchheim, Martin Broszat, Hans-Adolf Jacobsen, and Helmut Krausnick, *Anatomy of the SS State* (New York, 1968); Gerald Fleming, *Hitler and the Final Solution* (Berkeley and Los Angeles, 1984).

4. Karl Schleunes, *The Twisted Road to Auschwitz* (Urbana, Ill., 1970); Uwe Adam, *Judenpolitik im Dritten Reich* (Düsseldorf, 1972); Martin Broszat, "Hitler und die 'Endlösung': Aus Anlass der Thesen von David Irving," *Vierteljahrshefte für Zeitgeschichte (VfZ)* 25, no. 4 (1977): 739–75; Christopher R. Browning, "Zur Genesis der 'Endlösung': Eine Antwort an Martin Broszat," *VfZ* 29, no. 1 (1981): 97–109; Hans Mommsen, "Die Realisierung des Utopischen: Die 'Endlösung der Judenfrage' im 'Dritten Reich,'" *Geschichte und Gesellschaft* 9, no. 3 (1983): 381–420.

5. The conference papers and debate are published in Eberhard Jäckel

and Jürgen Rohwer, eds., *Der Mord an den Juden im Zweiten Weltkrieg: Entschlussbildung und Verwirklichung* (Stuttgart, 1985).

6. See Jäckel's remarks in Stuttgart, as well as his paper "Hitler und der Mord an den europäischen Juden im Zweiten Weltkrieg," delivered in Warsaw in April 1983; *Hitler in History* (Hanover, N.H., 1984); and *Hitlers Herrschaft* (Stuttgart, 1986).

7. Richard Breitman, "Himmler's Path to Genocide," and Charles Sydnor, "Executive Instinct: Reinhard Heydrich and the Final Solution to the Jewish Question," papers presented at the AHA convention, Washington, D.C., December 1987.

8. On 22 August 1939, at the Berghof, Hitler allegedly told his audience of generals: "Genghis Khan had millions of women and children killed by his own will and with a gay heart. History sees only in him a great state builder. . . . I have sent to the East my 'Death Head Units' with the order to kill without mercy all men, women, and children of the Polish race or language. Only in such a way will we win the vital space that we need. Who still talks nowadays of the extermination of the Armenians?" *Nazi Conspiracy and Aggression* (hereafter cited as *NCA*), 7: 753 (L-3). Another document from the same meeting, Canaris's notes on Hitler's speech, states: "Destruction of Poland in the foreground. The aim is the elimination of living forces, not the arrival at a certain line: Even if the war should break out in the West, the destruction of Poland shall be the primary objective. . . . Have no pity. Brutal attitude"; *NCA*, 3: 665 (1014-PS). Halder's notes were similar: "Goal: destruction of Poland— elimination of its living force. It is not a question of reaching a certain line or new boundary but of the destruction of the enemy"; Franz Halder, *Kriegstagebuch*, ed. Hans-Adolf Jacobsen (Stuttgart, 1962), 1:25. Heydrich proclaimed on 8 September that "the nobles, priests, and Jews must be killed." Helmut Groscurth, Helmut Krausnick, and Harold Deutsch, eds., *Tagebücher eines Abwehroffiziers, 1938–40* (Stuttgart, 1970), p. 201 (Privattagebuch, 8 September 1939). On 9 September, General Halder revealed that "it was the intention of the Führer and Göring to destroy and exterminate the Polish people"; ibid., p. 202 (Privattagebuch, 9 September 1939). When Canaris informed Keitel that he "knew that extensive executions were planned in Poland and that particularly the nobility and the clergy were to be exterminated," Keitel answered that the Führer had indeed decided upon a policy of "ethnic extermination" *(volkstümliche Ausrottung); NCA*, 5: 769 (3047-PS: notes by Lahousen from the diary of Canaris). On 18 September, Heydrich reiterated his list to the army Quartermaster General Eduard Wagner: "Fundamental cleansing [*Flurbereinigung*]: Jews, intelligentsia, clergy, nobles"; Halder, *Kriegstagebuch*, 1:79. Four days later Heydrich told Brauchitsch that "nobles, clergy, teachers, and legionnaires" were to be arrested and sent to concentration camps; Groscurth, *Tagebücher*, pp. 361–62 (Document no. 14, Groscurth memo on

verbal orientation from Major Radke, 22 September 1939). On 14 October, Heydrich ordered the "liquidation of Polish leadership"; National Archives Microfilm, T175/239/2728535-7 (conference of Heydrich's division heads, 14 October 1939). Three days later Hitler himself discussed the "devil's work" to be done in Poland, which included preventing a revival of the Polish intelligentsia as a ruling class. *Trials of the Major War Criminals before the International Military Tribunal* (hereafter cited as *IMT*), 26:378–83 (864-PS). Hitler continued to push the same policy into the following year, telling Hans Frank: "What we have now identified as the leading class in Poland must be liquidated." Hans Frank, *Das Diensttagebuch des deutschen Generalgouverneurs in Polen, 1939–1945*, ed. Werner Präg and Wolfgang Jacobmeyer (Stuttgart, 1975), pp. 209–12 (Polizeisitzung, 30 May 1940).

      9. The Polish historian Szymon Datner claims that 16,136 Poles were executed by the Germans by 25 October; *55 Dni/1.IX–25.X. 1939/Wehrmachtu w Polsce* (Warsaw, 1967), pp. 114–17. Czeslaw Madajczyk estimates about 20,000 victims; *Polityka III Rzeszy w okupawanej Polsce: Okupacja Polski, 1939–1945* (Warsaw, 1970), vol. 1, p. 58 [cited in Jan Gross, *Polish Society under German Occupation* (Princeton, N.J., 1979), p. 68).

      10. The simultaneous commencement of euthanasia in Germany only reinforces this point.

      11. See, for instance, the emphasis on the postwar testimony of Erwin Lahousen in Breitman, "Auschwitz and the Archives," *Central European History*, 18 (1985): 380; and Jäckel, *Hitlers Herrschaft*, pp. 95 and 172. Neither observes that Lahousen's postwar testimony is different from the entry he wrote for Canaris's diary on this day, in which Lahousen mentions only clergy and nobility, but not Jews, as targets for mass murder; *NCA*, 5: 769 (3047-PS).

      12. National Archives Microfilm, T175/239/2728513-5 (conference of Heydrich's division heads, 14 September 1939).

      13. Hitler with Brauchitsch on 20 September: Halder, *Kriegstagebuch*, 1:82; Hitler with Rosenberg on 29 September; Hans-Günther Seraphim, ed., *Das Politische Tagebuch Alfred Rosenbergs* (Göttingen, 1956), p. 81; Heydrich with Quartermaster General Eduard Wagner on 19 September; Halder, *Kriegstagebuch*, 1:79; Heydrich with Division Heads and *Einsatzgruppen* commanders on 21 September: National Archives Microfilm, T175/239/2729524-8, and *NCA*, 6: 97–101 (3363-PS: Heydrich Schnellbrief to *Einsatzgruppen* leaders, 21 September 1939); Heydrich with Brauchitsch on 22 September; Groscurth, *Tagebücher*, p. 362 (document no. 14: Groscurth memorandum on verbal orientation by Major Radke, 22 September 1939).

      14. Initially the *Judenreservat* was planned for the region east of Cracow, but its location was immediately shifted to Lublin after the border revision of 28 September placed this district in German hands.

      15. Heydrich's *Schnellbrief* or "express letter" to his *Einsatzgruppen*

commanders summarizing the results of his conference of 21 September discussed the steps to be taken to achieve the expulsion of the Jews. He made a distinction between the strictly secret ultimate goal or *Endziel,* and the short-term measure of concentrating the Jews in the cities along railway lines. Once again, this reference to a secret *Endziel* has been wrenched out of the wider context and claimed as proof that the Nazis, or at least Heydrich, were privy to the final goal of extermination. Only neglect of the broader documentation can lead to such a conclusion.

16. Robert Koehl, *German Resettlement and Population Policy, 1939–45* (Cambridge, Mass., 1957).

17. Helmut Krausnick and Hans-Heinrich Wilhelm, *Die Truppe des Weltanschauungskrieges* (Stuttgart, 1981), p. 75.

18. For the drop in Jewish population, see Yehuda Bauer, *American Jewry and the Holocaust* (Detroit, 1981), p. 6. For the deported Poles, see Hans Umbreit, *Deutsche Militärverwaltungen, 1938/39* (Stuttgart, 1977), pp. 217–18; and Yad Vashem Archives (hereafter cited as YVA), 0-53/48/650-2 (Umwandererzentrale Abschlussbericht 1940). On the gradual whittling away of the resettlement programs, see Christopher R. Browning, "Nazi Resettlement Policy and the Search for a Solution to the Jewish Question, 1939–1941," *German Studies Review* 9, no. 3 (1986): 497–519.

19. *Documents on German Foreign Policy,* D, VIII, 912–3 (Hewel memorandum on conversation of Colin Ross and Hitler, 12 March 1940).

20. "Einige Gedanken über die Behandlung der Fremdvölkischen im Osten," ed. Helmut Krausnick, *VfZ* 5, no. 2 (1957): 194–98 (NO-1880).

21. Ibid., pp. 195–96 (Himmler memorandum, 28 May 1940).

22. Leni Yahil, "Madagascar—Phantom of a Solution for the Jewish Question," in George Mosse and Bela Vago, eds., *Jews and Non-Jews in Eastern Europe,* (New York, 1974), pp. 319–32. Christopher R. Browning, *The Final Solution and the German Foreign Office* (New York, 1978), pp. 35–43.

23. Galeazzo Ciano, *The Ciano Diaries, 1939–43* (Garden City, N.Y., 1947), pp. 265–66; Paul Schmidt, *Hitler's Interpreter* (New York, 1951), p. 178; Klaus Hildebrand, *Vom Reich zum Weltreich: Hitler, NSDAP und koloniale Frage, 1919–1945* (Munich, 1969). In August Hitler told Otto Abetz, the German ambassador to France, that he intended to expel all the Jews from Europe at the end of the war; *Akten zur deutschen Aussenpolitik,* D.X, 389. Even American diplomats in Bucharest heard rumors of Hitler's mentioning the Madagascar Plan to Rumanian diplomats. *Foreign Relations of the United States* (1940), 2: 769.

24. Politisches Archiv des Auswärtigen Amtes (hereafter cited as PA), Inland IIg 177, Heydrich to Ribbentrop, 24 June 1940.

25. Frank, *Diensttagebuch,* pp. 261–63 (entry of 31 July 1940).

26. *Faschismus—Ghetto—Massenmord,* [Berlin (East), 1960,] p. 110

(excerpt of Schön report of 20 January 1941).

27. Frank, *Diensttagebuch*, pp. 302 (entry of 6 November 1940), 309 (entry of 2 December 1940), and 326–27 (conference of 15 January 1941). The Jews of Vienna were to be included through Hitler's explicit intervention: see 1950-PS (Lammers to Schirach, 3 December 1940).

28. YVA, JM 3582 (Umwandererzentrale Abschlussbericht 1941).

29. *Biuletyn Głownej Komisji Badania Zbrondni Hitlerowskich w Polsce*, 12 138F–39F (Müller to Königsberg, Gotenhafen, Posen, Lodz, Vienna, 15 March 1941).

30. Hildegard von Kotze, ed., *Heeresadjutant bei Hitler, 1938–1943: Aufzeichnungen des Majors Engel* (Stuttgart, 1974), pp. 94–95.

31. Jäckel, *Hitlers Herrschaft*, p. 97.

32. Hillgruber, "Die 'Endlösung' und das deutsche Ostimperium," pp. 98–99; Philip Friedmann, "The Jewish Ghettos of the Nazi Era," in Philip Friedmann, *Roads to Extinction: Essays on the Holocaust* (Philadelphia, 1980), esp. pp. 61 and 69; Isaiah Trunk, *Judenrat: The Jewish Councils in Eastern Europe under Nazi Occupation* (New York, 1972), esp. p. 61.

33. Broszat, "Hitler und die Genesis der 'Endlösung,'" pp. 753–55.

34. Mommsen, "Die Realisierung des Utopischen," pp. 410–11 and 414.

35. My arguments in this regard are more fully explored in "Nazi Ghettoization Policy in Poland: 1939–41," *Central European History* 19, no. 4 (December 1986): 343–68.

36. The Lodz ghetto was established between December 1939 and April 1940 for the express purpose of forcing the Jews to disgorge their allegedly hidden wealth in return for food. Warsaw was ghettoized in the fall of 1940, under the importuning of public health officials about the danger of spotted fever epidemic. Ghettoization in the southern district of the General Government followed in the spring of 1941.

37. YVA, 0-53/7876-82 (Palfinger's "critical report" of 7 November 1940).

38. YVA, JM 798 (Activity report for September 1940).

39. *Dokumenty i Materiały do Dziejów Okupacji Niemieckiej w Polsce*, vol. 3, *Getto Łódzkie*, pp. 102–4 (conference of 18 October 1940).

40. Cited in Philip Friedman, "The Jewish Ghettos of the Nazi Era," p. 69.

41. Frank, *Diensttagebuch*, p. 328 (conference of 15 January 1941).

42. Ibid., p. 334 (entry of 22 March 1941); YVA, JM 10016 ("Die Wirtschaftsbilanz des jüdischen Wohnbezirks in Warschau").

43. Frank, *Diensttagebuch*, pp. 343–46 (conference of 3 April 1941).

44. Ibid., pp. 354–55 (conference of 9 April 1941) and 359–62 (conference of 19 April 1941).

45. YVA, JM 1112, Bischof Aktenvermerk on discussion with Fischer, 30 April 1941. Götz Aly and Susanne Heim do not view this episode as a policy struggle symptomatic of the polycratic structure of the Nazi occupation regime in the General Government and indicative of the general lack of direction in Jewish policy at this time. Rather, they argue for a consensus among technocratic economic planners, who chose to pursue both starvation and productivity simultaneously. See their article "Die Ökonomie der 'Endlösung': Menschenvernichtung und wirtschaftliche Neuordnung," *Beiträge zur Nationalsozialistischen Gesundheits- und Sozialpolitik*, vol. 5, *Sozialpolitik und Judenvernichtung: Gibt es eine Ökonomie der Endlösung?* pp. 11–90, esp. 67–79. In my view they downplay the political context and exaggerate the significance of these economic planners in shaping Nazi Jewish policy in the General Government.

46. Christian Streit, *Keine Kameraden: Die Wehrmacht und die sowjetischen Kriegsgefangenen, 1941–1945* (Stuttgart, 1978), pp. 9–10.

47. On 26 February and 3, 17, and 30 March; Jürgen Förster, *Das Deutsche Reich und der Zweite Weltkrieg*, vol. 4, *Der Angriff auf die Sowjetunion* (Stuttgart, 1983), pp. 414, 416, and 427.

48. IMT, 31: 84 (2718-PS).

49. Förster, *Das Deutsche Reich*, pp. 413–47; Krausnick and Wilhelm, *Die Truppe des Weltanschauungskrieges*, pp. 116–41; Helmut Krausnick, "Kommissarbefehl und 'Gerichtsbarkeitserlass Barbarossa' in neuer Sicht," *VfZ* 25, no. 4 (1977): 682–738; and Streit, *Keine Kameraden*, pp. 28–59.

50. I am particularly indebted to Helmut Krausnick, Jürgen Förster, and Christian Streit for the conclusions of this paragraph.

51. Cited in Broszat, "Hitler und die Genesis der 'Endlösung,'" p. 749.

52. IMT, 38: 86 (221-L: conference of Hitler, Rosenberg, Lammers, Keitel, and Göring, 16 July 1941).

53. Broszat, "Hitler und die Genesis der 'Endlösung,'" p. 749.

54. Yehoshua Büchler, "Kommandostab Reichsführer-SS: Himmler's Personal Murder Brigades in 1941," *Holocaust and Genocide Studies* 1, no. 1 (1986): 13–17.

55. Jäckel, *Hitlers Herrschaft*, pp. 112.

56. IMT, 26: 266–67 (710-PS).

57. Bernhard Lösener, "Als Rassereferent im Reichsministerium des Innern," *VfZ* 9, no. 3 (1961): 303; Broszat, "Hitler und die Genesis der 'Endlösung,'" p. 750. Hitler did, however, approve Goebbels's request to decree the marking of the German Jews, which became effective 1 September.

58. H. G. Adler, *Der verwaltete Mensch: Studien zur Deportation der Juden aus Deutschland* (Tübingen, 1974), pp. 173–77.

59. Jäckel, *Hitlers Herrschaft*, pp. 117; Broszat, "Hitler und die Genesis der 'Endlösung,'" p. 751.

60. *Heeresadjutant bei Hitler, 1938–1943: Aufzeichnungen des Majors Engels,* p. 111. Engels dates this meeting to 2 October but Himmler was not with Hitler then.

61. Broszat, "Hitler und die Genesis der 'Endlösung,'" p. 751.

62. Christopher R. Browning, *Fateful Months: Essays on the Emergence of the Final Solution,* 2d ed. (New York, 1991), pp. 29–32.

63. Ibid., pp. 27–28.

64. For these two contrasting views, see Mommsen, "Die Realisierung des Utopischen," and Jäckel, *Hitlers Herrschaft.*

65. Arno Mayer, *Why Did the Heavens Not Darken? The "Final Solution" in History* (New York, 1988).

66. The recent literature on eugenics and euthanasia is immense. For the ideas of this paragraph, I am greatly indebted to Henry Friedlander's recent study of the fate of those caught at the vital conjunction of euthanasia and *Endlösung,* "Jüdische Anstaltspatienten im NS-Deutschland," Götz Aly, ed., *Atkion T4, 1939–1945: Die "Euthanasie"-Zentrale in der Tiergartenstrasse 4* (Berlin, 1987), pp. 34–44.

67. Raul Hilberg, *The Destruction of the European Jews* (Chicago, 1961), and *The Destruction of the European Jews,* revised and expanded edition in three volumes (New York, 1985); Christopher R. Browning, "The Revised Hilberg," *The Simon Wiesenthal Center Annual* 3 (1986); 289–300.

68. Heim and Aly, "Die Okonomie der 'Endlösung,'" pp. 11–90; and *Ein Berater der Macht: Helmut Meinhold oder der Zusammenhang zwischen Sozialpolitik und Judenvernichtung* (Selbstverlag, available through the Hamburger Institut für Sozialforschung, Hamburg, 1986).

69. This must not obscure the fact, however, that other elements of the anti-Semitic stereotype could also have murderous consequences. For example, the medieval notion of the Jew as disease-carrier was operative among the German public health officials in the General Government and set them on the path to mass murder. Christopher R. Browning, "Genocide and Public Health: German Doctors and Polish Jews, 1939–1941," *Genocide and Holocaust Studies* 3, no. 1 (1988): 21–36.

70. Indeed, I have argued elsewhere that, in facing the Communist-led uprising in Serbia and accepting the Jewish-Bolshevik equation as self-evident, the German military anticipated the Final Solution and began the mass murder of Jews on its own; Browning, *Fateful Months,* pp. 39–56.

71. Hilberg, *The Destruction of the European Jews,* rev. ed., p. 873.

72. Ian Kershaw, *Popular Opinion and Political Dissent in the Third Reich: Bavaria, 1933–1945* (Oxford, 1983), chap. 9; "The Persecution of the Jews and German Popular Opinion in the Third Reich," *Yearbook XXVI of the Leo Baeck Institute,* London, 1981, pp. 261–89; "German Popular Opinion and the 'Jewish Question,' 1939–1943: Some Further Reflections," *Die Juden im*

Nationsozialistischen Deutschland, pp. 365–86; Otto Dov Kulka, "'Public Opinion' in Nazi Germany: The Final Solution," *The Jerusalem Quarterly* 26 (Winter 1982): 34–45; O. D. Kulka and Aron Rodrigue, "The German Population and the Jews in the Third Reich: Recent Publications and Trends in Research on German Society and the 'Jewish Question," *Yad Vashem Studies* 16 (1984): 421–35.

11

The Genesis of the "Final Solution" from the Spirit of Science

Detlev J. K. Peukert

"Der Tod ist ein Meister aus Deutschland . . ."

If the unappealing episode of the *Historikerstreit* has had one redeeming feature, from a historical point of view, it is that after endless wrangles about "fascism" and "Hitlerism," "intentionalism" and "functionalism," attention has been concentrated on the single event around which any history of the National Socialist era must be written: namely, Auschwitz. [1]

Unfortunately, however, it must be said that the story of the *Historikerstreit* has been one of constant departure from, and evasion of, this central theme. The debate has been about the "Gulag" rather than "Auschwitz." Admittedly, in this respect it has not merely obeyed a certain inevitable logic of self-censorship. Even among writers who have been seriously and painstakingly concerned to understand how the policy of a "Final Solution" could emerge and be put into practice, the debate has inevitably widened out into a historical reconstruction of contexts and prehistories, despite the fact that categories of historical explanation break down in face of the horror of the policy's implementation. [2]

The effect of years of research has been that historians have moved away from a picture of the origins of the Final Solution that, while simplistic, also had the merit of simplicity: a picture of Hitler and his closest accomplices, stricken with racial mania, making deep-laid plans to translate their fantasies into reality, and then implementing these plans with demonic thoroughness, while keeping the facts from public knowledge throughout.

Today we know how complex and contradictory were the processes that led to the gradual and growing radicalization of Nazi racial policies and exter-mination methods, with their outcome in the murder of millions of Jews, Gypsies, subjects of the so-called *Ostvölker,* people with mental and physical handicaps, and the "unproductive" and "asocial."[3]

We also know that the Nazis' racial policies were inextricably bound up with both their domestic and foreign policies, and with the pattern—at first sight so normal—of German society: in other words, with everyday life, which, despite its banality, or even perhaps because of it, became literally deadly for millions of people.[4]

Speaking schematically, we can list a number of processes, deeply rooted in the everyday life of German society, that were contributory factors in causing these racial policies to be implemented in the form of practices of extermination. First, the escalation of the terror unleashed in the occupation of Poland and the Soviet Union led to mass-produced murder (the Commissar Order, the *SD-Einsatzgruppen,* and the treatment of prisoners of war). The forced employment of millions of foreign workers then meant that the *völkisch* hierarchy of *Herren-mensch* and *Untermensch* became a structural feature of daily life. This context made feasible the scheme of "annihilation through work" both inside and outside the concentration camps. Meanwhile, anthropological racism—with its centerpiece, anti-Semitism—became radicalized in the following stages: bans on emigration; deportations to the East; unsystematic mass killings; and, finally, systematic mass killings. Parallel to this intensified racial terror, eugenic or "social-hygienic" racism became radicalized—that is, the program of negative eugenics, proceeding via the mass compulsory sterilization of the so-called "genetically unhealthy" to the systematic murder of the allegedly incurable mentally or physically ill. Here the techniques of mass murder were tested out, ranging from selection and deportation to the gassing of victims and the conceal-ment of the facts from the public. Moreover, in steadily widening areas of social policy, health policy, educational policy, and demographic policy, a ruling paradigm and guide to action became established, whereby people were divided into those possessing "value" and those lacking "value." "Value" was to be selected and promoted, and "nonvalue" was to be segregated and eradicated. Large-scale social planning of a highly modern kind was harnessed toward the establishment of a racist utopia in which the social question would be "finally solved." No less important was the fact that the characteristic Nazi tension between the "normative" state and the "regulatory" state, the chaotic system of jurisdiction, and the rivalry among those who wielded power led to a growing reliance on ever more radical "solutions" to self-inflicted problems. Finally, behind this twofold radicalizing dynamism of form and content, there was the intrinsically unstable motive force of the National Socialist movement, forever taking flight into the future, and of the elite cartel led, in the movement's name, by Hitler. Since to have stood still would have meant a loss of identity, and since the positive meaning of the *Volksgemeinschaft* remained exceedingly vague, the regime inevitably drifted onto an increasingly radical negative concentration on the eradication of a world of enemies.

All of these factors, combined in various ways with regard to time, place, and subject matter, played a part in causing the racist Nazi utopia to come to fruition in the deadly machinery of the "Final Solution." All monocausal explanations of the origins of the "Final Solution," in other words, are inadequate. Nevertheless, we can and must ask whether this tangle of causes does not contain one central thread that might explain the origins of the decision, unparalleled in human history, to use high technology to annihilate certain abstractly defined categories of victims. Such a thread, according to the view to be argued in this paper, is not to be found in the traditional history of anti-Semitism and the persecution of the Jews, despite the fact that Jewish victims constituted by far the largest group on the charge-sheet of Nazi terror up to 1945. Rather, what was new about the "Final Solution" in world-historical terms was the fact that it resulted from a fatal racist dynamism present within the human and social sciences. This dynamism operated within the paradigm of the qualitative distinction between "value" and "nonvalue." Its complement in practical terms was the treatment of the *Volkskörper,* or "body" of the nation, by means of "selection" and "eradication." What emerged was an abstract process of selection based on this factitious racist definition of a holistic national entity, and a scheme for a high-technology "solution" based on cost-benefit analysis. The "Final Solution" was a systematic, high-technology procedure for "eradicating," or "culling," those without "value." It operated in terms of the dichotomies *healthy/unhealthy* with reference to the *Volkskörper, normal/deviant* with reference to the *Volksgemeinschaft*, and *Volk/Volksfremd* with reference to the nation and the race.

Recent research has shown that separate strands in the tangle of causes leading to the Final Solution were present in the most varied domains. The potential for good and ill inherent in the human and social sciences, and in the professions associated with them, was the central common factor. From this perspective, of course, the crimes of the Nazis are not the only historical event of relevance—if, that is, we regard these crimes not as a lethal outbreak of anachronistic barbarism, but as one among other possible outcomes of the crisis of modern civilization in general.

Recent studies of the development of psychiatry under National Socialism,[5] of the history of the compulsory sterilization program,[6] of genetics, eugenics, and medicine,[7] of social policy and demographic policy,[8] of education,[9] of the treatment of the "asocial" and of foreign workers,[10] of the persecution of the Gypsies,[11] of the persecution of the Jews in the context of everyday life,[12] and of racism as a form of cultural expression[13] have thrown up so many interconnected findings[14] that it seems legitimate to make a first attempt at an inclusive schematic interpretation. This author readily admits that his interpretation has arisen out of his own research in the area of the history of social-welfare education,[15] and that it must of course be subject to scrutiny and revision in the light of findings in the other individual areas mentioned. Nevertheless, any theory of the genesis of Nazi racism must transcend these individual fields, since racism itself transcended them both in its theory and in its practice.

The common racist factor in the disciplines and professions of the human and social sciences is the differential assessment and treatment of people according to their "value," where the criteria of "value" are derived from a normative and affirmative model of the *Volkskörper* as a collective entity, and biological substratum of "value" is attributed to the genetic endowment of the individual. This broad definition of racism deliberately includes the views of theorists and scientists who would certainly not have regarded themselves as "racists" merely by virtue of the fact that their theories and methods were centered on the tripartite model of "value," the *Volkskörper* as collective entity, and the hereditary character of the relevant attributes. To include them is to take account both of the point that the character of National Socialism in general, and of its racism in particular, was an amalgam of different inputs and tendencies, and of the historically vital fact that the process that evolved into the "Final Solution" was one of cumulative radicalization, in which the most deadly option for action was selected at every stage. In other words, the broad current that became the "Final Solution" was fed by numerous smaller currents that, taken singly, had perhaps never been intended, or desired, by their authors to lead to such a result.

In order to understand the specific role played by racist thinking in the history of the modern human sciences and the professions corresponding to them, we must go back to the turn of the century. This was the period that saw the rise of the theories, and—more important—the practices, involving a scientific approach to human beings, that have since put their stamp, for good or ill, on modern life.

The Human Sciences and the Utopian Dream of a "Final Solution"

By about the turn of the century, a scientific approach to the study of human beings and to the tackling of social problems had become a broadly practicable project for the first time. A breakthrough in scientific medicine had occurred, achieving notable success in combating epidemic diseases. This gave rise to the expectation that all the major diseases would be effectively combated, or even eradicated, in the foreseeable future. In a way analogous to the combating of disease, psychology and educational theory held out the prospect of scientific diagnosis of the personality and methods of therapy that would eliminate ignorance and social maladjustment. As prevention and cure spread through urban mass society, a new paradigm of social hygiene, targeted at the social causes of illness and deviance, became established. Increasingly, medicine took into its sights both the body of the individual and the collective "body" of the nation. As the state took it on itself, through social policy, to deal with risks to individual welfare such as illness, accident, and senile decay, so welfare services became professionalized and a new academically trained class of social workers was created and underwent rapid expansion.

Within a few decades, then, there had arisen a network of scientific and academic theories and methods on the one hand, and of social welfare institutions and practices on the other, designed to solve the "social question." The complexity of the issues involved meant that these new approaches were soon forced to reach out beyond the more restricted problem areas that had originally given rise to them. They now set themselves up, in terms both of self-image and of their mode of practical and administrative intervention, as key agents in the shaping and regulation of modern everyday life.

Increasingly, the scientific and academic disciplines and the social-welfare institutions and professions began to claim to be able to provide comprehensive solutions to all "social questions." To be sure, the frustrating fact had to be faced from the outset that means were finite and successes limited. Accordingly, much of the subsequent history of these disciplines and institutions swung between the dual poles of their claim to comprehensive validity and control on the one hand and the depressing fact of their limited efficacy on the other. It would have been possible to curb the sense of frustration by taking stock and scaling down the claims. It was also possible, however—and this was the more likely eventuality, given the astonishing breakthroughs made by the human and social sciences around the turn of the century—that the frustrating and recalcitrant features of social and human reality would be seen as obstacles that had to be surmounted or abolished by yet more rapid advance.

In the course of this evolution, the human and social sciences and professions acquired considerable new prestige, and the range of issues they were held competent to address was greatly enlarged. The emergence of the new social-scientific discourse in the domains of both theory and practice also coincided historically with drastic changes in social and living conditions at the turn of the century. We must outline these changes, albeit briefly, here.

The so-called "demographic transition" involved a major upheaval in key elements of the life-cycle.[16] Traditional death-rate patterns, with high infant and child mortality, the ever-present risk of death in adult life, and relatively early death in old age, gave way to the modern mortality pattern: low infant and child mortality, reduced risk of death in adult life, and very high old-age mortality in line with the increased mean level of life expectancy. Death, in other words, largely ceased to be an everyday phenomenon, and reappeared only at the far end of the life span in less comprehensible form. This alteration in the fundamental experience of life and death forced people to seek new existential answers; psychologically, indeed, we have still not come to terms with the banishment of death from daily life. The failure gave rise to a whole host of mechanisms of defense and repression.

The same applies to the role of the body, its health and sickness. Scientific medicine, public hygiene, and social-welfare insurance meant that concern with the body increased enormously. The new message was a "natural"—in this context, a rational scientific—attitude toward the body. The practical achievements of medicine, but more especially its faith in therapeutic progress, led to an idealization of youth and health;[17] the decline of the body through illness and aging was to be defied, or at least deferred, as long as possible. The tension between the bodily ideal and individual bodily decay was to be overcome not only by science but with respect to those individuals affected. The obvious move was for the actual target of scientific effort to switch from the individual, whose case was in the long run was always hopeless, to the "body" of the nation, the *Volkskörper.*

Bound up with these changes was the youth cult, itself fed from many sources. One of its wellsprings was undoubtedly the demographic transition, which first produced a quantitative rejuvenation on a scale hitherto unknown, and then, with the shift toward the two-child family, instigated a process of qualitative rejuvenation as parents became able to afford to devote more intensive care to their offspring. On top of this came the social and cultural thrust of innovation at the turn of the century, which made for a downgrading of the experience of the older generation and an identification of modernity with youthfulness.[18]

The youth cult reflected more than merely demographic changes. It signaled the decisive breakthrough of modern forms of life that occurred around the turn of the century and that entitles the period to be called (by analogy with cultural history) the beginning of the classical modern era. Industrialization, urbanization, mass society, and the permeation of technology into everyday life are merely some of the markers of this sociocultural modernization process. They were also the key concepts invoked in a vigorous process of self-scrutiny and debate conducted in the name of cultural criticism, social reform, and life-style reform. The debate was mirrored by the arrival of a new sense of vitality, not only among the avant-garde but also in the everyday lives of the masses. This in turn entailed unprecedented efforts at reorientation. Traditional sources of meaning and ritualized structures in everyday life failed to provide answers to the new questions. The drive for innovation devalued the experience of the older generation, yet for a long time it was unclear what new kinds of outlook would replace it.

Undoubtedly, these complex processes of upheaval in life-patterns were viewed favorably for the most part at the turn of the century, and were seen as indicators of the advancing realization of the Enlightenment ideal of the greatest happiness of the greatest number. It seemed that the human sciences and social professions would abolish the limitations of the human condition, or at least continue to loosen them.

Implicit within this faith in progress, however—which was very closely bound up with the new spirit of vitality in the new scientific and social professions—there was a fundamental sense of insecurity, as critical contemporaries were quick to point out. Illness, aging, and death might have been banished from modern day-to-day experience, but they lay in wait on the dark far side of the modern sense of vitality, more threatening and less understood than before, ready to usher in the extinction of the individual. Siegfried Kracauer, writing in 1929, diagnosed this phenomenon in his acute analysis of modern white-collar culture and its *neue Sachlichkeit* optimism in the brief span of the "golden twenties":

> It is, however, a mark of the *neue Sachlichkeit* altogether that it is a facade behind which nothing lies concealed. It has not been wrested from the depths; it is an aping of profundity. Like the rejection of old age, it springs from a dread of confrontation with death. [19]

A prime reason why the tabooing of death, the idealization of the body, the cult of youth, and the facade-like character of modern consumer culture so quickly became collective repositories of meaning was that the long-term historical process of secularization had by now reached the masses and everyday life. The cohesive force of Christian constructions of meaning was continuing to diminish, as was the influence of religious rituals on major life-events and the social environment.

At the turn of the century, then, the gap created by the decline of religious influence on everyday life in industrial society was so great, and the conquest of the world by secularized, scientific rationality was so overwhelming, that the switch from religion to science as the source of a meaning-creating mythology for everyday life took place almost without resistance. The result, however, was that science took on itself a burden of responsibility that it would soon find a heavy one to bear. In order that we may better understand the process through which a religious-based mythology of everyday life was converted into one legitimized by science, we should look for a moment at the question of the evolution of the world religions before the era of secularization.

Max Weber regarded theodicy as the central dynamic impulse behind the evolution of the world religions. The vindication of an omnipotent and just God in a world so obviously dominated by suffering and injustice generated repeated shifts towards rationalization, stretching the conceptual frameworks of the different world religions to their logical limits. We can see the evolutionary dynamism within the human and social sciences as analogous to the pressure toward rationalization generated by theodicy, with the sciences, as a result of the process of secularization, now promoted into the role of supplying the key concepts in the repository of everyday constructions of meanings. This science-based "logodicy" is equally the product of the borderline but universal experience of suffering and death. It asks the question: How can the rationalist, secular ideal of the greatest happiness for the greatest number be vindicated, given that it is rebutted in the case of each individual by illness, suffering, and death? The borderline, or extreme, experience of death cannot ultimately be explained away by means of scientific rationality, so long as death remains beyond science's reach. A "logodicy" of the human sciences accordingly drives the sciences into irrationality. It inevitably becomes fixated on the utopian dream of the gradual elimination of death, even while this dream is unfailingly confuted in the life of each particular individual. One obvious escape from the dilemma is to split the target of scientific endeavor into the merely ephemeral body of the individual, and the potentially immortal body of the *Volk* or race. Only the latter—specifically, its undying material substratum in the form of the genetic code—can guarantee the undying victory of science itself.

Naturally, this abstract, ideal-type process can be discerned only in partial and mixed form in the actual thinking of individual scientists and theorists. It need not be an ever-present influence governing thought and action. It is, however, basic and permanent, and has the corrosive force of existential doubt. It is also entirely subject to the trade-cycle of history. In periods of social and scientific growth and advance, it finds expression in an almost boundless faith in progress: obstacles are minimized, the future seems assured, the message is "Not yet, but soon." Indeed, the exact boundary between optimism and delusions of grandeur may not always be clearly apparent. Armed with the skepticism of hindsight, we are struck by the fantasies of omnipotence prevalent in the sciences and social professions at the turn of the century.[20] In times of crisis and decelerating progress, on the other hand, the grand designs are stalled as they repeatedly come up against insurmountable obstacles. The optimistic, utopian vision of the *Volkskörper* is stripped of its universality and is instead defined in negative, restrictive terms. The central concern now becomes that of identifying, segregating, and disposing of those individuals who are abnormal or sick.

The numerous varieties of racism, and particularly the institutionalized racism of the Nazis, added a ready-made armory of weapons to the science-based search for an irrational solution to the "logodicy" of death. The paradigm here was the *Volkskörper* qua object of scientific aid and cure. The body of the individual might indeed be an obstacle to therapeutic success, but all that was needed was a decision: whether it could be cured, and hence admitted to the ideal *Volkskörper*, or whether it should be eliminated—in which case the *Volkskörper* would again assume its ideal character after all.

Ideologically speaking, National Socialism offered a perfect validation of the primacy of the *Volkskörper*, with its doctrine of individual hereditary "value" and "nonvalue." Aesthetically speaking, it backed this up with its idealized body-images of steel-hard maleness, voluptuous femaleness, and, generally, youthful health with its promise of immortality.[21] The split between the individual and national "body" also allowed the borderline experience of death to be explained away. In this sense National Socialism reintroduced a language for negotiating the fact of death. In racist ideology, individual death and the ephemeral nature of individual existence are secondary to the eternal life of the *Volkskörper* and the perfectible genotype. Within the irrational logic that was National Socialism's hallmark, the nurture and improvement of the immortal *Volkskörper* in fact gave death a double significance: in the form of heroic death, and in the form of "eradication" *(Ausmerze)*.

The eudaemonistic sentiment that pervades Himmler's secret speeches justifying the "Final Solution" was, therefore, desperately serious. So too was the belief of numerous prominent scientists that concentration-camp experiments, euthanasia, and "criminal biology," while harsh in their effects on the individual, were justified not only because they affected solely those without "value" but also because they would secure the well-being of future healthy and normal members of the *Volkskörper*.

From Mass Well-Being to Mass Annihilation

It must be clearly emphasized that the ideal-type account given so far of the inner logic that led the human and social sciences to find their self-validation in racism depicts an extreme logical possibility: it does not imply that such an evolution was absolutely inevitable. On the contrary, it can be said that everyday mythologies, whether legitimized by religion or science, are only very rarely pushed to their logical limits. As a rule, it is an assortment of inconsistent and hence practicable half-measures, eclectically adapted to the inchoate structures of everyday life, that is used as a basis for action.

This was the case in the normal situation of work in the fields of science and social policy. A doctor, for example, might care selflessly for all of his patients and yet simultaneously cling to the utopian vision of a *Volkskörper* of the future, freed of all hereditary defects. Like Grotjahn, he might be a doctor concerned with public health and social hygiene, and impassioned champion of the welfare of those at the bottom of the social scale, and yet at the same time call for the sterilization of 30 percent of the population on grounds of genetic defects. Doctors and social workers who derived moral certitude from firm religious or other beliefs were able to remain relatively immune to racist ideas of "value" or at least to the barbarous consequences of such ideas. Historically speaking, this option remained open; such alternative ways of thinking and acting were possible. But there was also the racist option of the primacy of the *Volkskörper* over the individual, and of the "valuable" individual over the individual without "value."

My thesis is that the origins of the "Final Solution" can be established historically as follows: (1) we can show how the racist implications of the human and social sciences, in their function as constructors of meanings in everyday-life mythologies, might arise; (2) we can outline the possible alternatives that might result from these initial conditions, and those options that, in the actual historical context, did in fact result; (3) we can reconstruct the concatenation of circumstances within which the racist option prevailed; and (4) we can state the conditions in which the racist utopia was radicalized into a program for action and implemented in the form of the lethal technology of the "Final Solution."

The current state of research does not yet enable us to translate this scheme into a total history of racism in the Nazi state, one that includes an account of its roots in the nineteenth century. We know enough, however, to be able to point to parallel, if very varied, sets of racist processes in the most disparate scientific disciplines and social professions. The history of one such domain, which has been the subject of detailed study by this author, may serve as representative of many others. This is the field of social-welfare education.[22]

Social-welfare education evolved, as a halfway house between educational policy and social-welfare policy, to fill a gap in the system of social control of young people that had arisen within the contradictions of modern industrial society. This gap was to be filled by a higher cultural standard of youth-service provision and a battery of youth-welfare measures designed to rectify social deviance. The evolution of this system developed through a distinct set of phases.

First, the problem and a set of desired solutions to the problem is formulated in accordance with the social-reform aspirations and science-based progressivism of the 1880s and 1890s. This is followed by a phase of institutionalization, at first experimental and then very rapidly spreading to become the norm, still entirely governed by the optimistic goal of using state intervention to secure for "every" child the educational right to "physical, mental, and social fitness" (1900–1922).

There follows a phase of routinization and crisis of confidence, particularly when room for maneuver becomes financially restricted in the 1920s. The old optimism now survives side by side with a new sense of frustration, and the first seeds of an alternative vision to that of comprehensive educational provision begin to take root. Proposals are already being put forward for a law of "detention"—or, euphemistically, of "protection"—that will cover all those who fail to achieve the educational goal of "fitness," whether on objective or subjective grounds of "unfitness" or "ineducability." Legal schemes for compulsory detention of the "ineducable," however, break down both because of the unknown cost and because of internal self-contradictions in the attempted definitions of "ineducability." If the definition is kept narrow, then it does not catch all the social deviants intended, since they cannot be taken into custody as criminal or insane. But if the definition is made sufficiently wide to include them, then the overall number of those affected escalates so rapidly as to make a mockery of due legal process.

The search for new ideas by established educators disturbed by the contradictions thrown up by work in the field becomes intense in the crisis years 1928–33. The specific crisis within the field of youth-welfare education, symptomatized by revolts and scandals in young people's homes, coincides with a self-critical debate among educational reformers on the "limits of educability" and "limits of education." In turn, within the context of the general crisis in the welfare state, these changes affect, and are affected by, the new program of welfare retrenchment. Among the various alternative proposals generated by this crisis debate, a new way of viewing the educational problem gradually gains ground as welfare provision is cut back. Social and educational provision has to run the gauntlet of a cost-benefit trade-off. Services are allocated in accordance with their prospect of achieving immediate return, and the implicit guiding criterion becomes the "value" or otherwise of those receiving the services or the educational provision. "Lesser value" is not necessarily defined in terms of hereditary tendencies, but it may be. By the final years of the Weimar Republic, the new paradigm of selecting those of "value" and segregating those of "lesser value" has already begun to displace the previous paradigm of universality of provision and correction. This change of paradigm is reflected in the amendment to the Reich Youth Welfare Law of November 1932, when the "uneducable" are excluded from reform-school education. The racist doctrine of the genetic "value" of the individual gave the imprimatur of theory to practical policies that were already coming into effect.

When the Nazis come to power in 1933, the paradigm of selection and elimination, already dominant, is made absolute. What is new is not the paradigm per se, but the fact that its critics are forced into silence. In addition, through a voluntary preemptive act of obedience, racist terminology is elevated into the lingua franca of the human sciences and social-welfare professions. And, as yet another change, one single branch of modern social thought, namely racism, receives supreme state backing and is given ever greater scope to test its theories and methods and put them into practice.

After 1933 racism has an unprecedented operational license and is

systematically implemented on a colossal scale, as in the compulsory sterilization of the so-called "genetically unhealthy." Yet despite this, and despite the
constant establishment of new procedures of "special treatment" for the racially
stigmatized in concentration camps, the racist paradigm of selection and eradication encounters the same crisis of confidence as that faced by the universal-
provision paradigm ten years earlier. The "positive" racism underlying the
system of youth-welfare provision based on heredity rapidly comes up against
limits that rebut its utopian claims. Racist theorists accordingly start searching all
the more stubbornly for ways of vindicating their views through the "negative"
racism of segregation and eradication. While the image of an immortal, healthy
Volkskörper remains vague, the catalogue of deviances that are to be eradicated
becomes ever more detailed and specific. This negative radicalization of the
racist utopia becomes the vital guiding thread in the evolution of Nazi policy.
"Eradication" more and more overtly becomes the favored option, although up
to the outbreak of war no final choice has yet been made among the various ways
of implementing it, which range from physical segregation and sterilization, via
killing by neglect, to killing by design. [23]

    With the outbreak of war, and the issue of the order calling for the
systematic murder of those deemed "unworthy of life" (lebensunwertes Leben),
the crucial step is taken from the racist utopian dream to its realization in the
"Final Solution." It is no accident that this move occurs at the focal point of one
of the scientific professions. Indeed, the process through which the racist definition of the victims of the "Final Solution" is now expanded makes plain that it is
the eugenic, racial-hygiene variant of racism that has provided the key component parts in the machinery of mass murder: the notion of "nonvalue," removing
ethical status from those affected; the anonymity of the process of categorization
of the victims in terms of hereditary characteristics (largely specious in any case);
long-standing prior administrative practices involving institutions of segregation;
and, finally, the scientific and technological input involved in the construction
of the apparatus of murder itself. Anti-Semitism based on racial anthropology
supplies the graphic and traditionally legitimized scapegoat image that helps
serve as a basis for the expansion of the category of victim. But the specifically
modern character of the "Final Solution" derives from the swing to racial
hygiene in the human and social sciences.

    In the next phase, with the machinery of murder now running and
incorporating ever wider groups of people, the human sciences and social
professions are engaged in a parallel process of theoretical and institutional
generalization that is aimed at an all-embracing racist restructuring of social
policy, educational policy, and health and welfare policy. The debates and drafts
dealing with the "Law for the Treatment of Community Aliens" (Gemeinschaftsfremde), [24] the full implementation of which is abandoned in 1944 only
because of the state of the war, reunite the disorganized and conflicting separate

disciplines and agencies of the Nazi state, typically, in the negative project of identifying enemies.[25] The abortive projects of the 1920s to rescue progressivist welfare education by putting the "ineducable" into compulsory detention now resurface in the catch-all definition of *Gemeinschaftsfremde*, a category that potentially threatens everyone falling under it with police custody, if not imprisonment or death: "failures," "ne'er-do-wells," "parasites," "good-for-nothings," "troublemakers," and those with "criminal tendencies."

Nazi racism, the professed goal of which had been to secure the immortality of the racially pure *Volkskörper*, in practice inevitably became converted into a crusade against life. It found its fulfillment in the ever-expanding mass-production of murder of all those it defined as "unworthy of life." It found its final utopian refuge from the borderline experience of death in the unbridled infliction of death on others.

The fact that National Socialism followed this path does not mean that such a path was inescapable. On the contrary, several critical junctures and strategic shifts were required before the eudaemonistic utopian dream of the victory of science and social reform over mass poverty, ignorance, illness, and death was transformed into the mass-destructive utopia of racist purification of the *Volkskörper* through the "eradication" of lives of "lesser value." The strategic shifts included the following: (1) from the individual qua object of support to the social and national "body"; (2) from care for the needy to selection of those of "value" and eradication of those of "lesser value": (3) from the ideal of the greatest happiness of the greatest number to a cost-benefit accounting of provision and likely return, based on the "value" of those eligible for support; and (4) from self-indulgent delusions of technological and scientific grandeur to self-reproducing high-technology mechanisms of annihilation.

None of these shifts was inevitable, although all of them represented options implicit in the hybrid role of the human and social sciences in the modern world. It was owing to the particular character of historical change in Germany that the fatal sequence of choices was made, each in a specific historical situation, that led to the appalling logical extreme of the "Final Solution."

International comparisons can help explain which aspects of the crisis in the human sciences and of the mirage of a racist solution were specific to the German national tradition and which were bound up with the problems of modernization in general. Both crisis and solution, after all, were evident in other countries, albeit in different forms. Advance in the human sciences and in social policy was an international phenomenon, as was the growing, associated tendency for the scientific and social professions to assert their claims in the social field. Racism was international too, both in its more archaic guise as racial anthropology and in its more modern eugenic, racial-hygiene version.

As far as specifically German national factors are concerned, we can note the extraordinary acceleration in the process of modernization around the turn of the century and the correspondingly explosive debate on cultural criticism, social reform, and lifestyle reform. The level of institutionalization and bureaucratization within the social professions may well also have been particularly high. But distinctive national factors can really be discerned only in the crisis years of the late 1920s, when the general crisis of modernization in German society and the economy coincided with a deep-seated crisis of political legitimacy. And the vital factor leading to the radicalization of racism, and eventually to the "Final Solution," was the character of the Nazi dictatorship.

The German case was paradigmatic inasmuch as it revealed the lethal potential implicit in a general process of historical change; it was the product of national factors inasmuch as only the latter converted this potential into reality.

Let us pick out two critical episodes in the German case once again. First, the general crisis of modernization at the end of the 1920s promoted the change of paradigm to one of a policy of selection and eradication and then, with the Nazi seizure of power, gave racism a new institutional framework and a horrifying new source of energy. Second, the situation between the outbreak of the Second World War and the invasion of the Soviet Union, when the Nazis' racist utopianism became progressively more radical in the negative, "eradication" sense, gave rise to the appalling machinery of murder and the deaths of millions in the "Final Solution."

The process, it should be said, did not unfold without opposition. Resistance came from victims and their relatives; from a not inconsiderable number of scientists and members of the social professions; from individuals who could not, and would not, suppress their detestation of racism and the results to which it was leading; and indeed, although in varying degrees, from many nonfascist organizations, particularly the Catholic Church. Catholics, as religious absolutists, found it easier than Protestants, with their leaning towards nontranscendental rationality, to hold out against an ideology that sanctified the *Volkskörper* and deprived those of "lesser value" of their status as human beings. This fact can be explained if, as has been argued here, we view the roots of modern racism as lying in the problem of legitimation in a secularized world. A secularized world no longer provided final answers: it had no way of pointing beyond itself. Once the facade of a nontranscendent everyday mythology had been shattered by crisis, the search was on for "final solutions."

The "death of God" in the nineteenth century gave science dominion over life. For each individual human being, however, the borderline experience of death rebuts this claim to dominion. Science therefore sought its salvation in the specious immortality of the racial *Volkskörper*, for the sake of which mere real, and hence imperfect, life could be sacrificed.

Thus the instigators of the "Final Solution" finally achieved dominion over death.

After Auschwitz

The watchword for the human and social sciences in 1945, after the frenzy of the "Final Solution," was: "Back to normal!" The distinctive character of daily life in the last years of the war and the first years of peace was certainly part of the reason for this normalization. Millions had died in battle, at home, or as refugees, and these deaths were experienced by the survivors with a directness and intensity that overshadowed memories of the "Final Solution," which ostensibly had taken place far from home. Postwar distress encouraged people to turn inward and deal with the more manageable dimensions of their own fate, leaving the fates of the millions who were unknown to them to pale into insignificance. It was in similar fashion that the scientific and social professions, which had shed their inhibitions under National Socialism, now reverted rapidly to the routines of everyday inquiry.

Thus, apart from the small group prosecuted in the Nuremberg doctors' trial, most scientists and professionals who had committed or been implicated in crimes found it possible to resume a post-Nazi normality directly where their pre-Nazi routine had broken off. Since there were few prosecutions even of those who had been guilty of offenses in a juridical sense, those who had been involved in planning, establishing, testing, constructing, and operating the machinery of the "Final Solution," yet who were not technically liable to prosecution, could actually be pronounced "innocent."

At the same time, the destructive frenzy of the firing squads and gas chambers had furnished a *reductio ad absurdum* of the racist utopia of a "neat and tidy" final solution to all the questions besetting modern society. Disillusionment set in even among those who had been tempted by the utopian dream in the euphoric early years of the regime or during the period of German domination over the European continent.

Those, however, who tried, by returning to "business as usual," simply to evade coming to terms with the Nazi past—and most fell into this category— were also obliged to try to revert to a precrisis mentality as far as their respective sciences and professions were concerned. The sense of crisis that had been sufficiently unsettling, before the Nazi seizure of power, to infect the human sciences with racism, now had to be as firmly banished from consciousness as the Nazi years themselves.

Even among those scientists and academics, including some educational reformers, who had preserved their integrity and had been persecuted by the Nazis, coming to terms with the past took place in a selective fashion, either because there might be a sense of complicity or because of feelings of impotence. The result, with Nazi sympathizers and persecution victims in the scientific professions alike, was a blocking-off of any systematic analysis of the way in which their professions had been entangled in the history of racism in general and of National Socialism in particular.

There were ony few exceptions to this rule. One such was the publication of documents by Alexander Mitscherlich,[26] which was first vehemently criticized by members of the medical profession and then used as a pretext for abandoning any settling of accounts with the past. In the early postwar years there were also a good number of publications from a religious point of view that, not without reason, attacked National Socialism as part of a wider critique of secularism, but that never got beyond calling for a return to old Christian values and hence merely erected a moral and theological superstructure on top of a scientific base that was not itself called into question.[27] Altogether, it was far easier for Christian apologists in the 1950s to accede to the domination of science over everyday life by shutting out all problematical implications.

Just as the German economy in the 1950s resumed the path of growth abandoned in 1914, so the human sciences and social professions, by shedding their Nazi ideological baggage and the beliefs and attitudes acquired during the debate about "crisis" and "limits," returned to the unproblematical normality that they had abandoned in the quest for utopian final solutions in the 1920s.

What of the present day? What can we do now? We shall not find a way forward unless we continue with the task, so far only partially tackled, of restoring awareness of what actually happened in the past. The fact that a younger generation is now represented in all the disciplines and professions of the human and social sciences is a help here, not only because this generation bears no personal responsibility for the past, but also because, after a quarter of a century of normality, *Wirtschaftswunder*, and faith in progress, a sense of running up against limits is reappearing once again. This sense of crisis makes it possible—indeed, makes it imperative—to raise questions about the historical crisis that preceded the upsurge of Nazi racism. A purely factual reconstruction of past events is possible only if, at the same time, we engage in a theoretical debate about options and opportunities within the disciplines and professions of the human and social sciences, past and present.

In any case, skeptical questions are increasingly being raised about the viability and substance of our everyday mythologies; about our images of youth and age, illness and health, life and death; and about the moral categories we bring to bear in our dealings with others, notably those different from ourselves. Recent debates in West Germany about foreign migrants and AIDS present a conflicting picture. On the one hand, we can see the continuing survival of a discourse of segregation, untouched by any historical self-consciousness. On the other hand, however, there is a considerable body of opinion pleading for the tolerance and responsibility that spring from an awareness of German history and of the genesis of the "Final Solution" from the spirit of science.

Notes

1. *"Historikerstreit": Die Dokumentation der Kontroverse um die Einzigartigkeit der nationalsozialistischen Judenvernichtung* (Munich, 1987).

2. Dan Diner, ed., *Ist der Nationalsozialismus Geschichte? Zu Historisierung und Historikerstreit* (Frankfurt, 1987); Heide Gerstenberger and Dorothea Schmidt, eds., *Normalität oder Normalisierung? Geschichtswerkstätten und Faschismusanalyse* (Münster, 1987).

3. See the committed discussion by Hans Mommsen, "Die Realisierung des Utopischen: Die 'Endlösung der Judenfrage' im 'Dritten Reich,'" in *Geschichte und Gesellschaft* 9 (1983): 381–420.

4. *Alltagsgeschichte der NS-Zeit: Neue Perspektive oder Trivialisierung?* Kolloquien des Instituts für Zeitgeschichte (Munich, 1984); Detlev Peukert, *Inside Nazi Germany: Conformity, Opposition and Racism in Everyday Life* (New Haven, Conn., 1987); idem and Jürgen Reulecke, eds., *Die Reihen fast geschlossen: Beiträge zur Geschichte des Alltags unterm Nationalsozialismus* (Wuppertal, 1981).

5. Klaus Dörner, "Nationalsozialismus und Lebensvernichtung," in *Vierteljahreshefte für Zeitgeschichte* 15 (1967): 121–52; Ernst Klee, *"Euthanasie" im NS-Staat: Die "Vernichtung lebensunwerten Lebens"* (Frankfurt, 1983); idem, *Dokumente zur "Euthanasie"* (Frankfurt, 1985); idem, *Was sie taten, was sie wurden: Ärtze, Juristen und andere Beteiligte am Kranken- und Judenmord* (Frankfurt, 1985); Dirk Blasius, *Der verwaltete Wahnsinn: Eine Sozialgeschichte des Irrenhauses* (Frankfurt, 1990).

6. Gisela Bock, *Zwangssterilisation im Nationalsozialismus: Studien zur Rassenpolitik und Frauenpolitik* (Opladen, 1986), provides an outstandingly thorough source review and detailed historical account, and is also a penetrating theoretical study that will provide the underpinnings for future research. The present paper is greatly indebted to Bock's reconstruction of the international logic and phases of evolution of racism.

7. Gerhard Baader and Ulrich Schultz, eds., *Medizin und Nationalsozialismus: Tabuisierte Vergangenheit—Ungebrochene Tradition?* (Berlin, 1980); Benno Müller-Hill, *Murderous Science: Elimination by Scientific Selection of Jews, Gypsies, and Others, Germany 1933–1945,* (Oxford, 1988); Alfons Labisch and Florian Tennstedt, *Der Weg zum "Gesetz über die Vereinheitlichung des Gesundheitswesens" vom 3. Juli 1934* (Düsseldorf, 1985).

8. Hans-Uwe Otto and Heinz Sünker, eds., *Soziale Arbeit und Faschismus: Volkspflege und Pädagogik im Nationalsozialismus* (Bielefeld, 1986); Heidrun Kaupen-Haas, ed., *Der Griff nach der Bevölkerung: Aktualität und Kontinuität nazistischer Bevölkerungspolitik* (Nördlingen, 1986). The subtitle of this latter study gives an indication of the problems arising from the style of research it represents. Such work has the undoubted merit of recovering long-

neglected aspects of racial, health, and demographic policy as continuing historical processes and thus helping explain the specific shape they adopted under
National Socialism. The group of authors pursuing this line of research, however, centered around Karlheinz Roth and Götz Aly, repeatedly creates obstacles
for itself in reaching a balanced assessment of its own achievements by fusing
analysis with indictment and confusing continuity with identity. The constant
propagandist tone of these writers casts doubt on the reliability of the evidence
they cite and rules out the possibility of any nuanced, scholarly discussion.
Nevertheless, their findings must be taken into account by all serious historians
and used as a spur to new research. See especially the series *Beiträge zur
nationalsozialistischen Gesundheits- und Sozialpolitik* (Berlin, 1985ff.,) five
volumes of which are now available: *Aussonderung und Tod; Reform and
Gewissen; Herrenmensch und Arbeitsvölker; Biedermann und Schreibtischtäter;
Sozialpolitik und Judenvernichtung.*

     9. Ulrich Herrmann, ed., *"Die Formung des Volkgenossen": Der
"Erziehungsstaat" des Dritten Reiches* (Weinheim, Basel, 1985); Heinz-Elmar
Tenorth, *Zur deutschen Bildungsgeschichte, 1918–1945* (Cologne, Vienna,
1985).

     10. Wolfgang Ayass, "Es darf in Deutschland keine Landstreicher mehr
geben: Die Verfolgung von Bettlern und Vagabunden im Faschismus," diploma
dissertation (Kassel, 1980); Ulrich Herbert, *Fremdarbeiter: Politik und Praxis des
"Ausländereinsatzes" in der Kriegswirtschaft des Dritten Reiches* (Berlin, Bonn,
1985).

     11. Michael Zimmermann, "Die nationalsozialistische Vernichtung-
spolitik gegen Sinti und Roma," in *Aus Politik und Zeitgeschichte* 16–17 (1987):
31–45.

     12. Ian Kershaw, "Antisemitismus und Volksmeinung," in Martin
Broszat and Elke Fröhlich, eds., *Bayern in der NS-Zeit*, vol. 2 (Munich,
Vienna, 1979), pp. 281–348; see also the contributions by Mommsen, Allen,
Wiesemann, and Luchterhand in Peukert and Reulecke, eds., *Die Reihen fast
geschlossen.*

     13. Klaus Wolbert, *Die Nackten und die Toten des "Dritten Reiches":
Folgen einer politischen Geschichte des Körpers in der Plastik des deutschen
Faschismus* (Giessen, 1982); W. F. Haug, *Faschisierung des Subjekts: Die Ide-
ologie der gesunden Normalität und die Ausrottungspolitiken im deutschen Fas-
chismus* (Berlin, 1986); Hans Dieter Schäfer, *Das gespaltene Bewusstsein:
Deutsche Kultur und Lebenswirklichkeit, 1933–1945* (Munich, Vienna, 1981);
George L. Mosse, *Rassismus: Ein Krankheitssymptom der europäischen
Geschichte des 19. und 20. Jahrhunderts* (Königstein, 1978); idem, *Nationalism
and Sexuality: Middle-Class Morality and Sexual Norms in Modern Europe*
(Madison, Wisc., 1985).

     14. The first comprehensive accounts of the different racist policies in

their regional settings are given in: Projektgruppe für die vergessenen Opfer des NS-Regimes, eds., *Verachtet—verfolgt—vernichtet: Zu den "vergessenen" Opfern des NS-Regimes* (Hamburg, 1986); Angelika Ebbinghaus et al., eds., *Heilen und Vernichten im Mustergau Hamburg* (Hamburg, 1984); Jörg Kammler et al., eds., *Volksgemeinschaft und Volksfeinde: Kassel, 1933–1945*, vol. 1, *Dokumentation* (Fuldabrück, 1984); vol. 2, *Studien* (Fuldabrück, 1987). The total-history account by Norbert Frei, *Der Führerstaat: Nationalsozialistische Herrschaft 1933 bis 1945* (Munich, 1987), is the first adequate study of these complexities in the history of racism.

15. Detlev J.K. Peukert, *Grenzen der Sozialdisziplinierung: Aufstieg und Krise der deutschen Jugendfürsorge 1878 bis 1932* (Cologne, 1986).

16. Arthur E. Imhof, *Die gewonnenen Jahre: Von der Zunahme unserer Lebensspanne seit dreihundert Jahren oder die Notwendigkeit einer neuen Einstellung zu Leben und Sterben* (Munich, 1981).

17. Mosse, *Nationalism*.

18. Thomas Koebner et al., eds., *"Mit uns zieht die neue Zeit": Der Mythos Jugend* (Frankfurt, 1985).

19. Siegfried Kracauer, *Die Angestellten: Aus dem neuesten Deutschland* (1929; Frankfurt, 1971), p. 96. See also the stimulating essay by Erhard Lucas, *Vom Scheitern der deutschen Arbeiterbewegung* (Frankfurt, 1983).

20. Karl-Heinz Roth, "Schein-Alternativen im Gesundheitswesen: Alfred Grotjahn (1869–1931)—Integrationsfigur etablierter Sozialmedizin und nationalsozialistischer 'Rassenhygiene', " idem, ed., *Erfassung zur Vernichtung: Von der Sozialhygiene zum "Gesetz über Sterbehilfe"* (Berlin, 1984), pp. 31–56.

21. See n. 13 above.

22. See Peukert, *Grenzen de Sozialdisziplinierung*.

23. See Bocke, *Zwangssterilisation im Nationalsozialismus*.

24. See Peukert, *Grenzen der Sozial disziplinierung*.

25. Characteristically, a key role here was played by the Institute of Criminal Biology, directed by Dr. Robert Ritter, at the Reich Security Head Office. The Institute was the scientific body responsible for dealing with Gypsy persecutions, the Community Aliens Law, and the Moringen and Uckermark experimental youth concentration camps.

26. Alexander Mitscherlich and Fred Mielke, eds., *Medizin ohne Menschlichkeit: Dokumente des Nürnberger Ärzteprozesses* (Frankfurt, 1962).

27. Heinrich Kranz, "Lebensvernichtung und Lebenswert," in *Universitas, Dienst an Wahrheit und Leben*, Festschrift for Bishop Albert Stohr, ed. Ludwig Lenhart (Mainz, 1960), 2: 442–47; Bernhard Pauleikhoff, *Ideologie und Mord: Euthanansie bei "lebensunwerten" Menschen* (Hürtgenwald, 1986).

Appendix _____

Whatever Happened to "Fascism"?

TIM MASON

Tim Mason wrote this short essay on Fascism following the 1988 conference at the University of Pennsylvania from which this volume of essays derives. It is among the last of his writings before his tragic death in March 1990, and we publish it here as a tribute to his memory.

Before the final session of the conference, Tim had asked to be given time to offer his thoughts on an aspect of—or rather, an absence from—recent work on National Socialism that had begun to disturb him. This was the silent shift from the generic theory of Fascism that had shaped the political and historical debates of the 1960s and 1970s to a more restricted, localized, and ultimately less productive concentration on National Socialism alone. Tim worried that our discussions at the conference reflected a wider belief that Fascism, as he puts it here, "seemed to have become 'old hat.'"

This essay, which Tim wrote up from the notes of his final address to the conference, explains his disquiet at this tendency. He saw it as a retreat from engagement with the most fundamental and valuable questions that could be asked of this period of history. As a result partly of his move to Italy in the mid-1980s, Tim had begun to immerse himself in the history of Italian Fascism. He was already at work on the comparative empirical research he held to be so crucial for making sense of Fascism, and had published preliminary thoughts on workers' resistance to Fascism in Italy and on the theory of modernization. Had he lived, he would certainly have given us a uniquely informed comparative perspective for the further theorization of fascism. As it is, we have this brief essay— written in the pungent, challenging, intellectually rigorous style that always distinguished Tim's work: notes toward a project that he urgently wanted himself and others to work on.

The essay was first published in Radical History Review 49 *(Winter 1991). The text is unedited. The typescript contained embryonic footnote references that I have researched and completed as far as possible. I thank Geoff Eley and Ian Carter for their help in tracing some references.*

Jane Caplan

I want to argue in the notes that follow that an attempt to "reevaluate" the Third Reich in the late 1980s ought to have space for a slightly longer historiographical perspective than was evident in most of the papers and much of the discussion at the conference at the University of Pennsylvania in April 1988. Many different points could be raised in this context. I want to confine myself to one because it seems the most difficult and the most problematic: that is, the disappearance of theories, or articulated concepts, of "Fascism" from research and writing about the Third Reich since the mid-1970s. If it is used at all, the term now appears in the new literature (outside the GDR) in a loosely descriptive sense, devoid of theoretical baggage.[1]

I believe that this amounts to an enormous change, both in the conceptualization of National Socialism and in the directions of new research. This change should not be passed over in silence as though "Fascism" just melted away, but calls for some kind of stocktaking, toward which these remarks constitute a first fragmentary contribution. My own position on the issues involved is sufficiently muddled for me to try to write about them without having axes to grind: while I felt that the "Fascism" debates of the 1960s and 1970s brought enduring gains to the analysis of Nazism (see below), I never took a fully active part in them; I could never rid myself of basic conceptual doubts and confusions concerning *capital,* I always felt that a comparative dimension was missing from the writing on German "Fascism," and I thus usually preferred to use the terms National Socialism or Third Reich. This was true even of the notion of the "primacy of politics," in itself a very blunt instrument for a theoretical analysis of "Fascism."[2]

The consensus that theories of Fascism were possible and essential was once very wide. A full survey of the literature would be out of place here, but liberal and "apolitical" scholars were broadly represented in the discussions for a time. These discussions now seem closely linked with the *marxisant* writings of Kühnl, Kitchen, and the circle of *Das Argument,*[3] but it is well to recall that those who edited and contributed to the *Reader's Guide* to Fascism and to the massive *Who were the Fascists?*[4] also had a strong commitment to this type of approach, although they had intellectually and politically little in common with Marxist students of these problems. *The Nature of Fascism*,[5] to take the title of another eclectic book, offers further evidence, if it were needed, of the appeal the concept once had. In the late 1980s, however, such certainties (and my own old uncertainties) seem obsolete: most of the interesting new work is concerned specifically with Germany, Nazism, and the Third Reich, especially with the relationship between institutional structures and policy-making, on the one hand, and with biological politics (racism and eugenics), on the other. The most extreme peculiarities of German Nazism have thus slowly and silently come to dominate our moral, political, and professional concerns. When referred to at all at the Philadelphia conference, "Fascism" seemed to have become old hat. This amounts not to an organic development of a line of historical inquiry; it is much more like a fundamental change of paradigm.

I want to consider first of all what elements of the "Fascism" debate deserve to be retrieved and to be maintained in constant intellectual life and circulation. It seems then in place to speculate about why the debate faded away. Lastly, it is necessary to point out how the discussion is being revived, or rather, recast in a totally new form.

The first enduring achievement of the "Fascism" debate was the retrieval of a mass of contemporary (1920s and 1930s) Marxist and neo-Marxist writings on the subject. Whether our present concerns are with the movements and the regimes, or with the left-wing resistance to them, these works are too important simply to fall out of fashion. Second, the debate put class relations and class-state relations firmly at the center of the stage. Many historians never believed that they belonged there anyway, and have been provoked to write long, fruitful monographs to prove their case; and at least some erstwhile theorists of "Fascism" have come to doubt whether center stage is the right place for these issues. But I would argue very strongly that the themes should not be marginalized in the course of a hunt for novel research topics. One outstanding example of the ways in which the old conceptual apparatus can be fruitfully and discreetly married to new empirical research into the history of society and of ideologies is Ulrich Herbert's book *Fremdarbeiter*.[6] Class-class and class-state relations also call for constant critical inclusion into studies where they do not appear to be of primary importance, to be the engine of history—studies of gender roles, case studies in local history, etc. The present wave of doubts about and within Marxism has many justifications, but none of them should lead to a wholesale abandonment of the basic *questions*, however many of the "fascist" answers may need to be radically revised or abandoned.

The decline of the "Fascist" paradigm is not easy to chart. I can see little explicit evidence that the sustained, sharp, and comprehensive attacks on it by liberal and conservative scholars such as H.A. Winkler, H. A. Turner, and K. D.

Bracher[7] have had much persuasive effect—the debate was perhaps too con-frontational for there to be space for "conversions." For a possible long-term effect of these attacks, however, see below. At a purely intellectual level, it seems to me rather that "Fascism" theory ran into three dead ends in respect of the progress of empirical research within its own conceptual framework. The first dead end was self-inflicted, in the sense that theorists of "Fascism" did very little solid empirical work on their own home ground, that is, on the political economy of the period 1928–45; the territory that was theorized as being crucial was largely left to the research of other scholars, while secondary issues, such as fascist aesthetics and "faschistische Öffentlichkeit," aroused at least as much interest on the Left. The second dead end was Nazi racism, which was not studied systematically; this issue has always threatened to shatter generic con-cepts of "Fascism," and its highly uncertain treatment goes a long way towards explaining why German writings on "Fascism" received so little attention on the Left in Italy. This leads on to the third dead end: the weakness of the whole discussion in terms of comparative empirical work. A debate on these themes that did not refer continually to Italy, France, Rumania, or even Britain was bound to start revolving around itself in ever-decreasing concentric circles.

These intellectual constraints and limitations were clearly not trivial, but neither were they necessarily terminal—the work *could* gradually have expanded its basis and have continued to develop. Thus I tend to believe that the decisive reasons for the decline of the "Fascism" paradigm lay elsewhere—that is, in broader changes in the political culture. The first to note here is the slow decline and fragmentation of the movements of 1968. "Fascism" was very much a concept of these movements,[8] especially so in Germany where young people faced a parental generation, now in power, that had not resisted the Nazis and had not talked openly with their children about the Third Reich. There is a precise sense in which the German 1968 was a tragically belated (and thus to a degree misconceived) antifascist movement, not just contesting the parental generation per se but learning from and making good its terrible political errors. "Fascism," as I recall from many discussions in Berlin in the 1960s, was not just an epoch which ended in 1945, but was also something that the CDU and the right wing of the SPD was *then* trying to reinstate in a less barbaric form—"die formierte Gesellschaft" of Ludwig Ehrhard and Rüdiger Altmann, the mili-tarized police forces of West Berlin, etc. In the event, however, the SPD took control of the national government, there was a marked liberalization, and the 1968 movement went off in forty different directions, one of them terroristic. It was partly on account of this national sea change (which '68 itself did a lot to bring about) that the generic concept of "Fascism" lost its intellectual force among students and younger scholars on the Left.

The second major change that must be considered in this context is the development of feminism. This political-cultural movement of the Left has also helped to undermine the classical paradigm of "Fascism." Outside the works of Wilhelm Reich, there was little room in "Fascism" for such themes as gender and reproduction, and even Wilhelm Reich had little to say about the vast field of reactionary eugenics. Feminist inspirations and struggles have opened up very large, new areas of research into the historical reality of Nazism and German society in the twentieth century, themes that have burst the seams of older concepts of "Fascism" both in an empirical and in a theoretical sense.[9]

The third political cultural change that has worked in the same direction has been the steadily growing public awareness of Nazi genocide, above all the genocide of the Jews. This huge fact has come to dominate public perceptions of the history of Nazi Germany to an ever greater extent with the passing of the years, and in some measure scholarly research has followed this shift in public opinion.

At this point it may be helpful to try to relate the decline of "Fascism" to the vexed question of attempts to "historicize" the Third Reich; this effort may be doubly helpful in the sense that the meaning of "historicization" only becomes clear in the course of the practical use of the term. Most theorists of "Fascism" in the 1960s and 1970s understood Nazism *also* as a repository of possible lessons, warnings, and injunctions about economic and political developments in the near future; the Third Reich was "relevant." This is far from the concerns of those scholars who now wish to "historicize" it; the latter do not wish to deny its moral, cultural, and political *implications* for the present, but they do assert that Nazism belongs definitely to the past. "Historicization" has been presented as a novel idea, and threatens to become one in which methodological ruminations and moral sensibilities take command in a manner that can only lead to muddle.[10] The decline of that type of historical curiosity specifically associated with "Fascism" seems to me to be one example of "historicization" that *has actually taken place,* and a very important one.

However, this should in no way be understood as the happy triumph of the ivory tower over the seductions of politically committed history. Feminist history is politically committed, but the sustained and growing contribution to research and understanding that it has made, has, I would argue, in fact done a great deal to "historicize" Nazism by immensely broadening out notions of what it is that requires to be described and explained. If we now have some concrete notions of German society and Nazism, this is due as much to feminist work as it is to the proliferation of local case studies. And German society is the proper object of historicizing reflection and analysis. It is no paradox that this should be in part the outcome of a particular militancy in the present—historiographical progress normally occurs in this way. Normally, but not always: for the third political-cultural change noted above, the growing public preoccupation with genocide, may fuel the passions for research, but may also make critical distance more difficult, not less so. The scholarship on "Fascism" suffered both from a lack of critical distance and from a lack of comprehensive vision, both of them qualities essential to a "historicized" understanding of Nazism. The "Fascist" school failed to comprehend anti-Semitism, but it is no answer to read the whole of German history in terms of genocide, for that too contains elements of the "contemporaneity of the past" that can get in the way of critical moral discussion. [11]

This partial digression points toward the next observation, which is that no new paradigms have been put forward to take the place of theories of "Fascism." Those who wish to historicize Nazism may believe that we can do very well without *any* paradigms of that kind. To judge, however, from the essays in this volume and from other recent literature, there is something like a new consensus concerning the focus of research on Nazism. The most interesting new research takes it as axiomatic that the Third Reich was unique (in the radical sense of that word) and concentrates our attention on the broad gamut of Nazi biological politics (also unique), and on the institutions invented to implement them, often at the lowest administrative level (which also have a first appearance of uniqueness). It is thus impossible to conclude this section of these remarks without pointing to a paradox: the above position is the same as that put forward in outline, but insistently, by Karl Dietrich Bracher since 1970. Bracher has repeatedly argued that the Third Reich was unique, revolutionary, totalitarian, on account of the absolute preeminence it gave to biological politics. [12] I doubt very much that Bracher's direct influence has been great, since in the debate between functionalists and intentionalists he has aligned himself firmly with the latter, even on the issue of the Reichstag fire, whereas most of the new research feels itself much more indebted to various functionalist approaches. I can only note, not resolve, this paradox. It really does deserve to be noted, however, for it is a sign of how much things are in flux.

There are obviously no clear or simple ways out of these dilemmas. The Third Reich will go on being reevaluated, and new and old schools of interpretation will continue to shift in relation to each other. One limited but concrete way forward may lie in the making of systematic comparisons—above all with Fascist Italy; that type of work, that is, which the exponents of "Fascism" largely failed to do in the 1970s. One of the most remarkable features of that barren cultural episode that carries the name "Historikerstreit" is that the question of comparability was raised, to the best of my knowledge, only with respect to Stalin's Russia and Pol Pot, for example, and *not* with respect to Fascist Italy, which did, after all, provide Nazi Germany with a certain model and a loyal ally in war. Comparison (which is different from homologization) is an essential part of the historian's work, but like must be compared with like, and it is a distorting deviation to compare Nazi Germany with Stalinist Russia, a society that was at a completely different stage of cultural and political development and was pursuing radically different political goals. This negative part of the argument has been well stated, by Jürgen Kocka among others,[13] but the positive side of the argument has gone by default—that is, the argument in favor of systematic comparison with Fascist Italy.

The question of "Fascism" has reemerged in this new form. The old theories offer little by way of starting points, except perhaps for the political economy of 1922 and 1932–33 (i.e., the Italian Fascist and the Nazi seizures of power, respectively.) These theories tended to make Nazism look like Italian Fascism, without actually knowing what Italian Fascism actually looked like. Today, comparisons must commence with specific analytical questions that are capable in principle of empirical answers. The aim cannot be to reconstruct a "theory of Fascism" through the painstaking accumulation of comparative building blocks, for there are fundamental cognitive and methodological objects to the notion that theory can be constructed in this way. The goal must rather be to establish specific similarities and contrasts between the two regimes, and to establish the reasons for them, maintaining all the while a strict agnosticism with respect to the radical uniqueness of the one or the other. The themes available for such work are legion.

This may be illustrated first by two examples taken from the Philadelphia conference. Was there a strong eugenics movement in Fascist Italy? Yes, it was highly vocal and highly professional, but it ran up against the opposition of the Vatican (stronger in Italy than Bishop Galen in Germany!), and it lacked executive/administrative power.[14] Did denunciations play such an important role in enhancing the power of the various Fascist police forces as they did for the Gestapo? Almost certainly not, and this greatly diminished the repressive power of the Fascist dictatorship, which was unable, for example, to preempt the great strike wave that began in Turin in March 1943; but why this was the case calls for a lot of difficult research and analysis in both German and Italian cultural and social history: why should denunciation have been dishonorable in Italy, but not in Germany? There is no single answer, but the importance of the question is obvious.[15]

Such an approach to the question of Fascism and Nazism is not entirely new. Wolfgang Schieder has recently compared the stages of the seizure of power by the two regimes, coming to the conclusion that they were fundamentally similar.[16] MacGregor Knox has compared the relationship between the domestic and foreign policies of the two regimes, coming to the conclusion that both regimes used foreign policy to revolutionize domestic affairs;[17] one may argue that the relationship between the two spheres of state activity was in fact the opposite, but the author's method is impeccable and his conclusions consistently stimulating. Paolo Pombeni has executed a beautiful systematic comparison between the two parties, concluding that their functions and structure were basically similar.[18] Charles Maier has compared the Nazi and the Fascist economies, to the effect that the similarities outweighed the differences.[19] At a lower level of empirical research, I have tried to examine a contrast: the capacity of the Italian working class to launch a widespread strike in March 1943, of a kind that never came about in Germany.[20] I conclude that the difference had to do above all with the much greater administrative capacity of the Nazi regime, both in killing and providing welfare, than that of the Fascist state.

These essays indicate that the discussion can enter a new phase. Any less cautious formulation would be out of place. The question of Italian participation in genocide—against the Jews, in Africa, in the Balkans—remains hotly debated. Most Italian historians and publicists think that this issue marked off Italian Fascism from German Nazism in a decisive manner. But the problem is not resolved by counting corpses. What matters is the genocidal potential of the regime, and how one interprets in this light the various instances of mass murder that were committed in the name of Fascism. There is no doubt that the persecution of the Jews was carried out in Italy with less efficiency and enthusiasm than in any other country except Denmark. But the overall question remains open, in the sense that much research and analysis remains to be done. The fact that most Italians of all political colors are resistant to a positive comparison between "their" Fascism and German Nazism is a political-historical fact of great significance; it may also be an obstacle to historical work.

None of these remarks imply that the old concept of "Fascism" can, or should be revived. On the contrary, they point to a different program of work, which (alone, I believe) can identify just how peculiar (or typical) was the German road to organized inhumanity. If we can now do without much of the original contents of the concept of "Fascism," we cannot do without comparison. "Historicization" may easily become a recipe for provincialism. And the moral absolutes of Habermas, however politically and didactically impeccable, also carry a shadow of provincialism, as long as they fail to recognize that fascism was a continental phenomenon, and that Nazism was a peculiar part of something much larger.[21] Pol Pot, the rat torture, and the fate of the Armenians are all extraneous to any serious discussion of Nazism; Mussolini's Italy is not.

Notes

1. See, for example, Lutz Niethammer, *Lebensgeschichte und Sozialkultur im Ruhrgebiet 1930 bis 1980* 3 vols. (Berlin, 1983–86).

2. See Tim Mason, "The Primacy of Politics—Politics and Economics in National Socialist Germany," in S. J. Woolf, ed., *The Nature of Fascism* (London, 1968), pp. 165–95.

3. Reinhard Kühnl, *Formen bürgerlicher Herrschaft: Liberalismus— Faschismus* (Reinbek, 1971); idem, ed., *Texte zur Faschismusdiskussion: Positionen und Kontroversen* (Reinbek, 1974); idem, "Probleme einer Theorie über den internationalen Faschismus," *Politische Vierteljahresschrift* 16 (1975); Mar-

tin Kitchen, *Fascism* (London, 1976); *Das Argument* is a Marxist periodical published in West Berlin since the 1960s: for the 1960s debates on fascism, see especially issues 30, 32, 33, 41, and 43 (1964–67).

4. Walter Laqueur, ed., *Fascism: A Reader's Guide. Analyses, Interpretations, Bibliographies* (Harmondsworth, 1976); S. U. Larsen, B. Hagtvet, and J. P. Myklebust, eds., *Who Were the Fascists? Social Roots of European Fascism* (Bergen, 1980).

5. S. J. Woolf, *The Nature of Fascism.*

6. Ulrich Herbert, *Fremdarbeiter: Politik und Praxis des "Ausländer-Einsatzes" in der Kriegswirtschaft des Dritten Reiches* (Berlin, 1985). See also the survey by idem, *A History of Foreign Labor in Germany 1880–1950* (Ann Arbor, Mich., 1990).

7. See especially H. A. Winkler, *Revolution, Staat, Faschismus: Zur Revision des historischen Materialismus* (Göttingen, 1978); Henry Turner, ed., *Reappraisals of Fascism* (New York, 1975); Karl Dietrich Bracher, *Zeitgeschichtliche Kontroversen: Um Faschismus, Totalitarismus, Demokratie* (Munich, 1976), and idem, *The Age of Ideologies* (London, 1984).

8. A textual note here refers to "Jones," but I have been unable to trace the reference.

9. Feminist publications are now too numerous to mention in full, but important representative works in English include Renate Bridenthal et al., eds., *When Biology Became Destiny* (New York, 1984); and Claudia Koonz, *Mothers in the Fatherland* (New York, 1987); in German, see especially Gisela Bock, *Zwangssterilisation im Nationalsozialismus: Studien zur Rassenpolitik und Frauenpolitik* (Opladen, 1986). The text here also refers to two other works that have had a considerable impact on study of the social and ideological aspects of fascism: Klaus Theweleit, *Male Fantasies*, 2 vols. (Minneapolis, Minn., 1987–89); and Detlev Peukert, *Inside Nazi Germany* (New Haven, Conn., 1987).

10. See Ian Kershaw's essay in this volume.

11. Saul Friedländer, "Some Reflections on the Historicization of National Socialism," *German Politics and Society* 13 (February 1988): 9–21; see also the exchange of letters between Friedländer and Martin Broszat, reprinted as "A Controversy about the Historicization of National Socialism," *New German Critique* 44 (Spring/Summer 1988): 85–126.

12. Karl Dietrich Bracher and Leo Valiani, *Fascismo e nazional-socialismo* (Bologna, 1986).

13. Jürgen Kocka, "Hitler sollte nicht durch Stalin und Pol Pot verdrängt werden," in *"Historikerstreit": Die Dokumentation der Kontroverse um die Einzigartigkeit der nationalsozialistischen Judenvernichtung* (Munich, Zürich, 1987), pp. 132–42.

14. See MacGregor Knox, "Conquest, Foreign and Domestic, in Fascist Italy and Nazi Germany," *Journal of Modern History* 56 (March 1984): 1–57.

15. Robert Gellately, "The Gestapo and German Society: Political Denunciation in the Gestapo Case Files," *Journal of Modern History* 60 (December 1988): 654–94; Tim Mason, "Arbeiter ohne Gewerkschaften: Antifaschistische Widerstand in Deutschland und Italien," *Journal für Geschichte* (November 1985): 28–36.

16. I have not been able so far to locate this reference to a recent publication by Wolfgang Schieder, but see his collection *Faschismus als soziale Bewegung: Deutschland und Italien im Vergleich* (Göttingen, 1983).

17. Knox, "Conquest, Foreign and Domestic."

18. Paolo Pombeni, *Demagogia e tirannide: uno studio sulla forma partito del fascismo* (Bologna, 1984).

19. Charles Maier, "The Economics of Fascism and Nazism," in idem, *In Search of Stability* (Cambridge, 1987), pp. 70–120.

20. Mason, "Arbeiter ohne Gewerkschaften."

21. The reference here is to Habermas's contributions to the *Historikerstreit*; see *"Historikerstreit"*, pp. 62–76, 95–97, 243–55, and 383–87.

Notes on Contributors

CHRISTOPHER BROWNING is Professor of History at Pacific Lutheran University in Tacoma, Washington. He is the author of numerous articles on the Holocaust and Nazi racial policy. His books include *The Final Solution and the German Foreign Office* (1978) and *Fateful Months: Essays on the Emergence of the Final Solution*, 2d ed. (1991).

JANE CAPLAN teaches history at Bryn Mawr College. She is the author of *Government Without Administration: State and Civil Service in Weimar and Nazi Germany* (1988), and of articles on fascism, National Socialism, and the history of sexuality and gender. She is an editor of *German History, History Workshop Journal*, and the *Journal of Modern History*.

THOMAS CHILDERS is Professor of History at the University of Pennsylvania. He is the author of *The Nazi Voter* (1983), editor of *The Making of the Nazi Constituency* (1988), and has published many articles on the political history of National Socialism.

ROBERT GELLATELY is Professor of History at Huron College in Canada. He is the author of *The Politics of Economic Despair: Shopkeepers and German Politics, 1890–1914* (1974), and *The Gestapo and German Society: Enforcing Racial Policy, 1933–1945* (1990).

PETER HAYES is Associate Professor of History at Northwestern University. He has written widely on economics and politics in the Weimar and National Socialist periods. His most important work is *Industry and Ideology: IG Farben in the Nazi Era* (1987).

HAROLD JAMES is Professor of History at Princeton University. He is the author of numerous works on German economic history, including *The Reichsbank and Public Finance in Germany, 1924–1933* (1985) and *The German Slump: Politics and Economics 1924–1936* (1986). His most recent book is *A German Identity, 1770–1990* (1989).

IAN KERSHAW is Professor of Modern History at the University of Sheffield. His books include *Popular Opinion and Political Dissent in the Third Reich. Bavaria, 1933–45* (1983); *The "Hitler Myth": Image and Reality in the Third Reich* (1987); *The Nazi Dictatorship: Problems and Perspectives of Interpretation*, 2d. ed. (1989); and *Hitler: A Profile in Power* (1991).

CLAUDIA KOONZ teaches history at Duke University. She has published widely on the history of women in Weimar and Nazi Germany, and is the author of the prize-winning *Mothers in the Fatherland: Women, the Family, and Nazi Politics* (1987), and co-editor of *Becoming Visible* (1977).

TIM MASON taught at the University of Oxford for many years before his death in 1990, and was the author of *Sozialpolitik im Dritten Reich. Arbeiterklasse und Volksgemeinschaft* (1977; English translation forthcoming). An edition of his articles on German and European history is forthcoming.

HANS MOMMSEN is Professor of Modern European History at the Ruhr-Universität Bochum and has been Visiting Professor at Harvard, Berkeley, and the Hebrew University, Jerusalem. He is the author of *Beamtentum im Dritten Reich* (1966) and many other publications on Weimar and Nazi history, the resistance to Hitler, and the European labor movement. His most recent book is *Die verspielte Freiheit. Der Weg der Weimarer Republik in den Untergang* (1989; English translation forthcoming).

DETLEV PEUKERT taught at the University of Essen from 1978 until 1988, when he became director of the Hamburg Research Institute for the History of National Socialism. His many publications on the history of National Socialism and German social policy include *Die KPD im Widerstand* (1980); *Grenzen der Sozialdisziplinierung* (1986); *Inside Nazi Germany* (1987); and *Die Weimarer Republik* (1987; English translation in preparation). He died in 1990.

TILLA SIEGEL is senior researcher at the Institut für Sozialforschung in Frankfurt and is on the faculty of the Department of Sociology at the Freie Universität in Berlin. She is the author of several essays on National Socialist labor policy, and of *Leistung und Lohn in der nationalsozialistischen "Ordnung der Arbeit"* (1989).

Index